NO QUARTER

Random House

NEW YORK

NO QUARTER

The Battle of the Crater

— · 1864 — ·

Richard Slotkin

Published in the United States by Random House,
an imprint of The Random House Publishing Group,
a division of Random House, Inc., New York.

RANDOM HOUSE and colophon are registered trademarks of
Random House, Inc.

LIBRARY OF CONGRESS CATALOGING-IN-PUBLICATION DATA
Slotkin, Richard
No quarter: the Battle of the Crater, 1864/Richard Slotkin.
p. cm.
Includes bibliographical references.
ISBN 978-1-4000-6675-9   eBook ISBN 978-1-5883-6848-5
1. Petersburg Crater, Battle of, Va., 1864. I. Title.
E476.93.S58 2009   973.7'.37—dc22   2008036260

Printed in the United States of America on acid-free paper

www.atrandom.com

2 4 6 8 9 7 5 3 1

FIRST EDITION

Book design by Mary A. Wirth

For Iris, with love

If [war] was a perfect, unrestrained, and absolute expression of force . . . then the moment politics called it forth, [war] would replace politics . . . and follow its own laws: just as the explosion of a mine, at the moment it occurs, cannot be guided in any other direction than that given to it by the preparatory arrangements. . . . But it is not so. . . . War is not merely a political act, but also a real political instrument, a continuation of political commerce . . . by other means.

—CARL VON CLAUSEWITZ, *On War*

Preface

The Battle of the Crater, July 30, 1864, has gone into the history books as "a stupendous failure."[1] It was not the casualty list that set the battle apart. Losses were moderate by the bloody standards of Grant's 1864 overland campaign. What made the failure stupendous was the loss of a spectacular opportunity to capture the vital railroad junction of Petersburg, to drive Lee's army away from the Confederate capital of Richmond, and to end the war before Christmas.

The Federal Army of the Potomac had fought its way south at terrible cost, only to be stymied at Petersburg by Confederate forces fighting from behind an impregnable trench line. Then the ingenuity of a regiment of Pennsylvania coal miners in General Burnside's IX Corps created the opportunity for a breakthrough. Directed by their colonel, a mining engineer in civilian life, they dug a tunnel more than five hundred feet long, right up under a Confederate strongpoint, and packed four tons of blasting powder into galleries at its end. It was the longest military mine that had ever been dug, and when the powder was touched off, it would create what was the largest man-made explosion in history. To spearhead the infantry attack Burnside chose his 4th Division, nine regiments of African American soldiers—the largest Black military formation to that point in our history. The division was given special training in the maneuvers required to exploit the breach the mine would create.

The operation was designed to achieve a decisive victory. More than that, it was an operation that seemed to draw upon the unique strengths of the Union—its mastery of industrial technology, the voluntarism and skill of free labor, the moral and physical energy liberated as a result of its embrace of emancipation.

But all of this planning, labor, and high hope ended in embarrassing defeat. It was not just the skill and courage of the Confederate defenders that wrecked the Union assault, but the jealousy, intransigence, incompetence, and even cowardice of Federal generals. Hundreds of their soldiers were trapped in the huge sheer-sided crater left by the mine explosion, helpless to defend themselves. The closing phase of the battle was marked by a combination massacre and race riot, as White troops—both Union and Confederate—turned against the Black soldiers. To make matters worse, this debacle came just as Lincoln's reelection campaign was beginning. It intensified a growing crisis of public confidence in Lincoln's war policy and strengthened the prospects of the Peace Democrats, who opposed both the war effort and the emancipation of the slaves.

The failure was investigated by a military court of inquiry in August 1864, and later by Congress's Joint Committee on the Conduct of the War (JCCW). Historians have generally accepted the finding of the court, that Burnside and his division commanders were responsible for the fiasco. But the court was primarily interested in limiting the embarassment suffered by the army and its senior commanders. Instead of using the investigation to expose and correct the systemic flaws that crippled the Army of the Potomac, the court ignored and thereby perpetuated them. The court also ignored the unique features of the battle: the racially motivated killing of wounded men, the murder of POWs, and the White-on-Black violence within the Federal ranks.

The Battle of the Crater is worth a closer look. Its role in the campaign against Richmond was more significant than contemporaries realized, or most historians have allowed. The assault of July 30 was part of a larger, and largely successful, maneuver plan developed by General Grant, which modeled the tactics by which he would eventually break Lee's defenses. Few historians have taken a critical look at Lee's handling of the battle, yet there is good reason to think that Grant outgeneraled Lee in the lead-up to the Crater, and that Lee was lucky to have avoided disaster.

But the real interest of the Battle of the Crater lies in what it reveals about an American society at war with itself. The battle was fought at a moment of equilibrium in the struggle between two systems of thought and social organization—slavery on one side, free labor on the other. However, within each of the rival systems, transforming forces were at work. The South was faced with a radical choice between the preservation of slavery and national survival. Lincoln's reelection campaign presented supporters of the Union with stark choices about how the war should be fought and what kind of society ought to come out of it. Presidential politics would powerfully influence the decisions that produced the battle.

Above all, the Battle of the Crater is worth a closer look because the flash of its explosion illuminates the centrality of *race* in the tangle of social and political conflicts that shaped American life as the Civil War approached its climax. Because of the racial element, participants would remember this as the most intense and vicious combat of the war, and even the passage of time did not allay the bitterness it engendered. The animosities exposed on this battlefield were the same passions that would wreck postwar attempts to reconstruct the nation as a multiracial democracy.

My purpose in writing this book is to give the reader a clear and accurate account of the strategic setting and the battle action as it developed hour by hour, and to show how the culture and politics of that place and time shaped the way the soldiers fought and the meanings they saw in their experience of war.

Contents

PART FIVE
CONSEQUENCES

List of Maps

Part One

THE STRATEGIC SETTING

Chapter 1

Stalemate

PETERSBURG, JUNE 21, 1864

The opposing trenches zigzagged in a shallow four-mile curve across the countryside east of Petersburg. Between them was a junkyard of broken rifles, smashed kegs, scraps of blanket and uniform, bodies putrefying in the blast-furnace heat. This wrack marked the crest of a wave that had begun piling up seven weeks before and a hundred miles north.

The Union had started the campaign with high expectations. Its armies were under a new general in chief, Ulysses S. Grant, who as commander of the Union Army of the Tennessee had captured two entire Confederate field armies and driven a third from the battlefield in abject rout. The full strength of the Union was put forth in coordinated offensives on the two most critical fronts. Sherman in Georgia would drive against the Confederate Army of Tennessee with a hundred thousand men. (Union armies were named for the rivers associated with their operations, Confederate armies for the states they were assigned to defend.) Grant would oversee the advance of three different armies in Virginia. The Army of the Potomac with four infantry and one cavalry corps, under General George Gordon Meade and Grant himself, would go against Robert E. Lee and the Army of Northern Virginia. A small force under General Franz Sigel would advance from Harpers Ferry, West Virginia, to seize the supply-rich Shenandoah Valley. And the Army of the James (two army corps) under General Benjamin Franklin Butler would land on the south bank of the James River, where it could strike against the vital railroad lines that ran through Petersburg, carrying supplies for Richmond from the south.

On May 5, Grant's army crossed the Rapidan River and was immediately assailed by Lee's troops in a vast thicket of second-growth timber called the Wilderness. For two days the armies grappled in intense close-in combat. Blinded by the thick woods and dense undergrowth, troops blundered into one another, charge and countercharge broke up among the trees, the underbrush took fire, and the wounded lying between the lines screamed as they burned to death. On the second day the Union's General Hancock led a massive assault that nearly broke the Confederate line, only to see his corps routed by Longstreet's Rebel troops erupting out of the jungle on their flank. But Longstreet's counterattack broke against the Federal reserve line, and Longstreet himself was critically wounded. The Federals lost 17,666 men, the Confederates about half that many.

Yet instead of retreating after this tactical defeat, as his predecessors had done, Grant continued his offensive, marching his infantry east and then south to turn Lee's right flank and force the outnumbered Rebels to leave the forest and fight in the open. Once again Lee forestalled him, moving along the shorter line to seize the strategic road junction at Spotsylvania Court House, where his troops threw up strong field fortifications to offset the Federal advantage in numbers and artillery. Lee's position was in the form of an inverted *V*, pointing north.

Grant's strategy required him to maintain the offensive, and if he could not destroy Lee's army, he had to hold it in place so that Butler could operate against Richmond. So he pressured Lee's lines continuously with probes and threats against the flanks, and staged five major assaults, one of which (on May 12) smashed in the point of the *V*, wrecked one of Lee's infantry corps, and nearly succeeded in cutting the Confederate army in two. But after almost two weeks of fighting, Lee's lines still held, with losses for both armies climbing into the tens of thousands.

These losses might have been outweighed by strategic success if Butler and Sigel had carried out their assignments. But while Grant's army was fighting at Spotsylvania, Sigel's force was routed by Confederates in the Shenandoah. At the same time, Butler was making a botch of his campaign against Richmond, allowing his thirty-five-thousand-man army to be bottled up in the Bermuda Hundred peninsula five miles north of Petersburg.

Grant now altered his plan of campaign. He would try again to turn Lee's flank by swinging his infantry out to the east and south and forcing Lee's troops to scramble to stay ahead of him if they wanted to prevent

Grant from breaking their supply lines and keep him from getting between the Federal forces and the Confederate capital at Richmond. There was another battle when the Confederates headed Grant off at the North Anna River twenty miles south of Spotsylvania. But Grant simply made another sweep to the east and forced the Army of Northern Virginia back to the Cold Harbor crossroads, only six miles north of Richmond. There on June 7, Grant made his worst mistake of the campaign, ordering frontal assaults that the entrenched Confederates destroyed with shocking speed.

Undeterred by these losses, Grant now planned a complex series of maneuvers that, if successful, might lead to the capture of the vital rail nexus of Petersburg. With that city in hand, he could force Lee to choose between withstanding a siege in a starving Richmond or abandoning his trenches for an open-field battle against Grant's superior forces. On June 9, Grant sent most of his cavalry raiding to the west, to threaten the supply route from the Shenandoah and draw off Lee's cavalry. Then with one division of cavalry and the infantry of V and VI Corps, Grant repeated his by now predictable pattern of maneuvering around Lee's right flank, as if he intended to strike directly at Richmond through the swampy flatlands between the Chickahominy River and the north bank of the James River. Since Lee's army now stood with its back to Richmond, the Confederate general would have no choice but to shift his troops from Cold Harbor to block that threat. But the flanking maneuver was a feint, designed to hold Lee in the defenses of Richmond north of the James. Behind the screen set by V and VI Corps, the bulk of Grant's infantry and artillery were making a wider swing that would carry them all the way across the James River, by steamboat and pontoon bridge, to strike with overwhelming force the single division that held Petersburg and the Bermuda Hundred lines.

The plan was daring and risky, and it worked brilliantly. On June 15 the first of Grant's infantry corps—the XVIII under "Baldy" Smith—moved against the Petersburg forts, ten thousand infantry against a scratch force of twenty-four hundred. A division of Black soldiers led by General Hinks stormed one of the outer strongpoints and captured a Confederate battery. But the inner lines looked formidable, and Cold Harbor made Smith leery of storming entrenchments. He halted to wait for reinforcements. The next day he had three corps in hand, the II and IX in addition to his own, some forty-eight thousand troops. For a moment it seemed to the Union's soldiers that they might win the war at a stroke.

The low volume of fire, the look of the POWs, and above all the ease with which Negro troops had defeated White men told the veteran infantry that they faced outnumbered second-rank troops. Despite their ingrained fear of attacking entrenchments, many actually begged their commanders to send them in. [1]

Yet the generals still hesitated to attack positions that appeared so strong, and the endemic failings of the Army of the Potomac's command structure reasserted themselves. Orders got mixed, reinforcements arrived tardily, assaults lacked proper coordination. A soldier in the 14th New York Heavy Artillery described how it was: "[The] cry was forward . . . and forward we went & drove them like sheep & held the works for nearly 2 hours till we got out of ammunition then they charged us & away we went back as fast as our legs could carry us but rallied immediately & took them & held them & the rebs just got right up & skedadalded & our troops are advanced a good ways in advance of where the rebs was & they say petersburg is on fire."[2]

But in fact Petersburg was safe. By stripping his other garrisons Confederate General Beauregard managed to put fourteen thousand men into the forts, which were as formidable as they looked. They could not keep the Federals from storming their lines, but the cost they imposed in time and casualties prevented a breakthrough.

More Federal troops kept arriving, and General Meade assumed command, but in two more days of fighting (June 17–18) the Federals failed to break the Confederate defense. The heavy casualties of the previous six weeks had reduced both the number and the quality of the men in the ranks. The generals at the front had been demoralized by the futile and costly frontal attacks at Cold Harbor. Instead of obeying Meade's orders to attack in concert, the corps commanders kept questioning his management:

"Is it intended for the IX Corps to go forward simultaneously?"

"I do not understand the arrangements for my supports."

"Is the order to attack peremptory, or shall I be allowed some discretion?"

By July 18, with Lee's divisions finally arriving in front of Petersburg, Meade had exhausted his patience and resources. "What additional orders to attack you require I cannot imagine. . . . Finding it impossible to effect cooperation by appointing an hour for attack, I have sent an order to each corps commander to attack at all hazards and without reference to each other." It was a confession of failure and a fatal error of judgment.

Regiments and brigades attacking in succession had no chance against entrenched troops and artillery. The combat veterans knew their opportunity had passed, wrote their names on bits of paper, pinned them to their shirts so their bodies could be identified, and went forward with grim fatalism to face one last day of furious attack and bitter-end defense.[3]

Then the armies went to ground with a vengeance, in desperate haste scraping rifle pits out of the dry Virginia dirt, to hold the ground their violence and labor had won. Experience made them practical experts in field fortification. When dark covered them, they used pick and spade to turn rifle pits into breastworks, and then deepened the breastworks into trenches, six feet deep with logs laid along the parapet and loopholes for riflemen. Nightly details laid obstacles in front of the trenches: abatis, small trees cut and set in rows, trunks braced in the ground and tops interlaced facing the enemy to entangle and hold an attacking column, like barbed wire in later wars; and chevaux-de-frise, fences of heavy sharpened stakes, butts rooted solidly in the ground and spear points facing outward to impale an attacker. It would take weeks for the engineers of two armies to survey and perfect the lines, but after two days the infantry positions were already strong enough to break any frontal assault, and the area between the lines had become what a later generation would call a no-man's-land. The armies were locked in place, immobilized under the hammer of a blazing sun: "The heat and dust are intense and the streams and springs are fast drying up . . . the sufferings and loss in the line are something which I cannot think of without trembling. Our consolation must be a Christian one, that the enemy is probably even worse off."[4]

The military standoff marked a balance point in the war and, in the long political struggle that had divided American society into warring sections—a crisis of morale that tested the armies and the societies that had created them—tested their willingness and ability to sustain the struggle.

Civilian morale in the North was shaken by the terrible cost of Grant's operations: between 65,000 and 70,000 casualties in seven weeks, out of an army whose initial strength was 120,000. Yet Grant appeared no closer to destroying Lee's army than when he had begun; and if the position Grant had seized was indeed advantageous, it was not much different from the one McClellan had achieved in 1862 at far less cost. Voluntary enlistments were falling off, and the loss of confidence was hurting the sale of government bonds and the value of the currency, which was weakening the government's ability to sustain its armies. Opposition newspapers decried Grant as a "butcher," leading the nation's young manhood to slaughter to satisfy abolitionist fanatics.

Yet there remained in the North a hard core of support for the war. Abraham Lincoln was the voice and the agent of that determination. In the midst of the Petersburg fighting he told a Philadelphia audience: "We accepted this war for a worthy object . . . and the war will end when that object is attained. Under God I hope it never will until that time." As for Grant, he had won "a position from whence he will never be dislodged until Richmond is taken." The crowd cheered Lincoln.[5]

But victory depended on the army's effectiveness and its soldiers' willingness to fight.

Military Morale, North and South

At the start of the campaign more than half of Grant's hundred thousand men were veterans, with two or three years of service. Many of the three-year enlistees were eligible to be mustered out with honor in the spring of 1864. Yet despite the loss and suffering they had endured, more than half chose to reenlist for the duration. These were men who had outlived the spread-eagle patriotism of 1861. What they had left was pride in their regiments and an illusionless determination to finish the job that had already cost them and their comrades so much hardship and grief. Regiments of these Veteran Volunteers had carried the burden of combat since the Wilderness, spearheading every offensive, throwing themselves into every breach. To fill their depleted ranks, the federal government had resorted to conscription but allowed drafted men to buy "substitutes" to take their place. State governments, whose constituents feared and resented conscription, offered bounties for enlistment, which made volunteering somewhat more attractive but also created a new class of criminal: the "bounty jumper," who would take an enlistment bounty, desert, reenlist under another name (or in another state) for a second bounty, desert, and so on. The system maintained the army's numerical strength, but the army's quality was degraded as the Veteran Volunteers were replaced by men brought into the ranks by greed, coercion, or stupidity.

The quality of combat leadership was also seriously degraded. Casualties were heaviest among the veteran NCOs and junior officers who took the lead in assaults or stepped forward to rally men wavering or in retreat. The failures of the frontal assaults at Cold Harbor and especially at Petersburg had also weakened the soldiers' faith in the higher commanders. Colonel Stephen Weld of the 56th Massachusetts wrote to his father,

"The feeling here . . . is that we have been absolutely butchered, that our lives have been periled to no purpose, and wasted. In the Second Corps the feeling is so strong that the men say they will not charge any more works. . . . Father, it is discouraging to see one's men and officers cut down and butchered time and again, and all for nothing."[6]

Yet Weld did not want his father to think he was "croaking": he was still committed to the struggle, and thought the army would take Richmond if its generals would be less careless of the lives of their men. In spite of everything, the soldiers retained a "resilient, sometimes sullen belief in eventual Union victory." The mix of sentiments was most eloquently expressed by Captain Charles Francis Adams, Jr., scion of the presidential Adams family, now commanding Meade's cavalry escort. In a letter to his father, the American ambassador in London, Adams wrote: "Why is the Army kept continually fighting until its heart has sickened within it? . . . I have never seen the Army so haggard and worn, so worked out and fought out, so dispirited and hopeless *as now when the fall of Richmond is most likely* [italics mine]." What was wanted was not a change of generals but a change of tactics. "Grant will take Richmond, if only he is left alone; of that I feel more and more sure. His tenacity and his strength, combined with his skill, must, on every general principle, prove too much for them in the end."[7]

❧

On the other side of the lines the state of morale was very much the same. Despite Southern defeats at Gettysburg, Vicksburg, and Chattanooga, the Army of Northern Virginia had begun the 1864 campaign with high hopes. The Confederacy's two primary field armies had rallied after defeat. The Army of Tennessee, defending Georgia against Sherman, was now commanded by General Joseph E. Johnston, who was, after Lee, the most trusted senior general in the service. Defeat in the border states and the Mississippi Valley had driven Southern armies closer to the Confederate heartland, the seaboard states that were richest in population and resources. Conversely, Federal resources were stretched thin by occupation of captured territory, so it was possible for General Nathan Bedford Forrest, using guerrilla operations, to keep the Yankees from extending their hold in Mississippi. The deeper Sherman's army drove into Georgia, the more vulnerable its supply lines would become. It might well be possible to trap and destroy his force by a rapid transfer of troops down the railroads running south from Virginia.

But the results of the spring campaign were seriously disappointing.

Johnston was forced into a series of retreats that allowed Sherman to threaten the vital industrial center of Atlanta. The Army of Northern Virginia had suffered terrible losses: its thirty-five thousand casualties amounted to more than half the force with which the campaign had begun. Lee's counterstrokes had all been baffled; Grant had held the initiative and driven Confederate forces into a last-ditch defense of their capital. Like their opposite numbers in the Army of the Potomac, Lee's soldiers had been physically and emotionally exhausted by seven weeks of unrelenting engagement. If anything, they were more tired and hungry, because their commissaries were receiving inadequate supplies of food and clothing.

It was going to be extraordinarily difficult to replace those lost men. By 1864 the Confederacy had mobilized nearly all of its White military manpower. The new conscription law passed in February 1864 extended the age range for conscription to seventeen to forty-five years old. In the end the Confederacy would enlist more than 750,000 men, 75 to 85 percent of the military-age White male population. But it was impossible to draw very much more manpower without destroying the South's ability to produce food, manufacture weapons, and run its railroads. The Bureau of Conscription informed the War Department that "For conscription from the general population, the functions of this Bureau may cease with the termination of the year 1864."[8]

In addition to losses caused by death, wounds, and capture, desertion was becoming a serious problem. Inadequate food and clothing and incessant combat had a lot to do with this. But desertions also reflected the anxieties of soldiers whose distant homes were occupied or threatened by Yankee invaders, the war weariness of many Southern communities, and the impoverished conditions of soldiers' families left without a breadwinner for years at a time. The Confederacy too had mounted a drive to get three-year regiments to reenlist, but the effort did not last long enough to provide a precise gauge of troop morale. The Davis administration was unwilling to risk a failure of voluntarism, and it ordered all enlistments indefinitely extended—a measure we now call stop-loss. As in the Army of the Potomac, the combat power of Confederate veteran regiments had been degraded by losses among senior NCOs and junior and field officers. Yet veteran Confederate troops showed the same disillusioned commitment to cause and comrades as their Union counterparts. They had invested too much blood, health, fortune, and grief in the struggle to leave the job unfinished. A Mississippi infantryman wrote his fam-

ily, "I am getin very Tyred of this way of Living but such is the fate of
war. . . . I am not by any means willing to yield to the federal government
and surrender." As Sherman observed, Confederates were "plenty tired
of war, but the masses [are] determined to fight it out."[9]

WHY WE FOUGHT

The morale of Civil War regiments has been a wonder to historians and a
challenge to the military for a hundred and fifty years. What was it that kept
men with the colors when desertion and evasion of service were relatively
easy? What enabled those regiments to march, shoulder-to-shoulder with
loud cheers, into blasts of musketry and canister that they knew would
destroy one man in three—understanding that to be wounded was often
tantamount to a sentence of death, screaming through amputations without anesthetic or suffering the slow torture of gangrene? Perhaps the leaders who spoke for the interests of planters on the one side, bankers and
industrialists on the other, saw the war as a means of protecting their
property and vital interests. But for most private soldiers, military service
entailed serious economic sacrifice. Small farmers made up the bulk of
Southern rank and file. They had no slave property to protect, and left
their farms to be run by wives and children or aged parents. Fewer and
weaker hands meant less food for their families, less surplus to go to market, less cash to buy the things needed to maintain the farm and pay debts
or rent. Northern farmers faced similar difficulties. Northern factory
workers who enlisted gave up their jobs, with no assurance of reemploy-
ment should they return.

Whatever the differences that impelled their societies to war, many of
the motives that drove and sustained the soldiers were similar on both
sides of the Mason-Dixon Line. Young Americans were taught to think of
war as a normal and natural part of human experience, a necessary consequence of a people's political existence, "dreadful but inevitable [and
even] its horror is full of interest." The wars of the American nation were
widely seen as tests of national spirit and virtue, ordeals that purified and
regenerated people and state. The analogy between military and Christian sacrifice was recognized and embraced: the American nation had
been chosen as God's agent for advancing freedom, civilization, and true
religion, so that to serve the nation in war was a Christian as well as a civic
duty. There was a reciprocal relation between the individual's striving for
personal redemption and the nation's seeking to fulfill God's mandate. A

Southern soldier wrote, "If the hearts of our People will get right, God will give us Peace and not before." The same thought is echoed in the jeremiads of Northern preachers and the letters of soldiers, who saw the war as punishment for the nation's sins, and a means to their expiation. That faith strengthened both sides in the face of grief, discouragement, and the spectre of defeat. "Our cause we believe to be a just one and our God is certainly a just God, then why should we doubt." The sentence was written by a Southern soldier, but the sentiment was identical on the other side of the lines.[10]

One of the primary privileges and duties of the free citizen was to participate in the defense of his community and his country. But wartime service was more than a civic obligation. It was a test of one's personal character and social identity—a demonstration to yourself and your community that you were willing and able to live up to the expectations embodied in the concepts of "manhood" and "honor." There were differences in the way these values were defined in the different regions. In the Northeast, honor was closely bound up with a sense of civic and even national duty, where Southern honor was more likely to be vested in the family and the community. The common denominator was the belief that honorable service in war was a necessary attribute of manhood and of social respectability. Young men enlisted to affirm their identity, and they stayed with the colors to maintain their character.[11]

Among veterans on both sides, loyalty to the outfit and the army became synonymous with national patriotism. North and South, soldiers' letters are filled with assertions of their belief that their army is the nation's sole and best reliance. That loyalty was most intensely focused in the regiment. Civil War regiments were (for the most part) raised by communities, and they fused the intensities of local identity and national patriotism. This was as true of the Unionist North, with its ideological commitment to the national government, as it was of the South, whose political theory emphasized states' rights. By an act of imagination the soldier could see himself as defender of the nation and the flag that symbolized it. But in the heat of battle it was the flag of the regiment that was the focus of his passion and loyalty. He would give his life to advance it or to save it from capture or disgrace. His personal honor, and the honor of family and community, were vested in it.

It has been said that the determination of Southern troops was reinforced by the fact that they fought to defend their homes against an invading force. There is a good deal of truth in that view. As Mahone's

Confederate division marched double-quick through Petersburg to man the defenses on June 19, a woman with a child in her arms "sprang into the column and threw her arms around the neck of a soldier, so dusty and sunbrowned that you could scarcely tell whether he was white or black," weeping with joy and astonishment at the sight of the husband she had not seen in two years of fighting. One quick embrace and he rejoined the ranks and disappeared. Even those soldiers who had no immediate family in the town felt that, with Petersburg at their backs, they were defending "their" women and children from Yankee violence.[12]

For Northern soldiers, the object of defense was not so immediate. Yet their commitment to the seemingly more abstract cause of the nation was no less passionate and durable. North and South, White Americans shared the belief that the constitutional government established by the Founders was—and was meant to be—an instrument for assuring justice, political rights, safety of property, and personal dignity, to all citizens. The casting of ballots in an election was a secular sacrament, an affirmation and a guarantee of the individual's self-respect, moral independence, and social dignity. To be deprived of that right, that sacrament, was to be en-slaved. Young men on both sides were driven to take arms against one an-other because they believed the sacraments of government had been traduced, its just powers usurped, and that—imminently or inevitably—the other side meant to use the national government to enslave them.

To the South, the election of a Republican president signaled that the people of the North intended to pervert the power of the government by using it to undermine and ultimately destroy the slave-based system of plantation agriculture on which their culture, society, and politics were built. A transformation to which they could not freely consent would be imposed upon them, and to accept that result would be to acquiesce in their own enslavement. There was a corresponding belief in the North, which saw the "slave power conspiracy" using its control of the Demo-cratic party, the presidency, and the Supreme Court to make slavery na-tional—to overrule the decisions of Northern voters that had legislated an end to slavery in the Free States. Southern ideologues, such as Senator Hammond of South Carolina and the "sociologist" George Fitzhugh, lent credibility to that belief when they justified slavery by declaring that every civilized society rested on a mudsill class, a permanent proletariat of propertyless and dependent workers—an idea that treated the working classes of the North as little better than Negroes.[13]

The Northern ideal of American life was formulated in the ideology of free labor, most perfectly articulated by Abraham Lincoln: the man who this year works for wages may next year become a capitalist, hiring other men to work for wages and rise in their turn. That was how Northerners believed American life should be organized: no fixed or permanent classes, no proletarian mudsills and capitalist master races, but rather a continual movement of poorer men into the propertied classes, a system in which individual effort was guaranteed its reward under a government that assured each man an equal and fair chance to make his way. The South's secession was a resort to force to overturn the result of a free and fair election. To allow bullets to negate ballots would be to surrender the most essential political right and to accept enslavement by a Southern aristocracy. An Iowa soldier expressed the conviction of many veterans when he declared, "It may cost me my life, but If I cant live In a free country than I dont want to live at all. I was born & raised in a free Country & still intend to live under the old flag of our union or die in the defense of it."[14]

These feelings, powerful enough in themselves, were intensified by the fears and antipathies that attached to racial difference. In a nation half-slave and half-free, enslavement was more than a metaphor for a hateful condition of life; it was a living visible fact. To lose one's liberty, to have one's rights traduced, was to fall into the condition of the Negro, to lose one's social and racial identity—to become something less than human. Thus on both sides men were willing to kill and be killed to defend the fundamental ground of their identity, their personal and collective dignity—that is, their standing as free *White* men, their difference from Black people.

In the South, in the presence of slavery and of a very large Black population, that difference was formulated in unmistakable terms. As Governor Brown of Georgia told his constituents, slavery is the poor White man's friend because it assures "the poor white laborer . . . [he] does not belong to the menial class . . . [but] to the only true aristocracy, the race of *white men*." Newspapers editorialized that if the Yankee invasion succeeded, and abolitionism triumphed, "in TEN years or less our CHILDREN will be the *slaves* of negroes," and "Abolitionist preachers will be at hand to consummate the marriage of your daughters to black husbands." To submit to the Union was to "Submit to having our wives and daughters choose between death and gratifying the hellish lust of the negro!!"[15]

In the North, anxiety for White supremacy usually took more ambiguous forms: opposition to the Emancipation Proclamation and resistance to the recruiting of Negro troops or to using them in combat. But here too freedom and civil dignity were defined by a racial standard: White men had dignity, Blacks did not. The fear and hatred many Northerners felt for slavery was entangled with loathing for Black people, as if the degradation associated with slavery were a contagion Black people carried. Lincoln's home state of Illinois barred slavery but also forbade free Blacks from settling there. And the poorest of the North's poor Whites were as enraged by the prospect of competing with free Black labor as their counterparts in the South were. In July 1863, New York City had been the scene of a massive riot by its poor and laboring citizens, mostly Irish, which had begun as a demonstration against the draft and ended as a racial pogrom against the city's African Americans.

The North's use of Black soldiers brought those racial conflicts right onto the firing line.

THE HORSESHOE, JUNE 21, 1864

There was a sector, roughly in the center of the entrenchments that fronted Petersburg on the east, where the opposing trench lines were fewer than four hundred feet apart—easy killing range for the standard rifle-musket. Here the 2nd Division of IX Corps, commanded by General Robert Potter, had dug itself in at the high-water mark of the June 18 assault, creating a forward bulge in the Federal line that the soldiers nicknamed "the Horseshoe." Behind Potter's line the shallow ravine called Taylor's Run ran across the base of the Horseshoe from south to north. East of the run the ground sloped up to a low ridge on which IX Corps was constructing a fortified battery, soon to be named Fort Morton. The division acting as corps reserve was posted here and in the shallow cut of the Norfolk and Petersburg Railroad that ran across the face of the ridge. On the eighteenth of June that duty had been assumed by the 4th Division, General Edward Ferrero commanding—a division of Black infantrymen, the largest formation of Black soldiers that had so far been assembled, and the only such division in the Army of the Potomac.

Opposite the Horseshoe on higher ground to the west was a salient in the Rebel lines, a carefully engineered projection of the entrenchments, well fortified with logs and earth-filled gabions, equipped with a four-gun battery commanded by Captain Richard Pegram and protected by riflemen of Stephen Elliott's South Carolina Brigade. The Rebels in the salient could see a good deal of what went on in the Federal lines, and they were good at raiding picket posts in the dark. By the evening of June 19 the Rebels knew that the troops opposite belonged to a corps that included Negroes, "whereupon the Rebels vented, in an incessant galling and somewhat deadly fire, the bitter spite they felt against both negro soldiers and the white ones beside whom they fought." Elsewhere along the lines, soldiers on opposing sides "were even disposed to be friendly"; arranged temporary truces; and traded newspapers, coffee, and tobacco—but not on the IX Corps front. "Rifle shots and shells from batteries, forts, and mortars came among us continually, night and day, and we were constantly losing our brave men. Some were killed while asleep; some while forming in line at roll-call; some, while eating their 'grub.' " Burnside's corps lost an average of thirty-five men per day during the first week of the siege, and forty-eight per day during the second.[16]

The worst consequence of the Rebels' spite was that it became impossible ever to take an easy breath, to perform even the most ordinary act—eating, resting, defecating—in safety. "The spring is always bent; the nerves never have a chance to recuperate; the elasticity of courage is slowly worn out." On IX Corps' front the tension of frontline service was screwed tight and held hard, and the moral strength of men who lived under it would be steadily attenuated till they snapped. Even the anger and resentment they felt was complicated. They hated the Rebels for shooting them, but some of them also hated the Rebels for treating them as if they *chose* to associate with Negroes, and some hated the Blacks whose mere presence had brought this ordeal upon them.[17]

One of the long-service regiments in Potter's division was the 48th Pennsylvania, which held the sector closest to the Rebel salient. The members of the regiment had been raised in the coal mining districts of Schuylkill County, and there were many in the ranks who had worked the mines. They glared through the loopholes at the Rebel fort and the entrenchments that had defeated them, and the men were torn between wishing they could seize the entrenchments and kill their defenders, and fearing their generals would order them to attack again across the open ground.

And then somebody said, why didn't they dig their way across? Why didn't they tunnel under the fort and blow it up with gunpowder? The enlisted men and noncoms talked it over, and when their commander, Lieutenant Colonel Henry Pleasants, came to inspect, he heard them. Pleasants had been a mining engineer in civilian life, and he liked the idea: a tunnel a hundred fifty or even two hundred yards long was perfectly feasible, unless there were large springs to contend with. That night he made some sketches and drafted preliminary plans, and the next day he took them to his division commander.[18]

Brigadier General Robert Potter had also been thinking about ways to attack that fort thrust so tantalizingly close. He had been a lawyer in civilian life, had enlisted as a private in a New York militia regiment and had risen through the ranks. By the summer of 1863 he was in command of his division, which he led through the Vicksburg campaign, in the winter fighting around Knoxville, and through the battles of the overland campaign. Everything he knew about war he had learned on the job, but he was a fast learner. He adopted Pleasants's idea with enthusiasm and on June 24 endorsed it to his corps commander, General Burnside.

That was the start of the chain of events that would end in the Crater.

So far it was a process that would have pleased President Lincoln: a stratagem that would shape the conduct of the nation's greatest army, originating in the skills and desires of ordinary working-class Americans, given power by a free labor system equally respectful of officer and man, manager and worker.

But behind the lines a different order prevailed. As Pleasants's proposal passed up the chain of command it became enmeshed in the corporate and personal agendas of the officer corps, and in the clash of political and economic interests shaping the presidential campaign.

As it happened, President Lincoln himself was making a surprise visit to the battlefront at about the time Pleasants was writing up his proposal.

Chapter 2

"With as Little Bloodshed as Possible"

PARAMETERS FOR A FEDERAL OFFENSIVE, JUNE 21–23, 1864

Lieutenant General Grant commanded the united forces of Meade's Army of the Potomac and Butler's Army of the James. Butler's X and XVIII Corps held the northern sector: the lines across the Bermuda Hundred peninsula between the James and Appomattox rivers, and the bridgeheads at the river crossings. The lines in front of Petersburg were held by the Army of the Potomac, with IX Corps in the center and V Corps defending the southern flank. The II and VI Corps were retained as a mobile reserve. Sheridan's Cavalry Corps was still absent, on the return march from its raid toward the Shenandoah.

Grant and Meade were completing arrangements for their next move, a sweep by II and VI Corps around Lee's southern flank to seize the Weldon Railroad, when Grant was called away to meet his commander in chief on the dock at City Point. Lincoln's visit was a surprise, potentially an unpleasant one. It was implicitly an inspection by the man who would pass judgment upon the use Grant and Meade had made of the men and arms entrusted to them.

But Lincoln eased the tension, greeting Grant with great warmth and a heartiness. After polite inquiries and some joshing about Lincoln's seasickness, Grant proposed that the president visit the troops. Lincoln accepted enthusiastically and reassuringly, "Why yes, I had fully intended to go out and take a look at the brave fellows who have fought their way down to Petersburg in this wonderful campaign."[1]

GRAND STRATEGY AND PRESIDENTIAL POLITICS

Lincoln's warmth was sincere. It had taken him three years to find a general who shared his understanding of what had to be done to win the war. Despite the North's advantages in population and economic resources, it could never muster or sustain armies large enough to occupy the South. The Union could win only by destroying the Southern field armies. To do that it had to launch coordinated offensives on several fronts and persist in those offensives until Southern resources were exhausted. Grant had planned and executed that kind of all-out offensive, and by pinning Lee to Petersburg he had achieved a result that, in the long run, would ensure victory.

Ulysses S. Grant was a man in the prime of life, forty-two years old, with close-cropped sandy hair and beard. He was unimpressive at first glance, dressed for work in an ordinary soldier's blouse or jacket, usually rumpled, the only mark of his rank the three stars at his shoulders. But those who worked with him for any length of time recognized his strength of will and character, his courage and skill as a commander. He had weathered an unhappy childhood, early failure in military and civilian life, alcoholism, and a terrible apprenticeship as a Civil War general. He had become a master of his profession, with a perfect understanding of how an army should be organized and how it could be used, and the physical and moral courage to command under the stress of battle—a man stolidly certain of himself, no matter how great the responsibilities laid upon him. [2]

The Army of the Potomac tested the limits of his skill. The Army of the Tennessee, with which he had won his great victories, was Grant's own creation: a lean force, capable of long rapid marches and swift responses to changing tactical or strategic situations. (In that respect it resembled Lee's Army of Northern Virginia.) The Army of the Potomac was much larger, and its military culture had been formed by General George B. McClellan, who organized it along Regular Army lines. In action its reliance on hierarchy and bureaucratic procedures made its reflexes a good deal slower than the reflexes of the Army of the Tennessee. McClellan also politicized the army's structure from top to bottom. Like the head of any large institution, he favored those who supported his views and policies, and thereby fostered jealousies and resentments among those less favored. But this pattern was exacerbated by McClellan's grandiosity, by the cult of personality he created, and by his emergence as the leader of the conservative opposition to the Lincoln administration. His legacy to the Army of the Potomac was an officer corps divided between pro- and anti-McClellan cliques, each of which had entangling alliances with the political factions vying for power in Washington. Although the enlisted men and regimental officers were brave, dedicated, and effective soldiers, and the artillery units were superb, bureaucratization and politicization had hampered the army's performance.

Grant's appointment changed things for the better. He understood the Potomac Army's operations as part of a larger strategy and so did not overrate the significance of tactical setbacks. Among his gifts as a commander was the ability to focus with ruthless intensity on the military problem before him. The weakness in this virtue was that he sometimes failed to consider what the enemy might do. But it is possible that he didn't *care*. The hard experience of Shiloh had taught him that, given existing limitations of mobility and striking power, a Civil War army that stood its ground could not be destroyed on the battlefield. That being the case, when Lee attacked his army in the Wilderness, drove in both flanks and inflicted seventeen thousand casualties, Grant shrugged off the tactical defeat and resumed the offensive.

And when Grant attacked, he marshaled the largest, most powerful, and most successful combat assaults in the army's history. In the Wilderness and again at Spotsylvania these attacks had so threatened the Confederate army that Lee had been tempted to lead the counterattack in person. If Grant's assaults failed or fell short of their ultimate objective, he took it in stride. Each maneuver was part of an overall plan whose objectives were to hold Lee's army closely, to prevent a Confederate offensive or the shifting of troops to other theaters; to exhaust Southern reserves of troops and matériel; and ultimately to pin and besiege an immobilized Army of Northern Virginia in the defenses of Richmond.

On the day of Lincoln's visit it could be said that Grant had accomplished most of his primary objectives. Lee himself had admitted that once his army was compelled to stand a siege in Petersburg, defeat would be "only a matter of time."

But the "matter of time" was highly significant. Lee's defensive tactics had imposed such brutal costs on the Northern army that public faith in the leadership of Grant and Lincoln was shaken. Contemporary reports estimated that Grant's armies had suffered as many as seventy-five thousand casualties—ten thousand a week for seven weeks, a butcher's bill three times heavier than Gettysburg's. McClellan had failed to take Richmond in 1862, but he had gotten there at far less cost, moving his troops by sea directly from the Potomac to the James. Comparisons with McClellan were particularly dangerous, because "Little Mac" was slated to receive the Democratic nomination to oppose Lincoln in the 1864 presidential election.

Abraham Lincoln might not have read Clausewitz, but he thoroughly understood the Prussian theorist's central principle, that war is always an adjunct of politics. Military achievement meant nothing unless the North's political society was willing to bear the costs of victory.

On June 8, while Grant's army was burying the dead of Cold Harbor, Lincoln had been renominated for the presidency in Baltimore, as candidate of the National Union party. This was a coalition of those committed to the administration's war policy, ranging from abolitionist Radical Republicans on the left to "war Democrats" and slaveholding Unionists on the right. The twists and turns in Lincoln's handling of slavery had been designed to keep these dissident elements together, but the divisions were about to break into the open. A Radical caucus at the Baltimore convention refused to endorse Lincoln's platform. The more militant Radicals had already split with the administration and at their May 31 convention in Cleveland had nominated John C. Frémont. A third party might split the war vote and throw the election to the Democrats—a party dominated by its "peace" faction, willing to end the war on terms favorable to the South.

Lincoln believed that the success of the Union's cause depended on his reelection and was determined to use every resource of politics and publicity to ensure that result. In private, he was at pains to let Grant know that he had pushed to the limit the public's tolerance for heavy casualties. "Several times, when contemplated battles were spoken of, he said: 'I cannot pretend to advise, but I do sincerely hope that all may be accomplished with as little bloodshed as possible.' " But the public events of Lincoln's visit were scenes of political theater, designed to display his confidence in Grant, his enthusiasm for his "wonderful campaign."

One of the most significant scenes was staged at Grant's suggestion. The general knew Lincoln was intensely interested in Black troops and had staked the credibility of his racial policies on their performance. So when Grant proposed a visit to the division of Negro soldiers commanded by General Hinks, which had distinguished itself in the battles of June 15, Lincoln agreed enthusiastically. They rode out to the encampment, the president in his tall hat and long black coat powdered with

dust, trousers riding up his long, lean, pale shanks, "a country farmer riding to town wearing his Sunday clothes." The Black troops lined the road,
and "when they beheld for the first time the liberator of their race," they
broke ranks and mobbed around Lincoln's horse. "Always impression-
able, the enthusiasm of the blacks now knew no limits. They cheered,
laughed, cried, sang hymns of praise, and shouted in their negro dialect,
'God bress Massa Linkum!' . . . They crowded around him and fondled
his horse; some of them kissed his hands, while others ran off crying in triumph . . . that they had touched his clothes." Lincoln lifted his hat in
salute and sat with bared head, tears in his eyes, hardly able to speak.

In such moments Lincoln came face-to-face with the reality of the
revolution he had helped to make. Frederick Douglass understood its significance: "Once let the black man get upon his person the brass letters,
U.S., let him get an eagle on his button, and a musket on his shoulder and
bullets in his pockets, and there is no power on earth which can deny that
he has earned the right to citizenship in the United States."

But there were powerful parties working to keep Blacks from the citizenship they had earned, and not all of these parties were in the South.
The Peace Democrats were willing to return to slavery those Negroes already freed by the war if that concession would bring the South back into
the Union. It went without saying that they had opposed the recruitment
of Black troops and, when that had failed, had resisted their employment
in combat. These positions were supported by large sections of the officer
corps: the Regulars were generally conservative in politics, and of the officers who owed their appointments to politics, a very large percentage
were Democrats.[3]

Thus the "Negro soldier question" was a major issue in the presidential campaign, and for those of a Radical bent, it was a litmus test of commitment to the cause. They blamed McClellan for having imbued his
officers with a spirit of hostility toward the administration, and now that
McClellan was preparing to oppose Lincoln for the presidency, they
feared the McClellan faction in the Army of the Potomac would sabotage
Grant's efforts. Radicals were therefore determined to subject the army's
commanders to strict scrutiny, and to work for the promotion of political
generals with strong Radical credentials.

A prime example was Major General Benjamin Franklin Butler, commanding the Army of the James to which Hinks's Negro division belonged. In saluting Hinks's men, Lincoln was also saluting Ben Butler. To
make assurance more sure, Lincoln's plan for June 22 was to take a navy
steamer up the James River to visit Butler's HQ.

Ben Butler was a chimera—physically, morally, and politically. At forty-six he looked like an old man, his bald head set without apparent neck "immediately on a stout shapeless body, [with] his very squinting eyes, and a set of legs and arms that look as if made for somebody else, and hastily glued to him by mistake."[4] He suffered from strabismus, one eye cocked at an angle. This gave him a shifty appearance, which did not belie his character. He began political life as a Jacksonian Democrat, defending working people against exploitation by Massachusetts mill owners. Southerners dominated the party, and Butler curried their favor. By his own admission he was at that time contemptuous of the Negro race, and his constituents had no interest in freeing slaves to compete for their low-wage jobs. At the 1860 Democratic convention he nominated Jefferson Davis for president of the United States and voted for him fifty times, and when Southern extremists bolted the party and nominated John C. Breckinridge, Butler went with them. But when Breckinridge Democrats became secessionists, Butler came out for the Union. The Lincoln administration was passionately eager to recruit Democrats to the cause, and Butler's commission as general in the state militia was quickly translated into a Federal major-generalship.

As a field commander Butler never won a battle it was possible to lose. But he was as quick to recognize political opportunity as Grant was to spot military advantage, and was as ruthless in pursuing it. He "drew his sword and threw the scabbard away" and became (as his former colleagues saw it) the blackest of Black Republicans. In 1861 he had started the administration on the path to emancipation by the brilliant lawyer's device of identifying slaves as "contraband of war." This provided legal cover for Union armies to make use of slaves who fled to their lines and to confiscate the slaves of Rebel masters. Butler had humor, and enjoyed tying Southerners and their Northern allies into a conceptual knot: they could not challenge his ploy without contradicting the basic theory of slavery, that slaves were property rather than persons.

He saw the administration's handling of the Negro problem as the key to victory and to a successful reconstruction. He also understood that, for the Radical wing of his party, his display of active enthusiasm for the Negro's cause was a sign of his reliability and a ticket to influence and advancement. As military governor of Louisiana he sponsored the formation of Black military units even before Lincoln authorized them. (He also became a byword for graft and corruption in his handling of state and military business.) When he assumed command of the Army of the James, he sought to have Black troops assigned to him, and willingly used them in combat. On June 21, the day of Lincoln's visit to Grant, he wrote to Grant requesting that all the Black troops from the Gulf Department (Louisiana) be transferred to his army. When that request was turned down, he proposed that Grant transfer to his command the all-Negro 4th Division of Burnside's IX Corps.

His cynicism was tempered by pride in the noble sentiments that drew him to the cause of the oppressed, first White workingmen and now the Negro. As his experience with Black soldiers grew, as he saw their valor and loyalty displayed on the battlefield, his earlier feelings of contempt gave way to admiration of their loyalty and courage. An element of sincerity entered the mix of motives he brought to "the question," which made him all the more dangerous as a political force. It would have been hard even for someone as shrewd as Abraham Lincoln to decide whether Butler's advocacy of the Black man's cause was a principled act or a devious self-promotion.

What Lincoln and Butler discussed on June 22 is not recorded, but the purpose of their meeting was plain enough. Lincoln wanted Butler to refrain from joining the Radical opposition to his candidacy. Butler had not only been courted by the Frémont campaign, but he had also been entertaining proposals that he run himself: "Your style suits me and the North, and if, as some say, . . . you are not as honest as 'Abe,' . . . you could not steal more than Abe's friends do." However, Butler needed to retain Lincoln's support to forestall the efforts of the West Point crowd to remove him from command of the Army of the James. At the end of the day Butler remained loyal to the administration, and Lincoln left him in command.

Butler probably also contributed his mite to undermining Lincoln's confidence in General Meade, his rival for the role of Grant's chief subordinate. On the day of Lincoln's visit Butler wrote to his wife, "Hecatombs of men are slaughtered, and still no good result accomplished. Nor is it the fault of General Grant. It is the cursed system under which we are carrying on this war. In a word, it's the West Pointism of the Army, or the McClellanism, for he is but the representative of the system." In the Radicals' eyes, Meade was the senior member of the McClellan clique.[5]

General George Gordon Meade was seven years older than Grant, and looked it: thinning hair, grizzled beard, a deeply lined face with dark bags under slightly bulging eyes. He was tightly wound and irascible under the best of circumstances, and the intense and costly fighting of the past month had strained him to the limit. His staff feared to approach him, certain he would lash out with some angry and cutting remark. He was a man with a grievance. He had beaten Lee at Gettysburg and in the subsequent fall campaign had maneuvered and fought Lee to a standoff. His reward was a presidential rebuke for failure to pursue the defeated enemy, and Grant's decision to accompany the Army of the Potomac during the overland campaign—which implied official mistrust of Meade's abilities. As Meade feared, press and politicians blamed him whenever the army's execution fell short of Grant's intention. Add to this the suspicions of Radicals on the powerful congressional Joint Committee on the Conduct of the War and Meade's tenure of command was very much in question.

Lincoln's visit did little to soothe Meade's anxieties. Despite the president's assurance of sympathy and support, he had left the generals with a military conundrum: how to continue pressing an entrenched enemy without suffering the losses such offensives entailed. Meade suspected that if there was another disaster on the scale of Cold Harbor and the president needed a scapegoat, it would not be Grant who got the sack.

As it turned out, the attempt (June 21–22) to maneuver around the Confederate flank and seize the Weldon Railroad *was* a failure. The two infantry corps became separated in brushy woods, the Confederates counterattacked, and the infantry backed off—no panic rout, just worn-out soldiers walking away from a battle for which they saw no use. Meade's temper turned so savage that Charles Dana, the War Department's civilian observer, thought Grant would be forced to relieve him.

So when, on the twenty-fifth of June, General Burnside wrote to say he thought it feasible to mine the enemy salient on his front, Meade responded with unusual warmth: "I am delighted to hear you can do anything against the enemy's line, and will furnish you anything you want, and earnest wishes for your success besides." A successful mining operation might allow Meade's army to breach the Rebel line without staging a bloody and probably futile frontal assault. Even if the maneuver did not achieve a major breakthrough, it might well yield a significant local advance that would tighten the siege and demonstrate that the army was making progress. Moreover, it would take some time to dig the mine, and with such a prospect in view Meade might have a better chance of persuading Grant to allow the army a chance to rest and recover.

He immediately sent eight thousand sandbags to IX Corps and ordered his staff engineer, Major J. C. Duane, to look the project over and provide advice and assistance.

BURNSIDE'S OPPORTUNITY: JUNE 25–27, 1864

Ambrose Burnside was an impressive and attractive figure, forty years old, six feet tall with broad chest and shoulders, his massive head seemingly enlarged by the high bald dome above his brow. His well-fed face was dignified by a luxuriant double scallop of brown whiskers that framed his full cheeks and met above his mouth. Those whiskers were famous in their own right, immortalized in the barber's specialty called "burnsides." His manner was affable and ingenuous, so that even the waspish Meade found it hard to dislike him. In an army filled with officers hell-bent on self-promotion, he was remarkable for his modesty. Informed in the fall of 1862 that he had been appointed to succeed McClellan in command of the Army of the Potomac, he protested that the job was beyond his skill. It was too bad the War Department did not take him at his word.

He brought to his profession an odd mix of ingenuity and incompetence. He had a speculative bent that kept his mind open to innovative tactics and technologies, and with it came the speculator's tendency to plunge into everything in expectation of fabulous returns. He graduated from West Point in 1847, too late for active service in the Mexican War. In the boring routine of occupation duty his enthusiasm for gambling nearly ruined him. Faced with a run of bad cards, he could imagine no better play than to double-down on every hand. His postwar experience included fighting Indians in the West, where he recognized the army's need for a repeating carbine to replace the single-shot weapon then in use. He designed and developed the carbine in his spare time, took out a patent, and in 1853 resigned his commission to open the Bristol Rifle Works in Rhode Island. The Burnside was a very good weapon, but to make real money the maker needed a War Department order. He was active in the Democratic party, which got him a hearing with John Floyd, President Buchanan's ethically challenged secretary of war. Floyd gave him verbal assurance of a large order. He borrowed heavily to increase production, but Floyd gave the contract to one of his cronies and Burnside went bankrupt. In extremity he turned to schoolmate George B. McClellan, who had resigned his own commission to assume the presidency of the Illinois Central Railroad. By 1861 Burnside had paid his debts and was running the railroad's New York office.

He made an impressive record during the first year of the war. One of the mainsprings of Union strategy was the seizure of islands and ports along the Atlantic coast, to solidify the blockade of Southern shipping and to provide bases from which to threaten the interior. An army-navy operation had seized Fort Hatteras, which commanded the central point of entry to the North Carolina sounds. Burnside proposed recruiting an army corps, to be trained and equipped especially for amphibious operations, with which he would exploit the breakthrough. Promotion of the idea proved relatively easy. His friend McClellan had just been appointed to command the nation's armies, and Burnside had won the liking of President Lincoln. Burnside raised the regiments, got them equipped and trained, purchased or leased a fleet of transports, and under navy escort brought them out of the stormy Atlantic into the wide waters of the North Carolina sounds. With superior forces and command of the bays and rivers Burnside could strike wherever he wished, shifting forces far more rapidly than the road-bound Rebels. In a few months he had won two small battles and his troops controlled the sounds and all the coast from Beaufort to Plymouth.[6]

Then in the summer of 1862 Lee defeated McClellan in front of Richmond and opened an offensive toward Washington. Burnside's command, renamed IX Corps, was brought north to defend the capital. In the ensuing Battle of Antietam, Burnside was assigned the task of carrying a bridge and attacking the Confederate right. He fussed about his orders and delayed the assault. The "bridge of death" was eventually carried in a gallant rush, but too late to have a decisive result. Nevertheless, when McClellan failed to pursue Lee's army after the battle, Lincoln put Burnside in his place.

Army command was beyond him. Once again he began well, executing a swift march to the Rappahannock River crossing opposite Fredericksburg. But the pontoon bridge he ordered was delayed, and by the time it arrived, Lee's army held an impregnable position. All Burnside could think to do was plow ahead with the original plan, which now required a frontal assault against entrenched artillery and infantry. To make matters worse, his orders were so badly written that it was never clear what he intended his generals to do, and their assaults were uncoordinated. After the first waves were shot to pieces, it was apparent to everyone that further attacks were useless, but Burnside fought the battle the way he played cards, doubling the bet after every defeat, and he lost 12,600 men. Lincoln relieved him and sent him west with his own IX Corps to defend southern Ohio and western Kentucky.

His performance there somewhat redeemed his reputation. He did embarrass Lincoln by jailing a Copperhead (pro-Confederate) candidate for governor and closing an anti-administration newspaper—but this did him no harm with the Radicals. Two of his divisions under his chief of staff, John Parke, went to Mississippi to help Grant at Vicksburg, and saw hard service. Late in the summer, Burnside led his troops over the mountains to seize Knoxville, fulfilling Lincoln's wish to liberate East Tennessee and cutting the best railroad link between Virginia and the Confederacy's western armies. After having done so much so well, he then dithered when called upon to march to the aid of Rosecrans's army, besieged in Chattanooga. But he did stave off a Rebel siege of Knoxville, against an army commanded by James Longstreet. Summoned east to join Grant's overland campaign, he performed with earnest goodwill and acceptable efficiency—but neither Grant nor Meade were willing to entrust him with command of a major operation.[7]

So Burnside welcomed the mine project when Potter's note landed on his desk. He was eager to demonstrate his usefulness to Meade and Grant, who seemed inclined to parcel out his troops for supporting roles in the more active commands. It was a source of concern that his Negro division had been on loan for most of the campaign, guarding bridges and supply trains. He had just gotten them back when rumor informed him that Butler was politicking to gather all the Black troops into his Army of the James. On the day of Lincoln's visit Burnside proposed using the Blacks to make a surprise attack on the Confederate trenches. Meade turned him down. But a successful mining operation on his front would guarantee that IX Corps—presumably at full strength—would play the leading role.[8]

Burnside prepared a series of exacting queries for Colonel Pleasants, and came away thoroughly impressed by the young engineer's preparation, confidence, and technical expertise. The critical issue in a military mine of such length was ventilation, since drilling airholes to the surface would betray the operation to Confederate miners. Pleasants presented detailed sketches for a system of his own design, versions of which he had field-tested when digging railroad tunnels and in the mines. Burnside liked what he saw, made a quick inspection of the area to be mined, and then approved the plan and sent it up to army headquarters with his endorsement.

He was gratified by Meade's immediate and friendly response, but troubled by the decision to send Major Duane to look it over. Duane had literally written the book on military mining for U.S. forces, but he was a

McClellan loyalist and had been on bad terms with Burnside since Antietam. Duane's response confirmed Burnside's forebodings: he made a quick tour and told both Meade and Burnside that the project was "claptrap and nonsense." It was simply impossible to dig a military tunnel of that length. Duane therefore refused to supply Burnside with any of the sixty-odd pieces of specialized equipment that military mining required—pickaxes (common and short-handled), shovels (common and short-handled), push-picks, rakes, a windlass and rope, wheelbarrows, handsaws, boring rods, rammers, helves—though there were ample supplies at headquarters.[9]

But Pleasants had already started digging.

Chapter 3

The Miners

JUNE 25–JULY 2, 1864

Henry Pleasants was thirty-one, with olive skin and dark curly hair and mustache, a heritage from his mother, an Argentine heiress descended from Spanish nobility. His father ran guns to the Argentine colonists fighting for independence from Spain and, later, against the dictatorship of General Juan Manuel de Rozas. Henry's father died when Henry was eight, and his mother (fearing persecution by Rozas) sent Henry to be raised by a paternal uncle in Philadelphia. Pleasants never saw her again. He studied civil engineering and at the age of twenty-one took charge of a major railroad tunnel project. After a business dispute he shifted from railroads to mining, operating as an independent contractor in Pottsville, center of the soft coal region of Schuylkill County. There he married the daughter of Benjamin Bannan, editor of the region's leading newspaper (the *Miners Journal*) and a power in Republican politics. Henry's young wife died suddenly just before the firing on Fort Sumter, plunging him into a depression from which the war saved him. He threw himself into recruiting, training, and commanding Company C of the 48th. He became a good combat officer, jumped from captain to lieutenant colonel after Antietam, and at the start of Grant's overland campaign was given command of the regiment. A colleague wrote that: "This young and gallant officer was much valued by his . . . commanders. He was a soldier of true grit, possessed of more than ordinary ability as an engineer." But his personality was not that of the stereotypical plodding technician: his "Spanish blood" gave him an "impetuous nature, and quick, fiery temper," although his colleagues considered him "generous [and] good-hearted."[1]

The mine engaged his professional pride and his intense emotions, a combination that gave him the will and the energy to drive ahead regardless of obstacles or opposition. Even before going to see Potter he had had his adjutant draw up a list of the professional miners in the outfit. At noon on June 25, right after meeting with Burnside, he had his men begin the cut, starting in the face of a ravine about a hundred feet behind the front line, just above the bed of Taylor's Creek.

There were about one hundred professional miners in the regiment, out of the four hundred men who'd survived the spring campaign. The identification as a professional had a particular meaning in Schuylkill County. Professional miners became masters of vernacular engineering, because no mining could be done without careful and well-designed timbering of the shafts. The work was dangerous, nasty, and physically exhausting. Miners had to tunnel narrow shafts into the rock to get at the coal seams, doing intense physical labor in close quarters and inhaling coal dust and mephitic vapors. They were in constant danger of cave-ins, flooding by underground springs, and gas explosions. But for skilled miners the trade was also remunerative. Some worked for wages, and many worked as private contractors, leasing their place in a seam and delivering coal for an agreed upon price. Both classes of miners were relatively well rewarded, in an industry that continually expanded throughout the 1840s and 1850s to meet ever-growing demand.

Their work was supported by a large force of laborers, who did the unskilled labor of moving freed coal from the mine shaft to the railroad cars that carried it to market, or performed any of the hundreds of tasks required to keep the miners working: pumping water out of the tunnels, cutting and stacking timber, and so on. For this they were paid roughly a third of what a skilled miner could make, and worked twice as long to earn it. The edge of that distinction was sharpened by ethnic tension. The skilled miners and the owners who employed them were mainly Protestants of British or Welsh ancestry, the laborers mainly Catholic Irish immigrants. A Welshman new to the district might have to wait six to nine months to get "a place of his own" as a contract or wage-paid miner, while Irish miners had to wait years for the privilege.[2] By 1860 the Irish constituted a majority in many of the large towns of Schuylkill County. Most were Catholic peasants displaced by famine and rack rent, but the counties from which they came had different political and social traditions. The members of one of these subgroups, from Mayo and west Donegal, were accustomed to forming secret societies to resist landlords and government agents. In the coal fields such organizations brawled with the

Welsh and English, or operated as gangs in the harassment and intimida-
tion that was the currency of ethnic interaction. They were known as
"Molly Maguires," and were reputed (justly or not) to be the terrorist arm
of the labor movement in Schuylkill County.[3]

The mine owners, merchants, and well-to-do townsmen were Republican, against slavery and for free labor—by which they meant that
every wage worker had to see himself as an embryonic capitalist. That was
the editorial view of the *Miners Journal*, published by Colonel Pleasants's father-in-law, Benjamin Bannan (of Welsh ancestry). But the mathematics of free labor was flawed: industrial growth depended on the
existence of a large wage-earning force—it could not possibly continue if
every wage earner were to become an employer. Bannan blamed the existence of a mining proletariat on the flawed racial character of the Irish:
they were drunken, ignorant, lazy, superstitious, immoral, untrustwor-
thy—everything, in short, that Southern planters said about Blacks to justify their enslavement.[4]

But the 48th Pennsylvania had little trouble recruiting in the summer
of 1861. Their roster of enlisted men lists surnames reflecting the full
range of ethnicities and trades in the county: German farmers; Anglo
American lawyers and merchants; Scottish, Welsh, and Irish miners. The
Irish contingent included a scattering of names common in Mayo and
west Donegal—Dolan, Fisher, Boyle, O'Brien, Dougherty, Gibbons,
Kane, Kell(e)y, Kerrigan, O'Neil, Monaghan, Duffy, Carroll, O'Donnell—
names later associated with the Molly Maguires. They may have been exceptions to the political sympathies of their community, or they may have
been young men more excited by the roll of the drum than the bell that
rang at the pithead.[5]

The 48th were sent first to the North Carolina sounds, then Virginia,
and then Kentucky, Mississippi, and East Tennessee. For three years they
lived in a world apart, and their experience amalgamated them into a new
kind of community, a tight-knit military society absorbed in its own affairs. Some of the civilian hierarchy remained. Nearly all the field officers
were of either Anglo American or German ancestry, with a scattering of
Welsh, while the Irish were underrepresented in the ranks of officers and
NCOs. At the end of their three-year enlistment, when faced with the
choice of whether or not to reenlist as a unit, nearly all of the men affirmed
their loyalty to cause and comrades by signing on for the duration. In the
winter of 1863–64 they were therefore designated a Veteran Volunteer
regiment and sent home for a brief furlough before the spring campaign.

In the regiment's absence the county had been the scene of wide-spread violent resistance to conscription. The fact that a man could buy his way out of the draft for three hundred dollars was proof that this was "a rich man's war and a poor man's fight." Democratic politicians tried to link these local grievances to their national platform of opposition to Lincoln's antislavery measures. They described the August 1862 conscription as a measure "to enable abolitionist Capitalists to transport Negroes into the northern cities to replace workers who were striking for higher wages." That summer armed mobs attacked the sites where names were drawn. A year later, in the summer of 1863, there was a more serious wave of disorder in the county, on the heels of the huge Draft Riots in New York City—which also had a distinctly Irish character. Troops were sent to Pottsville to maintain order, and the Catholic bishop of Philadelphia came to preach against secret societies, especially the Molly Maguires. The mine owners were able to use the repression of seditious elements as a cover for suppressing all efforts at labor organizing.

The soldiers of the 48th must have known of the problems back home. In addition to letters, many subscribed to the *Miners Journal,* which covered (and condemned) the disorders. Although the violence had been suppressed before the men of the 48th returned for their furlough, state troops were still policing the region. Yet the only reference to these events in regimental histories or memoirs is oblique: the insistence that Schuylkill County sent as high a percentage of its men to war as any other county in the state. In fact, enlistments from the county were well below average. But regiments represented the honor and reputation of their communities: to admit disloyalty among the home folks was as shameful as admitting cowardice in their own ranks.[6]

DIGGING IN, JUNE 25–JULY 3

The 48th lived a solidarity their community had lost. It showed in the spirit with which they turned to mining in this new context. Every man in the regiment, miner or not, volunteered to help, and the work gave a boost to morale. It was a change from the crushing boredom of trench duties, and at the same time it was (for most of them) a reversion to their civilian identities. The job was also well-paid, not in money but in the privileges soldiers value: exemption from picket duty and fatigue details, a sup of whiskey when your shift was done, the expectation that the men who dug the shaft would not have to join the charge after the mine blew.

To supervise the work, Pleasants chose Sergeant Henry Reese, "a burly, red-headed Welshman from Minersville," known to his mates as "Snapper." He was born in Wales in 1835 to a family that had worked coal for generations—they sent young Harry into the mines at age eight. He immigrated to America as a young man, worked his way up to foreman, and joined the army in 1861. The coal dust he inhaled all his life settled in his lungs and would eventually kill him, but in 1864 he was still hale and strong, and he knew his business. The mine was his baby; he was around it all day and slept in its mouth at night so that no one came in or out without his knowledge.

He divided his workers into three-man teams, combining skilled miners to delve and set timber and unskilled laborers to shovel and haul dirt, and assigned regular shifts to use and also husband the strength of the men. In the Schuylkill mines the division of labor was a source of poverty and shame and the basis of exploitation, enforced by necessity and maintained by discrimination. In the regiment all men were volunteers, working for a common purpose and adding to their collective glory. On their first day they drove the shaft fifty feet into sandy clay, and added forty more on each of the next two days. To maximize speed and minimize timbering, Pleasants designed a tight tunnel structure, shaped like a pyramid with the top lopped off, four feet high from floor to ceiling and perhaps four feet wide at the base tapering to two feet at the top. Horizontal timbers would be sunk into the floor as a mudsill, and two props slanting inward would support a timber roof piece. Where the ground was soft or wet, this structure would be reinforced by plank retaining walls and flooring.[7]

The men not only worked with a will, they also used their knowledge and experience to forward the project, joining with officers and noncoms to improvise solutions to the difficulties that continually arose. They were using picks designed as entrenching tools, with long blades and shafts, suitable for swinging in the open air. They needed mining picks, with shorter heavier blades and shorter helves, but Major Duane and the army engineers said they had none to spare. So the skilled miners carried their tools to a nearby artillery battery, whose armorer modified their picks on his forge. The army would send no wheelbarrows with which to cart the earth out of the mine; so the men took empty hardtack boxes, reinforced them with metal straps, fastened on a pair of poles and made sleds that could be dragged along the ground, carrying three to four cubic feet of earth.

Three men at a time worked inside the shaft: one man cracking into the blank face of the clay with his pick, another with a short-handled shovel throwing the broken clay into a cracker-box sled, and the third man hauling it back down the tunnel to daylight. It was close quarters, the tunnel just four feet high and only about three feet wide at shoulder height. The men's movements were cramped; they were compelled to work at odd angles, lying down or sitting on an overturned keg or on their knees. They worked by the light of candles set in cap-lamps (also improvised). The disposal of the sand and clay they dug out of the mine was a perennial problem. At first they used it to fill sandbags to strengthen their trenches, but it soon occurred to Pleasants that excessive production of sandbags might give them away to Rebel observers. For the same reason, fresh dirt could not be dumped near their position. So it had to be hauled by night to distant ravines and covered with brush chopped by regimental details.

Pleasants did his improvising at a higher level. He had sent a requisition to Major Duane for use of an army theodolite, a surveyor's instrument for making precise measurements of distance and elevation. It was critical that he verify the direction and bearing of his tunnel, to ensure it would arrive under the targeted battery. When Duane failed to respond, Potter asked Burnside to second the request. This time the result was a flat refusal. Burnside had to write to a friend in Washington, asking him to send his own instrument down by the next supply boat.

The miners kept digging. At one hundred twenty feet in they hit a stratum of solid clay and the going got harder. At that point Pleasants halted the forward drive and supervised the construction of his ventilation system. At about the hundred-foot mark, he had the men dig a narrow chimney from the roof to the surface. They constructed a long square tube of boards along the floor of the mine, the near end opening below the chimney, the far end opening in the gallery where the miners worked. Below the chimney a small pit was excavated, in which a strong fire was kept burning. This created a draft or convection current that sucked out the used air and any noxious gases in the soil, and drew in fresh air from the tunnel mouth. When the length of the tunnel weakened the draft, Pleasants simply reversed the flow: he extended the wooden tube out through the mine entrance into the open air, and closed the tunnel mouth with heavy burlap. Now the fire created a vacuum at the near end of the mine, which sucked the air out of the deep end and drew fresh air down the tube to replace it.

The men inside escaped the furnace blast of Virginia sunshine, but in that confined space the air was heated by their bodies at work and by the candle flames, and clotted with the dust of their digging. They worked three-hour shifts at the start, shortened to two and a half as the work wore them down. Nor were they free from the usual perils of trench warfare—deliberate murder by snipers sitting in the trees behind the Rebel line, and the random butchery of mortar shells dropping from out of the blue. Theirs was the line closest to the enemy, and to make matters worse the Black troops of the 4th Division did another turn in the trenches from June 27 to July 3, which made the sniping and mortaring particularly vicious. General Burnside reported average losses of forty-eight men per day during this period—a rate he considered light.

On July 2 the miners hit an area some of them described as "quicksand"—in fact a layer of marl, a damp pasty soil with a consistency like putty. Instead of crumbling or shearing away from pick and shovel, it gummed and clung, and on contact with air hardened into a cement sturdy enough for the men to mold pipe bowls and knickknacks out of it. But timbers set into it would not hold, the mudsills sank, the props caved in, and the ceiling started to come down. Reese had to pull his men out and report to Pleasants that nothing more could be done unless they got a lot more timber and planking.

The colonel told Reese to send out details to scavenge timber, and wrote passes to cover their activities. Reese and his men scoured the rear areas, where they located a creek bridge and stole it, dismantling and packing it piece by piece into wagons liberated for the purpose. Another detail struck it rich: an abandoned sawmill—a supply of boards and timbers, and facilities for making more. Pleasants's men were fully employed with the work of mining, but there was a supply of surplus labor at hand: the Blacks of Ferrero's 4th Division, now coming off their stint in the trenches. For most of the campaign they had been employed as guards for the army's wagon train and other noncombat details. Why shouldn't the Negroes make boards for the mine?

Although the Irish back in Pottsville had no use for Negroes, the 48th had no particular bias against them. Still, most thought they were better suited as laborers than soldiers. General Potter put in the request, and General Ferrero sent some of his men to work at the sawmill making boards for the 48th.[8]

While the miners burrowed underground, the rest of IX Corps worked with pick and shovel to transform their fieldworks into entrenchments capable of maintaining a long siege. The core of their position was Fort Morton on the high ground where the ruined Taylor house stood, home to a fourteen-gun battery of heavy artillery firing from embrasures in a wall of earth-filled gabions and big timber. To the north, smaller fortifications protected mortar batteries, both the heavy type used to breach trenches and the lighter antipersonnel Coehorns. The Taylor house ridge provided some shelter for reserves and ammunition, although the rise was so shallow that Confederate gunners could drop shells into much of the rear area. Here there were straggling woodlots of pine that offered shade for troops off the line but limited protection from shell fire.

Burnside's engineers dug two "covered ways," one on each side of Fort Morton. These trenches were not literally roofed over. Rather, their zigzag course used inequalities in the terrain to provide cover for troops passing from the reserve areas to the front line. They were six to eight feet deep and about ten wide, so that (in theory) a regiment in column could be rushed down its length to reinforce the lines. As you approached the front, each covered way branched out in a delta of smaller trenches intended to feed different parts of the line. But at that point the cover became increasingly theoretical. The approach trenches debouched into the shallow marshy ravine of Taylor's Run, which was exposed to mortar shells and sniper fire from Rebels. To speed the crossing, the infantry, working under fire, laid "corduroy bridges" across the boggy ground: small logs trimmed and laid side by side in packed earth to make a solid roadbed, but they could do nothing to protect the ravine from hostile fire.

Once across the creek you were shielded from direct fire by the western bank of the ravine. The infantry dug shelters into this reverse slope, reinforcing the roofs with logs to make them bombproof. The larger bombproofs were headquarters for regimental commanders on the line. From the Taylor's Run ravine, approach trenches gave access to the main defense line, which at this point was a nearly continuous trench, six or more feet deep and six to eight feet wide. The infantry dug out the first three feet with pick and shovel, piling the dirt in front of the trench to make a parapet, which they reinforced with the heaviest timbers they could find. Sandbags were laid atop these head logs, with small spaces ("loops") left between them for the use of riflemen and officers making observations. At the foot of the trench wall was a wooden banquette of logs or planks, on which riflemen could stand to fire out the loopholes, or sit and rest during the interminable watches of the hot, boring, murderous day.

At twenty-foot intervals the main line was broken by a sharp angling of the trench or by the construction of a traverse, a barrier of earth and logs set at right angles to the trench wall. (The army's amateur soldiers sometimes used the word "traverse" to describe both the angle and the barrier.) The function of these devices was to defend against enfilade, or fire coming from the flank. Without traverses, such fire could sweep a trench from end to end. The traverses also compartmentalized, and so limited, the effects of mortar and artillery. Should an enemy succeed in storming some part of the line, the traverse was a defensive barricade to contain the breakthrough. So that officers and support troops could be quickly moved from one section to another, communication trenches were dug, parallel to the main line, and connected to it by short ditches or tunnels.

Forward of the main line was the picket line: a series of separate rifle pits manned by two or three men whose role was to repel raiding parties and give early warning of any attack. If you were out on picket, you lay all day in the "broiling sun" in a shallow rifle pit "about the size of a *common* grave though not half so well *furnished* . . . and everytime a man Show his head Zip . . . The bullets would just skim the top of the pit."[9]

Beyond or between the pickets were the obstacles, the brushy abatis and the spiked wall of chevaux-de-frise designed to hold an attacking enemy in the killing ground. On the forward edge of the Horseshoe the opposing lines were so close that IX Corps had no picket line, only the abatis. Beyond that were the enemy's obstacles, pickets, and main line.

Of the area just behind the Rebel line little could be seen, but beyond the front, the ground rose gradually to the long low ridge on which the Jerusalem Plank Road ran. Petersburg was just over the rise to the south. "It was an easy matter for us to see the steeples of Petersburg from some parts of our line, and the shrill notes of the car whistle and rumble of moving trains reminded us every day that the beleaguered town was alive and doing business at the old stand." At the northern end of the ridge was the higher bulge of the hill on which Blandford Cemetery was located. From Cemetery Hill a low ridge reached back down toward the trench line. There was a strong Rebel battery dug in on that high ground, five hundred feet behind the main line, whose guns could rake the forward trenches of IX Corps.[10]

Life in the trenches was squalid. Even in the open field, a two-day army camp smelled like a cross between a stable, an abattoir, and an open sewer. Now the army was in the Petersburg position to stay, and as days passed, that limited space had to absorb the waste of tens of thousands of human beings and animals, their rotting garbage, the offal of slaughtered livestock, and the amputated limbs and dead bodies of the men. Bad water and bad diet—desiccated vegetables, beans, salt pork, hardtack crackers fried in grease—gave the men "squitters" (chronic diarrhea). Camp diseases were rife: typhoid, dysentery—many of Burnside's troops, who had served in Mississippi, also had malaria—and now men were lost to sunstroke and heat prostration. The salty diet made some men prone to boils, "sick breaking out all about my body," which could easily become infected. The men wore woolen uniforms in the stifling heat, and between dust and sweat and unwashed bodily filth "our clothing became stiffened and caked with inground mud. Lice appeared, increased, swarmed . . . dropping upon us from the dried leaves of our bough-built shanties, and making life a disgrace as well as a nuisance."[11]

Above the filth the air was deadly dangerous. "With the patience of cats watching for mice the men would peer for hours at the [loop]holes . . . waiting a chance to shoot . . . and the faintest show of the crown of a hat above the hostile fortification, undistinguishable to the inexperienced eye, would draw a bullet." Sergeant Burnham and two of his buddies in the 9th New Hampshire had rigged a shelter tent over their trench as a sun shade, but a "saucy Johnny" on higher ground insisted on perforating it. The Rebel was shooting from a little notch in the top of an embankment. Burnham fired three or four rounds at it, and the Rebel quit. But that evening he started in again, and this time Burnham lay in wait for him: stuck his rifle out the loophole and let the Rebel take his shots at it. After the third, he got behind his gun, sighted on the notch, and when the Rebel's head appeared in it, "I fired, his hands and rifle went up in the air, and he fell back . . . with a bullet in his brain."[12]

Firing on the 9th New Hampshire's front was so incessant that a lone tree in front of their position was cut down by bullets. Rebel sharpshooters in trees behind the lines could and did kill men a hundred yards behind the line. They had a bead on every gap in the earthworks, every unobstructed passage or patch of open ground between the rear and the front lines, so that any movement, however innocent, carried the risk of death or maiming. Sergeant Rawson of G Company, "one of the brightest boys of our regiment, and beloved by all, in a playfull little scuffle . . . exposed himself to the ever watchful eyes of the Rebel sharpshooters, [and] was struck by a bullet in the head." A corporal in the 6th New Hampshire was in his tent making out E Company's payroll when a bullet cut through the tent wall and killed him. "His life-blood flowed over the pay-roll, which was forwarded to Washington . . . sealed with his blood." Men were killed or wounded in every unit every day.[13]

The men feared mortars above all. Mortars fired round shells in a looping trajectory, exploded by fuse, and when one of these burst in the contained and crowded space of a trench, it killed and mutilated men by blast and by the shrapnel of its iron casing.

The nervous strain was continual, the physical conditions appalling. The sun slammed down on the terrain day after day, and the heat solidified between the red clay walls. The drought made the clay friable, and the least movement stirred clouds of fine choking dust that dried the mouth and nose, which with the salted meat and dry crackers made unslakable thirst the besetting misery of life. After two weeks on the ground the men had drunk the nearby creeks and wells just about dry. Water details had to run the gauntlet of enemy fire going down to Taylor's Run or (if it was dry) crossing it to get to the rear area. Their comrades would "laugh & shout . . . to see them 'sail' dodging to and from one tree to another." Privates Park and Murray of the 57th Massachusetts, pinned down in their picket post with bullets zipping by and the sun pounding down, parched with thirst but unwilling to die for a drink of water, wrote out in all seriousness a request for immediate transfer to the navy. Though their reasons were excellent, the application was denied.[14]

Relief and variety in diet were sometimes provided by deliveries of fresh beef or vegetables, by parcels from home, and by visits from the Sanitary Commission. The latter provided Federal armies with a range of services, including nurses, reading matter, preachers and tracts to address spiritual needs, and healthful goodies like canned peaches, dried fruit and cabbages, and pickles—acidic to cut the taste of all that grease, and a preventive against scurvy. Men who had cash in hand could purchase treats from the sutlers, private contractors who sold tobacco, whiskey, canned goods, and notions from their wagons. But pay was often in arrears, and delivered in the form of "scrip," military chits that many sutlers refused to honor, so worthless that "One of the boys papered his tent all around with these sheets of scrip."

To maintain the strength and alertness of the men, units were rotated, two days up on the line and two days in the rest area. But Confederate gunners firing from higher ground could easily loft shells into the bivouac, and rifle bullets could be heard zipping through the pines and spent bullets dropping like bird shit from the branches. Officers and men dug their tents into the ground and set up log barriers on the side facing the enemy. The problem with that arrangement was that you couldn't see the shells coming. Their velocity was low enough that in the front lines you could often see them coming right at you. In the rear you had to keep one ear cocked for the sound of them whispering "quit, quit, quit" as they came "tumbling through the air." So in daylight, lookouts were posted to spot incoming rounds, and at their warning the men would drop flat to let the shrapnel whizz overhead. At night you could lie out and gaze at the stars and watch the rounds drop like meteors, fire trailing from their fuses.[15]

Captain George Washington Whitman of the 51st New York coped with these conditions through positive thinking. He wrote reassuringly to his widowed mother, "We live very well here, and are a great deal more comfortable than one would think." His attitude was not all feigned. He was one of those men who had found and bettered himself in the army. His roots were in the class of small farmers and artisans who were the core constituency of free labor, whose hope it was that every son would achieve a higher level of prosperity than his father. Whitman's father had been a dirt-poor farmer and carpenter. Of his six sons, three moved up and three fell out of the race, victims of alcoholism or mental deficiency. George trained as a carpenter, and then worked as an apprentice printer at the newspaper run by his brother Walt Whitman, the poet of *Leaves of Grass*.

The army brought out talents George had not known he possessed—courage under fire and the ability to manage and command. He had enlisted as a private and been promoted from the ranks. The life expectancy of such junior officers was short, as Whitman knew very well. As a city newspaper reported, "almost every week . . . has seen a funeral in New-York or Brooklyn of some officer or man of the Fifty-first, their bodies being forwarded to friends. Not an original officer remains." But George preferred to think about the captain's pay, $125 a month, that would enable him to buy his mother "that little house in the Country, where, Mattie, and Sis, and the rest of us can go and visit her, and where she will have nothing to do by feed chickens and make pumpkin pies and sich [*sic*] like, and tell her if she will only take things cooly and not worry, things will all come out right." He felt the same way about the war: "The ammount [*sic*] of it is Mother we all believe in Grant, and as far as I can hear the opinion is universal in the army."[16]

Officers and men also kept despair at arm's length with sardonic humor. They laughed at the water details who dodged bullets, laughed when a near miss sprayed clay on their cook and "peppered" the soup. In the part of the front usually manned by the 2nd Division there was an ice well, deep enough to hold a small precious store of ice down at the bottom. Men risked sniper fire for the chance to scoop a bucket of the stuff. On the fourth of July some officers of the 6th New Hampshire were enjoying the rare treat of lemonade, from fresh fruit supplied by the Sanitary Commission, cooled with ice brought out under fire from the ice well, when a random shell came looping over the trees and blew up a few yards away, burying the men in a cloud of red clay dust. They came out of it spitting and slapping at themselves, nobody wounded but looking "more like Indians than white men," their lemonade turned to muck. Captain Jones said to Captain Jackman, "That is the meanest thing I ever knew the Rebels to do."[17]

On another occasion a chance shell dropped into the middle of a card game, blowing up the pot and wounding five men. By some freak of ballistics a shard of shrapnel struck the blade of a shovel and flipped it end over end through the air till it struck a soldier—an older man who "straightened up, mad all through, and called out, 'Who the devil throw'd that shovel at me?' Of course the boys had to laugh at this," despite the wounded lying around. When a man could be hurt by such an absurd chance, what was there to do *but* laugh?

But after a few days in the hospital the old man's scalp wound turned gangrenous and killed him.[18]

TAKING SIGHTS, JULY 3-5, 1864

On July 3, Pleasants picked up the theodolite at Burnside's headquarters, carried it into the main trench line, and prepared to make his observations. A captain from Potter's staff came along to help.

The theodolite is a short telescope mounted on a staff or tripod, coupled with calibrated disks that measure horizontal and vertical angles. The surveyor chooses two points of observation and establishes the distance of a base line between them. At one of the chosen points he aims the telescope at the target; then he reads the horizontal disk to determine the angle of the target in relation to the base line. The vertical disk gives him the angle of its elevation above or below the chosen position. The surveyor then repeats the process at the second point of observation and uses trigonometry to compute the distance of the target and its elevation. This is easy enough for a surveyor laying out a boundary or a railroad right of way in open country. Pleasants had to make his observations under the watchful eyes of Rebel snipers. To increase the difficulty, the theodolite sent down by Burnside's friend was an old-fashioned model, clumsier than the modern instruments at Duane's headquarters.[19]

Pleasants camouflaged his upper body and the theodolite with burlap sacking and then squirmed into an angle of the trench line, followed by Potter's aide. He set the staff firmly in the ground and squinted into the telescope. The Rebel battery was a bulge in the line of turned earth, shaking in the waves of heat that baked up off the ground. He rotated the disks exactingly, careful not to jostle the instrument, and as he did, he heard a sharp crack like a board splitting and felt a dull wet splatter on his burlap cowl, and froze. He knew it was the sound of a bullet breaking the staff captain's skull and the splatter of his brains—but there was no second shot, so he kept on with his task while someone dragged the body away.

Then he crouched down the trench line to take his second observation.

When he returned to his headquarters that afternoon, he was surprised to find a lengthy dispatch from General J. G. Barnard, chief of engineers at Grant's headquarters—not Meade's. In a series of numbered paragraphs Barnard asked for specific information about every material aspect of the proposed mine, and for diagrams drawn to scale (longitudinal section and profile) of its structure and position. All questions were to be answered, with reference to paragraph and subparagraph, "without delay and as shortly as possible."

Pleasants was out of patience. The army engineers sniffed in superior fashion at his expertise, when he knew far more about modern mining methods. But perhaps Barnard's letter indicated that Grant's people were overriding Meade's people, expressing genuine interest in the project. So he replied quickly, if somewhat tersely, with all the technical details of the project, leaving unanswered those questions that were either premature (when the mine would be fired) or beyond his competence (i.e., how the attack should be organized).[20] He must have wondered why such operational questions would be asked of a mere lieutenant colonel of volunteers.

But in the meantime, he had figured out a solution to the marl problem. He told Reese to dig ahead on a rising angle, which would get them into the clay stratum above the marl. Then they could continue digging straight ahead.

⟳

Barnard's inquiry was the last in a chain, which had begun at ten-thirty that morning with a query from Grant to Meade: "Do you think it possible, by a bold and decisive attack, to break through the enemy's center, say in General Warren's front somewhere?" Grant had already begun a series of strategic moves, continental in scope, to bring overwhelming force to bear on the Petersburg front. He had reached all the way to Louisiana to order two divisions of XIX Corps shipped from New Orleans to City Point. That would give him enough force to hold the present lines *and* form an army strong enough to sweep around and past the entrenchments to overwhelm Lee's mobile reserve. But XIX Corps was weeks away, and Grant wanted to renew the pressure on Lee's army. Meade replied that he would have to consult Warren and Burnside, noting that Warren had already said he did not consider an attack practicable but that Burnside did. At noon Meade sent a confidential dispatch to Burnside, asking whether he thought his corps, supported by II and VI, could make a successful assault.

This was what Burnside had been hoping for. He had already stated his belief that a surprise attack, led by the Black division, had a good chance of breaking the enemy's line. That attack would be more certain to succeed if preceded by the explosion of the mine. But Meade was touchy about his authority, so Burnside's response had to be diplomatic as well as assertive. He began modestly: *if* his opinion were asked, he would advise waiting until the mine was ready to fire. But then he went a step too far: if Meade preferred to attack immediately, he thought IX Corps had a fair chance of succeeding, "provided my corps can make the attack and it is left to me to say when and how the other two corps shall come in to my support." After which it did him no good to declare that he had "the honor to be, general, very respectfully, your obedient servant."

Meade saw the proposal as an attempt to usurp his command, and he put Burnside in his place:

> Should . . . it be determined to employ the army under my command in offensive operations on your front I shall exercise the prerogative of my position to control and direct the same, receiving gladly at all times such suggestions as you may think proper to

make. I consider these remarks necessary in consequence of certain conditions which you have thought proper to attach to your opinion, acceding to which in advance would not in my judgment be consistent with my position as commanding general of this army.[21]

Burnside tried to make amends the following day, July 4, in a dispatch filled with the most abject apologies and confessions of personal unworthiness. But the harm had been done. Meade sent Burnside's proposal to Grant without endorsing it. Even so, Grant was interested enough to have Barnard send his questions to Pleasants, but Meade trumped that move by sending Major Duane and chief of artillery Henry Hunt to inspect, which guaranteed disapproval.[22]

Duane had already told Burnside he considered the project "claptrap and nonsense." So when, on July 4, Hunt and Duane arrived at Colonel

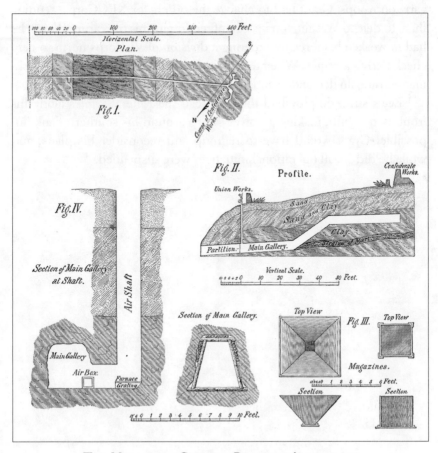

THE MINE, FROM COLONEL PLEASANTS'S DIAGRAMS

Pleasants's headquarters to question him on his operations, Pleasants was sarcastic. "[T]he great engineer at the head of the corps of so-called sappers and miners [said] that we couldn't go fifty feet into that hillside, and when I laughed in his face, didn't he want to know what caused my risibility? You bet he did." Pleasants had just come out after measuring the length of the tunnel, which was "precisely two hundred and sixty-four feet to say nothing about the odd five-eights of an inch," and dead true on Pleasants's bearing, aimed straight for the four-gun battery in the Confederate salient.[23]

But events elsewhere drew Grant's attention away from Petersburg. On July 5, a strong Rebel force, commanded by General Jubal Early, crossed the Potomac to invade Maryland. Early forced the citizens of Hagerstown to pay tribute to avoid the destruction of their town, and he was preparing to advance against Washington, which was protected by an inadequate force of garrison troops. Grant had to change the orders for XIX Corps, sending them to defend Washington instead of reinforcing his own army. Worse, he had to weaken his force by ordering a division of VI Corps north to help check Early's advance. When the Rebel force began to move against Washington, Lincoln demanded and got the rest of VI Corps.

Lee's strategic ploy had thus reduced the Federal armies along his front by one fifth, making a power sweep around his southern flank impossible. Grant would have to regroup and reconsider his plans, and while he did so, all operational initiatives were suspended.[24]

Chapter 4

Confederate Strategy

THE BEST DEFENSE . . . , JUNE 21–JULY 5, 1864

arly's invasion of Maryland was Lee's response to the strategic bind Grant had imposed on him. By pinning his army in the Richmond-Petersburg trenches, Grant compelled Lee's main force to stand on the defensive, where the attrition of siege warfare would eventually exhaust its resources. On June 21, while Grant and Lincoln conferred at City Point, Lee was writing to Confederate President Jefferson Davis: "I hope your Exc^y will put no reliance in what I can do individually, for I feel that will be very little. The enemy has a strong position, & is able to deal us more injury than from any other point he has ever taken. Still we must try & defeat them. I fear he will not attack us but advance by regular approaches. He is so situated that I cannot attack him."[1]

Robert E. Lee was more than just the commander of the Confederacy's most important army. For the officers and men who served under him, and for most of the Confederate public, he had become the personification of the nation for which they were fighting, the embodiment of the South's idealized self-image. He was fifty-seven, a tall man with steel-gray hair and beard, whose presence and manner somehow awed even men who were nominally his peers. He had the quiet self-assurance of a man who knows who he is; who has considered carefully what God, man, and conscience expect of him; and is satisfied that he has done all that duty and honor require. Some of that assurance was birthright: he was the son of Revolutionary War hero General Henry Lee, who had been a pillar of the Virginia Tidewater aristocracy—a class almost on the European model, not like the parvenu "aristocrats" whose cotton-based wealth was only a generation old. But Lee's father had squandered his fortune and reputation, and his son had had to regain them through a life of hard service and conscientious devotion to duty.

When Virginia seceded, he was faced with an agonizing choice of loyalties, but having chosen, he never looked back. Like Grant, his whole intelligence was concentrated on defeating the enemy. Beneath his noble calm and gracious reserve he was a passionate and determined fighter. Most generals "accept" battle; Lee sought it. Perhaps the most revealing thing he ever said was his remark at Fredericksburg: "It is well that war is so terrible, or we should grow too fond of it." Lee looked on every battle as an opportunity, not merely to check the enemy but to defeat him decisively. Those stunning victories in which Lee had beaten larger Federal armies had (with one exception) been won by a bold assumption of the offensive. Against Grant his methods had failed. After Longstreet's counterattack on the second day in the Wilderness, Lee was never again able to mount a corps-size infantry assault. He could not afford the losses such attacks entailed. As Grant moved inexorably closer to Richmond, Lee became almost desperate: "We must strike them a blow—we must never let them pass us again—we must strike them a blow. . . . Once let Grant reach the James River, and it is only a matter of time."[2]

Although he could not prevent Grant's reaching and crossing the James, Lee began adapting his strategy to the new conditions. If an offensive against Grant's main force was out of the question, he would entrench his lines and maintain a strong reserve, capable of rapid movement to any threatened point. He would also use a powerful detached force in the Shenandoah Valley to threaten an invasion of Maryland and an attack on Washington. A similar strategy had worked in 1862, when Stonewall Jackson's rampage in the valley had disrupted McClellan's campaign against Richmond.[3]

The Shenandoah was both a vital source of food supplies for Lee's army and a protected route for invading the north. The town of Lynchburg, at the valley's southern end, was the junction through which the valley's produce went by train to Richmond, one hundred twenty miles east. In June a Union army of eighteen thousand men under General David Hunter crossed the mountains from West Virginia and threatened to take Lynchburg. So on June 12, during the lull after Cold Harbor, Lee ordered his II Corps—three divisions under Jubal Early—by train to Lynchburg to drive Hunter out of the valley and, if possible, use the valley route to threaten an invasion. Early arrived at Lynchburg on June 17 and attacked

Hunter the next day, forcing him to retreat back into West Virginia. On June 21, while Lee was writing to Davis about the impossibility of attacking Grant's army, Early was reporting that the entire length of the valley was now open to a Confederate advance.

From Lynchburg the valley slants northeast to the town of Harpers Ferry on the Potomac River, with mountains on both sides to protect an advancing army from Federal attacks. With his small army in control of Harpers Ferry, Early could cut the Baltimore & Ohio Railroad, the rail artery linking Washington to the western states, and be in a position to raid Pennsylvania or threaten Washington. Lee wanted Early to seize the northern end of the valley, to protect the flow of food supplies to Richmond, and "to draw the attention of the enemy to his own territory," to relieve the pressure on Petersburg. He expected Early to act aggressively, so that Grant would be forced to weaken significantly the forces holding Lee in place, or would be goaded into making a premature frontal assault on the Richmond-Petersburg trench lines.[4]

The forces defending those lines comprised elements of two commands: I and III Corps of the Army of Northern Virginia commanded by Lee, and the Department of North Carolina and Southern Virginia—three divisions commanded by General P.G.T. Beauregard, which had defended the capital region until Lee's arrival. (Lee's Cavalry Corps, like Grant's, was en route to Petersburg.) There was also a small Richmond Defense Force under General Ewell. Though Beauregard retained nominal authority over the forces south of the James, Lee was effectively in control of all units.

The lines were divided into three sectors: the forts east of Richmond (north of the James); the trench line across the base of the Bermuda Hundred peninsula south of the James, between the James and Appomattox rivers; and the front of Petersburg, a trench line running south from the Appomattox to the Jerusalem Plank Road. The southern flanks of both the opposing armies ended "in air": that is, they were not anchored by a defensible geographical feature like a river or a ridge line. However, the southern end of Lee's line was partly "refused"—it curved back at an angle to face an attack from beyond the flank.

The Richmond front north of the James would later become the scene of major operations, but in June the Federals held only the bridgehead at Deep Bottom and a fortified camp at Harrison's Landing. The Richmond lines were held by Ewell's garrison troops, but Lee kept two divisions of his reserve close to the river crossings. The James River itself was a potential avenue for attack by the Union navy's ironclads, but they were checked by forts at Drewry's and at Chaffin's Bluff. Pickett's famous Virginia division held the Bermuda Hundred line against Butler's X and XVIII Corps. South of the Appomattox three divisions defended Petersburg proper. The post of danger on the southern flank was held by Mahone's veteran division, which belonged to Lee's army. Bushrod Johnson's relatively inexperienced division held the center of the line and Robert Hoke's the northern segment. (Both belonged to Beauregard's command.)

The combat effectiveness of Lee's forces had been degraded by losses and failures of supply, but perhaps the most serious weakness was at the higher levels of combat command. Lee's great offensive and counteroffensive strokes usually involved several divisions, and relied heavily on the skill of corps and division commanders. Grant's army wrecked Lee's command system by destroying the men who made it work. Since the Wilderness, Lee's army had lost twenty-two of fifty-eight general officers—eight killed, twelve incapacitated by wounds, two captured. The most severe loss was among the corps commanders. JEB Stuart, legendary commander of the cavalry corps, was killed; Longstreet, the best of the infantry corps commanders, was severely wounded. Generals Hill and Ewell, commanders of Lee's other two infantry corps, were weakened by illness. Hill's indisposition was intermittent, but Ewell had the kind of breakdown that disqualified him for field command. Lee had only limited confidence in Longstreet's replacement, Richard Anderson. His most trusted corps commander was Jubal Early, promoted from division command, who was now detached for the campaign in the Shenandoah.[5]

Lee maintained a strategic reserve of four infantry divisions, which would be augmented by three cavalry divisions as soon as the horsemen returned from their expedition to check Sheridan's raid toward the Shenandoah. The infantry reserve was vital to the defense. Federal forces outnumbered Lee's by a ratio of three to two—perhaps eighty-five thousand Federals against fifty-eight thousand Confederates. In the existing state of military technology, proper entrenchments could not be stormed unless the attacker had at least a three-to-one advantage in troop strength at the point of assault, and to exploit such a breakthrough an additional strong reserve was required. The Confederates also had the advantage of operating along "interior lines." Their lines were shorter than those of the Federals, and curved back on themselves, so that reserves could move to any threatened point along lines shorter than those along which the Federal attackers were moving. However, this advantage was offset by Yankee ingenuity and technology. Grant's engineers constructed a military railroad southward from the supply base at City Point, and thus speeded the transfer of men and supplies along the whole of the army's rear. They improved the lateral roads across Bermuda Hundred and bridged the Appomattox and the James at a number of points. When these arrangements were completed, Grant could move troops from the Jerusalem Plank Road at one end of his line to Deep Bottom at the other more swiftly and easily than Lee could shift forces from his center to meet them. So Grant could maneuver to achieve that three to one advantage at a chosen point of attack, or he could force Lee to retreat by pressuring the lines and sending an offensive column around his open flank.

To meet these threats, Lee distributed his reserve divisions so that every part of the line would have some support. Confederate divisions were identified by their commander's name. Of the infantry divisions, General Joseph Kershaw's was stationed closest to Richmond, with elements on the north side of the James at Chaffin's Bluff. The divisions of Henry Heth and Charles Field were positioned where they could move to either flank—by road to the south and west, and by the Richmond and Petersburg Railroad if they had to go north. Cadmus Wilcox's Division supported the southern end of the line, the most vulnerable flank; and he could draw on two or even three of Mahone's brigades, because the two-mile distance between Mahone's position and the Federal V Corps made a sudden heavy assault on this sector unlikely. Their teamwork checked the Federal attack on the Weldon Railroad on June 22–24. When the cavalry returned, it would patrol both flanks and provide a highly mobile strike force for operations beyond the trench lines.[6]

HOLDING THE PETERSBURG FRONT, JUNE 25–JULY 5, 1864

While Early marched north, Lee's army dug in. "Dig, dig, dig! is the word; while boom, boom, boom! from the mortars, & the shrill whistles of the minnies, alone, break the monotony of the tiresome, demoralizing, debilitating siege."[7] The Rebel picket line was not a series of separate rifle pits but a continuous line of lightly manned entrenchments that ran across the face of their main line, and were connected to it by communication trenches. Abatis and chevaux-de-frise were set as obstacles in front of it, creating two belts of resistance to derange and weaken an assault before it reached the main line. That line had a full parapet, and was broken by projecting angles and salients designed to give enfilade and cross fire during an attack.

Confederate officers continually studied and improved their entrenchments. They studied the enemy as well, trying to anticipate his moves by careful observation from posts in high trees, watching for dust clouds that might mark a wagon train or infantry on the march. They raided Yankee picket posts for prisoners, seeking intelligence on the state of Grant's army, on operations currently in the works. They watched the way the enemy developed his trench lines, in order to anticipate possible vectors of attack.

In late June, General E. Porter Alexander, artillery chief of I Corps, was inspecting the salient defended by Elliott's Brigade of Johnson's Division. Though sharpshooters were rife along this part of the front, scarcely any fire came from the positions a hundred yards to right and left of the salient. Alexander guessed that the Yankees there were trying to lull their opponents into a false sense of security while they worked some mischief. He made several visits to the spot, trying to puzzle out what they could be doing. Then on June 30 "suddenly a light broke in on me. They were coming, but it was not above ground. . . . They were coming underground. They were mining us!" If that was the case, countermeasures had to be ordered immediately: engineers detailed to probe for the Federal tunnel, reserves told to reinforce the point attacked, a coherent second line constructed out of the tangle of communication trenches and covered ways that scored the earth behind the main line.

Alexander's eagerness got the better of his judgment. Instead of returning to headquarters by the tortuous but sheltered communication trenches, he took a shortcut across open ground and a Federal sniper drilled him through the hand. The wound was serious enough to require a few weeks in a hospital. But he made a point of stopping at headquarters to warn Lee's aide, Colonel Charles Venable, about the threat to Elliott's Salient. With Venable was the distinguished British correspondent Francis Lawley, former governor of Western Australia and member of parliament, who had been covering the American war since 1862. When told the mine would have to reach five hundred feet, Lawley declared the project infeasible: "the longest military mine ever run was in Delhi" during the Sepoy Rebellion, and British engineers found it impossible to ventilate a shaft longer than four hundred feet. Colonel Pleasants would have been pleased by Alexander's response: he told Lawley there were coal miners in the Federal army who had ventilated deeper shafts and "were up to devices to which 500 feet would be only child's play." But Alexander could not stay to press his ideas, and his colleagues were absorbed in perfecting their entrenchments.[8]

A two-month drought had sucked all the moisture out of the soil, and every movement stirred the red clay dust into a stifling mist. The work was hard, and it undermined the strength and the morale of the men, diminished the energy and spirit that had once enabled them to move with speed and strike with power on the battlefield. The labor was made more onerous by lack of tools, lack of food (decent or otherwise) and clean water, and lack of medicines for the sick and injured. Shoes and clothing wore out and could not be replaced. The Confederate commissary general was a loyal supporter of President Davis, but he was no good at his job. Lee's forces had been chronically undersupplied throughout the war. With the army seated at the junction of the major rail and road routes, supply problems should have been easier to solve, but difficulties persisted. The rail lines to the Deep South were breaking down for lack of maintenance and repair, and closer to Richmond the Weldon line had been heavily damaged and was vulnerable to Yankee raiders. Supplies from the Carolinas and Georgia built up at the North Carolina depots until mid-July, when track repairs and an improvised wagon train delivered the goods to Petersburg. But the bonanza was short-lived.[9]

Officers were able to supplement their rations by buying such delicacies as jams and pies from sutlers or civilians in Petersburg. General Sanders, commanding Wilcox's Alabama Brigade in Mahone's Division, bought a batch of blackberry dumplings and pies for his officers, "better than we expected but not so good as they might be." The troops lived on hardtack crackers, corn pone, and salt pork, but were often on half-rations and bitter about it. To wash down the crackers and pork, and stave off dehydration in the heat, a man needed fresh water, but Yankee snipers shot up the watering details that went to get it.[10]

The least exposure at a loophole or above a breastwork was likely to get you shot. "Some of our regiment is killed our wounded every day," wrote Private William Faulkner of the 17th South Carolina (Elliott's Brigade). "All the men that are hit are shot in the head. If a man sticks his head above the breast works 'he goes up.' " These deaths were somehow more demoralizing than losses suffered in battle because they had "the chill of murder" about them. Lee tried to relieve the strain by giving every regiment a day or two each week to come off the line, to rest and wash and eat their scanty rations in peace. It mitigated the problem without solving it. Losses due to illness and desertion mounted.[11]

The strain was particularly hard on the divisions commanded by

Wilcox and Mahone, defending the army's vulnerable southern flank. Wilcox's command was continually shuttled between its reserve position and the Weldon Railroad. Mahone's men had to man a long trench line and periodically pull units out for maneuver against Federal flank attacks. A deserter from Mahone's Division who crossed the lines on July 4 told his interrogators that "Mahone's division is completely tired out in marching backward and forward down the railroad, and that Wilcox's division is now performing the same duty."[12]

Lee rated Mahone as one of his best division commanders, and had recommended him for promotion to major general, but in July 1864, Mahone was still a brigadier exercising a major general's command. He was born and raised in the Petersburg area and graduated from the Virginia Military Institute (VMI). Poor health kept him out of the Mexican War, and he made his career as a civil engineer and railroad entrepreneur. The Weldon Railroad, which he now fought to protect, had been his chief competitor. At thirty-eight he was a little below average height and seemed smaller because of his slight build, "as attenuated as an Italian greyhound [with] dainty" hands and feet. A bushy chestnut-colored beard covered his upper chest like a bib. He suffered from dyspepsia, and was sometimes forced to subsist on milk—he brought his own Alderney cow on campaign.[13]

His biographer describes Mahone's father as a merchant, prominent enough to be chosen lieutenant colonel of the local militia during Nat Turner's Rebellion in 1831. John Wise, the scion of one of the state's oldest families, took a less flattering view: "Billy" Mahone was the son of an Irish tavern keeper, who displayed "the most prominent characteristics of his race . . . brave, open-hearted, free-spoken, a free liver, and not overprosperous." Young Billy was known to have held a horse for his father's guests, and was "not, in his day, above taking in a tray of toddies" to a roomful of gamblers. He also rode jockey on his own racehorse. But though Wise patronized Mahone for his lack of social standing, he was eager to serve under him because of his reputation for gallantry.[14]

Mahone commanded five brigades: Finnegan's (Florida), Harris's (Mississippi), Wilcox's or Sanders's (Alabama), Wright's (Georgia), and his own Virginia Brigade now led by Colonel David Weisiger.[15] With the exception of the Virginians, his regiments represented the cotton states of the Deep South, whose people had been most enthusiastic for secession. Most were regiments of long service, formed in the heady early days of the war when volunteers had flocked to the colors and adopted names expressive of their enthusiasm and community identity. Some favored the "Ring-tailed Roarer" style of popular fiction, and named themselves "Wildcats," "The Cahaba Valley Boys" (Company C,10th Alabama), "Warsaw Rebels" (3rd Georgia), "Virginia Rangers," or "Isle of Wight Avengers" (Companies H and F, 61st Virginia). Some companies based on venerable militia companies were named for the traditional uniform of their units, "Jackson Grays" or "Bilisoly Blues." Most simply appended "Rifles" or "Guards" to the name of their town or county, or the captain who had sponsored their formation. The South had not attracted as many European immigrants as the Northern states, so there was no Confederate equivalent of the Army of the Potomac's Irish Brigade or the so-called Dutch (i.e., German) divisions of the XI Corps. But the 8th Alabama, which recruited near the seaport of Mobile, boasted an all-Irish "Emerald Guard" (Company I), and Company H was known as "the German Fusiliers."[16]

They were not professional soldiers but armed representatives of the little communities that offered them to the state. The 22nd Georgia's Company G had assembled on the green "where the Presbyterian church now stands" in the small Floyd County town of Silver Creek, in the hill country near Rome. "The day that we organized we chose a name for the company, the name of 'Fireside Defenders,' and the good ladies made up money, bought material and made us a beautiful flag, and Mrs. Lizzie Reese (*Nee* Hills) presented the flag to the company, with a beautiful address, and at the close of the address repeated a beautiful piece of poetry." As Private W. B. Judkins remembered, "The girls were all pretty, and much courting was done, for we had a fine good-looking company of mostly young men." They were told that their cause was a "just, and a religious, and a Godly one," and they believed it. Each man was given a large bowie knife, a foot long and weighing about two pounds, with which they expected to carve up Yankees in hand-to-hand combat.

The 22nd Georgia got to Virginia in time for the Seven Days' Battle and were shot to pieces charging Yankee guns on Malvern Hill. The larking ended and they learned the hard lessons of their new trade: threw away the big knives, which were cumbersome and useless on battlefields dominated by rifles and artillery; thought twice before answering the call to "Charge!" The unending search for food became as great a concern as battle. Private Judkins's memoirs, written more than forty years later, are filled with vividly recalled episodes of meals forgone and enjoyed; of foodstuffs found, given, begged, or stolen; of devices for hiding purloined

pork from inquisitive officers. His recall of the terrible fighting at Sharpsburg (or Antietam) is overridden by his memory of how Gib Leigh stole a
chicken and a four-gallon pot of lard, and how Judkins both cooked the
chicken and ate it for him. "The ground was covered with apples where
we fought, shot off the trees. . . . We got quite a lot of apple butter and
preserves out of a house at Sharpsburg, it was nice with our hardtack and
tough beef."

The jaunty and defiant names remained, but by 1864 losses to combat and disease had whittled the Fireside Defenders and Isle of Wight
Avengers down to remnants, and their identity was now largely invested
in their standing as members of Mahone's Division, Army of Northern
Virginia. As Private Judkins put it, "the men [were] all disheartened and
tired of the war, but we were into it."[17]

The Virginia regiments of Mahone's Brigade (now commanded by
Colonel David Weisiger) were mostly recruited in the Tidewater counties
around Richmond, Petersburg, and Norfolk. They had fought as a single
command since facing off against Burnside in North Carolina in 1862.
Between July and September 1862 they fought in five major battles and
were force-marched from the Richmond suburbs to western Maryland,
and halfway back again. At the Wilderness and Spotsylvania they twice
broke up Federal offensives that threatened to cut the army in half. Mahone's Brigade was also known for the proficiency of its sharpshooter detachment, a battalion of picked marksmen specially trained in scouting,
skirmishing, and sniping. At Petersburg they became adept at infiltrating
and raiding Yankee picket posts at night, bringing back prisoners to be
questioned by the staff.[18]

The 12th Virginia were literally "fireside defenders." Ten of twelve
companies were raised in Petersburg, and the church spires of their
hometown overlooked the trenches they manned. Most Southern regiments drew 80 or 90 percent of their men from farmers and country laborers, with officers from the landed gentry. In the 12th, 80 percent were
city workers: clerks, bookkeepers, iron molders, blacksmiths, machinists,
railroad engineers, or brakemen. The level of literacy in the regiment was
far above the average for the Confederate army. Their officers were urban
professionals and businessmen: the colonel a commission merchant, and
his subordinates lawyers, newspaper editors, and the like—most with
some college education. Membership in the regiment was (at least at the

start) socially exclusive. Very few factory workers were enrolled, largely because they were thought to be unfit to associate with respectable citizens—analogous to the "poor whites" in rural districts. However, there were men of education and social standing among the privates and non-coms. George Bernard was a lawyer but served two years as a private before being promoted to sergeant. His friend Emmett Butts, also a lawyer, remained a private soldier in the outfit. Unlike the rugged, unlettered individualists of the rural and mountain districts, whose homes were scattered across the countryside, these townsmen lived within a square mile of one another, "worked for the same employer, boarded at the same house, ate at the same restaurants, went to their choice of three or four leading churches." They felt their battle losses keenly, and that sense of loss was sharpened when they returned to see their once prosperous hometown gone to seed, its commerce ruined by war and blockade, and the whole Yankee army clamoring to break in.[19]

The trenches immediately to Mahone's left were held by General Alfred Colquitt's Brigade, borrowed from Robert Hoke's Division to ease the burden on Mahone's hardworking troops. Colquitt's troops were the link with Bushrod Johnson's Division, which held the central sector of the Petersburg front.

Johnson had served as a brigadier in the western campaigns and had no reputation to speak of in Virginia. He was a West Pointer and had served in the Mexican War but had resigned because of his involvement in a shady business deal. His combat record was undistinguished, and he was not an active division commander. "Seldom if ever was the man seen in the trenches; he was barely known by sight to his men; toward him they felt no affection, of his prowess they had no evidence, and in his ability they felt no confidence." His three infantry brigades had been brought together only a few weeks earlier as part of the hastily assembled army with which Beauregard had blocked Butler's advance against Richmond.[20]

Wise's Virginia Brigade held the line immediately next to Colquitt. The brigade's ancestry was distinguished, its battle record less so. It had been organized by Henry S. Wise, whose long record of public service included a term as governor of Virginia, during which he oversaw the hanging of the abolitionist John Brown. The regiments of his brigade had been in service since the early days of the war. One had been part of Wise's Legion, which had campaigned ineffectively in West Virginia in 1861–62.

Others had served as garrison troops in the Richmond area, an assignment so easy that one frustrated warrior nicknamed them "the life insurance brigade." They had participated in small actions in the Richmond area, at Charleston, South Carolina, and in northern Florida, and had performed well in the heavy fighting around Bermuda Hundred in May. The brigade was now commanded by Colonel J. Thomas Goode while Wise took charge of the Petersburg garrison.[21]

On June 22 Wise's son John, a seventeen-year-old graduate of VMI, visited his father's old brigade and recorded his impressions of life in the trenches. It was "indescribably monotonous and uncomfortable. In time of sunshine, the reflected heat from the new red-clay embankments was intense, and unrelieved by shade or breeze; and in wet weather one was ankle-deep in tough, clinging mud." For shelter from the sun and protection from Yankee mortar bombs the men used bayonets and tin cups to carve burrows into the sides of the trench. If there was an alarm, "At the sound of the drum, the heads of the soldiers would pop up out of the earth [like] prairie-dogs or gophers."

Sniping was vicious and unremitting. Two soldiers, Blake and Newman, tried to make life in their two-man picket post more comfortable. They set up a small mirror on the back wall, facing the loophole in their position. Then they could sit and play cards, glancing now and then in the mirror for an indirect, and therefore safe, view of the Yanks. They got a little too comfortable, indulged in a little horseplay after a disputed hand, and as Blake's head passed the embrasure, a sniper drilled him through the brain, the bullet smashing the mirror when it exited.

Sometimes the high commands called a temporary truce, which allowed the ladies of Petersburg to visit the trenches. The Yankees would act civil and call out, "Hello, Johnny! It's ladies' day, ain't it?" The enlisted men sometimes made informal truces and crossed no-man's-land to meet and talk, the conversation often descending to what young Wise regarded as the vulgar and obscene. And they'd trade, Yankee coffee for Rebel tobacco, Blue rumors for Gray gossip, copies of the *Richmond Enquirer* for the *New York Herald* or *Tribune*. Both armies got a good deal of their intelligence by reading each other's newspapers.

Supplies were scanty—even ammunition ran short. General Johnson set the men to scavenging spent bullets and shards of shrapnel from burst mortar shells, offering a furlough in Petersburg for the men who recovered the most metal. It was said that the competition got so keen that as soon as they saw a shell looping in, men would jump out of their holes and start for its likely landing place. The strain and hardship of their life could drive men to acts of suicidal daring—leaping up on the parapet and daring the enemy to shoot him—anything to escape "such intolerable life," to provoke the storm and break the tension of its eternal impending.[22]

⸲⸱⸲

To the left or north of Wise's Brigade, in the center of Johnson's divisional line, was Stephen Elliott's South Carolina Brigade, which held the position known as Elliott's Salient. Ironically, the brigade's history closely paralleled that of the Union IX Corps, which now held the lines opposite. Its five regiments had been organized in South Carolina in 1861. The 23rd was recruited in Charleston, but the 17th, 18th, 22nd and 26th were formed of companies from various parts of the state. South Carolina had led the secession movement since the 1830s and was the first state to secede; enthusiasm for the Confederacy ran high.

The line between gentlemen and ordinary White men was clearly drawn in South Carolina. Captain Samuel Lowry and his fellow officers of the 17th went to war with their Black menservants. Captain Wilson brought his cook Dick, and Lieutenant Avery brought his man Noah, "a stoutly built Mulatto, full of fun and as faithful as the day is long." Lowry's "boy" was named Horace; "he was about 40 years of age, and one of the best and most faithful negroes." In the field, their servants aided them in new and surprising ways. Colonel McMaster's Sam kept him supplied with fresh-baked pies during that summer in Petersburg, given to him by a "*fine woman of color* who had fallen in *love* with Sam." When Colonel Dantzler of the 22nd was killed in action, his manservant, Caleb Glover, brought his body home.[23]

The South Carolina Brigade began their service defending the coast of their native state against Federal amphibious operations and then went north under Brigadier General Nathan "Shanks" Evans to join Lee's army at the Second Battle of Bull Run and Antietam. Then it was back to coastal defense, in North Carolina against the force that had replaced Burnside's at New Bern. In the summer of 1863 they went west to join the army attempting to relieve Vicksburg, and once again faced off against part of IX Corps. Then back to North Carolina, where they played a supporting role in General Robert Hoke's recapture of Plymouth.[24]

The wanderings of the brigade undermined their health, and tried their loyalty. Many of the men were reluctant to fight outside their home state because it seemed to violate the states' rights orthodoxy on which they had been raised. But Confederate patriotism proved stronger, and they fought well at Bermuda Hundred in May, when Beauregard defeated " 'Beast' Butler—the cowardly old skunk!" Along the way they were relieved of Brigadier Evans (a quarrelsome alcoholic), but his replacement had been captured in his first battle and they were now commanded by Brigadier General Stephen Elliott.[25]

Elliott belonged to a distinguished family with large holdings in the Sea Islands. His plantations grew the fine long staple cotton for which the region was noted, a variety that could be chancy to grow but for which English manufacturers would pay a premium. He had attended Harvard and had graduated from South Carolina College in 1850, had earned local celebrity as a sportsman, and had served in the legislature and the militia. His first command was the defense of his hometown of Beaufort, which was captured by Union troops in the first winter of the war. Thereafter he served in the defense of Charleston until appointed to Evans's Brigade. In the meantime, the Sea Islands were occupied by the Union, and became the scene of a notable experiment in social reconstruction: some of the lands were turned over to the slaves that had worked them, and Northern educators set up schools to teach literacy, husbandry, and civics to the freedmen.[26]

General Elliott was not impressed by his brigade. He thought the men lacked discipline, and thought the regimental commanders were mediocrities at best. He compared Colonel Hudson to Iago, and thought Colonel McMaster (whom he had known at school) a poltroon: "If you do not think well of a man in college the chances are that you never will."[27]

At Petersburg on June 16 Elliott's Brigade came up to support Wise's Brigade just as a Federal assault drove the Virginians out of an entrenched line. Elliott ordered a countercharge with bayonets that retook the line and made the Federals recoil. Then they pulled back to a new trench that had been prepared as a secondary defense line. "Those were the lines we held until Petersburg was evacuated." The brigade dug in and engineers constructed a battery in the outthrust known as Elliott's Salient. Private William Faulkner of the 17th described the life they lived after that:

> July 3rd: This is a miserable place, lying in the fortifications in the sun and dust, with the enemy two hundred yards in our front continually popping away at us every minute day and night and our men returning the fire. We are so close we can talk to each other, but it is against orders. . . . We get little or no sleep. Three men out of every

company stands or shoots all the time through the night. I stood up from midnight until day this morning and shot until my gun got so warm I could hardly hold it. If the roar of our guns would stop, we would soon get orders to pitch in. This beats anything of war I have ever seen. . . . I have got so used to it I can lie on the ground and sleep, the guns not disturbing me.

Captain Lowry shared the discomfort with his men. "We have had no rain in about two months and the dust is stifling. Living on corn bread and bacon, with cow peas occasionally. Will not be apt to get anything better this summer." His "boy" Horace had died the year before, of a camp disease.[28]

COUNTERMINE: JULY 1–11

During the first week of July, picket line gossip hinted that the Yankees were digging a mine against Elliott's Salient. John Wise would wander over from the Virginia Brigade, put his ear to the ground, and listen—and thought he could hear the dull pounding of picks. The possibility roused more curiosity than concern among the infantry. But headquarters recalled Porter Alexander's warning and sent Captain Henry Douglas to supervise a counter-mining operation.

Douglas thought the likely point of attack was somewhere between Elliott's Salient and another salient a half mile north. Since he had no idea of the direction from which the Yankees were digging, he had to probe at several different points simultaneously. Starting on July 13, at each of the two salients, Douglas's men sank three shafts, each six feet deep, and then carved out galleries to the right and left. His ninety men were divided into six detachments, each of which worked a twelve-hour shift. They were urged to make as little noise as possible with their picks lest the Yankees hear and muffle their own operations. They were to stop work every fifteen minutes and listen hard for the enemy. Because the shafts went straight down, Douglas had to rig a windlass at the top of each to lift out heavy buckets of earth one at a time. He was careful to conceal his operations, using the excavated clay to fill sandbags or dumping it in hidden positions to the rear. But the work had to be done in the front line, at the top of a slope rather than behind the wall of a ravine, so his men took casualties from sniper and mortar fire. He had to set some of his troops to deepening the communication trenches and to constructing covered ways—communication trenches so sited that they were "covered" or hidden from observation and line-of-sight fire.[29]

It was hard for the infantry to keep its anxieties focused on the possibility that a mine might blow some of them up. The routine of trench life was stultifying, the direness of particular threats buried under the pervasive atmosphere of misery, boredom, and unrelieved tension. There were so many false alarms, bombardments that spread for no reason up and down the lines, "Chinese demonstrations" (harmless fireworks displays) presaging assaults that never came. Douglas's operations reassured the troops by their display of diligence—and their negative findings. A joke made the rounds to the effect that Grant was tunneling into Petersburg, and had got as far as Sycamore Street, the main thoroughfare of the town. The Yankees even had a railroad down there, and if you put your ear to the ground, you could hear the engine chuffing, and see its smoke rising through the spaces between the cobblestones.[30]

Some soldiers wished the Yankees *would* try something. Private Faulkner wanted a chance to fight back: "If the Enemy advances on us somebody will be hurt. Our men have not any idea of giving up the works." Higher up the chain of command the feeling was the same. Lieutenant Colonel William Pegram, who commanded the artillery battalion supporting Elliott's Brigade, wrote, "I would like to have this kind of warfare broken up, and get to field fighting once more. . . . I believe that such is the wish of every thinking man in the army."[31]

But unless Grant's army was substantially weakened, Lee could not go on the offensive. Their hope was that Early's invasion of Maryland would force Grant to detach large forces to defend Washington or force him to attack Petersburg—which might give Lee a chance for a decisive counterblow.

⌇⌇

Early had gone north with one cavalry and four infantry divisions, fifteen thousand to eighteen thousand men. On July 4 he closed on Harpers Ferry, forcing Federal troops to abandon the place. On July 5 he crossed the Potomac and established a base of operations near Sharpsburg, Maryland, where he resupplied his men (especially with shoes) and prepared to strike at Washington. Hunter's West Virginia force was too far away to stop him. Grant put Ricketts's division of VI Corps on a steamer and rushed it north. An anxious Union War Department scraped up a force of militia and garrison units, added Ricketts's veterans, and sent it out under the command of Major General Lew Wallace. On July 8, Early pushed east through the South Mountain passes and moved on Washington, and Grant was ordered to send the rest of VI Corps to save the capital. They embarked at City Point on July 9, and Grant was also constrained to redirect XIX Corps, en route from Louisiana, from Virginia to Washington. Later that day, Early attacked Wallace's command at the crossing of the Monocacy River, and in a hard daylong fight forced it off the high road to Washington.

On July 11, Early's advance passed through Silver Spring, and by the twelfth his main body had reached the outskirts of the capital. The forts here looked impregnable, with high thick parapets and huge cannons jutting from the embrasures, but they were manned by an inadequate garrison, augmented by armed clerks and convalescents. Early might have been able to break into the city if he had attacked at once. He hesitated, supposedly because it was rumored that reinforcements had already arrived. In fact, General George Wright and the rest of VI Corps would not get there until midnight. But even if Early had attacked, he could have done little more than embarrass the Lincoln government at prohibitive cost to his army. He would have taken heavy casualties attacking the forts, and would have had difficulty extricating his command from the city, with VI Corps arriving and other forces—Hunter's command, Wallace, the militia—moving up behind him. His main task was to maintain a strong force at the northern end of the Shenandoah Valley, to protect its farms from Yankee depredations, to disrupt the Baltimore & Ohio Railroad, and to distract Grant by continually threatening a raid or invasion. On July 13 he began pulling back toward South Mountain, and by the fourteenth he had safely recrossed the Potomac, shadowed but not impeded by Wright's pursuing force.

Early had achieved a great deal, but Lee had wanted more. On July 11 he wrote Davis: "I had hoped that General Grant, rather than weaken his army, would have attempted to drive us from our position." The inevitable repulse might have allowed Lee to counterattack and win a decisive victory. But with Grant standing on the defensive, "I fear I shall not be able to attack him to advantage."

At Petersburg the situation remained unchanged: "We wore through a weary month of guard duty, mortar shelling, and sharpshooting, watching and waiting for the affray . . . but no assault was made."[32]

Part Two

~

THE CHOSEN
INSTRUMENT

Burnside Selects the Spearhead

Despite the way in which Meade had put him in his place, Burnside was convinced the army would have to make use of his mine. Some means had to be found to break (or at least threaten) Lee's fortified line, and with Grant's forces reduced by the absence of VI Corps, the only conceivable way to do that was by the combination of a mine explosion and an infantry assault. So Burnside, with admirable professionalism and initiative, began to develop an operational plan.

The fact that Pleasants's mine was of record length increased the likelihood that its explosion would take the Rebels by surprise. To augment its effect, Burnside planned to create an explosion of unprecedented size by packing twelve to fourteen hundred pounds of gunpowder into the mine. This would not only blast a huge breach in the Confederate line, but would also produce what we would call "shock and awe," causing nearby troops to flee in panic. Thus the primary tactical problem was how to use infantry to exploit the breach. Two critical issues were beyond his authority to resolve. No attack could succeed if Lee's reserve divisions were in position to be thrown into the breach. Grant would have to create some sort of diversion to draw those reserves away from the Petersburg front. Burnside's attack would also need support from the corps on its flanks. But Meade had made it painfully clear that Burnside was not to presume to dispose of corps other than his own. So Burnside concentrated on plans for his own infantry.

His objective was the low crest line along which ran the Jerusalem Plank Road, with Blandford Cemetery Hill above its northern end.

Troops on that high ground could take the main Confederate line from the rear, and would have an excellent position from which to repel counterattacks. The Union artillery would dominate the streets of Petersburg and the bridges by which Lee's forces south of Petersburg were supplied. Lee's army would be split, the main body forced to retreat over the Appomattox under fire. Confederate units south of the breach might be cut off and destroyed.[1]

The most critical assignment would fall to the division chosen to spearhead the attack. It would have to maneuver around the crater and the mass of debris produced by the explosion, secure the breach against counterattacks by Rebel troops in the adjoining trenches, and lead the advance on Cemetery Hill, the key to the whole position. The other three divisions would follow, support the spearhead's advance, and seize the crest line south of Cemetery Hill on which the Jerusalem Plank Road ran. The spearhead assignment required regiments with enough energy and morale to storm high ground under fire, and enough coolness and skill to carry out the complicated maneuvers required to pass the breach and organize for the assault. Which division should Burnside select?

IX Corps was the smallest of the four infantry corps in Grant's army, with only two brigades (rather than four) in each division, and the heavy losses suffered in the overland campaign had further degraded its combat strength. The 3rd Division was commanded by Orlando Willcox, a Regular Army officer with the longest experience in division command—he had even commanded the corps when Burnside was absent. He was competent, but not especially energetic as a combat leader. The 2nd Division was commanded by Robert Potter, an amateur soldier but an able and fearless field commander. They were Burnside's strongest subordinates, and their divisions contained the highest proportion of veteran regiments. But the quality of those regiments had been degraded before the campaign had begun by a flawed system of obtaining replacements.

The experience of the 6th New Hampshire Veteran Volunteers is representative. The regiment reenlisted after three years of service in the winter of 1863–64, but it had been reduced to fewer than three hundred rifles. So the state filled their ranks any way it could, half with volunteers and half with conscripts, substitutes hired by draft evaders, and bounty jumpers. Fully half the replacements deserted before they reached the front. Many of those who stayed could not be trusted with picket duty. Their brigade mate, the 9th New Hampshire, had 466 of 885 recruits desert—444 of them before ever reaching the regiment. The rage felt by

Captain Jackman of the 6th against these worthless soldiers blended with his distaste for immigrants: "They represented six or eight nationalities. Some were blind, some deaf, and others so lame they could scarcely march at all; and many of them could not speak or understand a word of English." But he felt still more bitter against the native-born, who sent "this scum of other nations . . . to represent the Old Granite State . . . while her own sons who were drafted stayed at home, taking their comfort and—some of them—getting rich out of fat government contracts."[2]

Some of the "scum" proved decent soldiers, as even Jackman admitted, and one performed at a level beyond the call of duty. Abraham Cohn, a Jewish immigrant from Prussia, had moved to Campton, New Hampshire, after being invalided out of the 68th New York. In January 1864 he reenlisted as a private in the 6th New Hampshire, "five feet five and ½ inches high, florid complexion, blue eyes, black hair," and by the time they got to the Wilderness had been promoted to sergeant major. On the second day the 6th New Hampshire joined Hancock's massive assault on the Confederate right, which was broken up by Longstreet's flank attack. Under heavy fire, Sergeant Major Cohn was able to rally soldiers from his own and other regiments and form them into a defensive line that checked Longstreet's advance. He would receive his first Medal of Honor for "conspicuous gallantry" in the action.[3] Battle brought out the strengths of the soldiers, and developed their skills, but it also broke them down. Sergeant Cohn's moment of glory was succeeded by weeks of stubborn blunted assaults and forced marches that winnowed the regiment down to its most solid elements—then went on and on, relentlessly grinding those elements down. They were at a third of their authorized strength when they reached Petersburg, and the attrition continued. By June 30, the 6th and 9th combined could barely muster four hundred twenty rifles.

James H. Ledlie, commander of the 1st Division, was a newcomer to the corps, a "dark-eyed, pudgy little man with a huge black mustache," a civil engineer with no prior field experience who probably owed his promotion to seniority and political influence. Most of his regimental commanders, and the Regular officers assigned to his staff, thought him incompetent and unstable, and suspected him of getting drunk before every action. At the crossing of the North Anna, on a drunken impulse, Ledlie had ordered an unsupported frontal assault against an entrenched position held by Mahone's Brigade, causing heavy and needless casualties. On June 17 at Petersburg, when part of the division was pinned down under heavy fire, Ledlie failed to respond to repeated pleas from

Colonel Stephen Weld for ammunition and support. When Weld later reported to Ledlie, he found him asleep on the ground. His adjutant
"kicked him awake, poked him," and got him to attend "in a hazey-dazey
sort of way." Told that his men had been driven back and scattered, he
"drew himself up" and remarked that "there are thousands of men all
around here," which was not at all to the point; he "then tumbled down in
a drunken sleep again." Yet Weld did not prefer charges, because Ledlie
"has always treated me kindly and I don't care [to say] anything against
him." He also feared that Ledlie or his personal staff might retaliate
against him: the staff protected Ledlie's reputation outside the division,
and he reciprocated by excusing them from exposure to danger.[4]

The result was that word of Ledlie's incompetence had never
reached Burnside. From the corps commander's perspective, Ledlie's
failures were just what one would expect of a new commander with a division of half-trained troops. Of the divisions made up of White soldiers,
the 1st had the smallest proportion of veteran to rookie regiments. Ledlie's 1st Brigade teamed three new regiments from Massachusetts with
three understrength veteran outfits. The 2nd Brigade combined two understrength infantry regiments with a pair of heavy artillery regiments, the
14th New York (NYHA) and the 2nd Pennsylvania Provisional (PPHA).
These were oversize units, recruited and trained to man big guns in fixed
fortifications, now compelled to serve as infantry. The poor performance
of the division early in the campaign is partly attributable to the fact that
so many of its units had to get their training in combat.

The experience of Ledlie's 57th Massachusetts typifies the development of the rookie regiments who joined IX Corps in April. It was recruited in the small cities of Worcester and Fitchburg, and the farming
and mill towns of that region. Its personnel profile resembles that of Petersburg's 12th Virginia—fewer than 25 percent were farmers. However,
unlike their Southern counterpart, the 57th was not ethnically or socially
exclusive. Its ranks included small businessmen, clerical workers, artisans, and a large number of railroad workers and factory operatives, especially shoemakers and boot makers. A large percentage were foreign-born,
with the Irish predominant. As in the 12th Virginia, the officers were
drawn from the educated classes, a mixture of old or aristocratic families
with men and professionals, but among the field officers were a clerk, a
machinist, and a storekeeper.[5]

The colonel was William Francis Bartlett, a scion of the Boston aristocracy, which was mercantile rather than plantation-based. Frank Bartlett

was a handsome six-footer, blond, blue-eyed and athletic, a Harvard student but more the man-about-town than the scholar. He was no abolitionist—on the contrary, he thought the South had the better constitutional arguments. But family honor and the wish to live usefully led him to enlist right after Sumter. He became a skilled and dedicated officer who led from the front and paid the price: a bullet smashed his knee at Yorktown, and his leg was amputated. He returned to action hobbling on a cork leg, and had his wrist shattered by a minié ball at Port Hudson, Louisiana, in June 1863. On his recovery he was appointed colonel of the 57th.

The regiment had only sixty days of training, mostly close-order drill. There was no opportunity to learn battalion or regimental maneuvers, let alone those needed for action as part of a brigade or division. Like all new regiments the 57th was decimated by camp diseases, and on the eve of the Wilderness was reduced to half-strength. They plunged into that blind struggle in which even veteran regiments lost direction and cohesion, and made up with energy for lack of skill. Bartlett was struck in the temple by a spent bullet and knocked out of action. The regiment almost broke when routed troops came running through their position, but they were rallied by Color Sergeant Leopold Karpeles, a Jewish immigrant from Hungary. Karpeles won the Medal of Honor, and Lieutenant Colonel Chandler took over the regiment, but they had lost 262 of the 548 men they'd taken into action.[6]

In six weeks of fighting the 57th became a solid combat unit. But by June 20 the regiment had been "nearly destroyed," fewer than three hundred remaining of the original thousand. By July 4 sickness and snipers had them down to 181 rifles. Though some of their sick and wounded would return, they would never again muster more than half of their original strength, and their leadership was decimated by combat losses. Chandler was killed at the North Anna, and Karpeles was seriously wounded. Lieutenant George Barton saw only two ways out. One was for "some three or four of the Rebel leaders including Jeff. Davis" to come within mortar range. The other was for Grant to "pursue the same course that he did at Vicksburg. *Under mine* them and blow them up. I understand that something of that kind is really under way *good if true.*"[7]

As Burnside ran over the state of his divisions, it seemed to him that his White troops had lost the élan required to storm a strongpoint. Their units were all understrength, the men physically and morally exhausted by the losses and hardships of the overland campaign and the siege, and they had become entirely too canny about attacking entrenchments. On the other hand his Colored division had suffered hardly any losses from combat, because it had been relegated to guarding the army's wagon trains and bridges.

The source of its strength was also its weakness: its troops had no battle experience, and there was no way of knowing how they would behave under fire. Of course, the same was true of any rookie outfit, and no one hesitated to throw untried White troops into combat. While some would break at the first crisis, others were capable, in their ignorance, of attempting and achieving extraordinary deeds of valor, and the average of their performance was generally good enough. But with Black troops the difference of race superseded every other consideration. The question for Burnside was not whether inexperienced troops could do the job but whether Negroes were capable of meeting the requirements of the battlefield.

Burnside's racialism was of the moderate variety. He had actively sought to have a Black division in his command and had assisted its recruitment. He did not think they were "fully equal" to White soldiers in intelligence or self-reliance, but he thought their racial character made them more amenable to discipline and unquestioningly loyal to those they saw as benefactors.[8] He was sure they would fight if properly led. And giving them the spearhead role would have some intangible advantages. If nothing else, using the Colored division as the spearhead would prevent Ben Butler from stealing the division. But if they scored a notable success, its symbolism would be extraordinarily powerful in a presidential election contested, in large part, over opposing solutions to "the Negro question." The 54th Massachusetts's gallant failure at Fort Wagner in Charleston Harbor (July 18, 1863) had made legends of the Black men and their commander. What would be the impact of a successful assault, on Lee's army, by a whole division of Negroes? And what would the public think of the general who had made it possible?

Burnside thought well of the division commander, Edward Ferrero. He was an amateur soldier whose prewar experience was limited to militia drills and instructing West Point cadets in the art of social dancing. His father was an Italian expatriate, a friend of Garibaldi and other exiled nationalists, who ran a fashionable dancing school in Manhattan. Edward developed this into a highly profitable business, patronized by the city's social and financial elite. He had a modest fame as a performer, as an originator of popular dance figures, and as author of *The Art of Dancing, Historically Illustrated, to Which Is Added a Few Hints on Etiquette,* published in 1859, regarded at the time as definitive among works in English. He was darkly handsome, with olive skin and black hair and beard, something of a dandy in his dress, a "paragon of neatness" even in the field. He had been with IX Corps for three years and had been put in command of the 4th Division at the start of the year, although his appointment as brigadier general had not yet been confirmed by Congress.[9]

So on July 4, Burnside summoned Ferrero to his headquarters near the Shand house and asked whether he thought his men were up to the assignment. When Ferrero said they were, Burnside tasked the division commander to develop a tactical plan and begin training his men to execute it. Ferrero made only one request: that his division be exempted from the incessant demand for fatigue details, which had scattered his units all over the army's rear area. Among the tasks from which they were relieved was that of running the sawmill that made planks for Colonel Pleasants's mine.

THE BLACK DIVISION PREPARES

Ferrero met with his brigade commanders to sketch a plan of attack. The 1st Brigade was commanded by Colonel Henry Goddard Thomas, twenty-seven years old, a lawyer from Maine who had fought as a private at Bull Run and then taken a commission in the 11th U.S. Regulars— which technically made this civilian-soldier the first Regular officer to command Colored troops. He served briefly as colonel of the 19th United States Colored Troops (USCT) before getting command of the brigade. The 2nd Brigade was commanded by Joshua Sigfried, formerly colonel of the 48th Pennsylvania, who had been reluctant to take command of Colored troops, accepting only out of "disinterested patriotism." Perhaps because Sigfried had more combat experience than Thomas, his brigade was chosen to lead the advance.[10]

On July 5, Thomas and Sigfried went up to examine the ground from the frontline loops. Sigfried was accompanied by his two most trusted regimental commanders, Colonels Delevan Bates of the 30th and Seymour Hall of the 43rd USCT, whose units would lead the brigade into action. To keep from being killed by sharpshooters they had a soldier put a hat on a stick and poke it up over the parapet, waited for the local sniper to shoot, and then snatched a look while he was reloading. They could see the no-man's-land between the trenches and the top of the high ground beyond the Rebel lines, but little of the crucial four hundred yards immediately behind the Rebel front. Additional observations made from platforms set in trees behind the Union lines added only a little more to the picture. But using the best information they could get, they drew up a plan of attack.

The obvious place to strike was through the breach made by the mine explosion. But Ferrero concluded that the mass of earth thrown up by the explosion would make coherent troop movement impossible. Moreover, the flanks and rear of troops passing through the breach would be exposed to fire from Confederates holding out in the trenches to the left and right. He therefore decided to strike the Confederate lines between Elliott's Salient and the smaller battery (Davidson's) to the south. If the troops jumped off immediately after the explosion and dashed across the hundred yards that separated the opposing trench lines, they might carry the line before the entrenched riflemen recovered from their shock. The threat to their left rear would then be eliminated, and the mine would have erased the threat from the right rear, allowing them to advance directly onto Cemetery Hill.

The division would form with the 2nd Brigade in front and the 1st behind it, in "a double column of regiments closed in mass." That is, each brigade would assemble in two columns side by side, each column consisting of two regiments in line formation, one regiment behind the other, drawn up close together. A regiment "in line" actually consisted of two lines of riflemen, one behind the other, so each column of the brigade would consist of eight lines of infantry. After passing the Rebel lines, the lead regiments of the 1st Brigade would peel off to right and left, to take the defenders in the flank and rear and clear the trenches on either side of the breach. The other seven regiments, still in their double columns, would dash for Cemetery Hill and the Plank Road, drive off Rebel defenders at the point of the bayonet, dig in, and hold until the rest of the corps arrived to support them.[11]

Burnside approved the plan, and on July 9 the training of the 4th Division began. (That same day Early's force defeated Lew Wallace's force on the Monocacy.)

Unfortunately, Ferrero himself was not able to see the division through its preparation. During the first week of training he was notified that Congress had not confirmed his appointment as brigadier general of volunteers, without which he could not remain in command. Burnside tried his best to get him confirmed, and Grant wrote Chief of Staff Halleck on his behalf, warmly praising Ferrero's work and concluding "I do not know how he is to be replaced." But Congress adjourned without taking action, and on July 20, Ferrero took ship for Washington to make a personal appeal to the president and the War Department. Brigadier General Julius White, who had served briefly with IX Corps in East Tennessee, took administrative charge of the 4th Division. But he had little connection with its training.[12]

In Ferrero's absence, his plan was modified by Sigfried and Thomas, perhaps in response to problems discovered during practice runs. Ferrero had envisioned an attack on the entrenched line between the (presumable) crater at Elliott's Salient and the next salient south. But there could be no certainty that the troops holding these lines would be panicked by the mine, and if a significant fraction of them stayed to fight, they would certainly delay the divisional spearhead and might stop it in its tracks. Speed was essential—it was imperative that the division seize the hill before Confederate reserves could arrive. The brigade commanders therefore decided to advance through the breach created by the mine, avoiding the crater itself but passing over the rubble field thrown out to either side by the explosion. The broken ground would cause some delay and disorganization, but not as much as a manned trench line. The absent Ferrero was not informed of the change.

The brigade and regimental commanders in the 4th Division were pleased and honored to have been chosen to lead the assault. It was an acknowledgment that they had succeeded in making their units fit for combat service. More than that, it was an opportunity to fulfill the special mission to which they had committed themselves: "Both officers and men were eager to show the white troops what the colored division could do." They took heart from the proverbial wisdom "that there are times when the ardor, hopefulness, and enthusiasm of new troops, not yet rendered doubtful by reverses or chilled by defeat, more than compensate, in a dash, for training and experience."[13]

But that was theory. As veterans they knew how chancy it was to trust raw troops for such an attack. Rookies were capable of attempting, and sometimes achieving, seemingly impossible assaults, because they underestimated the obstacles and opposition. But that same inexperience might lead them to overestimate the danger of any one of the million unexpected things that could happen on a battlefield—sudden fire from an unexpected quarter, disorientation in the battle smoke, a voice crying something that sounds like "We're flanked!"—and they might break and run back faster than they went up. Practically every infantry unit in both armies broke at one time or another—it was a necessary survival mechanism. One of the things that made Civil War armies all but indestructible as organizations was the soldiers' willingness and ability to rapidly escape the jaws of destruction—then stop, rally, and reform their ranks. Veteran troops could be balky about undertaking an attack that looked to them like a losing proposition. But they were less likely to panic in action, because they expected the unexpected, and had learned to discriminate between real and imaginary threats to their safety. If they broke and ran, they also knew how far to retreat and when to stop, reform, and check the enemy's pursuit. With rookies it was likely to be all or nothing: either they'd storm your fort or run themselves off the field.[14]

And that was how it was with White rookies. No one could be sure how it would be with Blacks. But the officers of the United States Colored Troops had bet their lives on the premise that Negroes could do as well as Whites.

Chapter 6

"Guide on de Army"

AFRICAN AMERICANS GO TO WAR

Colonel Henry Thomas had told Ferrero that his men were eager for the chance to prove themselves in battle, but he seems to have had some doubts. He told his regimental commanders to make the announcement, and then stood at the edge of the bivouac listening to learn how they took it.

He knew his troops had their own way of responding to impending action. An encampment of Whites would have been abuzz with speculation and argument. "Not so with blacks; important news such as that before us . . . was usually followed by a long silence." As the word went around, the soldiers separated into small circles, perhaps of men from the same district or community, "sitting on the ground intently and solemnly . . . 'studying,' as they called it." It was an active and collective meditation.

Most of the men in Thomas's brigade were from Maryland and Virginia, ex-slaves rather than free Negroes from the North, and they assimilated the news in the style of those often surreptitious religious meetings that took place in the slave quarters. "They waited, like the Quakers, for the spirit to move; when the spirit moved, one of their singers would uplift a mighty voice, like a bard of old, in a wild sort of chant." The singer might begin by offering lines from songs already known. There was a marching song that Whites sang, about how they would "gird on the armor," which Black singers enlarged to "We'll guide on de army and be marchin' along." Or someone might propose a song of liberation, "No more driver's lash for me, / Many thousand gone." White officers thought such solemn and spiritual themes were most characteristic, but Black sol-

diers had other moods. During its training, the 30th USCT had made up
a song full of jaunty defiance and a sardonic appreciation of their peculiar
situation:

> *Jeff Davis says he'll hang us*
> *If we dars to meet him armed*
> *Berry big t'ing, but be not t'ht all alarmod;*
> *For fust he's got to gotch us—*
> *Dat am berry cla'r;*
> *And dat's what's de matter*
> *Wid de Colored Voluntar.*

During the Wilderness battle they were razzed by units of V Corps,
and improvised a call-and-response on the spot. One man took the lead
and chanted in syncopated rhythm, "Will *you,* will *you* / *Fight* for de
Union?" and the whole regiment responded, "Ah-*ha*! Ah-*ha*! / We'll *fight*
for Uncle Sam!" V Corps actually gave them a cheer.

But the news of the mine action was without precedent. Only new
words, improvised for the occasion, would suffice. Finally a deep voice
began to sing:

> *We-e looks li-ike me-en a-a-marchin' on,*
> *We looks li-ike men-er-war.*

The singer repeated the verse again and again, varying the music
slightly. "The rest listened to him intently; no sign of approval escaped
their lips or appeared on their faces. All at once, when his refrain had
struck the right response in their hearts, his group took it up," and in
short order the song had spread through the regiment, "half a thousand
voices . . . upraised extemporizing a half dissonant middle part and bass."
It was a stunning and moving expression of communal thinking and feeling, because it was clear to Thomas that through this musical improvisa-
tion, this call-and-response, his men had considered the task that had
been laid upon them and chosen it as their own.[1]

Thomas was attentive and sympathetic—but he did not participate
in the emotion his men shared. It was a spectacle, something exotic, a
glimpse into an alien life. The music was "as weird as the scene," the men
themselves alien and unaccountable, "these dark men, with their white
teeth and eyes and full red lips, crouching over a smouldering camp-fire,
in dusky shadow, with only the feeble rays of the lanterns of the first ser-

geants and the lights of the candles dimly showing through the tents."[2] That alienation was characteristic of the relations between White officers and Black troops. The officers would write journals, letters home, and postwar reminiscences filled with anecdotes of their experience with individual Black soldiers, but the persons are rarely identified by name. In White regiments, comradeship persisted long after the war, was renewed at annual reunions, and often led to the production of a regimental history to which many individuals contributed. In the USCT comradeship between officers and men ended with the war. There were no reunions, and the few regimental histories that were produced were mainly by and about the officers. As a result, most officers remembered their soldiers simply as instances of racial character, as Negroes rather than persons.

USCT: The Officers

A sense of mission was almost a prerequisite for commanding United States Colored Troops. You had to volunteer for that service, and most USCT officers transferred out of the units that were, in a double sense, their homes, in order to serve with a "despised race." Some were motivated by discontent with conditions or personal relations in their original unit, some by the prospect of promotion, others by the hope of avoiding battle (since some commanders used Black troops only for garrison duty). But most chose the service in the belief that the success of Black troops was essential to the war effort. The army and administration had made that appeal in an intense publicity campaign, so successful that it drew into the USCT many staunchly Unionist officers who had opposed the administration and emancipation earlier in the war.

Few of the officers had been abolitionist activists, though many from the Northeast had sympathized with the movement and were connected to it by family and friendship. Joseph Glatthaar's study of these officers shows that a high percentage came from regions affected by the prewar waves of evangelical revivalism, including New England, New York's "Burnt-over District," and northern Ohio. Men reared in this religious tradition saw the defense of the Union not merely as a civic duty but as an affirmation of faith in sacred principles that the Union embodied. They brought to the task of training Black troops a reformist and missionary spirit, a sense that by working with Negroes they were somehow engaging the problem at the root of the Civil War. But there were also large numbers of men who had been (and remained) unsympathetic to the Negro or to emancipation, who took commands in the USCT out of a sense of civic and patriotic duty.[3]

The method of appointing officers in the USCT was unique. In a White volunteer regiment, officers were appointed by state governors and/or elected by their troops. But officers of the USCT had to qualify for commissions by passing a rigorous examination, which tested their knowledge of tactics, regulations, history, geography, mathematics, and much else. This was as close to a true merit system as any in American history. As in the modern system of examinations, tutorials and study guides were offered to aspirants. The vast majority of officer candidates were veterans of field service, who brought experience as well as book knowledge to the table. As a class, the officers of the USCT were probably better qualified for their commands than officers in the average volunteer regiment.[4]

It took a special kind of courage to lead Black troops in action. The Confederate government had officially declared that officers of the USCT would not be treated as prisoners of war but as criminals fomenting slave rebellion—an offense punishable by death. Fear of Federal retaliation prevented open execution of that policy, but Confederate Secretary of War Seddon encouraged field commanders to apply its principles unofficially, "red-handed on the field or immediately thereafter." Reports of the killing or imprisonment of captured officers, and the massacre or re-enslavement of Black POWs, had been rife since the fights at Milliken's Bend and Fort Wagner in the summer of 1863. On April 12, 1864, the most notorious of these massacres was perpetrated at Fort Pillow, Tennessee, by troops under the command of General Nathan Bedford Forrest. It provoked a firestorm of outrage in the Northern press, and an investigation by the Committee on the Conduct of the War. Fort Pillow was followed within the month by reports of massacres at Poison Spring, Arkansas, and Plymouth, North Carolina. It was generally assumed that an officer of the USCT could not expect to receive quarter from the enemy.[5]

Those who volunteered for the USCT often had to face the contempt and hostility of their home communities, neighbors, and even families. There was strong public opposition to the use of Black troops. A New Jersey newspaper urged the state to refuse to enroll Blacks as soldiers: "Those who would arm the negro population with weapons of war and turn them against their masters' throats would proclaim a world of terror such as the world has never seen."[6]

The high command of the Army of the Potomac was particularly hostile to the idea of incorporating Black regiments. Many officers shared McClellan's opposition to emancipation. Seymour Hall had earned the respect of his brigade and division commanders in three years of service. But when he spoke of his intention to accept command of the 43rd USCT, "A staff officer of high rank said to me: 'Hall, you know we do not want any "nigger soldiers" in the Army of the Potomac, but if any ever do come I hope your command will be the first.' . . . A very distinguished general, on whom I called to say good-bye, said: 'I am sorry to have you leave my command, and still more sorry that you are going to serve with negroes. I think it is a disgrace to the Army to make soldiers of them.'" Hall answered that "good fighters were needed, and that such would not disgrace the service whatever their color." The general, a "gallant and distinguished" officer, replied that he didn't care about color but believed Negroes were unfit for combat. He would accept the government's policy but "without changing . . . one jot of my former judgment."[7]

Theodore Lyman, an officer on Meade's staff, thought it a shame that White men should have to call on Negroes to help them. "As I looked at them my soul was troubled and I would gladly have seen them marched back to Washington. Can we not fight our own battles, without calling on these humble hewers of wood and drawers of water, to be bayonetted by unsparing Southerners? We do not trust them in battle." Even after the success of Hinks's division, and the good work done by Ferrero's men during the campaign, Lyman still felt nothing but contempt. On July 1, he was escorting some visiting French officers on a tour of the camps, and "I took advantage of the propinquity of the nigger division . . . to show the unbleached brethren to my imperial commissioners. . . . There was turned out for them a regiment of darks. The sun was intense and the sable gents looked like millers, being quite obscured except when they stood perfectly still. They did remarkably well. . . . [The] Frog officers . . . were in ecstasies over their performance."[8]

Lyman's use of "nigger" is representative of attitudes that were nearly universal among Whites, in the North as well as the South. The term was a vulgarism, not normally used in polite conversation. Nevertheless it was commonly employed by middle- and upper-class Whites in a variety of private and public settings. Newspaper editorialists and politicians routinely used it to denigrate or deride "nigger equality," "nigger rights," and "nigger soldiers." It was even used by some USCT officers, sometimes ironically, sometimes in a spirit of self-mockery, but often as a way of expressing their sense of distance and difference from the men they commanded. At bottom, "nigger" was a word expressive of contempt at best, loathing at worst. It described a being without dignity, abject, physically repulsive, unfit for association with Whites, eligible for ridicule and humiliation. "Nigger" defined the color line as a definitive border between the dignity of citizenship and degradation or social death. Even in the Free States, Black people were excluded from participation in the basic activities of citizenship. They could not serve on juries, vote, hold public office, or (until 1863) join in the common defense.

To approach the "nigger" was to risk contamination, and anything that tended to blur the color line threatened pollution to the larger society. For the "distinguished general," incorporating Negro troops disgraced the Army of the Potomac by suggesting a likeness between its White soldiers and "niggers." Officers like Hall had been reared in that same tradition, and had to struggle with it when they made the decision to transfer to the USCT. One made a joke of it, writing to his daughter, "Zetty. What do you say to it. Aint you afraid your pa will get black[?]" One White officer wrote that he was "well aware that . . . with some I should loose [sic] caste by becoming an officer in a colored regiment," but thought it was his duty to assume that task. His brother responded with the prayer that he should "flee from its presences . . . 'A chaplain of a *nigger* regiment!' My god! . . . I had much rath[er] you had not asked my opinion, or even informed me, that you were making yourself so willing, to accept a degraded position, (I wouth rather clean out S__t houses at ten cents pr day.)." His father warned that one day he'd find himself alone with a hundred "mutinous" Blacks—rather than lose a single company of White men, his father would have preferred to see the whole race exterminated.[9]

Similar attitudes were rife among the rank and file of the regiments from which the new officers came. This is significant because most of the USCT officers were enlisted men, noncoms, or junior officers before their transfer. White soldiers routinely looted slave cabins as well as plantation houses, and abused refugees in the contraband camps, which included rape or coerced sex with Black women. When the government began enlisting Black troops, there were exaggerated reports of regiments laying down arms and deserting, "swearing they will not fight to free the Negroes." The men of the 48th Pennsylvania accepted the necessity of enlisting Blacks, but "many doubted whether the colored boys would prove faithful under fire." That attitude changed when the White men passed through the trenches captured by Hinks's Black division and saw dead

Black men lying on the parapets. But even this acknowledgment preserved the essence of racial distinction. If the dead had been White, the 48th would just have said that they'd belonged to a good outfit. Whatever Blacks did, whether good or bad, it was seen as proof of something about the whole race.[10]

Most Northern soldiers had never seen a Black person before they went South, and many reacted with "aversion and often with loathing." Linton Smith of Delaware was of Quaker origin and was antislavery, but his impression of Southern Blacks comprised "Dirt, filth, grease, essence of nastiness. Thick lips, wooly heads, dirty noses and peculiar smelling, and ungrately [sic] for favor conferred, as men can be."[11] Perhaps a more typical reaction was the naïve response of Lieutenant Freeman S. Bowley of the 30th USCT, a seventeen-year-old Massachusetts boy who had lied about his age to get a commission. At the first sight of his company he was shocked by "How black the men were. I never imagined that men could be so black."

But after a few days of working together Bowley's men "did not seem so black, nor so much alike as they did at first." The men learned to respect "the little lieutenant," because he knew his job, and because he worked *with* them instead of standing apart. Bowley was one of the few USCT officers whose memoirs are full of references to named individuals—not just "my Negro sergeant" but Thomas Festus, John Offer, Percy Gibbs.[12]

One way for USCT officers to cope with the public hostility was to identify passionately with the mission of transforming slaves into freedmen. A skeptical observer noted that the USCT officers "are enthusiasts and think they would rather drill & discipline black men than white." In many regiments officers or chaplains taught their men to read, write, and cipher as well as the manual of arms. They were struck by what seemed to them a willingness to accept discipline and instruction that was most unlike the fractious resentment of hierarchy that characterized White volunteers. That quality led many officers to echo the colleague who declared, "I would rather have command of negro troops, with the same opportunities of improving themselves in drill, than of the ordinary white recruit one gets." George Walcott was another of the 30th Regiment's "boy lieutenants," exempt from service because he was a widow's only son, but moved to enlist by a Christian's "chastened enthusiasm" for the cause of freedom, and the uplifting of the Negro race. He idealized his men, finding them "Generally . . . more moral than white soldiers, they never grumble: give them an order and they obey it. No profanity or sabbath breaking. I would not change my position for the same in a white regiment."[13]

Lieutenant Robert Beecham of the 23rd had a more realistic but no less positive view of his men. Beecham was a veteran of the famous Iron Brigade, with an enlisted man's ironic view of military protocol. After two years of the hardest service, he was disgusted to have risen no higher than "eighth corporal" in the 2nd Wisconsin: "Think of it, ye ambitious sons of the great republic who long for military honors." So he applied for the USCT, worked and bluffed his way through a series of bureaucratic catch-22s, and got his commission. He did not think his men were saints. They were mostly from D.C. and Baltimore, and included "some pretty hard cases," but no more and no worse than one would find in a similar number of White city men. "[As] a rule the men were sober, honest, patriotic and willing to learn and fulfill the duties of soldiers." He admired his men, and the race they represented, because "the Afro-American [had come] forward cheerfully and volunteered his strength, his brawn, his heart's blood to save the honor of the flag that to him and his race had been the symbol of every dishonor." Beecham took some pains to contradict the racial stereotypes associated with Blacks. It was not true that Negro feet were disproportionately large—Beecham had wrangled for hours with a quartermaster who would not supply proper shoes because he thought "no shoe too large for a Negro." They would drink liquor when they could, but not to excess: "The 2d Wis. was not as sober and temperate as the 23d U.S. Colored Troops." Likewise, "there never was an organization of 1,000 men in all this broad, free America where a woman was held in greater esteem or her honor more sacred." Above all, they were "not filthy": rather the opposite, "and for that reason if for no other, I would prefer to command a company or regiment of black, rather than white soldiers."[14]

Beecham was not unique. The experience of living and working with Blacks at close quarters was often a cure for the false pride of White supremacy. One company commander, who had approached his troops with a skeptical but open mind, came to believe that a few weeks' experience would disabuse White people of "the idea that the entire negro race are vastly their inferior. . . . I *know* that many of them are vastly the *superiors* of those (many of those) who would condemn them to a life of brutal degradation."[15]

But most officers of the USCT brought to their new task a consciousness shaped by the culture of White supremacy. They understood what "nigger" signified, and most of them used the word. If their understanding of race was to be transformed, it would have to develop *through* the language of racism. The colonel of one Colored regiment defined his project in just these terms: "yesterday a filthy, repulsive 'nigger,' to-day a nearly-attired man; yesterday a slave, to-day a freeman; yesterday a civilian, to-day a soldier." Officers typically saw their troops as charges rather than fellow soldiers, superstitious in religion, primitive in their understanding of social and personal relations. Indeed, they shared the Southern view that Negroes "will have to have some one to look after them like that many children or else they will starve to death."[16]

Racial difference transformed every virtue into a liability. Officers who were pleased to find Black troops more amenable to discipline than Whites typically concluded that Blacks lacked the pride and self-reliance of the superior race—a lack that explained their supposed acquiescence to enslavement. Captain Charles Francis Adams thought they lacked "the pride, spirit, and intellectual energy of the whites," in part because of their experience as slaves, but mostly by their nature. More to the point, he thought they lacked the most essential quality of soldiers: "After all a negro is not the equal of the white man . . . he cannot stand up against adversity. . . . Retreat, defeat and exposure would tell on them more than on whites. . . . He cannot fight for life like a white man." But if Blacks showed ferocity in combat, it became testimony to their supposed primitivism or "savage" nature. One officer thought Blacks so "excitable" they would "throw themselves forward to the cannon's mouth; and in their rage, will even tear their opponents with their teeth." Another feared, "I do not believe we can keep the negroes from murdering every thing they come to." Yet many officers were equally afraid that the race was too servile to confront their former masters in battle.[17]

The Maryland Regiments

There were nine regiments in the 4th Division's order of battle. Four were raised in Maryland and the northern counties of Virginia (the 19th, 23rd, 30th, and 39th USCT). The rest were raised in the Free States: the 43rd in Pennsylvania, the 31st in New York City, the 27th in Ohio, the 28th in Indiana, and the 29th in Illinois.

When the South seceded, four slave states (Delaware, Maryland, Kentucky, and Missouri) stayed with the Union. Their slaves were not freed by the Emancipation Proclamation, which applied only to districts controlled by the Confederacy. Unionist slave owners resisted all proposals for voluntary and compensated emancipation, fruitlessly hoping to preserve their property despite the overthrow of Southern slavery. Most were therefore unwilling to let their slaves enlist, since enlistment conferred freedom. The situation was somewhat different in Maryland, where the governor and a legislative majority had read the writing on the wall and begun the process of abolishing slavery within the state. When Maryland started raising USCT regiments, it offered owners a bounty of three hundred dollars per man for every slave who enlisted—the standard fee paid by a drafted man for hiring a White substitute. Faced with the eventual uncompensated loss of their property, the owners now saw financial advantage in encouraging, or even persuading, their slaves to enlist.[18]

But Marylanders remained deeply ambivalent about Black soldiers. When the 19th paraded through Baltimore, "some of the more rabid of the Rebels in our midst gave vent to their spleen. . . . One female . . . thought it had come to a pretty pass when she had to stand to allow 'niggers' to pass and that they were a nice crowd to send to fight against white men."[19] Only one native Marylander took a commission in the USCT. Of the Maryland regiments in the 4th Division, the 39th was commanded by Colonel Ozora P. Stearns, a Minnesota lawyer and political leader, later a U.S. senator. Delevan Bates of the 30th and Cleaveland Campbell of the 23rd were New Yorkers. Bates was a combat veteran—an old man of twenty-five who was dismayed to find that many of his junior officers were mere boys, including Lieutenants Walcott and Bowley from Massachusetts. Captain Rickard of the 19th was a Rhode Island businessman who served two years in the 18th Connecticut, a regiment of schoolteachers and their students. He was proud that his regiment was "composed entirely of slaves," and thought "No man desiring the speedy overthrow of the rebellion . . . could have looked upon [them] with other than feelings of satisfaction." His colleague Lieutenant Lemuel D. Dobbs was a Pennsylvanian, from Armstrong County in the western part of the state—a farmer studying to be a schoolteacher when the war broke out. At twenty-two he was a veteran of three years' service in the famous "Pennsylvania Reserves," and may have been a POW for a short time. He was a newlywed, married in February to a Baltimore woman—perhaps someone he met while the regiment was mustering.[20]

Although there had been enthusiastic volunteering for the first Colored units, such as the 54th Massachusetts, the 1st Kansas Colored, and the 1st South Carolina, recruiting for the USCT proved more difficult than anticipated. To a man like Captain Charles Francis Adams, this showed the Negro's servile reluctance to fight for his own liberation. The slow pace of recruitment was better explained by the extremely small population base (less than 1 percent of the North's total military manpower) but also by a degree of politically self-conscious resistance. Although African Americans in general supported the Union cause as the best means of ending slavery, it was by no means certain at the start of 1864 that a Northern victory would lead to complete abolition, let alone civil equality. Fugitives from those border states that still protected slavery believed that if they enlisted, their masters would be able to locate and recover them; and their old masters could and did hold their families hostage to prevent enlistment. Black troops were paid less than White—ten dollars a month instead of thirteen dollars—and in most states were ineligible for the bounties given to White soldiers. Blacks resented both the material discrimination and the racial insult this symbolized. Until the last months of the war, all line officers in the USCT were White. No Black man, whatever his ability, could win a line commission—a deterrent to enlistment by Black men of property and accomplishment. Nevertheless, in the end some thirty-four thousand free Blacks would enlist in the Union armies, roughly 15 percent of the total free population, and a much higher proportion of the Black community's military-age manpower.[21]

The 23rd and 39th USCT were raised in and around the cities of Baltimore and Washington, D.C., the 19th in rural southern Maryland, and the 30th on the eastern shore, where the bulk of the state's enslaved population resided. Slaves in Maryland worked as field hands on farms and small plantations and as unskilled laborers in the cities and towns. There was also a sizeable free Black population that engaged in skilled trades and services as well as day labor. Slaves were often hired out by masters, as laborers (skilled and unskilled) and as field hands, so that slavery in Maryland blended into wage labor at the margins. Still, the vast majority of the Maryland soldiers were laborers or field hands.[22]

Just like their White counterparts, African Americans tended to enlist in groups of family, friends, or neighbors. The Dorseys, who came from the Baltimore–Ellicott City area, were well represented. Charles, Decatur, James H., James W., and Prestley all served in the 39th, and John H. and Moses Dorsey in the 19th USCT. Decatur Dorsey was probably released by his master to serve in the 39th, although it was later claimed that he had escaped from slavery. Whatever his original status, he had a gift for soldiering. He enlisted in March, by May he was a corporal, and in July he was color sergeant. The latter was a position of danger and responsibility. The regimental commander usually kept the color near him; the flag was the guide the regiment followed in the attack and marked the place to rally after a repulse. So the color was usually the target of enemy bullets, the object of any bayonet attack. It was also the visible symbol of the regiment's spirit and honor: it could never be allowed to fall or be captured by the enemy. Only a powerful, courageous, and absolutely trustworthy man was fit to be a color-bearer.[23]

Officers in these Maryland regiments got surprising insights into the workings of the slave system when they tried to help their men deal with the complications of their new status. Some still thought of themselves as belonging to their original owners, though enlistment had made them free. In many cases the soldier's wife and child were indeed still enslaved, and correspondence between them was mediated by the owner or members of the master's household. Perry Gibbs, a free Black farmer from Anne Arundel County, proudly informed his lieutenant that he was the father of nine children, "all as black as crows; no milk and 'lasses ones in dat fam'bly." It was his boast that none of the master's blood tainted the heritage of his children, and (by implication) that his wife's honor had never been compromised by a master's lust.[24]

With the rest of the division, the 19th and the 30th guarded the army's wagon trains from the Wilderness to Cold Harbor, and twice fought off attacks by Rebel cavalry. The 19th performed well in its brief turn at trench duty. The night before they began training for the crater, a patrol went out to protect some sappers. "When they got well out, the Rebels came leaping over their works four lines deep and charged them. The blacks stood their ground manfully and inflicted upon the chivalry very severe damage, although suffering much themselves."[25]

THE FREE STATE REGIMENTS

The other five regiments were raised in Free States. Their enlisted ranks therefore showed a different mix of trades, different proportions of free and slave. There were also differences in the political processes that created the regiments.

The 31st was one of three Colored regiments raised in New York

City during the fall and winter following the July 1863 Draft Riots. The city's Democratic administration was at odds with the Republican governor over war policy, but the two parties agreed on the necessity of keeping peace in the streets. Like White volunteer regiments, USCT outfits were raised under state sponsorship, and recruits were credited to the state's draft quota. But as soon as USCT regiments were recruited, they were adopted into Federal service. (A few states did raise their own Colored regiments, but these were exceptions.) By filling New York's quota with Blacks they could minimize the demand for White conscripts, depriving the mobs of their primary grievance, and at the same time reduce racial competition in the local labor market.

Blacks were recruited from the city and neighboring counties and assembled on Rikers and Hart islands, off the coast of the Bronx. For African Americans from the city, the act of enlistment had some ironic implications. On the one hand, it was a gesture affirming the link between war and emancipation, and a rebuke to the antiwar mob that had attacked them. On the other, their enlistment allowed the Irish to avoid serving.

The 31st was the last regiment to be organized, and was commanded by Colonel W.E.W. Ross. The mix of trades represented in the outfit reflects Black participation in the economy of a large port city: boatman, sailor, cart man, teamster, cook, spoke maker, butcher, carpenter, tailor. Nevertheless, 60 percent were farmers or day laborers. The city's racial complexity is suggested by the fact that at least two and as many as six of the enlisted men may have been Asian.[26]

By the time the 31st was organized, the pool of Black manpower in the state had been drained. So to fill out its ranks the regiment incorporated a few companies from the 30th Connecticut (Colored), which had also fallen short of completion. With them came a company of Pequot Indians, survivors of a once mighty tribe in the Thames River Valley, many of whom had intermarried with Blacks. They had enlisted under the false presumption, promoted by recruiters, that they were eligible for conscription. The Mohegans, who lived farther upstream, were more cognizant of their rights and had refused to serve.[27]

❧

The 43rd was raised in eastern Pennsylvania, and its creation represented a victory for Black activism in the state. There was a relatively large community of free Blacks in Philadelphia, with a century of political engagement in the antislavery movement, supported by the powerful Quaker and

Moravian communities in the state. The governor was a Republican, but Democrats remained powerful, and the state was not considered safe for a party committed to emancipation.

From the beginning of the war, African American organizations agitated for the right to join in the defense of the Union. In Pittsburgh and Philadelphia they organized and armed three volunteer companies: "We consider ourselves American citizens. . . . Although deprived of all political rights, we yet wish the government of the United States to be sustained against the tyranny of slavery." The Philadelphia companies were rejected by the state, but the Pittsburgh contingent was enrolled as Company I, "Zouave Cadets," in the 12th Infantry. However, no precedent was set, because the 12th was enlisted for only ninety days and mustered out without seeing action. For two years Black leaders unsuccessfully lobbied Harrisburg for permission to serve, and won only when Washington, D.C., weighed in on their behalf.[28]

The state established Camp William Penn near Philadelphia and began recruiting. To speed the process of providing officers, a school was opened to prepare candidates for their examinations. Recruits also came from other states, especially New Jersey, which refused to form its own Black regiments. Educated Black men in the 43rd were solicited by agents from other states seeking noncoms for regiments recruited among freed slaves. Very few transferred, even with the promise of promotion. Like White volunteers, they wanted to serve with men from their own communities. But there was also some caste feeling involved. One Pennsylvania soldier wrote of the "men who has Been in Bondage . . . we cant expect them to Do as well as a man that has Been free."[29]

Colonel Hall took over in March 1864, determined to prepare the 43rd for combat in the four weeks before they were to join the army. He began an intensive regimen of battalion drill basic to combat operations, deploying from column into line, wheeling right or left, breaking and re-forming by companies. He also put them through endless repetitions of the manual of arms, fixing and unfixing bayonets, repeating the nine steps for loading, aiming, firing, and recovering the muzzle-loaded rifle-musket. With Chaplain Mickley, Hall instituted a school to provide basic education and to demonstrate Negroes "are very susceptible of intellectual and moral culture."[30]

Mickley was a man of radical principles who believed his regiment would prove that. Yet Mickley's history mentions only one Black man by name: Sergeant Major R. B. Forten, a Black man born in London, an "intelligent and cultivated" man whose character stands in "most favorable comparison with our own race." But another sergeant, John Brock of Carlisle, Pennsylvania, was an active correspondent of *The Christian Recorder,* a Methodist newspaper, which published his letters from camp. Brock was twenty-one years old, a member of the African Methodist Episcopal (AME) Church, and a graduate of its Sabbath school who served as commissary sergeant. He proudly described the 43rd's march into Maryland, which was "once under the despotic sway of slavery," and welcomed the assignment to Burnside's corps: "We are proud to be under such a distinguished leader, and we hope . . . to burn the sides of the rebels."[31]

In Washington the 43rd marched in review for President Lincoln, saluting "gracefully with their colors and [giving] loud hurrahs for the Great Emancipator of their race." Colonel Hall kept them up to the mark all the way down to the Rapidan, where they joined the army. He felt it was essential to impress his former colleagues with the discipline and spirit of his men, not simply for his own pride but to convince them that Black troops could be trusted in combat. They had few chances to show what they could do—mostly endless fatigue and guard duty, punctuated by skirmishes with Rebel patrols and brief turns in the dangerous posts of the picket line.[32] But Sergeant Brock was well satisfied. He wrote to *The Christian Recorder* about the five hundred slaves liberated by the regiment. More than that, he believed that the presence of his regiment on the battlefield redeemed the reputation of the race: " No longer can we be reproached as being afraid to take up arms for the defense of our country. No longer can it be said that we have no rights in the country in which we live, because we never marched forward to the defense."[33]

⁓

The 27th USCT was raised in Ohio, and like the 43rd drew recruits from a free Black community with a long history in the state. Ohio had a tradition of abolitionist activism, dating to the evangelical revival of the 1820s and centered on the Oberlin College community. As happened in Pennsylvania, agitation for Black enlistment began early in the war. A volunteer company in Cleveland declared its people were as ready to serve now "as in times of 1776 and the days of 1812," and the Cincinnati community began organizing a Black brigade. But Ohio also had a large and active Copperhead movement, and a tradition of virulent anti-Black racism, especially in the southern part of the state. African American recruiters in Cincinnati were verbally and physically intimidated by Whites, and forced to close their recruiting stations. The police officially informed them, "We want you damned niggers to keep out of this; this is a white man's war." John Mercer Langston had a national reputation among African American leaders—Governor Andrew of Massachusetts sought Langston's aid in recruiting Blacks for the 54th Massachusetts. But Ohio's Republican governor, David Tod, was afraid that if Blacks were allowed to fight for the Union, it would become morally and logically impossible to deny them political rights—and Tod was not ready for that. He rejected Langston's proposal to enlist Blacks, declaring: "This is a white man's government; that white men are able to defend and protect it, and that to enlist a negro soldier would be to drive every white man out of the service." As a result, many of Ohio's most militant Blacks traveled east to join up, and when Tod finally agreed to form two regiments, the 5th and the 27th, the manpower pool had been drawn down. Because of this, even though Black Ohioans enlisted in numbers exceeding their proportion of the state population, the regiments went to war understrength.[34]

Three quarters of the men listed their occupations as either farmer or laborer, but their political ideas were well formed—they would fight to free their enslaved brethren and to vindicate their own manhood. Langston told them that they had enlisted to support the government in its supposed determination "to recognize the citizenship of the native-born colored American."[35]

The 28th and 29th regiments were organized in Indiana and Illinois, Free States in which a dislike of slavery went hand in hand with virulent antipathy for Blacks. The southern counties in both states had been settled by emigrants from the South, small farmers unable or unwilling to compete with plantations worked with slave labor. Both states had adopted Black Codes, which limited the rights of free Blacks to settle and barred them from attending public schools, voting, jury service, giving sworn testimony, or serving in the militia. Nevertheless, each state had small communities of free Blacks—many of long standing—that were centers of religious life and political agitation. The Indiana communities tended to form in counties with large Quaker populations—a denomination active on behalf of abolition. As in Ohio, Black community leaders in Indiana and Illinois began petitioning for the right to military service early in the war, and here too they were rebuffed. Although Republicans had majorities in both legislatures, and held the governorships, Democratic conservatives and Copperheads controlled large constituencies. They opposed Black enlistments, declaring "the proposition to arm the slaves of the South is an insult to every American citizen" that would encourage Negroes to "shoot the men, ravish the women and strangle the children of the South indiscriminately."[36]

Official opinion reversed itself in the summer of 1863, and popular opinion followed, in response to the government's institution of conscription in states that failed to meet their volunteer quotas. Now Black enlistments became a politically useful instrument for forestalling the rage of White voters. Instead of enforcing the Black Codes against Negro settlement, Indiana and Illinois competed vigorously to recruit Blacks, both in the states and in nearby contraband camps. Both states offered bounties to Black volunteers to offset resentment over the lower pay offered by the Federal government. William Fishback, chief of Negro recruitment for Indiana's Governor Morton, called on the state's Black men to "Show yourselves worthy soldiers, and the petty prejudices that weak and wicked men have endeavored to excite against you will be forever swallowed up in the gratitude of a nation that will own and applaud your heroic deeds." Illinois's Governor Yates called for a regiment that would "stand as much hardship, and fight as desperately, and kill as many Rebels in battle, as any equal number of men of the purest Anglo-Saxon blood." Others urged them to "drive home and clinch the re[f]utation of the slanders that have annulled their race and to prove in their own persons . . . that beneath the black skin rest the great qualifications now needed by the Republic." If they did their duty like men, they would "sink the opprobrious epithet nigger into eternal oblivion." But racial attitudes remained the same. Both governors spoke disparagingly of Negroes and opposed liberalization of the Black Codes.[37]

Some Black leaders urged their men to refuse to enlist so long as they were denied basic civil rights, but most advocated enlistment. In Indiana, leadership was provided by two AME ministers, William Revels—brother of Hiram Revels, who would serve as a reconstruction-era senator from Mississippi—and Garland White, a semiliterate but eloquent preacher who had been the slave of Confederate leader Robert Toombs and escaped to Canada. Revels put his call to arms in revolutionary terms: "Hereditary Bondsmen! Know you not that he who would be freed, himself must strike the first blow?" White returned to Indiana to help recruit the 28th and serve as its chaplain.[38]

In both states, the free Black population was a small fraction of the whole, 0.5 percent in Illinois and smaller in Indiana. But after 1861, Blacks liberated or escaping from Southern plantations augmented the manpower pool. In a sample company of 155 men from Indiana's 28th USCT, only forty were from the Free States. The remainder were from border or Confederate states and were either freed or fugitive slaves—at least forty-six of these were fugitives who refused to name their community of origin. In Illinois the percentage of fugitives was still higher. Slaves from Kentucky and Tennessee had easy access to the southern part of the state, and most of its western border faced the slave state of Missouri. This presented Illinois officers with some unique problems. They frequently had to negotiate with former owners in Missouri, who used the enslaved families of soldier fugitives as hostages to compel a return to slavery. Medical examiners also found the marks of slavery on the bodies of their recruits: "left ear cropped . . . Scarred heavily on back from whipping." "Some of them were scarred from head to foot where they had been whipped. One man's back was nearly all one scar, as if the skin had been chopped up and left to heal in ridges." Putting on the uniform and learning to wield weapons transformed their attitudes and self-image: "They walk erect, and bear themselves as men who have rights and dare to maintain them."[39]

The 28th USCT was commanded by Massachusetts-born Charles S. Russell, thirty-three years old. Little is known about his prewar career. He served a hitch in a three-months Indiana regiment and then returned to Boston and was commissioned as captain in the 11th U.S. Regular Infantry, which helped restore order in New York after the Draft Riots. As colonel of the 28th he was hampered by the lack of officers, both line and staff. He was joined by two junior colleagues from the 11th Regulars, both German-born. There were a number of German immigrants in the USCT, some of whom were "Forty-eighters"—liberals who had fled to the United States after the repression of the revolutions of 1848. But Captain Johann Hackheiser and Lieutenant Jacob Scholl had come for economic opportunity. Scholl was the son of the mayor of the small town of Wurmberg; he had emigrated at age sixteen, "having heard many tales of better opportunities [in] . . . that land of promise." He moved to Indiana, became a citizen, and served in the militia. He enlisted in 1861 because "he had already learned to love his adopted country, and was ready to assist in preserving her unity." Hackheiser was an Indianapolis store clerk before enlisting in the Regulars. He had a fiancée, Sarah Kinder, to whom he wrote warm and chatty letters. In June, with the sound of cannonading from Petersburg in his ears, he seized "the only chance perhaps to write you a letter, so I took the morning for it and I hope I will hear from you soon (and often)." He was in good health, and so were the men, but "it is hard work to make good soldiers of the Negro, it takes time and patience." Still, "I hope we will be in Richmond by the fourth of July. I would like to bee ther on that day, [to take] dinner in the Capitol City of the Rebles [*sic*]."[40]

⁂

The commander of the 29th was John A. Bross, thirty-eight, a noted Chicago lawyer and public official who had led troops in battle at Perryville and Stones River. Bross had been a Douglas Democrat before the war, strongly opposed to abolition and "nigger equality." His acceptance of a command in the USCT reflected the radicalizing effect of the war for the Union. Bross was a serious Christian whose beliefs had been shaped by Francis Wayland's *The Elements of Moral Science:* to be valid, moral conviction must be expressed in action. He allowed experience to modify his racial prejudices—and found free Blacks to be a "more intelligent class of men" than contrabands, which suggested the educability of the race. His men seem to have liked and respected him. One soldier wrote that he "found in Colonel Bross a friend, one in whom every member of the regiment placed the utmost confidence. . . . He was loved by every one, because he was a friend to every one."[41]

Chicago gave the 29th a big send-off in April. Speakers praised Bross for his moral courage. That "a white man of good family, of culture, and of social position, does not hesitate to place himself at the head of a regiment of blacks" set an enlightened precedent that (if followed) might lead to the moral regeneration of the state, and an end to the infamous Black Codes. Not all who watched their departure were so proud. One man wrote his newspaper that he was "glad the darkies have left Pike County and joined the army of the Lord," and he hoped the last one would go "and take all his relations with him."[42]

It was widely assumed, in the North as well as in the South, that Confederates would show no mercy to armed Blacks or their officers. The regiment's departure coincided with news of the massacre of Black troops and their White comrades at Fort Pillow. A local editorial declared, "These colored troops should take no prisoners until the massacre at Fort Pillow is avenged." Bross echoed that sentiment in his response: "When I lead these men into battle, we shall expect no quarter, and shall not ask for quarter. . . . I ask no nobler epitaph, than that I fell for my country, at the head of this black and blue regiment." The *Chicago Tribune* echoed, "Let it be understood that they are to expect no quarter, and they will give none."[43]

Bross's pledge was no mere verbal flourish. By the beginning of June 1864, it was widely accepted on both sides that when White soldiers clashed with Black, neither could expect to receive quarter, and therefore neither was obliged to give it. Long before Fort Pillow, a Rebel POW taken at Vicksburg declared that Southern troops "would rather fight two Regiments of White Soldiers than one of Niggers. Rebel citizens fear them more than they would fear Indians." By word and example, Southern leaders had indicated their belief that the use of Black troops was a crime against civilization and humanity, and that its perpetrators were not entitled to protection under the laws of war. Union officers expected their Black soldiers to respond in kind, in part because that would be a natural and "manly" response to such a threat, but also because they saw Blacks as more "primitive" and *Southern* in their values—less imbued with the civility of Northern Christianity. Charles Francis Adams thought that "the cruelty of Fort Pillow" explained why the "darkies fought [so] ferociously" in Hinks's assault on June 15: "Now [the Rebels] dread the darkies more than the white troops; for they know that if they will fight the rebels can expect no quarter. Of course, our black troops are not subject to any of the rules of civilized warfare. If they murder prisoners, as I hear they did, it is to be lamented and stopped, but they can hardly be blamed."[44]

From that premise, some officers drew the conclusion that exhortations to remember Fort Pillow and to fight without expecting or granting quarter would give their "darkies" the extra goad they needed to make them good fighters.

TRAINING THE SPEARHEAD, JULY 9-25, 1864

Although Burnside had promised Ferrero to relieve his men from other duties so that they could train for the assault, it was never possible to bring the whole division together for training. Each regiment was drilled individually. Although every regiment in the division would receive some training, two regiments were drilled intensively—the 30th and 43rd USCT of Sigfried's brigade, which he chose to lead the attack and then wheel outward to sweep the flanks clear.

The 43rd was commanded by Colonel Seymour Hall, a superb citizen soldier whose combat experience included every campaign of the Army of the Potomac from Bull Run to Mine Run. He was twenty-eight years old, from a farming family in upstate New York, the only son of "a very patriotic widow." In 1861 he had raised a company from among his fellow students at Genesee College and led them into the 27th New York Infantry (later incorporated with the 121st). He would be awarded the Medal of Honor for his bravery at Gaines's Mill (1862) and Rappahannock Station (1863). He started as a private, rose through company command, and was promoted to colonel on his transfer to the USCT. Sigfried told him he was chosen because "I knew I could rely on you in any emergency. You had full control of all your men, the discipline in your regiment was high up, your officers and men had implicit confidence in you." Sigfried must have had comparable confidence in Delevan Bates, colonel of the 30th USCT, who was only twenty-four but had distinguished himself in the fighting at South Mountain and Fredericksburg. He had been taken prisoner at Chancellorsville, and had joined the USCT after his exchange. Bates had served with Hall in the 121st New York, a bond that would help them work together.[45]

Hall's regiment was stationed in the rear area for much of the time before the attack, and was able to drill on prepared ground. Bates's men spent much of their time picketing the army's southern flank, in a line of entrenchments that ran through an area known as Second Swamp. Unlike Thomas, Sigfried and his regimental commanders did not make it generally known that they were training for an important assault. Even the junior officers in Bates's regiment were left in the dark, although the veterans among them sensed something was up. "Depend upon it," Captain Smith told Lieutenant Bowley, "this division is going to be put in somewhere to make a desperate charge."[46]

Hall and Bates had to concern themselves as much with the military spirit and psychology of their men as with the complex footwork of their maneuvers. They had to imbue them with a fierce commitment to attack, enable them to feel they were part of a large and powerful machine utterly bent on storming the high ground and closing with the enemy. To begin that process, they would have given their troops a refresher course in the manual of arms. Most of the men had been wielding nothing more deadly than a shovel for the past month. They needed to recover their sense of being soldiers.

The muzzle-loading rifle-musket used a conical lead bullet wrapped in a paper cartridge containing gunpowder. It was loaded in nine steps. First, with your weapon grounded before you, you would take a cartridge from the leather box on your belt and tear the paper with your teeth (the grains were salt-bitter grit) to expose the powder. (If you were missing too many teeth, you could cut the cartridge with a knife.) You'd then pour the powder down the barrel and thumb the bullet (pointy end up) and the paper into the barrel. Next you'd draw the ramrod from its slot under the barrel, ram bullet and paper down to the breech (the paper acted as a wad to contain and compress the powder), and then return the rammer to its slot. Now you'd raise the piece and prime it. In the old flintlock days, this meant pouring a little powder into the touchhole, but the modern weapon used a copper-jacketed percussion cap. So you'd half-cock the hammer and set the cap on its nipple. Next you'd raise the piece, draw the hammer to full-cock, and on the order "Ready!" lock it into your shoulder. On "Aim!" you'd aim, and on "Fire!" you'd squeeze the trigger. There would be a deafening *Slam!* and the butt would kick your shoulder socket as the line fired and bitter black powder smoke stung your nostrils. With practice you would be able to load and fire twice every minute.[47]

For the advance through the breach, it was vital that officers and men become thoroughly familiar with the movements they would have to make. There were two potential choke points where the difficulty of the maneuver might throw the inexperienced troops into confusion. The first would come in getting out of their own trenches and forming for the advance. The second and more critical problem concerned the lead regiments, which would have to pass through the debris field around the crater and then wheel left and right "by companies" to widen the breakthrough. The wheeling maneuver was complicated, and if the men of the lead regiments became confused, they would derange the whole advance. The two regiments next in the column would have to be trained to resist their natural inclination to follow the leader; they'd have to keep advancing straight ahead after the leaders peeled off to left and right. Noncoms and enlisted men alike had to understand the plan of maneuver and know how to keep it going under the stress of enemy fire if their commanders should be killed or wounded.[48]

For the 43rd, at the head of the right-hand column, the movement was "right companies right into line wheel, left companies on the right into line," and the 30th would mirror those movements to the left. Picture the 43rd advancing in two lines, one behind the other, each line consisting of four companies. At a point chosen and marked by their regimental commander, the companies on the outside of the two lines were to pivot to the right (the rightmost file closer was the turning point) and stand in place. The next companies inward to their left were to continue marching until they had passed the first companies. Then they also were to wheel to the right and march up level with the first two companies, and so on until the regiment was once again in a double line, facing at a right angle to its original line of march.[49]

Now picture them doing that over ground churned and broken, under fire from rifles and artillery.

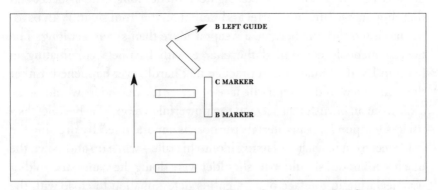

"ON THE RIGHT, INTO LINE" —BY FIRST LIEUTENANT IAN STRAUS

Source: http://www.6thtx.org/Maneuver_On%20the%20right%20into%20line.htm

Close-order drill in the modern military is a way of inculcating discipline. In 1864 it was training for combat. The infantry was armed with single-shot rifle-muskets, and the only way to deliver significant firepower was by massing them shoulder-to-shoulder to deliver their fire. The only way to break a line of riflemen was to concentrate shoulder-to-shoulder a mass of men with bayonets against a single point in the firing line. It was not only the tactics, but also the fighting morale of the Civil War unit that was based on close order. "Men fight in masses. . . . To be brave they must be inspired by the feeling of fellowship. Shoulder must touch shoulder. As gaps are opened [in an advancing line] men close together, and remain formidable." These drills gave the men their first opportunity to see themselves as part of a massive assembly of armed Black men. "A strong feeling of pride and esprit de corps sprung up within the hearts of the blacks, and they began to think that they too might soon have the opportunity to win some glory for their race and their country." Repetition reinforced that sense of belonging to a powerful human machine, and imbued the men with an understanding of the pattern their movements ought to follow. Colonel Hall declared, "From the time of my assignment to the day before the assault, I practiced these movements till they could have been executed as perfectly in the dark as in the light."[50]

For Hall, the critical moment would come after the regiment completed its wheel and stood behind the enemy trenches, ready to "take him in the flank and roll up his line with the bayonet," clearing the way so the rest of the division could storm the crest.[51]

"Fix bayonets!" This was the order that chilled the heart. The bayonet was a three-sided steel spike, eighteen inches long, with a socket end that slipped over the rifle barrel and caught on the front sight. With bayonet mounted the rifle became a weapon more than seven feet long. The tactical manuals envisioned the charge with bayonets culminating in hand-to-hand combat, but in practice that hardly ever happened. Either the attackers would recoil in the face of fire or the defenders would break away from an onrush that seemed too powerful to stop. The bayonet "is a useless weapon for slaughter; its purpose is a moral one." By drawing the cold steel from his belt and fixing it onto his rifle—while up and down the line his comrades shoulder-to-shoulder were doing the same—the soldier was declaring in the face of all men his determination to close with the enemy, no matter what. It was a gesture he could not conceal or take back. To augment the moral force of the bayonet charge, most officers ordered their men to remove the percussion caps from their rifle-muskets before the charge. As Colonel Weld explained, "If we made a charge and the men had caps on their guns, when we got within a few yards of the works the men would stop and fire and then turn and run and that would be the end of it. The only chance was to keep on the steady jump and rush them right over the works."[52]

But the gesture was not always sufficient. The line advanced against fire, the ranks were ripped by bullets, comrades (townsmen and kindred) dropped away, a man could hear the bullets strike the body of the man next to him, a sodden thump, a crack when bullet struck bone. The racket was deafening the closer the line got to the enemy. In every attack there was a point at which the soldiers sensed that the power of their mass was withering and the fire against it was rising to the intolerable. There was an "invisible 'dead-line' . . . beyond which no one could force himself to step." The line would waver to a halt, and the men would stand and answer fire with fire. If that failed to tip the balance, they backed off, individuals stepping back and their comrades keeping line with them—until they decided the whole thing was hopeless and walked or ran back out of range.[53]

What could carry a regiment through that deadline was the sense that their own force was overwhelming in its numbers and, more important, its determination. Some regiments discovered in themselves, or developed through early success, a belief in their invincibility. Outfits like the Army of the Potomac's Iron Brigade were able to storm objectives or hold positions against fire and in the face of losses that would have broken most regiments. The officers of the 4th Division could not know whether or not their troops had that capability, and most probably doubted whether "the Negro race" possessed that kind of morale. One did what one could. There were devices for instilling that kind of determination. Exhortation was effective with troops of that era, when powerful oratory from the stump and the pulpit was central to public life. The officers of the 4th Division could stir their men by naming them liberators of their enslaved kindred, by asking whether or not they were ready to prove their own manhood and the manhood of their race, were ready to win equality with their own strength. And they could remind them that theirs would have to be a fight to the death, that once committed there was no turning back. "Remember Fort Pillow, remember that the enemy will show no mercy and grant no quarter. How will you answer that threat?"

At the crucial moment, when it was either break and run or charge with bayonets, the men had to shout, had to give voice to their battle cry, whether it was a slogan such as "Remember the Alamo," the wordless roar of the Yankee "Hurrah!" or the shrill keening of the Rebel yell. When you heard it, you were aware of all the men behind and around you, with you, and when you joined the yell, it was your final commitment to close with the enemy or die trying.

So finally after days of practice a time would come when it would all go like clockwork, and every private in the ranks now could feel, as he lined up, that the whole outfit was with and around him, every man knew what he was doing and why and how he was going to do it.

Then the order was "Port arms!" and each man held the weapon across his body, the butt down to the right, the barrel and bayonet up to the left, and the advance began, regular marching pace to set the alignment. Then on the order, the quickstep and the advance would accelerate, the whole long line pressing through the shrinking space between you and the trench line, and at the word "Right by companies!" you and your comrades would wheel in perfect time like gears turning one another in succession as the other companies rushed past to extend your power out and out. . . .

Then you'd stop for one dead silent bump of the heart.

Then the captain would yell "Charge bayonets!"—and in the front rank the bright sharp blades would swing level in terrible unison, and as you began the forward rush you would feel all eight hundred boots pounding the earth behind you, and you would yell and he would yell and everyone would yell, "Fort Pillow! No quarter!"[54]

Chapter 7

The Politics of Race

WASHINGTON AND RICHMOND, JULY 1864

T he stakes of battle were extremely high for the soldiers of the 4th Division. From the enemy in their front they could expect no quarter. What made that risk worth taking was the hope that victory would mean freedom for the slaves and civil equality for the race. But it was by no means certain that restoration of the Union would bring full emancipation and civil rights. The coalition that sustained Lincoln in his prosecution of the war was threatening to split upon that very issue.

To maintain public support for the war Lincoln had to appease a broad constituency that ranged from Radicals to War Democrats to "loyal" Southerners in Arkansas, Tennessee, and Louisiana. As a matter of both practical politics and constitutional principle, he believed that once Federal authority was reestablished, Southerners would have to be persuaded to again give their free consent to be governed as part of the nation. Without that consent it would be impossible to maintain civil peace in a section whose people were embittered by defeat and fearful of social change. So in the wake of his advancing armies Lincoln fostered the restoration of normal patterns of trade and civic organization, on the theory that old habits would reassert themselves and Southerners would begin trading, talking, and finally acting like Americans again. He also set easy conditions for Southerners in areas under Federal control to begin the process of restoring their states as self-governing parts of the commonwealth.

To the Radicals this policy seemed likely to restore control of a reconstructed South to the Democrats, and even to secessionists. On July 2, as

Early's army was crossing the Potomac into Maryland, Congress passed a bill cosponsored by Senator Benjamin Wade of Ohio and Congressman Henry Winter Davis of Maryland that gave Congress the power to control reconstruction. The ex-Confederate states would be treated as territories, to be governed by Federal appointees until they had (re)qualified for statehood. The interval of Federal control would be used to reconstruct Southern society, breaking up the plantation system to create an economy based on small farms, with White men and freed slaves sharing economic benefits and political rights. Lincoln may have agreed with the Radicals' ultimate goals, but he disapproved of their methods, and with Lee's and Johnston's armies holding their ground and Early at the gates of Washington, Lincoln thought it premature to be wrangling over postwar reconstruction. On July 8 he killed the Wade-Davis bill with a pocket veto, leaving it unsigned as the session expired.

Lincoln's own combination of civic and military action was working rather well. For a year now Jefferson Davis had been complaining that planters in his native state were effectively submitting to Federal authority because it allowed them to sell their cotton. Loyalist constituencies had emerged in Union-controlled territory, allowing Lincoln to authorize a new state in West Virginia; new legislatures in Louisiana, Arkansas, and Tennessee; and local governments along the coast of the Carolinas. There was significant resistance in the occupied South, but guerrilla warfare never seriously threatened the Union's hold on these semi-reconstructed regions.[1]

But the core problem, the issue most intractable in the politics of persuasion, was race. Lincoln pleaded in vain with his loyalist regimes in Louisiana and Arkansas to begin the process of granting political rights to the freedmen. He failed to persuade Kentucky, Delaware, and Missouri to accept compensated emancipation, despite the plain evidence that slavery as an institution would be swept away by the war. The fundamental contradiction on which every vision of reconstruction foundered was the impossibility of reconciling democratic theory and practice with the preservation of White supremacy.

Lincoln himself was certainly a racist, in the sense that he shared the nearly universal nineteenth-century belief that mankind was divided into distinct physiological types gifted with particular aptitudes, and that some races might (on average) be more poorly endowed than others. He also believed that the theory of human nature set forth in the Declaration of Independence was absolutely right: that all humans, of whatever race, were equally endowed with the desire and the *capacity* for self-government. He had been slow to accept the idea that it was both right and necessary that Negroes should achieve self-government as Americans, rather than as colonists in Africa or the Caribbean. He was still willing to compromise on the timing, pace, and legal specifics of the transformation of Negro slaves into citizens of the republic. But he was also determined to begin that transformation by sponsoring specific legislation, by using the power of his office behind the scenes to negotiate on behalf of civil rights, and by using his own considerable powers as a campaigner to persuade the public that African Americans were entitled to freedom and (eventually) citizenship.

It was not only the South that needed persuading. The opposition Democratic party had adopted a platform described by one of its partisans as "the Constitution as it is, the Union as it was, *and the Niggers where they are.*" Conservative Democrats stood on the doctrine that Stephen Douglas had articulated in his 1858 debates with Lincoln: the American government was founded on "the white basis . . . by white men, for the benefit of white men and their posterity forever," and neither Indians nor Negroes were entitled to any place therein. These views were perfectly consonant with the Confederate concept of nationality. Alexander Stephens, vice president of the Confederacy and an author of its constitution, declared that the "cornerstone" of the new government was "the great truth that the negro is not the equal of the white man; that slavery, subordination to the superior race, is his natural and moral condition." Or, as a Georgia secession commissioner put it, "Our fathers made this a government for the white man, rejecting the negro, as an ignorant, inferior, barbarian race, incapable of self-government, and not, therefore, entitled to be associated with the white man upon terms of civil, political, or social equality." Since Democrats agreed with the South on the fundamental issue of White supremacy, they saw no reason why Confederate leaders should refuse to negotiate with them for a peaceful restoration of the Union. (The Davis administration encouraged them by soft-pedaling its determination to settle for nothing short of full independence.) The Democrats were calling for an armistice, followed by a negotiated settlement with the South that they hoped would lead to restoration of the Union. To make that possible, they would rescind the Emancipation Proclamation and restore to slavery the Blacks that had been freed by it.[2]

Their position had strong appeal in the North. In 1860, Lincoln had won election by arguing that the perpetuation of Negro slavery would lead, in the end, to the economic degradation of White workingmen. The Democrats now turned that rhetoric around. By changing the war for the Union into a war to free the Negro, and by conscripting poor White men to fight it, Lincoln was enslaving the White man for the sake of the Black. That claim hit home with two large classes of Northern poor Whites: the "butternuts," Midwesterners of Southern origin, and the Irish Catholics of the cities and mining districts of the Northeast. In the summer of 1863 those resentments had been exacerbated to the point of insurrection by the military draft.

New York's working poor, predominantly Irish, resented the idea of being conscripted to fight a "rich man's war," especially since it had become a war to free the slaves. In the city's hierarchy of race and class, the Irish were but one step above the Blacks. They competed for the same unskilled day labor jobs, and native-born employers discriminated against the Irish, treating them as an alien and unwanted race, similar to Blacks in their unfitness for American citizenship. The Irish feared emancipation would bring hordes of Blacks to the city, to run down their wages and reduce them to the kind of social abjection that properly belonged to "niggers." The Draft Riots began with the destruction of the halls in which the draft lottery was conducted, and then morphed into a race riot. Individual Blacks were murdered or lynched, and an attempt was made to burn the Colored Orphan Asylum together with its inmates. It took a division of Federal troops from the Army of the Potomac to restore order. The mob did not want to fight in the war, but it was willing to fight to preserve the color line.[3]

Conscription was also going to be a major liability for Lincoln in the 1864 campaign, because the losses suffered by Grant's army had to be made up. On July 18, Lincoln was compelled to issue a call to the states for half a million new volunteers, with the understanding that if volunteers were not forthcoming, the deficit would be made up by an intensified conscription. The editor of New York's leading Catholic weekly declared that if the "President called upon them to go and carry on a war for the nigger, he would be d—d if he believed they would go." Democratic publicists sought to strengthen public distaste for racial equality by elaborating the vile associations that attended the word "nigger." The New York *World,* a Democratic paper that supported McClellan, produced a pamphlet, *Miscegenation: The Theory of the Blending of the Races,* that purported to be a Republican policy paper calling for the forced amalgamation of the Irish and Negro "races" to produce a new, racially debased working class. Other Democratic journals published editorials and cartoons of similar purport. A New Jersey paper warned that "those who would arm the negro population with weapons of war and turn them against their masters' throats would proclaim a world of terror such as the world has never seen." It characterized the president's party as Black Republicans who prayed for emancipation because it would allow "illustrious, sweet-scented Sambo [to] nestle in the bosom of every Abolition woman, that she may be quickened by the pure blood of the majestic African." A Catholic weekly dubbed Lincoln "Abraham Africanus the First," and suggested that he had a "taint of negro blood," which explained his "brutal" and "obscene" habits. Thanks to him, "Filthy black niggers, greasy, sweaty, and disgusting, now jostle white people and even ladies everywhere." Their propaganda exploited, and risked arousing, the racial rage that had produced the Draft Riots one year earlier.[4]

There were also Republican conservatives no less interested in preserving White supremacy. In the fall of 1863 Montgomery Blair, postmaster general in Lincoln's cabinet, had secretly reached out to Democratic leader (and McClellan booster) S.L.M. Barlow. He wanted Barlow to convince his fellow conservatives to abandon the hopeless defense of slavery and join with Republican conservatives to support policies "sustaining this exclusive right of government in the white race." The opinions of such a man, and of the public opinion he represented, could not be ignored.[5]

To persuade men who thought as Blair did about the Negro, Lincoln had to show an inescapable link between the preservation of the Union, emancipation, and the extension of civil liberties to Blacks. That link was symbolized by the Black soldier. Lincoln challenged conservatives directly and explicitly on this issue: "You say you will not fight to free negroes. Some of them seem willing to fight for you," and when victory finally comes, "there will be some black men who can remember that, with silent tongue, and clenched teeth, and steady eye, and well-poised bayonet, they have helped mankind on to this great consummation; while, I fear, there will be some white ones, unable to forget that, with malignant heart, and deceitful speech, they have strove to hinder it." But if the ideals of the Declaration of Independence were to be realized, those who would use Blacks as soldiers had to also recognize them as fellow men, entitled to the exercise of natural rights: "But negroes, like other people, act upon motives. . . . If they stake their lives for us, they must be prompted by the strongest motive—even the promise of freedom. And the promise being made, must be kept."[6]

Democratic conservatives, Copperheads, and Confederate political agents understood that the enlistment of Black soldiers implied recognition that African Americans were entitled to the rights of citizens. That summer, Confederate agents in Canada were advising the Copperhead wing of the party to include a plank demanding that "All negro soldiers and seamen to be at once disarmed and degraded to menial service; and no additional negroes to be, on any pretence whatever, taken from their masters."[7]

The Black soldier was a central symbol in the presidential contest. That was why Ben Butler was working so hard to gather all the Black regiments in front of Petersburg under his command, and why proposals for using Black troops roused the hopes and ambitions of generals such as Burnside and made General Meade queasy.

RACE AND THE CRISIS OF CONFEDERATE NATIONALISM

The Black soldier was a powerful political symbol in the Confederacy as well—and not a simple one. In theory, the Confederacy was a White man's republic. But as more White men were drawn out of the civil economy into the army, Blacks and women became more critical to the maintenance of production—and the rising demand for their labor created the potential for enhancing their status and power. As battle losses drained the South's White manpower, White Southerners were forced to consider whether it might be necessary to use Black men as soldiers. But the political culture of the Confederacy made it extraordinarily difficult to deal rationally with the problem.

The founders of the Confederacy imagined their nation not merely as a civil compact but as an organic unity. At his inauguration in 1861, Davis greeted his fellow citizens as "Brethren of the Confederate States of America—for now we are brethren, not in name, merely, but in fact—men of one flesh, one bone, one interest, one purpose, and of identity of domestic institutions . . . we shall have nothing to fear at home because we shall have homogeneity." In the words of a popular marching song, "We are a band of brothers, and native to the soil, / Fighting for the property we gained by honest toil."[8]

The cultural and political leadership of the South envisioned their society as an alternative to the liberal, polyglot, competitive, and commercial society of the North. The theory behind such a society had been elaborated over decades by intellectuals such as George Fitzhugh and political ideologists such as John C. Calhoun and James Hammond. But the essence of their vision, and the common understanding of their ideal, was eloquently expressed by young John Wise, the teenage cadet who was spending time in the trenches with his father's brigade. The Wises traced their lineage back through the first families of Virginia to the gentry of Devon in England. Wise recalled the family home in the Accomack peninsula as a region of "princely" homes and the "most highly cultivated people. . . . In all America, there is no spot more emphatically English than the Kingdom of Accawmacke."

> Near at hand, or far away upon the hillsides, one beheld the working-bands of slaves, well clothed, well fed, and differing from other workmen . . . chiefly in their numbers and their cheerfulness and their comfortable clothing. . . . Those slaves, over whose sad fate so many tears have been shed, went about their work more joyously than any laboring people I ever saw.

This was the South of Southerners' finest imagining: a pastoral utopia ruled by an aristocracy kindly, noble, and wise; not merely a civil compact but an organic society, analogous to a family, under the paternalistic care and guidance of a planter elite. It was a stable society in which the poorer classes deferred to their betters instead of trying to outdo and displace them. This was as true for poor Whites as for Blacks. Wise believed that his soldiers were "but children of a larger growth. . . . Without constant guidance and government and punishment, they become careless about clothes, food, ammunition, cleanliness, and even personal safety." Wise would have said much the same things about his Negroes.[9]

There were some parts of the South, notably in the tidewater communities of the seaboard states, where society took something like that form. But the reality of Southern life did not match the ideal. The supposed "homogeneity" of the South was a political fiction, of the kind all nationalist movements create for themselves. For thirty years before the war, Southern separatists had tried to define a different genealogy for Northern and Southern Whites. It was said that the Southern colonists had been Cavaliers while Northerners were Puritan Roundheads; that Northern Whites were merely Anglo Saxon, while Southerners were Anglo Norman—descended from the aristos who'd conquered Saxon England in 1066. This was nonsense. Southern settlers reflected the same mix of ethnicities as their Northern counterparts—English, Welsh, Scots-Irish,

German, Huguenot. There were plenty of Northern pioneers among the founders of those huge Mississippi Valley plantations.

The South differed from the rest of the nation in its dependence on slave labor rather than wage labor to produce goods for the market; and the plantation system gave Southern politics, social divisions, and culture some distinctive qualities. Nevertheless, Southern planters were no less engaged than Northern entrepreneurs in the pursuit of capitalist development, seeking always to develop and exploit market advantages, to expand access to economic resources, to get a better return on investment, to manipulate taxes and tariffs to benefit their enterprises. The inevitable result was that social and political divisions, based on economic interest, disrupted the harmony of Jefferson Davis's band of brothers.[10]

The stresses of war revealed the weaknesses of Confederate political theory and the fault lines in Southern society, and the Confederate political system was not well equipped to repair them. Secession had been justified by an extreme interpretation of the "sovereign" powers of the states, and the Confederate Constitution limited the powers of the central government. Davis supposed that state governors would consent to "national" measures if he appealed to that homogeneous body of interests and values that united Southerners. But governors were jealous of their authority, especially on the crucial issue of conscription. Those in states threatened with invasion wanted to keep their troops at home; Davis wanted the troops with the armies in Virginia and northern Georgia, where the war would be won or lost.[11]

Though the entire South had an interest in slavery, that interest was radically different in the Confederacy's various subregions, and rich and poor had a very different kind of stake in the system. The vast majority of Southern Whites were small farmers who owned no slaves and were often in competition with planters concerning land use, land ownership, taxation, and the funding of internal improvements. The war aggravated these tensions. Planters sought draft exemptions for their overseers and resisted taxation, leaving the middle and poor classes of Whites to bear the brunt of both military service and runaway inflation. Many of the army's growing number of deserters left the ranks to go to the aid of families impoverished by rising prices and the absence of menfolk to work the farm. In April 1864, a letter writer who identified himself as "For the Poor Man" complained to Davis that the government was "grinding down the face of the poor and seem to care not if they starve to death." The poor were the "main defense of the Land" but were charged "extortion prices" and high taxes; "the rich around us have plenty to spare but we cant get it. At the same time our sons and Brothers are fighting to save their Negroes and their property. . . . We were free before [the war] began but we are not so now." A North Carolina private complained to Governor Vance that planter-exemption laws "made a distinction between the rich man who had something to fight for, and the poor man who fights for what he never will have. . . . Poor soldiers who are fighting for the 'rich man's negro' [were] tired of the rich mans war and the poor mans fight." A group of Georgia soldiers wrote President Davis they were "tired of fighting for this negro aristockracy."[12]

Yet resentment of planter privilege never led Southern poor Whites to oppose slavery as an institution. In the end, most were willing to defend other men's Negroes because they had a deep social and psychological investment in White supremacy. If Blacks should be freed from slavery, their numbers alone would allow them to contest and seek to overturn the material supremacy of Whites, and the Republican propaganda of equal rights would rouse their political will. When the seceding states of the Lower South sent commissioners to persuade the Upper South to join them, that was the chief fear to which they appealed. In a society dominated by large planters, the civic dignity and equal standing of poor Whites was dependent on the difference in status between themselves and Black slaves. Thus, to grant equality to Blacks was, in effect, to "degrade" Whites to the level of Negroes, and merge them—first symbolically, and then actually—with an inferior race. As a secession commissioner from Georgia put it, Republicans "have demanded, and now demand, equality between the white and negro races . . . equality in representation, equality in the right of suffrage, equality in the honors and emoluments of office, equality in the social circle, equality in the rights of matrimony. . . . Freedom to the slave [is] eternal degradation for you and for us." If the South were to stay in the Union, her people would ultimately have to "flee from the land of their birth, and from the slaves their parents have toiled to acquire as an inheritance for them, or to submit to the degradation of being reduced to an equality with them, and all its attendant horrors."[13]

Violence was the only imaginable response to such a threat of personal and racial "degradation." Africans were savages by nature; they sought freedom because their "black blood" was aroused by "the pleasures of spoil and of the gratification of yet fiercer instincts." Emancipation would leave White women exposed to the "brutal lust" of liberated Black men, or to a legal regime that (in ways not specified) would somehow compel White women to take Black husbands. As early as 1784, Thomas Jefferson had opposed the abolition of slavery on the grounds that hostility between the races—based on remembered grievances and differences in nature—would lead inevitably to "convulsions . . . ending in the extermination of one or the other race." However, most Southern spokesmen believed that an American race war would follow a course opposite from Haiti's: not the Whites (a well-armed majority) but the Blacks would be exterminated. The maintenance of slavery was, in effect, the Negro's guarantee against genocide. Thus Jefferson Davis could describe the Emancipation Proclamation as "a measure by which several millions of human beings of an inferior race, peaceful and contented laborers in their sphere, are doomed to extermination."[14]

But the Confederacy was discovering that a modern nation-state could not fight a total war while at the same time excluding between 30 and 40 percent of its male population from its military manpower. Some Southerners had recognized the problem early in the war. A Mississippi petition had argued, "[The] population of the Southern States is a complex one, consisting of two races," and it was folly to "attempt the defense of the country with only one of the elements of its power." Until 1864 this weakness was masked by the South's ability to mobilize most of its White military-age population, while slave labor maintained the productive economy and assisted with the construction of fortifications. But the Emancipation Proclamation gave slaves a vested interest in Union victory, and wherever there were Union armies, slaves deserted to them in large numbers, diminishing their contribution to the Southern economy. When the North began recruiting ex-slaves as soldiers, the South's Black population became a reserve of manpower for its enemies. And this was occurring as the South was reaching the end of its White military manpower.[15]

In January 1864, General Patrick Cleburne made the most radical and detailed proposal for the enlistment of Black soldiers. It had behind it the moral authority of one of the Confederacy's best and bravest generals, whose patriotism was beyond question. Cleburne argued that slavery had become a liability to the Confederate cause. Its existence prevented England and France from recognizing Southern independence. Conflicts of interest between planters and small farmers weakened army morale. Planters collaborated with the enemy to protect their slave property. Negroes attracted by the promise of freedom added their strength to the Union forces. All these liabilities could be transformed into assets if the South would immediately free a quarter million slaves and arm them in defense of the state. But Cleburne's program required emancipation. "It is a first principle of mankind that he who offers his life in defense of the State should receive from her in return his freedom and his happiness. . . . If we arm [the Negro] and train him and make him fight for the country in her hour of dire distress, every consideration of principle and policy demand that we should set him and his whole race who side with us free." This would impose serious losses on the planting interest. But "As between the loss of independence and the loss of slavery, we assume every patriot will give up the latter—give up the negro slave rather than be a slave himself."[16]

The problem with all such proposals was that they undermined White supremacy, the cornerstone of the nation. As Georgia's Howell Cobb told Davis, "The day you make soldiers of them is the beginning of the end of the revolution. If slaves will make good soldiers our whole theory of slavery is wrong." If Blacks were by nature as soldierly as Whites, as capable of self-government and patriotism, then the law of nature and of nature's God could not sanction their perpetual enslavement. What bound the Confederacy's rich and poor together, what united the "brethren" in spite of political and economic conflicts, was not their fictitious homogeneity but their actual fear and revulsion at the prospect of an abolition of slavery that would degrade them to a level of equality with their Negroes. Most of the Deep South plantation states had found the mere presence of free Negroes so subversive of order that they required all slaves freed by their owners to leave. They had much more to fear from having among them the contagious example—not to mention the power— of a class of freedmen who had been armed and trained as soldiers, and shared battlefield honors with Whites. As one non-slaveholder wrote President Davis, "We have but little interest in the value of slaves, but there is one matter in this connection in which we feel a very deep interest. We are opposed to Negro equality. To prevent this we are willing to spare the last man, down to the point where women and children begin to suffer for food and clothing; when these begin to suffer and die, rather than see them equalized with an inferior race we will die with them. . . . Let us not sacrifice at once the object for which we are fighting."[17]

Davis recognized some of the force of Cleburne's arguments. In February 1864, he went so far as to assert that the national government had authority to draft slaves for use in building fortifications—an invasion of property rights that drew down the wrath of states' rights fundamentalists such as Alexander Stephens. But further than that Davis would not go. He feared that the planter class, the dominant force in the secession movement and Confederate politics, would withdraw support from a state that no longer protected its property interest. Desertion might increase if the soldiers came to believe that the sacrifices they had made to prevent "Negro equality" were being thrown away by the government. So Cleburne's proposal was suppressed and he was denied the promotion to corps command that his achievements warranted.

Instead of adapting racial policy to the necessities of national survival, the political and military leadership of the Confederacy used the racial menace of the armed Negro as an instrument of propaganda, to convince war-weary people that they had to fight to the death to save themselves and their families from degradation. That propaganda required that Negroes armed as soldiers, and the Yankees who led them, be treated as odious criminals, be discredited and destroyed by any and all means. The troops defending Richmond were warned that the Federal army opposing them contained Black regiments, and this embodied the spectre of Negro equality with "all its attendant horrors." The Richmond *Examiner* published an account (probably provided by a Copperhead correspondent) of the departure of the 29th USCT from Chicago, which asserted that: "White women were there in attendance, to bid farewell to black husbands, around whose necks they clung long and fondly! Black women, too, and men almost white, were locked in each other's arms, some weeping while others were shouting, praying, or singing."[18]

By word and example, Southern leaders indicated their belief that the use of Black troops licensed the most extreme measures. Battlefield massacres were committed by poor White enlisted men enraged by the mixed emotions of combat and racial antipathy. But the principle of massacre was condoned by some of the Confederacy's best and brightest. Davis's proposal to try Union officers as inciters of slave rebellion was among the more moderate. The Confederate Congress considered a bill for "raising the *black flag*, asking and giving no quarter" in future battles. General Beauregard was most eager that the bill be enacted: "Has the bill for execution of abolition prisoners after 1st of next January passed? . . . It is high time to proclaim the black flag. . . . Let the execution be with the garrote." Congress did not pass the bill, fearing retaliation against Confederate POWs. But Secretary of War Seddon told commanders in the field to see that Black soldiers or their officers were "dealt with redhanded on the field or immediately thereafter."[19]

With his superiors waving the black flag, demanding the garroting of captured officers, and condoning the murder of POWs, it is not hard to understand the young Mississippi soldier who wrote his mother of his fear that, if he should ever "see a Negro soldier," he could not be "a Christian soldier." He was not vaunting his rage but reflecting the depth of a revulsion, shared with his comrades and kinfolk, that was strong enough to test the strength of his faith and conscience. Events would show that he had reason for his fear.[20]

In the summer of 1864, the pressures that were moving North and South to consider opening the door of citizenship to African Americans had a paradoxical effect on race relations. The greater the perceived need for including Blacks in the defense of the nation, the more violent was the resistance. That pattern was evident in the New York Draft Riots, and it appeared in the South as well—most painfully in the ranks of Robert Ransom's North Carolina Brigade, Johnson's Division, which was manning the Petersburg trenches on the left of Elliott's Brigade.

THE PEACE MOVEMENT AND RACIAL POLITICS IN RANSOM'S BRIGADE

North Carolina had been the most reluctant of the seceding states in 1861, and though it sent more troops into Confederate service than any state but Virginia, accommodationist sentiment remained strong. In the winter of 1863–64 a political movement emerged that openly favored a peace settlement with the North on the basis of a reconstructed Union. The motives and constituencies of this "peace" movement were mixed. There was some lingering pro-Union sentiment in the mountainous areas in the west of the state (where there were few slaves) and along the coast where farmers and planters had been collaborating with the occupation since 1862. War weariness was a factor in a state that had lost so many men in battle. Conscription was a sore point in North Carolina, just as it was in New York: poor and middling Whites resented the exemptions granted to planters and their employees.

The movement for a peace settlement was hitched to the gubernatorial candidacy of William W. Holden, editor of the *Raleigh Standard*. To free his movement from any taint of Black Republicanism, Holden and his supporters turned states' rights rhetoric on its head. Their movement was a protest against the "centralizing" tendency of the Richmond government and was "rather an excess of loyalty to the State" than disloyalty to the Confederacy. Holden also played the race card, affirming his belief that "This is a white man's government, and intended for white men only." He drew on rumors about Cleburne's proposal and used them to accuse Davis of undermining White supremacy by (supposedly) planning to free Negroes for use as soldiers. North Carolina provided the Army of Northern Virginia with thousands of soldiers, and its farms and factories were that army's richest source of supply. If the state withdrew from the war, the effect would be catastrophic. Already, popular discontent was reflected in the high desertion rates among North Carolina troops. In the piedmont region, deserters, draft resisters, and "peace" men were numerous enough to defy the civil authorities, and the winter of 1863–64 saw considerable violence between them and the Home Guard.

Governor Zebulon Vance of North Carolina, a Davis supporter, at first tried to co-opt the movement. He asked Davis to approach Lincoln with an offer to negotiate, knowing Lincoln would reject it and so discredit Holden's platform. When Davis refused, Vance went back to basics. He would beat Holden by outdoing him as an enemy of "nigger equality." Vance warned Carolinians that if in their war weariness they voted to return to the Union, "Instead of getting your sons back to the plow and the fireside, they would be drafted . . . to fight alongside [Lincoln's] negro troops in exterminating the white men, women, and children of the South."[21]

The Richmond government backed Vance by assembling a military expedition, directed against the Federal garrisons Burnside had established in 1862 to hold the sounds and the tidewater counties—garrisons that contained large numbers of Black troops. A division of North Carolina troops was assembled, commanded by Tar Heel General Robert Hoke. The reconquest of the coastlands would force collaborationists to return to Confederate allegiance and would open fresh districts to conscription. It might also restore the North Carolinians' military morale by pitting them against invaders of their own soil—invaders whose forces contained a large and active contingent of Black troops.[22]

The backbone of Hoke's little army was Ransom's Brigade. Many of its units (especially the 25th and 26th North Carolina) had been recruited in the piedmont and mountain counties, where Holden's candidacy was strongest, and the Vance-Holden political split was reflected in the ranks. Political differences tracked with class differences. Officers in Ransom's Brigade put forward a resolution expressing "mortification . . . at the course of our people at home" and condemning the editorial stance of Holden's newspaper, and published it as an expression of troop sentiment. But several enlisted men claimed that the "resolution" was bogus, the officers had forced it through without discussion. One man wrote to the *Standard* that he was "a peace private . . . and two-thirds of the regiment are the same way." But political differences were set aside when they went into action against Black troops.[23]

On March 9, Ransom's Brigade marched through Suffolk, Virginia (on the Carolina border), to attack the 2nd U.S. Colored Cavalry. The ladies of the town "were standing at their doors, some waving handkerchiefs, some crying, some praying, and others calling to us to 'kill the negroes.' Our Brigade did not need this to make them give 'no quarter,' as it is understood amongst us that we take no negro prisoners." A private in the 49th North Carolina wrote that he expected the Negroes to run if they could, but to "fit if they aire hem[m]ed sow they cant run . . . for they know that it is deth eny way if we got hold of them for wee have no quarters for a negro."[24]

Plymouth, North Carolina, had been in Federal hands since Burnside captured it in 1862. It was a seedy ruin, abandoned by most of its original citizens, occupied by a Federal garrison of fewer than three thousand armed troops. In addition to organized military units, there was a large number of White "loyalists" who fled there for protection, and two thousand or so former slaves from local plantations. Some of the loyalists (called "Buffaloes") and Blacks were organized into companies, others were listed as unorganized recruits, and a number of civilians in both categories were armed and prepared to defend themselves against recapture.

Hoke attacked the town on April 17, 1864, with superior forces, augmented by the fire of the ironclad *Albemarle*, which drove off or sank the Federals' naval support. On April 20, he summoned the Federal commander to surrender, implying that if he stormed the town, he would show "no quarter." The capitulation rapidly degenerated into violence and disorder. Many of the Blacks and the Buffaloes did not believe the capitulation's terms would protect them from punishment or execution. Some continued to fight; others tried to escape to the woods and swamps. Many of these, including numbers of Black women and children, were pursued by Ransom's men and were shot as they fled. An Alabama artilleryman stated it was "a well known fact that for three weeks after the place was captured negor [*sic*] bodies were seen floating out of the swamp into the river. The sight was sickening." The best modern study of the battle suggests that the number of Blacks killed in the town after the surrender was probably about twenty-five, with another forty shot as they fled, and perhaps forty more hunted down and killed in the swamp. Fifteen Black POWs were deliberately shot by firing squad on the Plymouth docks three and four days after the battle, on orders from Richmond. The other Black prisoners were treated as fugitive slaves rather than as POWs. Those who could be identified were returned to their owners. The rest were taken into possession by the state and were set to work on fortifications. President Davis was well aware that this policy violated understandings earlier reached with the Federal government on the treatment of prisoners. He had General Bragg tell Governor Vance to keep the matter "out of the newspapers" so that the Federals would not retaliate against Southern prisoners.[25]

Word soon spread that Rebel troops had massacred hundreds of Blacks, including soldiers who had surrendered. The news resonated with, but was partially eclipsed by, news of the larger massacre that had occurred the previous week at Fort Pillow. Not all the exaggeration was on the Union side. Confederate soldiers expressed their rage against the enemy, and Negro equality, by writing bloodthirsty letters to their hometown papers. While these statements falsified the actual size of the massacre at Plymouth, they constituted a public endorsement of the principle that Blacks in arms against the South ought to be killed without mercy. The letters also reflected a more subtle aftereffect for those who acted out the imperatives of racial rage. Whatever sense of vindication and empowerment they gained was offset by the recognition that by breaking the moral code that limited even military violence, they had made themselves liable for retaliation in kind. "Ransom's brigade never takes any negro prisoners. Our soldiers would not even bury the Negroes—they were buried by negroes. If any of us should be captured by them, our fate would be hard." So atrocity begot the expectation of atrocious retaliation—an expectation that would justify still more atrocious violence at the next confrontation.[26]

After Plymouth, the brigade was rushed north to defend Petersburg, and took over the lines north of Elliott's Brigade. The hardship and stultification of life in the trenches intensified the disaffection in the ranks and led to increased rates of desertion. When engineer Captain Douglas commandeered some of Ransom's men for labor on his countermines, two were so disgusted they crossed the lines and deserted to the Yankees on July 17. They told their interrogators that "They belong to the Forty-ninth North Carolina and state that if the soldiers were allowed to vote Holden would get nearly all the votes of the privates." They also told them that their engineers had been counter-mining, probing for the Yankee tunnel all along the front.

The tension between war weariness and fear of Negro equality remained unresolved in their ranks. The "peace privates" were tired of the war, but like the New York draft rioters they would fight to preserve the color line. Vance would overwhelm Holden, his appeal to negrophobia helping him win nearly 90 percent of the vote. Even so, disaffection among North Carolina troops was so serious that Vance's supporters had to resort to fraud and coercion to ensure the votes of soldiers in the line. In some companies, officers simply reported a unanimous vote without consulting their men. In others, votes were taken but not reported. On the evening of July 29, two more deserters from Ransom's Brigade wriggled into II Corps' lines: "They deserted because they were not allowed to vote yesterday. They say that in very few cases . . . were any allowed to vote that did not vote for Vance. These men both voted for Sheriff but were not allowed to vote for Governor."[27]

But it would have been a mistake to conclude that morale in Ransom's Brigade was ready to collapse. Those who had supported Vance had chosen a fight to the bitter end. Those who supported Holden were still willing to fight to stave off "nigger equality"—"it is understood amongst us that we take no negro prisoners."

Part Three

BATTLE PLANS

Chapter 8

Setting the Stage

JULY 15–29, 1864

While Early marched on Washington and retreated to Winchester; while the 4th Division trained; while Lincoln wrestled with the politics of war, liberation, and reelection, the miners on both sides kept digging.

On July 16, the tunnel dug by the 48th Pennsylvania reached the 511-foot mark, which by Pleasants's calculation put it right under Elliott's Salient. With the tunnel finished, they began to carve the lateral galleries that would extend across the width of the salient and hold the powder charge. The next day headquarters passed on to Colonel Pleasants the intelligence delivered by the deserters from Ransom's Brigade, that the Rebels were countermining.

That afternoon he went into the tunnel with Captain Winlack and another officer. They crouched their way to the end of the shaft, making as little noise as possible. With one officer in each gallery and Pleasants at the junction, they extinguished their lamps, lay down on the damp ground, and listened intently in the absolute dark. They could hear through the thickness of earth a muffled intermittent pounding. It might be picks chopping out a countermine probe, or hammers pounding nails into planks to make a floor for the battery overhead. Pleasants listened patiently for half an hour, and concluded the sounds were too random to indicate a countermine. A whispered conference with Captain Winlack confirmed it: "The rebels know no more of the tunnel being under them than the inhabitants of Africa." But Pleasants's nerves were overwrought. When the second officer replied in an inaudible mumble, Pleasants told him to speak up, Pleasants himself speaking in a voice that "rang from one end of the gallery to the other."

The next day Pleasants told Harry Reese he could complete the excavation of the lateral galleries. The men were to work as quietly as possible and pause at frequent intervals to listen for countermining.[1]

On the Confederate side, Captain Douglas kept crews at work at four different points, digging deep pits and then carving lateral shafts that groped outward toward the picket lines in front of Elliott's Salient. A day and night of work could extend these shafts between six and nine feet. Douglas himself had all he could do to keep up with the myriad problems of running a large and complex operation with an inadequate number of engineers, supplemented by a lot of disgruntled infantrymen. He was short of equipment and even food for his men, and the lack of medicines meant that every man he sent to the hospital was permanently lost. Notwithstanding all this, the total distance excavated in his four mines now amounted to two hundred ninety feet.

On July 18, he stooped his way into one of the galleries with an earth auger and began drilling holes toward the Yankees. The bores would amplify any sounds, and there was a chance that the drill might break through the stiff clay and turn freely in the open air of the Yankee mine itself. If the Confederates could locate the mine, they would dig a shaft as close to it as possible, fill it with gunpowder, and collapse the walls and ceilings with an explosion.

But the auger cranked nothing but clay, and the bore holes opened on silence. Douglas repeated the process at all the shafts with no result.

The next day was "dull and sultry." The clouds burst, unloading an all-day and all-night rain on the parched entrenchments. Water rose ankle-deep in the trenches and countermine shafts, driving rats out of their hidey-holes, and the red clay turned to paste. Douglas had to suspend work. But the following night—July 20—the officer in charge of the detachment at Elliott's Salient heard the sound of picks, checked to see that no pick work was being done in his own lines, and then reported to Douglas. The sounds had seemed to come from the left of the salient, so Douglas ordered his men to begin a new shaft to that side of the battery.[2]

The downpour that swamped the trenches percolated through the clay, boring downspouts into the roof of the mine and swelling the under-

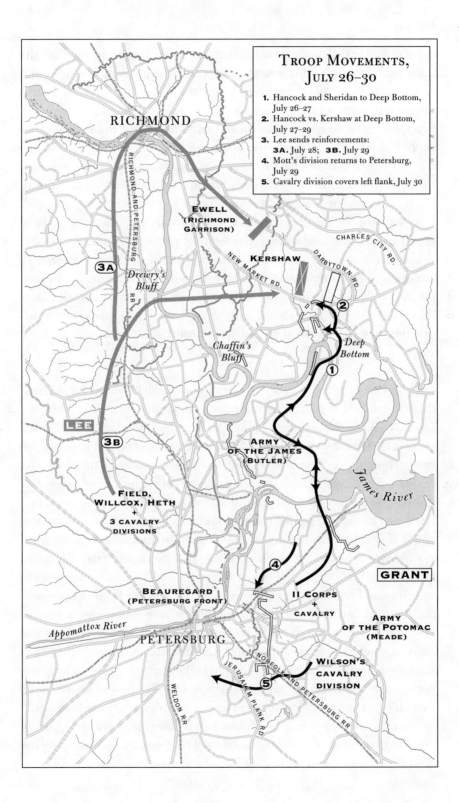

TROOP MOVEMENTS,
JULY 26–30

1. Hancock and Sheridan to Deep Bottom,
   July 26–27
2. Hancock vs. Kershaw at Deep Bottom,
   July 27–29
3. Lee sends reinforcements:
   3A. July 28; **3B.** July 29
4. Mott's division returns to Petersburg,
   July 29
5. Cavalry division covers left flank, July 30

RICHMOND

RICHMOND AND PETERSBURG RR

EWELL
(RICHMOND
GARRISON)

CHARLES CITY RD.

NEW MARKET RD.

KERSHAW

DARBYTOWN RD.

3A

*Drewry's
Bluff*

DREWRY'S BLUFF RR

②

Deep
Bottom

①

*Chaffin's
Bluff*

ARMY
OF THE JAMES
(BUTLER)

James River

LEE

3B

FIELD,
WILLCOX, HETH
+
3 CAVALRY
DIVISIONS

④

GRANT

BEAUREGARD
(PETERSBURG FRONT)

II CORPS
+
CAVALRY

ARMY
OF THE POTOMAC
(MEADE)

Appomattox River

PETERSBURG

NORFOLK AND PETERSBURG RR

⑤

WILSON'S
CAVALRY
DIVISION

JERUSALEM PLANK RD.

WELDON RR

ground springs. Reese's crews had to set more timber to stabilize the walls and floor, and reinforce the intervals with planking—tedious and time-consuming work, especially when they had to be careful not to pound too loudly with their mallets. The wet also made digging more difficult, the damp air was unpleasant and unhealthful, and the suction of the ventilating system was weakened by distance.

On July 21, the miners in the right gallery heard a dull persistent thumping from above. Work stopped again and Pleasants went down to listen. This time he thought there was something systematic to the sound. It might have been made by the firing of field pieces in the battery above their heads, but it might also have been the picks of counterminers. He decided to curve the shaft away from the sound, and reemphasized to Reese the need for quiet and attentive listening by the miners. But he kept pushing the work, intent on finishing as quickly as possible, fiercely determined to show up Major Duane and the self-important brass hats at headquarters who had doubted his judgment and skill.

❧

Captain Lowry of the 17th South Carolina wrote in his diary: "It is feared that the enemy are tunnelling under our lines, and . . . we are preparing for such a device by digging a tunnel all along the whole face of the battery to meet theirs if they have any." Measures were also taken to improve the entrenchments and provide secure secondary positions to which the troops could retreat. There was a long ravine, made by a small creek, that sloped down from the high ground and along the base of the ridge that ran down to the east from Cemetery Hill. Engineers improved it to provide a sheltered route or long covered way from the rear area to the front line. Midway between the Plank Road and the front, a lateral ravine branched off at a right angle from the creek bed to create a natural entrenchment. Plans were made to improve this into a fully developed secondary line, but even in its natural state it was suitable as a reserve position. Closer to the front line, engineers constructed a cavalier (also called a gorge line) across the rear of Elliott's Salient, about 125 feet behind the main line. A trench was dug to half the usual depth, with a parapet of earth-filled baskets (gabions) in front of it. Troops driven out of the trenches by a mine explosion or a Federal assault could rally behind the cavalier, where they would be standing on a higher level and firing down into the exposed rear of the captured line. Gorge lines were also dug behind the two salients that bulged out of the main line north of Elliott's, held by the 49th and 25th North Carolina of Ransom's Brigade, and a web of communication trenches linked them to the long covered way. These diggings turned the ground behind the line into a labyrinth of intersecting ditches.[3]

But after that flurry of anxious activity—nothing. Division commander Bushrod Johnson wanted more artillery on the high ground behind his line, for fire support in case of an assault. New mortar and artillery batteries were promised but were slow in arriving. He also wanted engineers to build a second defensive line along the Plank Road, but engineers were in high demand everywhere. In their new countermines Douglas's crews repeated the process of digging shafts, hauling the dirt out by windlass and bucket and hefting the buckets to where they could be dumped unseen, boring holes with the earth auger, and hushing the chatter and clatter of the troops so they could listen in silence for something more than silence. Douglas meticulously reported the distances dug and timbered by his crews each day, but after June 21, they never heard another sound. Whatever the Yankees were planning, there did not appear to be an imminent threat of danger.

On July 25, Captain Lowry noted in his diary, "All quiet" on the front. It would be his last entry.[4]

In fact, the 48th Pennsylvania was finishing the lateral galleries some twenty feet below the gun trails of Captain Richard Pegram's battery. On July 23, Pleasants made a final inspection and reported to General Potter that the tunnel and its lateral galleries were complete and ready to receive the powder.

There was no powder. No decision had yet been reached on when or if the mine was to be used. Until an operation was ordered by Grant or Meade, there was nothing to do but wait.

But for Pleasants and his men, doing nothing was not an option. They had to maintain the mine's viability for the day of battle—police its length and shore up places weakened by springs, rotting timber, or the pressure of earth. If the galleries were to remain usable as chambers for gunpowder, they had to be kept dry. So the steady accumulation of spring water and seepage from rainstorms on the nineteenth and twenty-first had to be kept at bay by men scooping out muck and trucking it out in handbarrows—while still from above they could hear the counterminers at work, probing for them through the earth.

On the twenty-fourth of July there was another heavy downpour that soaked through the clay and spattered between the ceiling planks in the left lateral gallery. The timber braces seemed to be sliding out of line in the wet earth, and when the battery twenty feet overhead fired its guns, the jolt could be felt. By the morning of the twenty-sixth it appeared that the left gallery might be caving in. Pleasants had the timbering reinforced, but if the mine were not used soon, it might become unusable, and all that labor would have been for nothing.[5]

The dispatch that would answer his prayers was already on General Burnside's desk.

BATTLE PLAN: GRANT'S HEADQUARTERS, JULY 22–26

Grant wanted very much to resume the offensive. Once Early had been forced out of Maryland, Grant ordered VI and XIX Corps to return to Petersburg, where they would give him the numerical superiority he needed. He would leave the small army commanded by General Hunter to defend Maryland against a repetition of Early's invasion. This was the same force that had been driven away from Lynchburg in June. It had made a demoralizing retreat over the mountains, and a long hard hike back up to Maryland. On July 22, as Hunter advanced toward the valley town of Winchester, VI and XIX Corps began their march for Washington and the steamboats that would take them to City Point.

But on June 24, Hunter's force was routed by Early and retreated back across the Potomac. The Confederate army was once again in control of the northern end of the valley. The order for VI and XIX Corps to return to Petersburg had to be rescinded.

Lincoln was out of patience with Grant's neglect of the situation. He wanted a competent general to organize the units collected on the Maryland border and lead them on a systematic campaign to eliminate the threat from Early's force. But Grant was reluctant to engage in the political and bureaucratic infighting in which this appointment was enmeshed, and his attention was absorbed by his own evolving plan for action on the Petersburg front. Grant kept passing the decision off to Chief of Staff Halleck, who was incapable of decisive action. Lincoln had recently laid down the law with his fractious cabinet, silencing them with the stern warning that "I must myself be the judge, how long to retain . . . and when to remove any of you." He now sent a similar message to Grant, appointing Halleck to command in western Maryland. It was a purely symbolic gesture—Halleck could not and would not exercise field command. But it was the first significant military appointment Lincoln had made without at least consulting Grant.[6]

So Grant had to consider his next operation at a moment when the president's confidence in his leadership was in doubt, and his force seriously reduced. On July 23 he asked Meade to consider two possible operations: another strike beyond the flank to cut the Weldon Railroad or an attack on Burnside's front. In either case "Burnside's mine will be blown up," if not as prelude to a frontal assault then as a diversion in favor of the flanking move. He also laid down a general principle that would govern any attacks in the near future: "If this is attempted it will be necessary to concentrate all the force possible at the point in the enemy's line we wish to penetrate. All officers should be fully impressed with the absolute necessity of pushing entirely beyond the enemy's present line if they should succeed in penetrating it," and—with Lincoln's warning against incurring heavy casualties in mind—"of getting back to their own present line promptly if they should not succeed."[7]

Meade and Major Duane inspected Burnside's front and advised against leading an assault from there. Troops attacking Elliott's Salient could be enfiladed by artillery fire from other salients to the north and south. Moreover, it seemed most likely that the Confederates had a second fortified line, to which troops could retreat if driven from the front line. No second line had actually been seen, but Meade concluded that from "the evident necessity of there being such a line, I am forced to believe we shall find one there." He also thought it was too dangerous to strike at the Weldon, with only the II Corps and the cavalry as a maneuver force.[8]

Grant immediately put forward a different plan, to attack on the Richmond side of the James River. The city was held by a garrison under the command of Richard Ewell, backed by Kershaw's Division of the Army of Northern Virginia. Grant proposed sending II Corps and two cavalry divisions under Sheridan (roughly twenty-five thousand men) rapidly and secretly across to the north side of the James. Major General Winfield Scott Hancock, commander of II Corps and the best offensive general in the army, would be in charge. II Corps would drive back and pin the Confederate infantry defending Richmond while Sheridan's horsemen swept around their flank to make a sudden surprise assault on the weak Richmond garrison—"surprise the little garrison of citizen soldiery now in Richmond and get in." If the direct attack failed, Sheridan was to raid out north of Richmond to destroy the railroad linking the city with the Shenandoah.

The chances of actually storming Richmond might have been slim, but Grant wanted a strong effort made. He had assigned the mission to his two most offensive-minded subordinates, and his orders were a goad to boldness and swift action. There was to be no "cautious movement, [such as] developing our force, and making reconnaissances before attacking." Hancock and Sheridan had to strike fast and hard if they hoped to succeed. The rest of the army would be concentrated for a supporting strike on the south side of the James. Grant lacked the superiority required for a frontal assault, but Burnside's mine was the equalizer. A few tons of gunpowder planted under a Rebel fort could do what no amount of artillery could accomplish: blast a large and exploitable breach into a fortified trench line. With that in mind, Grant told Meade to "direct the loading of the mine in front of the Ninth Corps. I would set no time when it should be exploded, but leave it subject to orders." If Hancock and Sheridan succeeded in breaking into the Richmond defenses, the explosion of the mine and an infantry assault through the breach would prevent Lee from sending his reserves to Richmond. On the other hand, even if Hancock and Sheridan failed in their main mission, their expedition might "cause such a weakening of the enemy at Petersburg as to make an attack there possible." Then the springing of the mine and a follow-up assault by massed infantry might achieve a decisive breakthrough. A large force planted on Cemetery Hill and the Jerusalem Plank Road would be in position to roll up the Confederate lines across the whole front of Petersburg. Even if Lee's army succeeded in reforming its defense north of the Appomattox, four of the five railroads feeding Richmond would have been cut, Confederate logistics would rapidly deteriorate, and Lee might be compelled either to abandon Richmond or to leave his entrenchments for a stand-up fight in the open.[9]

But the Hancock-Sheridan expedition was to be the primary line of operations. On July 25, Grant ordered Meade to assemble the force for a night march across the rear of Butler's lines on Bermuda Hundred, then over the James by pontoon bridges to the area known as Deep Bottom. Troops from X Corps set to work improving the pontoon bridges between Bermuda Hundred and Deep Bottom, and a force was sent across to hold the James River bridgehead. The operation was to be kept as secret as possible so it could not be betrayed by picket line gossip. The mine was to be ready for firing no later than Wednesday afternoon, July 27, so it could be used as part of a diversionary attack to prevent Lee from sending his reserves to stop Hancock.

Since it was now certain that Burnside's mine would be used, Meade and Duane made another inspection of that sector on the morning of the twenty-sixth, this time from a new signal station on a timber platform in the trees. They noted entrenchments at various points on the forward slope of Cemetery Hill and the crest line where the Plank Road ran, but now they saw that these were detached works with unfortified spaces between, not a continuous line of entrenchments. This increased the odds of success for the mine assault. Meade also received intelligence, gleaned from a Richmond newspaper, that Lee had already sent two additional divisions to Richmond, which seemed to indicate that Lee had anticipated Hancock's march and moved to block his attack. This increased the likelihood that the Deep Bottom expedition would be downgraded from main thrust to diversion, and an attack by IX Corps in conjunction with the mine might become the start of an all-out offensive.[10]

BURNSIDE'S PLAN, JULY 26, 1864

General Burnside's lunch was disrupted by two urgent dispatches. The first from Meade began with words Burnside had been waiting for: "I wish you to submit in writing your project for the explosion of your mine, with the amount of powder required, that the preliminary questions may be definitely settled." If Burnside would designate a safe place for delivery, Meade would have the gunpowder sent forthwith. The second dispatch was from Grant's chief of staff, inquiring whether the mine was in imminent danger of discovery. If it was, Burnside was to prepare to fire it the next day, July 27, at four in the afternoon. There would be no assault in connection with such an explosion. (It would serve as a diversion in favor of Hancock's expedition, though Burnside was not informed of this.) If the mine were *not* in danger of discovery, Burnside was to preserve it "for use at some early future day . . . in connexion with other operations."

Burnside had been planning this operation for nearly a month. The difficulty was to frame it in a way that would allow him to command the attack, without presuming on Meade's prerogatives as he had on July 3. He began by telling Grant and Meade that the Confederates had not found his mine but he could not guarantee its safety beyond two or three days. He deferred to them on the question of when and how the mine should be used, "but it may not be improper for me to say that the advantages reaped from the work would be but small if it were exploded with-

out any co-operative movements," such as an infantry assault by IX
Corps.

He provided the technical specifications of the mine: more than five
hundred feet long with side galleries extending forty feet to either side.
He would have Pleasants construct eight "magazines" or powder chambers, two at the far end and two at the near end in each of the two lateral
galleries, each magazine a wooden crate filled with gunpowder. The magazines would be linked by wooden troughs also filled with gunpowder.
Five or six fuses would be run from these troughs to the surface—a redundancy of fuses to make firing more certain. Once the fuses were laid,
the main tunnel would be "tamped" by filling the last hundred feet with
sandbags. This would contain and compress the explosion, forcing it upward. The fuses would burn at a predictable rate until they reached the
exposed gunpowder in the trough and flashed, simultaneously detonat-
ing all eight magazines. The prevailing doctrine among military engineers called for eight thousand pounds of blasting powder in a mine of
this size and depth. Burnside proposed using twelve to fourteen thousand pounds, to maximize its destructive power and its moral effect on
nearby troops.[11]

The crux of his plan was the infantry assault. The best time to explode the mine would be just before dawn or at five in the afternoon.
Burnside would "mass two brigades of the colored division in rear of my
line in columns of divisions—double columns closed in mass; the head of
each brigade resting on the front line." They would charge right after the
explosion, and as they passed the breach, the lead regiment of each
brigade would peel off to right or left and "come into line perpendicular
to the enemy's line . . . and proceed down the line of the enemy's works as
rapidly as possible." The remaining regiments of the Colored division
would deploy into columns of regiments and advance immediately on the
high ground, the column on the right moving directly onto Cemetery
Hill, that on the left seizing the crest line along the Jerusalem Plank Road
left of the hill. The other three divisions of IX Corps would be massed in
readiness to be "thrown in" to support the Colored division. Once the
rest of the corps had come up to the crest line, Burnside wanted to "throw
the colored division right into the town." Of course, supporting attacks by
other corps would be necessary, but Burnside was careful not to infringe
on Meade's prerogatives: "There is a necessity for co-operation, at least in
the way of artillery, of the troops on my right and left; of the extent of this
you will necessarily be the judge."[12]

Burnside's maneuver plan differed from Ferrero's original design and from the tactics practiced by the division since July 9. Ferrero had wanted the brigades to form one behind the other and charge the entrenchments between the mine crater and the battery to the south. Then the lead regiments of Sigfried's brigade (the 30th and 43rd) would peel off left and right while the rest of the division advanced. The revised plan called for the attack to pass through the breach made by the mine. This approach would avoid the danger of storming a line still held by Rebel troops and would shorten the distance to Cemetery Hill. But the adaptation still called for the brigades to form one behind the other, which—in an attack through the breach—presented problems for command and control. Each brigade would have to split into diverging columns to pass around the sides of the crater, and each column would mix elements of different brigades.

Burnside's plan called for the brigades to form side by side in parallel columns. One brigade would pass around the crater to the right, the other to the left. The lead regiment of each brigade would peel off to clear the trenches on either flank while the rest deployed into line and advanced on Cemetery Hill and the Plank Road. The chief advantage of Burnside's plan was that each brigade would preserve its unity from start to finish. Burnside's "column of divisions" was also better suited than Ferrero's "column of regiments" for rapid movement through the breach and speedy deployment of the flanking regiments. In this formation each regiment would be formed in two parallel "columns of companies." Each of these columns would consist of a series of companies, one behind the other, each company formed in line. As the head of the column passed around the crater, it would present a two-company front to any Confederates capable of resistance. On the far side the companies of the outer column (the one away from the crater) would wheel outward "by companies," while those in the inner column would simply right-face or left-face into line behind them. The regiment would then be ready to make its flanking sweep along the Rebel line. This was a simpler and faster maneuver than the original plan of sending a regiment-wide line of battle through the breach and then having them perform the complex "wheel by companies." The only problem with Burnside's plan was that it was not the one the troops had been practicing. So the critical and difficult maneuver of turning the Rebel flank on the left would be entrusted to an unrehearsed regiment from Thomas's brigade.[13]

It was not strictly necessary for Burnside to specify which division would take the lead, since only a general description of his plan was called for. Perhaps he wanted Meade to know that he had had the prescience and professionalism to train a division for the specialized tasks of the assault. He may have thought it necessary to identify this as the Colored division because his claim to that division had been undermined by Meade's habit of detaching it for duty with other corps and by Butler's campaign to consolidate Black troops in his Army of the James. On some level he was probably aware that *everything* having to do with Colored troops was politically loaded, and he wanted Meade's approval in order to mitigate the political risks of giving Negro troops the central role in a major operation.[14]

But Meade would not respond to Burnside's dispatch until he had overseen the start of the Deep Bottom offensive.

DEEP BOTTOM, JULY 26–28, 1864

On the afternoon of the twenty-sixth, the cavalry and II Corps infantry were recalled from fatigue duty or roused from rest and assembled in their camps to draw food, ammunition, and equipment. At 4:00 P.M. they began their march to the James River crossings. They marched on roads well behind the Federal front, in light field order—no wagon trains, just their batteries and ambulances trailing the troops. It was late evening when they crossed the Appomattox by the bridge at Broadway Landing and full dark as they marched across the rear of Butler's positions. Cavalry patrols were posted there to manage traffic, and small bonfires illuminated the crossroads.

The Bermuda Hundred peninsula was shaped like a hand making a gesture of derision—the two-finger sign of horns associated with cuckoldry. Each finger was shaped and wrapped by a sinuous curl of the James. The western or upstream finger was Jones' Neck, and at its tip Butler had constructed a pontoon bridge to the area called Deep Bottom on the northern bank, with a second bridge about a mile downstream. Engineers covered both bridges with hay and straw to muffle the sounds of horses, caissons, and marching men as they crossed in the dark. Between the two bridges were a pair of gunboats, armed with heavy mortars to provide artillery support.

Upstream from Jones' Neck was Chaffin's Bluff, a fortified hill on the north bank of the river that, with the Drewry's Bluff fort on the south side, closed the river to Federal ironclads. Chaffin's Bluff was also the anchor of the advanced trench line that protected Richmond on the east. The river twisted a deep S curve between Chaffin's Bluff and the Deep Bottom crossing, but the distance between them was much shorter by road. Grant's plan called for Hancock and his infantry to cross the Jones' Neck bridge, take the first road to the left (the New Market Road), and surprise and storm the garrison at Chaffin's Bluff. Sheridan's cavalry would cross at the downstream bridge and ride farther to the north on the Long Bridge Road and then turn west and strike toward Richmond on either the Darbytown (also called the Central) Road or the Charles City Road. With speed and luck Sheridan might be able to break through the lightly defended fortifications and attack Richmond itself, or at least outflank the troops at Chaffin's and force them to retreat. Failing that, Sheridan was to ride out to the north and west and wreck the Virginia Central Railroad, over which supplies and reinforcements moved between Richmond and the Shenandoah.

Hancock and Sheridan arrived at the pontoon bridge at 2:30 A.M. and crossed ahead of their troops to confer with General Foster, who commanded the division of X Corps in the Deep Bottom bridgehead. The ground there was marshy and wooded. Foster's line was set close to the riverbank, anchored on the west or left by the ravine of Three Mile Creek and on the right by the span of open water formed by the confluence of Four Mile and Bailey's creeks. Beyond his line was a strong Confederate force—Kershaw's Division of the Army of Northern Virginia—that held the junction of the New Market and Long Bridge roads. Chaffin's Bluff itself was now held by half of Cadmus Wilcox's division, with the other half just across the James as additional support.

The Confederate position on Foster's front was also anchored on the creeks and could be taken only by frontal assault. Hancock and Sheridan therefore decided to cross by the lower bridge and move north as rapidly as possible to get around the left flank of the Confederate position. But with the lower bridge as their only crossing, cavalry and infantry could not move at the same time. Hancock's infantry went first, while Sheridan's horsemen had to wait and follow. Moreover, the Federal troops would have to move cross-country until they reached the New Market Road, which would further slow their advance. Finally, Bailey's Creek cut across all three of the approach roads to Chaffin's Bluff and Richmond, providing the Confederates with strong defensive positions. Still, the initial strength of the Federal force was upwards of twenty-five thousand, opposed by fewer than half that number of Confederates.

Hancock got his troops over the bridge in the dark, rested them briefly, and at daylight advanced to the New Market Road and turned west. The division led by Francis Barlow led off on the road itself, with Gershom Mott's division moving through the woods on the right and John Gibbon's division in reserve. Barlow ran into a line of breastworks manned by Kershaw's troops just this side of Bailey's Creek. The Federal troops deployed into line and a firefight spread out toward the flanks. Barlow's artillery came up and opened on the breastworks, and the gunboats chipped in, lobbing huge hundred-pound mortar shells over the trees to descend with a sizzling sound like water seething in a kettle to burst in and around Kershaw's position, where "great trees a foot and a half in diameter were snapped off like pipestems."

Meanwhile, on the right, Régis de Trobriand's brigade led Mott's division through the woods, its skirmishers searching for the key junction where the New Market intersected the Long Bridge Road coming up from the Jones' Neck bridge. De Trobriand's brigade collided with a Confederate line of battle in front of Bailey's Creek. Rebel fire was intense, but the Federals kept working forward, threatening the Rebels and holding them in place. Kershaw thinned the middle of his line to send help, and Barlow saw the weak spot. He ordered a charge by Nelson Miles's brigade, which broke the ranks of Humphreys's Mississippi Brigade, drove them back, and captured a four-gun artillery battery. The whole Rebel line unraveled as the infantry fell back across Bailey's Creek. Kershaw's Division had suffered a galling defeat and serious losses—perhaps three hundred men and four guns. But it was able to reform in breastworks prepared on the other side of the creek, and Hancock's men had to pause and regroup.

In the meantime Sheridan's two divisions moved swiftly up the Long Bridge Road and then swung west between the Darbytown and Charles City roads. The area was lightly defended, and Sheridan drove as far as the headwaters of Bailey's Creek. If he had been able to continue, he might have struck Kershaw's command in the flank and rear and destroyed it outright. But the Rebels had "refused" their line of fieldworks— bending the outer edge back at right angles to face an attack from the flank—and Sheridan was stopped.

In mid-afternoon Hancock's troops made a halfhearted attack across Bailey's Creek—they were simply too tired from their all-night march (not to mention months of hard service) to go farther that day. Hancock spent the afternoon deploying his divisions along the Bailey's Creek line and tying in with Sheridan. Grant made a brief visit to Deep Bottom, assessed the situation, and modified Hancock's mission. The strike against the Virginia Central Railroad was off. It would take Sheridan too far from the critical scene of operations. Hancock and Sheridan were to operate together against Kershaw, take Chaffin's Bluff, and drive Confederate forces back into Richmond. In addition to II Corps, Hancock could use Foster's division of X Corps and a brigade of XIX Corps that had not yet taken ship for Washington.

But the Confederates were also reinforcing. Hancock's advance had been reported to Lee early on the morning of the twenty-seventh, and it was clear the force north of the James was inadequate to stop it. Lee ordered General Richard Anderson, Longstreet's replacement as commander of I Corps, to take over on the north side. Heth's infantry division and two divisions of cavalry were assembled by the tracks of the Richmond and Petersburg, where more than a dozen trains were waiting to carry them north. They got their orders at 1:30 P.M., and it took them seven hours by rail and road to reach Chaffin's Bluff, where they would form Anderson's reserve for the fighting on the twenty-eighth. That left only Field's Division and part of Wilcox's for a reserve on the south side. To bolster the Petersburg defenses, headquarters finally agreed to Bushrod Johnson's request for artillery. On the evening of the twenty-seventh, the seven guns and twelve mortars of Colonel John Haskell's artillery battalion were hauled into position along the crest line west of the Jerusalem Plank Road. Sixteen barrels were sited to bear on Elliott's Salient and the area just behind it.[15]

❧

July 27 was a busy day at Burnside's headquarters. In the morning they began to take delivery of the powder and fuses sent up from City Point—but there were problems. Major Duane predictably objected that Burnside's plan to use twelve thousand pounds of powder was contrary to military doctrine. Burnside countered that experiments he had conducted in the course of his business as an arms manufacturer had led him to believe that the greater charge would increase the lateral force of the blast, producing a wider but shallower crater. However, that aspect of the plan also brought serious objections from Burnside's own subordinates. Their troops would be massed for the assault only one hundred or one hundred fifty yards from the explosion, where they might be deluged with the fallout from the larger blast. Burnside again appealed to his earlier experiments to assure them of their safety but failed to mollify them. He may well have been correct in thinking that the larger charge would produce a shallower crater, which might have been less of an obstacle to the advance. But his subordinates' worries were well founded.

Meade resolved the issue in Duane's favor: eight thousand pounds was all Burnside would get. Unfortunately, in their absorption with the powder controversy, Burnside and his staff failed to inspect the crate of fuses that Duane had sent.[16]

By early afternoon the powder was at hand, and Burnside ordered Pleasants to begin charging the mine. It was a laborious task, and a dangerous one. The wagons carrying the powder were parked a mile from the mine head, out of sight from Rebel observers. There were three hundred twenty kegs, each containing twenty-five pounds of black powder. Carrying parties were detailed from the 48th and other regiments in Potter's division. Pleasants had had his men prepare dozens of canvas slings, with pockets at either end. With a keg in each pocket, a soldier would shoulder the sling and trudge off to the mine, following a route made devious by the need to hide the operation from Confederate observers, under the heat hammer of the Virginia sun. (Burnside had wanted to make the transfer at night, but Meade wanted the mine charged as soon as possible.) The deliveries had to be paced to prevent a too-rapid pileup of kegs at the mine head, because the narrowness of the tunnel and the limited ventilation prevented more than half a dozen men at a time from working in the mine.

At the mine head teams of two or three would sling their pairs of kegs and stoop their way down the length of the tunnel, the weight of the kegs increasingly painful to bear because they could not stand erect. Their way was lit not by cap-lamps but by the dull flicker of candles set in niches in the wall—a man carrying fifty pounds of blasting powder does not want an open flame anywhere about his person. At the end of the tunnel they would turn into the side galleries and deliver their kegs to a miner stationed there. He would pry open the kegs and pour the contents into one of the plank box magazines. Every step of the process was dangerous. If a keg were dropped or otherwise damaged in transit, a trickle of powder could leak, and a spark of any kind—the flash from a hobnail boot striking rock or from the static electricity in the hot dry air—would blow the bearer into fragments and perhaps set off a chain of explosions and wreck the mine. That danger was redoubled in the galleries, where candle flames flickered in the presence of large heaps of powder poured out in the open. Extreme and anxious care was required of everyone involved, from Pleasants down to the last man in the ranks.

The job was completed in six hours—a tribute to the management of Pleasants and Harry Reese, and to the cooperative spirit of the men who did the work.

Now it was Pleasants's task to place and fill the wooden powder troughs in the floors of the galleries, and to lay the fuses linking them to the surface. When he opened the crate of fuses sent by Duane's department, he was disgusted to find not safety fuse but ordinary blasting fuse, cut into various lengths (some only ten feet long) instead of the thousand-foot lengths he had requested. Safety fuse was designed for setting off blasts underground or across long distances. It came in long lengths and was treated to be moisture-resistant. Ordinary fuse was susceptible to damage by the moisture in the tunnel, especially if its use were postponed for a day or two. Moreover, there was not enough fuse for the redundancy needed to maximize chances for a successful detonation. What there was would have to be spliced at many points to achieve the proper length, and at every splice it was possible for the fuse to sputter and go out. If such a break were to occur in the tamped portion of the tunnel, it could not be reignited without dismantling the sandbag barrier. And whoever went down to reignite a broken fuse would be in danger of blowing up with the mine.[17]

Perhaps some functionary at the supply depot had misread or ig-nored Burnside's specification of safety fuse. Even Pleasants found it hard to believe that Major Duane had sabotaged them out of spite—although, judged by its effect, incompetence can be indistinguishable from malice. But Pleasants had learned not to dwell on such frustrations. He extended the powder troughs into the main tunnel, filled them, and laid three lengths of fuse side by side on top of the powder. He piled a small heap of powder where the two new troughs met and then ran the three fuse lines back ninety feet down the main tunnel. Every one of these fuse lines was spliced in several places, and any one of these splices might be flawed, but by tripling the lines and heaping extra powder at the most critical junc-tions, Pleasants was increasing the odds that at least one of the lines would work.

The portion of the fuse that would run through the tamp was shel-tered in a tube made of boards. Then Pleasants set the men to labor again, teams of three hauling sandbags into the mine and packing them together to tamp the tunnel. This too had to be done with care to avoid breaking the fuse line, and small air passages had to be left between the sandbags to ensure there was enough oxygen in the mine to feed the explosion. Probably Reese or one of the professional miners stayed in the mine to oversee that part of the work. Burnside had wanted a hundred feet of tamping, but the shortage of fuse led Pleasants to reduce that to thirty feet, which he deemed sufficient.

The mine had to be fired by someone stationed four hundred feet into the tunnel, at the place where the last ninety feet of fuse line ended. The fuse burned at six feet per minute, a rate that would allow the firing team fifteen minutes to get out of the hole before the blast went off.

It took all night and most of the next day to finish the job, but at 6:00 P.M. on July 28, Pleasants was able to report that the mine was ready to fire. It was the only piece of good news Burnside received that day.

THE ELEVENTH HOUR

At noon on the twenty-eighth Burnside had ridden to Meade's headquarters to confer about his plan for the infantry assault. Meade had already rejected Burnside's request for the extra-large powder charge—now he disapproved the maneuver plan. The long campaign had taught Meade to distrust the ability of his generals (Hancock was an exception) to carry out complex maneuvers under combat conditions. The string of botched offensives that had begun in the Wilderness had culminated in the organizational breakdown of July 18–19, when Meade had been utterly unable to get his corps commanders to move in concert. Of all his corps commanders, Burnside was probably the one whose skills Meade distrusted most. He therefore forbade splitting the lead regiments out to the flanks— forbade all special formations and any attempt to change formation during the attack. The lead division must simply "rush" for Cemetery Hill, with the other divisions advancing in support.

Then Meade completed his demolition of Burnside's proposal by ordering him not to use the Colored division as his spearhead. He gave as his reason that "he could not trust them because they were untried."[18]

Burnside surrendered the other points, but this one seemed indispensable. He argued strenuously and in detail his reasons for choosing the Colored division. Chief among them was his belief that his three White divisions were played out as assault troops. They had been decimated by the losses of the campaign, especially among officers. They had now spent a month in the trenches, where exhaustion, disease, and daily casualties had reduced their numbers, physical strength, and morale. Trench warfare had also habituated them to seeking shelter at every opportunity. If asked to charge Cemetery Hill, they would go to ground as soon as they saw that Rebel artillery had their range. The Blacks were fresh, their ranks had not been ravaged by battle losses. By all reports their discipline was good and they were eager to prove themselves. As Meade well knew, it was often possible to get inexperienced troops to carry out assignments veteran troops would balk at. Although their combat experience was limited, they had been trained especially to meet the problems and stresses of the assault—they and their officers were the men best prepared by training, health, and morale to lead the offensive.

Meade was well aware that any decision affecting Black troops was fraught with political complications, especially for a supposed "McClellan man" like himself. So he chose his words carefully, to avoid any breach (actual or implied) of what we might call political correctness. It was not that he "had any reason to doubt, or any desire to doubt the good qualities of the colored troops." But "the operation was to be a coup-de-main, . . . his assaulting column was to be as a forlorn hope, such as are put into breaches," and Burnside should therefore "assault with his best troops." By "best" Meade presumably meant "experienced," but in context with Burnside's assessment of his corps the statement also implied that wornout White troops were better than fresh well-trained Black ones.

Burnside refused to give up. He was (Meade noticed) "very much disappointed." His sympathy for the condition of his troops was genuine, and his emotion lent force to his objections. He also expressed concern for the Colored division and their officers: their arbitrary removal from the spearhead role might seriously damage their morale. He may have implied that Meade's decision reflected a prejudice against Colored troops. So to show his appreciation of the strength and sincerity of Burnside's objections, "and in order to show him that I was not governed by any motive other than such as I ought to be governed by," Meade agreed to "report the matter to the lieutenant general [Grant]; state to him my reasons, and those of General Burnside's [sic], and let him decide."[19]

Burnside was satisfied with this promise. He assumed Meade would fully and fairly represent his arguments for leading with the Black division, and that those arguments would be compelling. Grant was known to be a supporter, if not an enthusiast, of the use of Black troops in combat. Burnside had reason to think that Grant thought well of the 4th Division. The lieutenant general had praised its progress in his letter recommend-

ing Ferrero's promotion. Burnside returned to his headquarters to receive
Pleasants's report on the completion of the mine and to invite his most experienced division commanders, Potter and Willcox, to a conference the
next morning to get their advice on preparations for the attack. Since he
received no further word from Meade that evening, and the attack was
scheduled for the morning of July 30—only some thirty-six hours away—
he went to bed believing that his plan to use the Colored division would
not be overruled.

⸎

Grant had gone north of the river to assess the progress of his thrust
toward Richmond. The second day of fighting was drawing to a close.
Richard Anderson now commanded the Confederate force, all of whose
elements had been drawn from Lee's strategic reserve. Kershaw's Division and two of Wilcox's brigades had been posted there earlier in response to Foster's establishment of the Deep Bottom bridgehead, and
now Heth's infantry division and two cavalry divisions had arrived from
the south side during the night. Anderson took the initiative, pulling
Wilcox's two brigades and one of Kershaw's out of line and marching
them north under General Connor to strike Sheridan's cavalry on the
Union's right just below the Charles City Road. Federal observers spot-
ted the movement, and the gunboats harassed it by dropping mortar
bombs into the trees. Connor's troops reached Sheridan's front at 10:00
A.M., formed with the three brigades abreast, and advanced. Cavalry in the
open, armed with short-range carbines, were at a disadvantage against infantry with rifles. Sheridan's first line was driven back three hundred
yards. They took shelter in some farm buildings, and supports came up
on either side. When the Confederate infantry came on again, advantages
were reversed. Firing from shelter, the cavalry's repeating carbines produced a storm of bullets that broke the assault. The cavalry rose up and
counterattacked, the rattle of the repeaters making them sound like twice
their number, and Connor's troops were driven backward for a mile, losing two hundred prisoners, several battle flags, and 158 dead.[20]

But Hancock had not been able to dent Kershaw's line behind Bailey's Creek. The attack on Sheridan had caused Hancock to order Gibbon's division north in support. Before the division could move, Sheridan
had driven Connor's troops from the field. Hancock gave Gibbon, once a
friend as well as a colleague, an undeserved tongue-lashing for not moving sooner. Then he ordered him to entrench a line to protect their south-

ern flank—scouts reported a Rebel column moving from Chaffin's Bluff to cut them off from their bridgehead. That attack never materialized. But Gibbon's division was Hancock's reserve, and while it was distracted, he was unable to use it for the powerful strike his orders envisioned.

Hancock was not the man or the general he had been. The serious wound he had received at Gettysburg had never properly healed, and it drained his resiliency of mind and body and made him testy. He could no longer inspire in his junior officers and enlisted men the kind of energy and initiative that had made his II Corps the elite assault force of the army. But then, the men who had made II Corps what it was were mostly dead or disabled. As Gibbon himself said, its troops, who "at the commencement of the campaign were equal to almost any undertaking, became toward the end of it unfit for almost any."[21]

When Grant and Meade arrived in the late afternoon to look things over, Hancock's line was no farther advanced than it had been twenty-four hours earlier, and Sheridan was no closer to turning the Confederate flank. It was clear that nothing decisive could now be achieved on this front. Nevertheless, Hancock and Sheridan had done considerable damage. In two days of fighting they had inflicted more than 600 casualties—killed, wounded, or missing—at a cost of only 488 of their own men. That success, coupled with the apparent size of the force and with Hancock's reputation as an offensive general, had led Lee to conclude that Richmond was the objective of a large and dangerous Federal offensive. After dark on the twenty-eighth he ordered Charles Field's infantry and Rooney Lee's cavalry division to march for Chaffin's and cross the river above Drewry's Bluff. By the evening of July 29, three and a half of the four infantry divisions that constituted Lee's strategic reserve were north of the James River, along with nearly all of his cavalry. On the south side, two brigades from Wilcox's Division held the fort at Drewry's Bluff—available for action north of the river but too far from Petersburg to help there. Pickett's Division was the sole defense of the Bermuda Hundred front. The lines defending Petersburg south of the Appomattox were manned by the infantry divisions of Hoke, Bushrod Johnson, and Mahone, with no strategic reserve.

The dispatch of Field's Division was a questionable decision. Neither Hancock nor Sheridan had been able to make much headway on the twenty-eighth, but Lee may have been fooled into thinking Hancock's advance was the precursor to a still heavier blow. It is also possible that Lee was hoping to use the additional troops for a counteroffensive against

Hancock. Throughout the Petersburg campaign he would treat nearly every Federal venture in the open field as an opportunity to destroy or cripple a segment of Grant's army. He saw that tactic as his best hope for cutting down the odds against him and for embarrassing the Federal army and the Lincoln administration. Perhaps he even dared to hope that some fortunate combination of circumstances would allow him to turn one of these counterblows into a decisive battle.

Although Grant would not learn of Field's movement until the following day, by the evening of July 28 he already had enough information to know that the Deep Bottom expedition had succeeded in its secondary purpose of inducing Lee to strip most of the reserves from his Petersburg lines. With luck, and a show of energy by Hancock and Sheridan on the twenty-ninth, Lee might be induced to send still more. That would create an opportunity to do something decisive on Burnside's front. The mine was now upgraded from a potential diversion to the centerpiece of the offensive against Petersburg. With that in mind, Hancock was to send Mott's division back to Petersburg that night. The rest of his and Sheridan's commands would skirmish heavily against the Bailey Creek line until nightfall on the twenty-ninth and then, as secretly as might be, march back to the Petersburg front and form a reserve to exploit a possible breakthrough.

Meade would write the orders for these and the other movements that would position his divisions for the Battle of the Crater. But first he had to resolve his disagreement with Burnside over the use of the Black division. He gave Grant the gist of Burnside's thinking about the condition of his White divisions, and both Grant and Meade were aware that the Black troops had been given some training for the assault. Meade probably rehearsed his objections to the use of inexperienced troops for such an operation, but what Grant recalled as the central point of their conversation was simply this: "General Meade said that if we put the colored troops in front . . . and it should prove a failure, it would then be said, and very properly, that we were shoving those people ahead to get killed because we did not care anything about them. But that could not be said if we put white troops in front." Grant concurred. He understood as well as anyone that Black soldiers were a highly charged political symbol, dangerous no matter how one handled them. To accept them as soldiers was offensive to conservatives, to reject them a sign of disloyalty to Radicals. To refuse to use them in battle risked the accusation of "McClellanism," but to send them into a slaughterhouse was worse.[22]

The decision to demote the 4th Division was political rather than military.

EVE OF BATTLE, JULY 29, 1864

July 29 was another scorching summer day. North of the James, Hancock's and Sheridan's men worked hard to convince General Anderson that the Bailey Creek line was about to be assailed in strength. Cavalry and infantry launched vigorous probing attacks, as if searching out weak spots for the grand assault. Sudden gatherings of blue-coated infantry would lunge out of the trees as if to say *This is it* and then spread out, exchange fire, and withdraw. Artillery would tune up, indicating that those earlier exercises had been feints to set the Rebels up for the real thing. Anderson did not feel entirely secure until late afternoon, when the first elements of Field's Division came marching in from Chaffin's Bluff. But Mott's division had already left the north side and was marching across Bermuda Hundred to relieve John Turner's and Adelbert Ames's divisions of Butler's army in the trenches just south of the Appomattox River.

At 10:30 that morning Burnside welcomed Generals Potter and Willcox to his headquarters tent, and the three sat down to discuss plans for the assault the next day. Among the problems they faced was the fact that General Ferrero was still absent in Washington, trying to get his commission confirmed, and the 4th Division was under the temporary command of Julius White. Burnside confessed that he "had been very much worried and troubled the day before lest General Meade would overrule" his plans for the Colored division. But because he had received no further communication in the twelve or fifteen hours since Meade had conferred with Grant, "I took it for granted that [Grant] had decided to let [the plan] remain as it was."[23]

That hopeful presumption was hardly uttered when Meade himself rode up, accompanied by General Ord. Burnside immediately asked what Grant had decided about the use of Black troops. Meade was surprised. He had had his chief of staff send Burnside an official dispatch less than an hour earlier, but Burnside had not yet received it. No matter—Meade had always known he would have to reinforce that written order in person. Burnside could be stubbornly resistant to unwelcome instructions and had (as Meade saw it) displayed a disposition to usurp his command prerogatives. So he stated the case flatly, "I saw General Grant, and he agrees with me that it will not do to put the colored division in the lead."

Burnside was stunned. "I felt, and I suppose I expressed, and showed, very great disappointment . . . [and] asked General Meade if that decision could not be changed."

"No, general, it cannot; it is final, and you must put in your white troops."[24]

Burnside reiterated his reasons for not wanting to use those troops—their physical weakness, their reluctance to fight outside entrenchments. But he weakened his case by a too-clever elaboration of his argument: the opinion that, should the Blacks take the lead and suffer repulse, his White troops would still have enough will and discipline to continue the attack; but if the Negroes saw White men repulsed, they would not be willing to go forward. If that were the case, the Whites *were* capable of making the attack, and Negro morale *was* too weak for the hard service Burnside demanded of them. But Meade was through arguing: "You must detail one of your white divisions to make the advance." Burnside replied, "Very well, general, I will carry out this plan to the best of my ability."[25]

Meade and Ord then rode off to inspect the ground to be crossed in the attack.

Burnside was stymied by this unexpected reversal of the course of action he had planned so long, so meticulously, and so well. Colonel Harris, his ordnance officer, reflected in his diary the surprise and frustration of Burnside and everyone on his staff:

> Thus, at the eleventh hour . . . the Negro division & its gallant commander, who believed they would be invincible & who had learned their duty by constant application to this single idea for the previous month, were informed that "it wasn't best" and they must be replaced by white troops who had already their own instructions to do an entirely different thing.[26]

Burnside was a general who relied on the advice and support of loyal and long-tried subordinates, and Potter and Willcox were his most trusted colleagues. But now they were reluctant to offer the advice that would enable Burnside to choose a White division to lead the assault. Each man had excellent reasons for thinking his own division unfit for the task—they were the same reasons Burnside had given Meade. On the other hand, it would have been unseemly for either man to suggest that the task should fall to the other. They spent some time talking themselves into an impasse before it occurred to them that Burnside "had better send for General Ledlie." Ledlie was summoned, but he was no less reluctant than Potter and Willcox to put his division forward. The discussion was stilted and evasive, since no man was willing to claim the task or demand that another man's people undertake it. Burnside could not bring himself to make the choice.[27]

After some two hours of this, Meade reappeared to find the question unresolved. He took the opportunity to impress upon Burnside and his division commanders what was, for him, the most crucial element of the operation. Whichever division was chosen to lead, it must move immediately after the explosion and advance to Cemetery Hill with the greatest possible speed. "[I]f immediate advantage was not taken of the explosion of the mine, and the consequent confusion of the enemy, and the crest immediately gained," the enemy would bring up reserves and contain the advance to the vicinity of the crater. Since that position was overlooked by a semicircle of batteries, it could not be held. He also reiterated the principle that Grant had laid down on July 24, when the operation was first conceived: if the attack did not succeed swiftly and immediately, it should be abandoned in short order and the troops withdrawn before heavy losses were incurred.[28]

Meade's interruption did nothing to clarify Burnside's problem. Up until the afternoon of July 29 he had done everything a good corps commander ought to do. He had shown initiative and intelligence in seizing the opportunity presented by the proximity of a regiment of miners to the Confederate fort, had undertaken and sustained the mine from his own resources, had developed a tactical plan for the infantry assault, and (on his own initiative) had begun training a division as his spearhead. But Meade had stripped him of his best and longest held ideas, and all the alternatives were stale second bests. The arguments Potter, Willcox, and Ledlie made against the use of their divisions were all too persuasive. Burnside could not bring himself to settle the issue by fiat.

As he puzzled things out, it seemed to him that the most important issue was not the military quality of the divisions and their commanders but one of *fairness* to these well-liked colleagues sitting at his table. So he looked round the table and said, "It will be fair to cast lots."

It was a gambler's decision, not a general's.

He tore three strips of paper and put them into his hat, one shorter than the rest, "and so they did cast lots, and General Ledlie drew the advance." Ledlie rose and "at once left my headquarters in a very cheerful mood to make his arrangements."[29]

Preparation for Battle

JULY 29, 1864

G rant's orders had set this operation in motion, but the conduct of
the battle itself would be entirely in Meade's hands. In the early
phases of the overland campaign costly mistakes had resulted from the
uncertainty about each general's area of authority and responsibility.
Grant was in command of all the Union's armies, and he was the senior
general on the scene, but Meade was the designated commander of the
Army of the Potomac. They had worked out an arrangement under which
Grant, as general in chief of the armies, decided the strategic objectives
and the direction, timing, and pace of large offensive movements, while
Meade (or his designee) took responsibility for all operational details. A
corollary of this arrangement was that once Meade had begun an operation, Grant would not intervene or interfere in its conduct. Unity of command was essential in battle. Officers on the line had to be able to rely on
the authority and integrity of their chain of command. If Grant made a
habit of interfering, Meade's subordinates would second-guess every
troublesome order and the operation would fall apart.

Meade's orders for the attack went out to his corps commanders in
mid-afternoon, all movements to begin after nightfall to conceal them
from the enemy. General Burnside was to recall the two brigades of his
4th Division from their present tasks and mass them behind the three
White divisions, which were to form ready for the assault. He was to have
his engineers clear the way for the advance by preparing passages through
the trench parapets and abatis, which meant cutting gaps in the obstacles
and providing ladders and stairs for troops to use when exiting the

trenches. He was also instructed to send pioneers with the attacking columns, instructed and equipped for the tasks of destroying enemy obstacles, cutting passages, and filling entrenchments to allow artillery to be brought forward and to enable the storming party to dig in on Cemetery Hill. General Warren, commanding V Corps on Burnside's left, was to concentrate ten thousand infantry to support Burnside. General Ord was to draw out three divisions of the Army of the James, two to hold Burnside's reserve trenches and one to join the attack. General Hancock was to complete his disengagement from Deep Bottom, recross the river, and take position in reserve behind the right of the Union line. Sheridan was to bring his cavalry back and position it behind Warren's V Corps at the southern end of the line. At dawn the troopers were to strike west toward the Weldon Railroad and threaten to turn the enemy's southern flank while Burnside assailed them in front. (This task was later shifted to General James Wilson's lone cavalry division, which was already in position.)

Burnside would make his headquarters in the bombproof behind his fourteen-gun battery (Fort Morton), less than a thousand feet behind his front line. Meade would move from his headquarters near City Point to Burnside's HQ near the Shand house, about a mile northeast of the front. From the Shand house Meade would have a clear line of horseback communication to Warren and Hancock, at the far extremes of his line. But on this static battlefront Meade enjoyed the advantage of a telegraph link between his headquarters and those of his corps commanders. It seems not to have occurred to him that this technological innovation would have worked just as well from Fort Morton—a position that overlooked the point of attack, where he would have been in closer touch with events as they unfolded.

The mine was to be exploded at 3:30 A.M., and Burnside's columns were to assault immediately after. More than a hundred artillery pieces had been concentrated in the area, and when the mine went up, every battery was to open fire, taking deliberate aim and being careful not to impede the infantry's advance. Burnside's lead division (the 1st) was to charge directly for Cemetery Hill, without hesitating to deal with threats from its flanks. The two other White divisions (2nd and 3rd) were to support this advance by covering its flanks, with the Colored division as a corps reserve. Though their final objectives were not specified, it was presumed that all or part of these supporting divisions would eventually join the 1st Division on the Plank Road line. From that high ground they would so menace the rear of the Confederate line and the city of Petersburg that the Confederates would be forced to retreat all along the line. "Promptitude, rapidity of execution, and cordial co-operation are essential to success."[1]

In its general outline, the plan anticipated the methods that would later be used to break trench lines on the western front during the Great War: a powerful spearhead is driven through a weakened spot in the enemy line, outflanking or isolating the enemy's strongpoints. But unless the attackers can substantially widen their initial breach, the momentum of advance cannot be sustained and the advancing forces find themselves holding vulnerable salients, with enemies rallying on their flanks and threatening their lines of supply. Burnside's rejected plan had envisioned the use of his two lead regiments to clear the trenches to either side of the crater, allowing the supporting divisions to advance on a wider front. The allotted force had probably been inadequate, but the idea had been sound. Under Meade's plan, the Union divisions would have to move, one after the other, through the narrow breach created by the mine, an arrangement that would slow the advance and allow the Confederates holding on the flanks of the breach to turn it into a bottleneck.

Meade did not include in his orders the cautionary guidance he had given Burnside that afternoon: that if the attack did not lead to a quick and decisive result, it was to be retracted before the investment of lives became exorbitant. But that caution affected his orders to Ord and Warren: until their own observations assured them of Burnside's success, the decision to engage was left to their discretion, in consultation with Meade's headquarters. This was in fact a structural weakness in the plan. Even if Burnside succeeded in passing one or two divisions rapidly through the breach, their advance to Cemetery Hill had to be made upslope across open ground, every foot of which was exposed to artillery crossfire from batteries on the Plank Road up ahead and on the spurs of higher ground to either side. These flanking batteries could be silenced or diverted only by an infantry attack, and if Burnside's divisions were committed to the capture of the Plank Road–Cemetery Hill line, these supporting attacks had to come from V Corps on the south and Ord's troops from the Army of the James on the north. But Meade was unwilling to commit himself to such a comprehensive plan of assault. He would see how far Burnside succeeded and then supplement his efforts on an ad hoc basis. He did not convey to Warren any sense that the operation required an all-out commitment to the offensive; rather, he conveyed a feeling that avoidance of heavy losses was as important as success.

Warren had once been considered one of the best corps commanders in the Army of the Potomac. At the start of the campaign, Grant had thought him the best man to replace Meade should that become necessary. But the unrelenting combat of the overland campaign had exposed unsuspected weaknesses in his mind and character: "For thirty days now it has been one funeral procession, past me; and it is too much!" He had become reluctant to risk *any* decisive action, could see only the possibilities for disaster in every proposed offensive. For the past month he had thrown a wet blanket over every proposal for action considered at Meade's HQ: "All our efforts are attended with such great difficulties that I believe no one can regard any future operations . . . with anything but the deepest anxiety and solicitude." He would not even advise, let alone undertake, offensive action without positive orders. In an army strategically compelled to take the offensive, that made Warren a perpetual drag on operations.[2]

Burnside's orders went out shortly after Meade's. Produced amid a crush of business and administrative complications, and in a mood darkened by disappointment, they were (as Burnside's orders often were) unclear and incomplete in some critical respects. He missed the assistance of John Parke, his able chief of staff, who was in the hospital recovering from an attack of malaria.

Among the complications was the sudden and unexpected reappearance of General Ferrero. His commission had finally been confirmed less than twenty-four hours earlier. He had grabbed passage on a supply ship and arrived at Burnside's headquarters shortly after the drawing of lots. Ferrero was immediately returned to command of the 4th Division, displacing General Julius White. To mollify White, Burnside appointed him temporary chief of staff, but this probably diminished the efficiency of IX Corps staff work, since White was unfamiliar with the personnel and routines of the corps. Ferrero was left at loose ends. He had been completely out of touch while in Washington, but no one had any time to brief him, and he seems not to have attended the meeting at which Burnside gave verbal instructions to his division commanders. He had no idea of the several modifications imposed on his original plan and until late that evening supposed his original plan was in force, and his men were to lead the attack.[3] The division itself was dispersed in several detachments that had to be recalled to their assembly point.

Burnside mistrusted his powers of written composition. He preferred to give his division commanders their instructions face-to-face and resolve any questions at once. His orders were general: he relied on his subordinates to make appropriate judgments about the details. Colonel Pleasants was to explode his mine at 3:30 A.M. General Ledlie would "immediately upon the explosion of the mine move his division forward as directed by verbal orders this day, and if possible crown the crest at the point known as Cemetery Hill, occupying, if possible, the cemetery." General Willcox would form his division behind Ledlie's and advance in its wake and to the left to protect Ledlie's advance on that side. Potter was to advance on Ledlie's right and protect his flank by seizing the long ravine or creek bed (i.e., the "long covered way"). In the written orders, sent out later that evening, Burnside instructed Ferrero to occupy the trenches vacated by the advancing troops; then, when Ledlie had "crowned" or entrenched a line on the hill, Ferrero was to advance through Ledlie's position and try to seize the small village of Blandford, a suburb of Petersburg. This was a forlorn remnant of his original grand design, which had called for the Colored division to capture the city.[4]

Some critical elements were missing from both the oral and the written instructions. He gave no orders for leveling the parapets of his trenches, or removing the tangle of abatis that formed a protective barrier along his front. Nor did he order his engineers to construct sandbag ladders or other devices to enable troops to climb quickly out of the six- to eight-foot-deep frontline trenches. He rejected the requests made by Meade's chief of artillery Henry Hunt and by General Warren that he have his engineers cut down two small groves of trees that stood between the lines on either side of the designated assault path. These obscured the artillerymen's line of sight and impaired their ability to fire effectively in support of the attack. He reasoned that to do so would warn the enemy an attack was imminent and lose the advantage of surprise. Meade thought that risk of negligible importance. The fact that the Rebels were countermining meant they were alerted to the chance of an attack on Elliott's Salient. But Meade lost this round: Burnside ignored his instructions.

Burnside also neglected parts of Meade's order that ran no risk of compromising the surprise but were in fact essential to the success of his operations. If Ledlie's division succeeded in gaining the crest, his men would need to throw up fieldworks as protection against the inevitable counterattack. That was why Meade wanted Burnside to detail engineers, equipped with entrenching tools, to accompany the infantry. Burnside would also need to bring field artillery forward to support the infantry on the high ground. That was why Meade wanted Burnside to detail engineers to prepare passages across their own and the Rebel entrenchments. Perhaps Burnside forgot to give these orders. Perhaps his staff, in the rush of business, somehow failed to communicate them. Or perhaps these were the kinds of details Burnside left to his division commanders. Whatever the reason, the parapets and abatis remained in place, no preparation was made for the artillery, and only Potter sent engineers forward with his troops.[5]

Burnside also did not specify where his division commanders were to station themselves during the action. This was a critical matter. Burnside's battlefield appeared small and open enough to allow him direct observation over most of the ground, but the appearance was deceptive. There were gullies and ravines, hidden trenches, folds of ground, and horizon lines from behind which the enemy might suddenly burst. His vision was bound to be limited as the day went on by heat haze, clouds of dust, and gun smoke generated by the fighting that would pile up in the windless air. But even if he had a clear oversight of the action, he would have the gravest difficulty getting his instructions to the battle line in a timely manner. Orders would have to be given to a staff officer, who would make his way to the front on foot, since he could not go horseback through the trenches. If the officer used the covered ways linking Fort Morton to the front line, he would have to thread his way through throngs of troops, some pushing forward to get into the fight, others wounded and coming back. Then he would have to make the dash across no-man's-land, dodging bullets and shell fire, worm his way through the breach, locate the appropriate commander amid a fog of battle smoke and hideous confusion . . . by which time events were likely to have outrun his orders. The same difficulties would impede the sending back to headquarters of the battlefield intelligence on which decisions could be based.

So it was of utmost importance to have on the battle line one or two generals with the experience and skill to read the shifting rhythms of the fight and to maneuver large units to meet changing exigencies. That is the job description for a division commander: someone capable of maneuvering several brigades, not just the handful of regiments a brigadier commanded. Moreover, the battlefield presence of senior generals was of peculiar importance to the morale of the volunteer army. Soldiers identified with their regiments, which were extensions of the communities from which they came. In battle, their awareness of things shrank radically to the space immediately around them and the comrades at their shoulder. Under that stress they would heed even the most doubtful orders—to storm a trench, to rally after a repulse—if given by officers of their own regiment. And they readily extended that recognition to higher officers known to them and tried by experience—the colonel acting as brigade commander for example. But they would balk at such an order given by an officer from another brigade, or one strange to them—unless that officer was recognized as a *general.* The general represented "the army," the powerful agency that sustained the regiment and gave it purpose, and his gestures could make men storm a trench who had good reason to think it would get them killed—could make men who had had enough and were walking away from the battle turn around and face the enemy.

Some corps commanders took that sort of responsibility themselves and stayed close to the front: it was Hancock's way, and it had gotten him shot at Gettysburg. There were very good arguments for the view that a corps commander ought to stay well in the rear, to oversee the totality of his operation. Burnside's view from Fort Morton was better than that on most Civil War battlefields, and while he was there, he could use the telegraph to call on support from Warren, Ord, and Meade. But if Burnside himself would not go forward with his troops, it was vital that one, some, or all of his division commanders stay close to the action. Best of all would have been to designate one senior officer to exercise authority on the other side of the breached line. The absent John Parke would have been ideal for the role: he had commanded most of the corps in the Mississippi campaign. Burnside could have chosen one of his division commanders for that role—but he presumed his division commanders knew their jobs, and left it to them to decide whether or not they would follow their men through the breach.

However, he did assign his two senior staff officers to accompany the lead divisions. Staff officers were the commanding general's vicars, responsible for informing headquarters of developments at the front and for seeing that their general's orders were carried out. They were also entrusted with their general's authority to alter orders and redirect troop movements. Burnside had always intended for Colonel Charles Loring, inspector general of IX Corps, to go in with the spearhead division. Loring had worked with Ferrero and his brigadiers during the planning and training stage of the operation. When the spearhead assignment was shifted to the 1st Division, Loring made plans to attach himself to Ledlie's headquarters. However, he did not join Ledlie until 2:30 A.M., just before the attack was to jump off, so he was unacquainted with the state of preparation in Ledlie's division. Major Van Buren was assigned to Potter's division, which was tasked to oversee the firing of the mine and to follow Ledlie's assault.

The attack would jump off from the forward bulge in the lines known as the Horseshoe, whose center approached within 125 yards of Elliott's Salient, which lay due west. The ground was open across two thirds of the Horseshoe's face, but the northern third of its arc was masked by the thick growth of timber that filled the space between Taylor's Run and the Rebel main line—one of the groves Burnside refused to cut down. The Horseshoe was about five hundred yards wide. Its southern end was marked by a small stream that flowed down from the Confederate positions, through the Federal lines, to merge with Taylor's Run. That creek turned and ran through a steep-sided ravine across the rear of the Horseshoe, making a natural gorge line or reserve trench behind the main line. Those waiting to join the attack were instructed to stay under cover and to use the covered ways to move from the rear area to the jump-off point. Burnside knew very well that all of the open ground behind his lines was vulnerable to shell fire and even to rifle fire, and he was concerned that the Rebels might bombard and break up support troops formed in the open. But requiring troops to use the covered ways meant that two thirds of his infantry would shuffle toward the action in a queue down a thousand feet of zigzag trench six to eight feet deep.

THE DEFENSE

Meade had some sixty thousand troops south of the Appomattox, facing about twenty-five thousand Confederates. However, most of Hancock's and Sheridan's men had just returned from Deep Bottom and were too worn out for immediate offensive duties. Mott's division of II Corps and Hinks's division of XVIII Corps held the northern third of the Federal line, facing Robert Hoke's Confederate division. On the southern flank, Warren's V Corps held an extended front opposite Mahone's Division, but ten thousand of Warren's men were massed on Burnside's left to support his attack. In the center, Burnside's IX Corps (perhaps twelve thousand effectives), augmented by seven thousand troops from the Army of the James, fronted the three brigades of Johnson's Division (Wise's, Elliott's, and Ransom's). In the critical sector, centered on Elliott's Salient, some seventeen thousand Federal troops were massed against perhaps four thousand Confederates. The latter would have to contain any Federal assault long enough for Lee to bring in reinforcements from Hoke's and Mahone's divisions.[6]

Lee had to know that by sending Field's Division north of the James he had stripped the Petersburg defenses to the bare minimum. He certainly knew Burnside was mining Elliott's Salient, which made it likely the Federals would attack in this area. He must have calculated that the defenses were adequate to defeat an attack by a Federal army corps between fifteen and twenty thousand strong. The overland campaign and especially the June assaults on Petersburg had taught the officers of both armies that well-planned entrenchments could break any offensive. Simply crossing several belts of entrenchment could exhaust the attackers, and a minimum of defenders could inflict losses heavy enough to prevent the attackers from achieving a decisive breakthrough.

The Confederates had shaped the terrain in and around the salient into a deceptively powerful defensive position. The ground on which the critical action would play out was a space no more than twelve hundred yards square. That was the approximate distance from the fourteen-gun battery (Fort Morton) on the east to the Jerusalem Plank Road–Cemetery Hill line on the west. The northern limit of the battlefield was set by the low ridge that sloped down from Cemetery Hill to Taylor's Run. The southern boundary was marked by Davidson's battery, just south of where the Baxter Road passed through the Confederate lines.

Three salients projected from the lines on Johnson's front. In the center was Elliott's, with its four-gun battery. Five hundred yards to the south and seven hundred yards to the north, other salients bulged farther to the east than Elliott's, and their fire would enfilade the ground in front of it. (This was the feature that had led Meade to speak of Elliott's position as a "re-entrant" rather than a true salient.) To avoid that fire, attackers would have to advance on a narrow front and cross no-man's-land very rapidly. The Confederates had a picket line across the front of their whole position—a line of shallow trenches manned by small parties of riflemen whose job was to warn of an attack and to take some of the steam out of the assault before it hit the main trench. The Federal lines were protected by the brush tangles of abatis, the Confederate by chevaux-de-frise, sharpened stakes bristling outward, which an assault force would have to break through.

To an observer in the Union lines, the terrain between Elliott's Salient and Cemetery Hill—the designated path of attack—appeared to be open ground, rising gradually to the Plank Road. It was overlooked on three sides by higher ground on which Rebel artillery was planted, but the differences in elevation were mathematically slight. The cemetery at the northwest corner of the field was the highest point and was no more than thirty feet higher than the Confederate main line. The crest line along which the Plank Road ran (the western boundary of the battleground) was ten feet lower, and the high ground that closed the southern side was lower still. Moreover, the upslope to the Plank Road was very gradual, so it appeared that an attacking battle line could advance against it at a quick-march without much derangement of its ranks.[7]

The level appearance of the field was deceptive. The small differences in elevation between the Confederate main line and their artillery positions in the rear were still large enough to allow their guns to fire down onto their own main line and all of the ground behind it. Ever since the discovery of the Federal mining operation, Lee, Beauregard, and their staffs had anticipated an attack here and had created an arc of artillery positions to defend against it. The southern anchor was Davidson's battery, on the main line south of the Baxter Road: its three guns could sweep no-man's-land from end to end, and could even be brought to bear on Elliott's Salient. One gun, in a detached position, was located fewer than two hundred feet south of the salient and could fire canister point-blank into the salient and the ground in front of it. To the west, on the Plank Road crest line, were the six guns of Flanner's and Langhorne's batteries and Lamkin's eight mortars, all commanded by Colonel John Haskell. The cannons were protected by detached earthworks, but the mortars were simply ranged behind the crest line—their looping trajectory allowed them to fire over it. Haskell had additional mortars and cannons in a reserve park behind the hill.

To the north of Lamkin's mortars was the opening of the long covered way, and Cemetery Hill, the highest point and the steepest slope on the battlefield. From the hill a ridge sloped eastward down to Taylor's Run, with the long covered way following the streambed at its foot. This ridge was steeper and higher than the ground over which the attack would pass, was very difficult for infantry to attack, and was a perfect platform for the eight guns in the batteries of Ellett and Letcher that were dug into a V-shaped earthwork on the ridge back. These guns had line of sight on every square inch of the battlefield. Closing the arc on the north, Wright's four-gun battery was entrenched where the ridge touched the Confederate main line, angled so that its guns could sweep both no-man's-land and the Confederate rear area.[8]

The most distant guns were only six hundred yards from Elliott's Salient. Using explosive shells or spherical case shot, these guns could reach every portion of the battlefield, and over much of the field their fire would interlock. Case shot was an effective weapon against infantry at distances greater than four hundred yards: a lead or iron ball packed with seventy to eighty lead balls and an explosive charge (detonated by a fuse) that sprayed the lead balls downward.

But the most effective shell against infantry was canister, a thin metal container filled with layers of lead or iron balls (more than one hundred) packed in sawdust. The container disintegrated when the gun was fired, and the bullets sprayed out like the blast from a monstrous shotgun. It was the deadliest element in the Civil War arsenal. Its killing power, especially against infantry advancing in close order, was immense. Ideal range for canister was four hundred yards or less, but it could be effective at distances up to five hundred or six hundred yards. At the longer range, Confederate gunners could sweep every inch of the field with canister, and with the exception of a five-hundred-foot-deep strip of ground across the back of Elliott's Salient, the entire battlefield was within *ideal* canister range from one or more batteries, with interlocking fire on any troops approaching Cemetery Hill.

The ground behind the Rebel lines was not as open as it appeared. About twenty-five yards behind the salient was the cavalier, or gorge line trench, which cut across the base of the salient. If the Rebel troops were driven out of the salient, they could rally there. The cavalier trench was dug only half as deep as most and was protected by a low parapet, so troops in it would be higher than those in the salient and could fire down on any troops that had captured the salient. The cavalier was tied into the main line on the south and was connected on the north to a labyrinth of communication trenches and defensive traverses. This labyrinth filled much of the ground along the rear of the main line between the salient and the base of the ridge to the north. These trenches offered protected secondary positions in which the defenders could rally if driven from the main line. Even if lightly defended, the maze of ditches would be a serious obstacle to advancing troops. None of this was visible from Federal observation posts.

Along the base of the ridge, the long covered way provided yet another fallback position for troops driven out of the main line. But its primary value was as a protected route for reinforcements. Troops could be assembled behind the crest line, invisible to Federal observation, pass through a tunnel that had been dug under the Plank Road, and reach the northern end of the line without being vulnerable to enemy fire.

Halfway down this long covered way—perhaps two hundred fifty yards behind the salient—a lateral ravine intersected the south side of the covered way at a right angle. This ravine made a natural secondary trenchline, about three hundred yards long—a barrier to any advance, set midway up the slope between the salient and the Plank Road. The sides of the ravine were sloping rather than steep, which meant that a line of troops defending it would have to form where the ground broke downward, and fire from a prone position—not ideal for defense but clearly better than fighting in the open. If an attacking force seized the salient, fire from this ravine could prevent it from using the cavalier trench, which was entirely open to fire from above and behind. Fire from the ravine could also sweep the ground over which any attack through the salient would have to pass.

The natural terrain, as improved by Confederate engineers, made the position a lot stronger than it looked, and the artillery defending it was ample in quantity and was well sited. The weakness of the position was the lack of infantry. Grant's strike at Deep Bottom had drawn all of Lee's mobile reserves to the Richmond lines. It would take most of a day to bring any substantial number of them south, even with the aid of the railroad. To defend against a possible surprise attack, Hoke and Johnson kept almost all their men in or just behind the front lines, with perhaps one regiment from each brigade recuperating from its shift in the lines and available as a local reserve. So the task of providing a reserve for the whole Petersburg front fell to Mahone's Division. Its trench line curved away from the Federals, to provide a margin of safety against a flank attack. Since much of his command was not in immediate contact with the enemy, Mahone could draw two or three brigades out as a mobile reserve. However, the assembly point for that reserve was more than a mile to the south of Elliott's Salient. It would take more than an hour for them to reach the site of any breakthrough.

The five regiments of Elliott's Brigade occupied some four hundred yards of trench line centered on Richard Pegram's battery in the salient. Behind it was the cavalier trench, and then nothing but a small open flat and two hundred yards of naked slope to the shelter of the lateral ravine. The 18th South Carolina defended the battery. On its southern or right flank were the 22nd and 23rd, on its left the 17th and 26th South Carolina. South of Elliott the trenches were held by the Virginia regiments of Wise's Brigade, commanded now by Colonel Goode. Behind Goode's trenches the ground rose slightly, so that troops on it could fire down into

Elliott's sector. Colquitt's Brigade from Hoke's Division had been slotted into the south of Goode's troops, forming a link between the divisions of Mahone and Johnson. North of Elliott's position, some six hundred yards of trench were held by Ransom's North Carolina Brigade, which also belonged to Johnson's Division. The 49th and 25th North Carolina defended the front between Elliott's line and the foot of the Cemetery Hill ridge. Their position was extremely strong: at the top of a slope, partly shielded by the uncut trees in no-man's-land, and backed by the guns of Wright's, Letcher's, and Ellett's batteries. Moreover, their rear area was the maze of intersecting trenches that connected the covered way to the front, from which they could defend themselves against an attack from the flank or even from the rear. However, Ransom too had had to put every one of his regiments into the line, with none to spare for a reserve. Because of the vulnerability of the position, troops were told to maintain exceptional alertness. Lee himself visited the infantry lines on the morning of the twenty-ninth, and was fired on by a sharpshooter.[9]

Moving Up: Evening, July 29, 1864

On the Petersburg front it was business as usual: no heavy bombardments, no reconnaissance raids, just the continual sniping and random bursts of artillery that typically harassed this front. As always the mortar fire was vicious near Wright's battery, and Captain Floyd was relieved when the 18th South Carolina shifted to the trenches around Captain Richard Pegram's battery. Pegram (a cousin of Lieutenant Colonel William Pegram, who commanded the artillery battalion in this sector) believed Douglas's countermining had foiled the Yankees' attempt to blow up his battery. But that did not diminish the possibility of an infantry assault while their forces were thinned, so he gave orders for his gunners to keep watch all night. All three brigades in Johnson's Division were in a state of high alert.[10]

Out on the southern flank, General Mahone was concerned. He had to guard against a possible flank attack and also be prepared to shift units north if the Yankees attacked Johnson's front. Since the twenty-eighth he had been warning his brigadiers to have their men ready to march or fight on short notice. On the evening of the twenty-ninth, with the Petersburg front at its weakest, Mahone ordered the men be called to arms at three in the morning. But the measure was merely precautionary. He saw no sign that a Yankee attack was imminent.[11]

The bland façade maintained by Burnside's troops masked the frenzy of activity behind Federal lines. At army and corps headquarters generals and their staffs were writing and dispatching orders for infantry, artillery, cavalry, and engineers, dealing with the million unanticipated problems and questions such a process generates. North of the James the troops of Hancock and Sheridan were putting the finishing touches on Grant's diversion, marching the same troops round and round to suggest the arrival of reinforcements, while their engineers were covering the pontoon bridges with moss and leaves to muffle the sound of tramping when they marched south that night.

South of IX Corps, Warren was concentrating two divisions to support the left of Burnside's assault. The rest of his corps was spread thin to man the entrenchments protecting the southern flank. Mott's division was preparing to move into the section of trenches next to the Appomattox, on Burnside's right. They would be joined by a brigade of USCT troops from Hinks's division. That would relieve three divisions of the Army of the James to participate in the assault, under the command of General Ord of XVIII Corps. Turner's division of X Corps would join in the attack. Ames's division (XVIII) would defend the reserve trenches around Fort Morton. One brigade of Burnham's division (XVIII) would take over the trenches connecting Burnside's flank with V Corps, and two brigades would garrison a gorge line that ran across the rear of the Horseshoe.

The army's base at City Point, the little peninsula jutting into the James River estuary, was a hive of activity. Supplies were being continuously unloaded from ships at the waterfront and stacked onto wagons or the cars of the United States Military Railroad for shipment to the front. All around the little port were depots jammed with barrels of gunpowder and bullets, pyramids of artillery shells, cartons and kegs of rations, piles of sandbags for fortification—every depot shrinking as it dispensed its goods to the details charged with transporting them to front, where new reserve depots of ammunition and supplies began to accumulate.

Clara Barton landed at City Point with a boatload of medical supplies and found herself in the middle of it all. The hospital she ran was at Point of Rocks, on Ben Butler's side of the Appomattox, and every road between City Point and the Broadway Landing pontoon bridge was clogged with traffic. So she decided to spend the night at the Army of the Potomac's depot hospital, south of the town. In partnership with a host of charitable and service organizations—the U.S. Sanitary Commission, the

Christian Commission, the Masonic Mission, and numerous state relief commissions—the army had constructed a hospital tent city, which at full capacity could care for twelve thousand patients. The hospital for Black soldiers was segregated, but under the supervision of a young woman named Helen Gilson it had become "an object of pride." The tents were close enough to the estuary to sometimes enjoy a breeze, but not today. It was sweltering under the canvas, where nurses and sick or wounded men were plagued by clouds of flies, mosquitoes, and gnats. Outside, the sun was fierce and the air choked with dust from the interminable lines of wagons going by, feeding gunpowder and hardtack to the front. Barton's colleagues told her it was for the big battle tomorrow morning. The news gave her reason for concern about her cousin George Barton, an officer in the 57th Massachusetts. She stayed to help the hospital staff prepare for battle, stocking lint for bandages, renewing their supply of opiates, readying bone saws and knives for use by the surgeons. Twelve thousand beds—in the life of this army there had been several days when that many men had been shot.[12]

Potter's division had been holding the Horseshoe trenches, so they were nearly in their attack positions. After dark Simon Griffin's brigade sidled north to make room for Ledlie's troops on the forward edge of the Horseshoe. The brigade would go forward after Ledlie, in support of his right flank. Zenas Bliss's brigade assembled in the creek bed behind them. Potter would stay close to Pleasants until the mine was fired, to deal immediately with any problems that might arise. Pleasants himself was afire with nervous energy. An operation involving the entire Army of the Potomac depended on his having placed the mine properly, and his ability to fire it at the stated hour. He was confident his mine would work exactly as planned and could not bear the thought of letting the consequent operations go forward without him. He asked Potter to allow him to serve on his staff and carry orders to the front, and Potter agreed. Pleasants's men were equally appreciative when (as reward for their labors) Potter designated them provost guard, which meant they were excused from the attack.

The 6th New Hampshire was resting in the rear after helping the 48th load the mine. They got their orders after supper on the twenty-ninth and "We all knew what it meant. It was an anxious night, and but few closed their eyes at all." Officers and men gathered in small groups to talk things over, like the neighbors and friends they had always been. Several had presentiments of death, including Captain Crossfield, who told

Captain Ela that "he dreaded the coming battle more than he had all the others in which the regiment had been engaged, though he did not know why." The severity of those battles is suggested by the fact that Ela, only a captain, was commanding what was left of the regiment. After dark the 6th marched down the covered way and rejoined Griffin's brigade on the front line. They were joined by their brother regiment, the 9th New Hampshire—fewer than two hundred men, commanded by Captain Hough.[13]

The 31st and 32nd Maine moved up with them. They were rookie regiments but had lost as many men in one year as the 6th had lost in three. They had started with a thousand men each, recruited from the farmers, lumberjacks, stonecutters, and shipwrights of southern Maine. By mid-July the 32nd had "fought itself to death"—it was reduced to two hundred seventy men. The 31st had suffered similar losses. One of its surviving "men" was actually a woman, Mary Brown, who had adopted male disguise in order to serve—one of at least two women hidden in the ranks of IX Corps.[14]

Lieutenant James Chase of the 32nd Maine had no forebodings. He was a farmer's son, seventeen years old, commissioned when he was sixteen. He got sick at the start of the overland campaign and had only been back for a week. He was appalled to see what had happened to the 32nd in the weeks he had been away—three quarters of its people gone, the remnant tired and dirty, wearing worn-out shoes and uniforms. Although his sick leave was valid until August 2, he volunteered to serve before then because he wanted to rejoin his friends and comrades. Up at the front he barely had time to shake hands when a mortar shell killed the lieutenant commanding his platoon. Chase took over the unit, reduced to two sergeants and ten privates. They had been expecting orders to attack since the twenty-eighth, but no special preparations were demanded, so they spent the twenty-ninth picking "graybacks," or lice, out of the seams of their uniforms. That evening, as they marched through the rear area to the entrance of the covered way, Chase noticed the corps surgeons setting up field hospitals in a grove of pines, with "amputating tables" side by side, a row of ambulances, and "a wagon loaded with picks and shovels to bury the dead." The sight did not affect his pleasure at being back with his unit, or his youthful feeling of invulnerability.[15]

Captain Samuel Sims of the 51st New York, Bliss's brigade—George Whitman's friend and colleague—had a more mature understanding of the possibilities, and prepared for them. On the twenty-seventh he had written to his mother:

I wish to assure you all that I am fully conscious of what might happen to me and believe that I can meet *any event* as you would have me. . . . I trust that mercies may still be continued to me. . . . I would like to be in the midst of peace again, that is that the whole country was at peace. For I have the same feeling now as at the start of the war. We have a brave enemy to contend against, and many hope the struggle will be continued yet a long time. I pray not, for the desolation caused is terrible to think of and this campaign *alone* has taken all the "glory hunters" spirit quite out of them.

Having faith in God, who doeth all things well, I remain.

Your affectionate son,
Saml[16]

The mood was darker in Ledlie's division. They had spent less time in the lines than the other White divisions and perhaps for that reason had given less thought to the role they might have to play should the mine be exploded. They were utterly unprepared for the part assigned to them. Worse, officers and men regarded General Ledlie with mistrust and active dislike. Those who had seen Ledlie in action thought him incompetent, unstable, often bizarre—as when he ordered a regimental band to play the same tune round the clock, till the repetition became maddening. On the battlefield his performance had verged on the disgraceful.[17]

When Frank Bartlett returned to the division on July 23 as a newly promoted brigadier general, his colleagues had begged him to step forward as Ledlie's replacement. Bartlett demurred. He thought he should lead a brigade before taking over a division. He had been in a hospital since the second day in the Wilderness, when as colonel of the 57th Massachusetts he had been hit in the head by a spent bullet, which had given him a severe concussion and had permanently damaged his sight. It was the least serious of his wounds. One wrist had been smashed by a bullet at Port Hudson and his leg had been amputated after the battle of Yorktown in 1862. He tried in vain to resist a foreboding of personal disaster, writing to his mother: "You must be prepared to hear the worst of me at any time. God grant it may not come, for your sake, and for the sake of all I love and who love me at home. *But you must be prepared for it.* It is wearing to body and mind, this being constantly under fire." He thought his brigade was in poor physical condition, though its morale seemed solid.[18]

At 3:00 in the afternoon on July 29, Bartlett and his fellow brigade commander, Colonel Elisha Marshall, met with Ledlie and his staff to receive their orders. They were to form after dark and proceed down the covered way to their position in the front line. Marshall's brigade (the 2nd) would lead. It would form in a column of battalions, three lines of four hundred men each. Bartlett's 1st Brigade would take the same formation behind Marshall. When the mine was exploded at 3:15 or 3:30 A.M., they would exit the trenches and seize the Confederate lines to (respectively) the left and the right of the crater. Then they were to defend their lodgment and secure it by digging trench lines to connect their position to the Union main line. The 2nd and 3rd Divisions would come in on their right and left and protect their flanks, and the Colored division would pass through them and attack Cemetery Hill.[19]

Bartlett took the orders as a virtual death sentence. It seemed to him they were called upon to make another of those suicidal frontal assaults. He wrote in his diary, "We storm the works tomorrow at daylight. Our Division leads. I hardly dare hope to live through it. God have mercy." His only regret was that he could not ride his horse and that, stumping about on his cork leg, he would not be able to lead effectively and from the front. But he would give his best and his all, as he always had.[20]

After Bartlett and Marshall left, Ledlie informed his staff that he would not require the officers with volunteer commissions to go forward with the advance. They could remain in the rear, leaving the dangerous work to the staff who had regular commissions. The senior of these, Major Powell, was disgusted by this latest display of Ledlie's lack of professionalism. But Ledlie's personal staff had deflected or covered up reports of his behavior that might have discredited him with Burnside, and this was probably a return of the favor.

What Powell, Marshall, and Bartlett could not know was that the orders Ledlie gave them were not the same as those he had received, verbally and in writing. Burnside had made it plain that the task of storming Cemetery Hill belonged to Ledlie's division, not the Colored division, and that the storming party was to advance as quickly as possible, without waiting for the 2nd and 3rd Divisions to support its flanks. The idea of having engineers connect Ledlie's lodgment to the existing lines had been expressly ruled out by Meade's verbal orders, and Burnside had never suggested the possibility. Ledlie had seized upon one unfortunate phrase in Burnside's written order: that after capturing the positions around the crater the 1st Division should advance on the hill "if possible." Ledlie chose to assume that his troops would have done all they could when they captured the Rebel line, that a further advance would *not* be possible, and that the only logical alternative was for the Colored division to do the job.

It is conceivable that Ledlie never fully understood Burnside's orders, either because he was drunk or because panic diminished his ability
to attend. None of those who left accounts of Ledlie's meetings with
Burnside and with his regimental officers noticed signs of inebriation, but
alcoholics often learn to mask their symptoms, and this was an army in
which hard drinking was a norm. But it seems more likely that Ledlie deliberately falsified his orders to evade the dangers inherent in his assignment, and explained them to his officers in a way that gave a plausible
rationale to their assignment. Whatever the reason, Ledlie's actions were
a criminal dereliction of duty, which would have a crippling effect on the
entire operation.[21]

HANGING FIRE: UNION LINES, 10:00 P.M.–3:30 A.M.

Unlike the other divisions of IX Corps, the officers and men of the 4th Division were prepared to carry out the tactical plan of the operation and
were eager to get at it.

Thomas's brigade had been on fatigue duty of various kinds, including the digging of trenches to protect the army's southern flank. To keep
up their fighting edge, Major Rockwood of the 19th had used the occasion to drill his men in clambering out of a trench and forming a battle
line. With the rest of the brigade, they were recalled on the afternoon of
the twenty-ninth and assembled behind Fort Morton in the early evening.

In the bivouac of the 29th USCT, Colonel John Bross prepared for
battle by having his servant shave off his full beard, leaving only the twin
scallops of whisker that were Burnside's trademark. He unwrapped the
full dress uniform of a lieutenant colonel of infantry, which he had just received from home: dark blue frock coat bound with a yellow sash, the
lower sleeves ornamented with a triple loop of gold braid, gold epaulets
with twin oak leaves, a black hat wound with braid and the gold bugle of
the infantry on the front of the crown. He would command from the front,
and meant to be instantly recognizable to any man in his or any other regiment as a figure to heed and follow. Perhaps he hoped that some would
mistake him for Burnside—soldiers usually responded well when they
saw high commanders leading the charge. But of course he was also making himself a preferred target for Rebel marksmen.

His one concern was that the regiment had still not received its full
complement of men or, more important, of officers. Four would-be lieutenants had been at his headquarters for weeks, waiting for commissions
that were interminably delayed. To Bross's profound satisfaction, all four

agreed to serve in the battle, although their unofficial status might create serious problems for them should they be captured.[22]

Sigfried's brigade had been up on the line, manning the trenches and performing picket duty, and was withdrawn to the railroad cut on the afternoon of the twenty-ninth. There Colonel Bates of the 30th USCT finally explained to his junior officers the reason for their intensive drilling out in the Second Swamp. They had been selected to lead the assault on Cemetery Hill at three the next morning, and "it is hoped and expected that Petersburg will be captured." He had kept the mission secret to protect its security, and he now told them that "The information that I have given you you will keep to yourselves." Captain Smith, who had suspected something like this was in the wind, told Lieutenant Bowley, "We are to lead, and we will catch the butt end of it." The two exchanged the addresses of their families, to be notified if "anything happens," but Bowley was eager for action and "ate supper with my usual relish."[23]

Bates divided the regiment into two-company divisions, assigned commanders, and told them to keep their men moving and to "shoot any man who leaves the line." The company officers then told their men that the hour was at hand for which they had prepared, "each giving words of advice and encouragement according to his idea." Bowley liked the spirit in which his men took the news. When one soldier complained about carrying so many cartridges and wished he had a chance to shoot 'em off or a mule to tote 'em, his friend replied "Reckon yo'll git all de chance yo' wants." Other officers roused the temper of their troops by admonishing them to " 'Remember Fort Pillow,' and not to give up or surrender under any circumstances, for it would mean sure death, as no quarter could be expected from the rebel soldiers." Similar advice was given in other regiments.

Bates knew that his men would look to their preachers and men of eloquence at such a moment, and he wandered through his camp to listen. A sergeant from the Eastern Shore was exhorting his men. This was going to be a great fight, he told them, the greatest they had ever seen. If they took Petersburg, most likely they'd take Richmond, destroy "Mars Gin'ul Lee's big army" and end the war. So every man was admonished to lift himself up in prayer for a strong heart and, as brethren, to remember the poor Colored folks in bondage. Then he reverted from preacher to sergeant. Generals Grant, Burnside, and Meade would be watching them, and *he* would have his eye on them, and the first "nigger" that goes "projeckin' " would get *this* bayonet in him, "'Fore Gawd." Bates thought "such speeches as these from men of their own color were perhaps of more practical value to the common soldier than all that was said by the officers."

> But, be this as it may, every man in the 30th U.S.C.T., both white and colored, felt that a great event for the 4th Division of the Ninth Army Corps was near at hand and that the results of the coming fight would either place the colored troops side by side with their comrades of lighter hue, or else they would never again be given such responsibilities as were now before them.[24]

The men turned in to get as much sleep as possible before the expected summons at three in the morning, and Thomas and Sigfried went to division headquarters to get their orders. They were pleasantly surprised to see General Ferrero back in command. But what Ferrero told them was a terrible disappointment: the division would wait in the rear rather than lead the attack. Beyond that, Ferrero had little guidance for them. He himself was disoriented by the rapid turn of events, having been restored to command only hours earlier, and having missed (or been left out of) Burnside's conference with division commanders.

Thomas returned to the bivouac "dejected and with an instinct of disaster for the morrow." He summoned his regimental commanders to give them the news, and saw his own emotions mirrored in their faces. But he told them not to wake the line officers—let them have their rest. Sigfried said nothing to anyone, thinking it pointless to disrupt his officers' sleep merely "to be informed of what would do them no service."[25]

❧

Just before midnight, Ledlie's troops drew extra ammunition and rations for three days and began moving silently down the covered way. These zigzag trenches were more than a thousand feet long, and the men moved down them slowly, in long columns four abreast. The heat was stifling even in the dark. There was a three-quarters waning moon that set shortly after midnight. After that it was pitch-dark. Marshall's brigade filed into the section of the front line directly opposite Elliott's Salient. Marshall was a West Pointer, class of 1850, with ten years' service in the Regulars, mainly on the Western frontier. He had used hard discipline to make infantrymen out of the 14th New York Heavy Artillery (NYHA), whose men frankly complained that that was *not* what they had enlisted for. He formed his men in three lines, with the 2nd Pennsylvania Provisional

Heavy Artillery (PPHA) in the front, the 14th NYHA behind it, and two small infantry regiments (3rd Maryland and 179th New York) in the rear. Bartlett's 1st Brigade crowded in behind them. To improve his tactical control, Bartlett divided the brigade into wings. The right, under Colonel Gould (29th, 57th, and 59th Massachusetts), was packed in alongside the two small regiments in Marshall's third line. The left wing (100th Pennsylvania, 56th and 21st Massachusetts), commanded by Colonel Stephen Weld, formed outside the trench, right behind the 179th New York.[26]

The trench was packed tight. Men stood or sat in ranks on the firing step or the mud floor of the trench to wait for morning. Talk was hushed so Rebel pickets would not be alerted to the concentration building in front of them. The mood was morose and anxious. Colonel Weld thought "the officers and men were disappointed and discouraged at having to lead, as we had heard all along that the negroes were to do this, and we had no confidence in Ledlie." They knew enough about the mine to know they were right next to it. Word had got out about the colossal powder charge Burnside had asked for, and there seemed every reason to think that when the mine blew, it would drop the remains of the Rebel fort right onto their heads. The 57th Massachusetts was close to the mine head, and the men took note of Colonel Pleasants's pacing up and down or climbing the parapet to gaze across at the fort, continually checking his pocket watch. They resented him as the man whose headstrong pursuit of this project had doomed them to face this moment. As a unit, they were close to unraveling—fewer than a hundred left to stand in line, and their officers radiating pessimism. Major Albert Prescott, their commander, worried obsessively about the suffering and hardship his family would face if he should be killed, a concern universal enough to draw most of the regiment's survivors into gloomy sympathy.[27]

At around 2:30 A.M., Colonel Loring of Burnside's staff joined Ledlie outside a bombproof near the mouth of the south covered way. Until the previous afternoon, Loring had assumed he would go in with Ferrero's troops, with whom he had been working. Since then he had been totally engaged by headquarters business. So he was unaware of the way in which Ledlie had altered Burnside's orders and did not know how Ledlie had instructed his brigadiers.

In the moonless dark no one noticed that no ladders or sandbag stairs had been provided for them to climb out of the six- to eight-feet-deep trench, over the top of the parapet, and into no-man's-land. Burnside's staff should have ordered it done by the engineers. Failing that, Ledlie's staff or the brigade commanders themselves ought to have noticed and made sure of it. But this assignment had fallen to them without warning, at the last minute, and their attention was absorbed by the rush of orders and preparations for moving up. By now it was 2:45 A.M.—it had taken more than three hours to get into position, and the explosion was to take place in forty-five minutes.[28]

⌘

Over on the Confederate side of the lines, staff officers in Lee's headquarters were awake, monitoring developments on the Richmond front. Lee had begun to suspect that Hancock's move was a feint. At 2:00 A.M. on July 30 he issued a warning to all headquarters on the Petersburg front to expect an attack as early as the following morning.[29]

⌘

Willcox's division had to wait for Ledlie's men to pass before they could follow them down the covered way. The 20th Michigan and 1st Michigan Sharpshooters had been picketing the army's southern flank, and their supper was interrupted by Burnside's order. After a four-hour march they reached the assembly zone and were told to get some rest, but few did. "Troops were moving all about us, and artillery was rumbling past, going into position." Lieutenant Colonel Cutcheon was wakeful, the "probable moments of life seemed too short to be wasted in sleep." He ordered the cooks to prepare coffee for the men and bring it forward at daylight.

Attached to his brigade was a battalion of the 1st Michigan Sharpshooters, expert marksmen specially trained as scouts and snipers. Among their ranks was a company of Native Americans, recruited from the Ottawa, Chippewa, and other Native American tribes of the Upper Peninsula. These tribes had fought against the "Big Knives" in every frontier war from Pontiac's Rebellion (1763) to the War of 1812. The government had taken most of their land and had tried to remove them to the Indian Territory. Yet they responded readily to the recruiting efforts of a young Ottawa leader named Garrett Gravaert, described as "an educated half-breed." In their poverty the prospect of a substantial cash bounty undoubtedly appealed to them, but they were also moved by tribal interest. An 1855 treaty had broken their reservation up into private holdings, and by 1861 a number of Ottawa communities had been reorganized as regular townships, whose people were voting citizens of the state. Yet they remained Ottawa, and wanted to renegotiate the 1855 treaty so they could maintain tribal control of their counties. Their leaders promoted enlistment in the Sharpshooters, hoping to influence Federal negotiators by a display of loyalty. Though their political concerns were unique to their situation as Native Americans, they repeated a pattern common in the North. They were willing to fight for the Union because they saw participation in democratic politics as their best hope for achieving security and justice. The Indian company had fought with extraordinary valor in the Wilderness, at Spotsylvania, and in the June 15–18 assaults on Petersburg, suffering heavy casualties. Among them was Lieutenant Garrett Gravaert, mortally wounded, and his father, Sergeant Henry Gravaert, killed outright. Now the Sharpshooters made their own special preparations for battle, following tribal custom even though most were Christians.[30]

Willcox's 1st Brigade was commanded by Colonel John Hartranft, his 2nd by Colonel William Humphrey. Hartranft was an engineer and a lawyer, and Humphrey a Michigan businessman, but both were veterans of combat command. The explosion was scheduled for 3:30, and it was nearly that time when Hartranft's men started down the covered way. Humphrey's brigade didn't move till sometime between 3:30 and 4:00 A.M. The entrance to the covered way was behind the ridge on which Fort Morton sat. In the lee of that ridge Colonel Cutcheon of the 20th Michigan saw the men of the Colored division waking to their breakfast, and beyond them the camp of Turner's division from X Corps. These two divisions were reserves for the assault, but neither was ready for deployment.[31]

∽

In the railroad cut, Sigfried's brigade was roused from sleep for the movement to its assembly point. Lieutenant Bowley thought the Rebels were preternaturally alert: although his men counted off in whispers, they drew fire from Rebel pickets, which grew to a brief artillery exchange. The outfit hunkered down to wait it out and promptly fell asleep. By 3:00 A.M. it was quiet again, and the brigade filed back through the covered way to the rear of Fort Morton, where they unrolled their blankets again and tried to get some sleep. No one thought it odd that the brigade slated to lead the attack should be moving farther to the rear. The army's ways were often inexplicable.[32]

∽

General Meade and the army staff had arrived at the vacated tents of Burnside's Shand house headquarters at around 2:30 A.M. and made their arrangements by lantern light. It was thick dark—so much so that at 3:20 A.M. Meade telegraphed Burnside: "As it is still so dark, the commanding general says you can postpone firing the mine if you think proper." Burnside's response came almost instantly: "The mine will be fired at the time designated. My headquarters will be at the 14-gun battery." So the telegraphic connection was working, and Burnside was in place. Another ten or fifteen minutes and they would all get to see the elephant.

In the meantime there was always a tremendous amount of work to be done by the army staff, concerned not just with this operation but with the maintenance and supply of eighty or ninety thousand men and at least that many horses. When 3:30 came and went, there was not much concern: the burning of fuse cord in a damp cave could hardly be timed to the tick.[33]

⌾

At 3:00 A.M. Colonel Pleasants was at the mine head with Lieutenant Jacob Douty and Sergeant Harry "Snapper" Reese, ready to light the fuses. Although the 48th had been excused from the attack, many men found reasons to come see for themselves the result of their hard work. Pleasants estimated that his triple line of fuse would take about fifteen minutes to reach the powder chambers in the lateral galleries. The sky was still black—it was scarcely darker in the mine shaft than in the ravine where they waited. The three men lit candle lamps and crouched their way down the tunnel. The fuse ends were some four hundred feet in. Ninety feet of fusing ran on the open floor of the mine and then entered the tubing that carried it through the thirty feet of piled sandbags with which the mine was tamped. There were several splices in the exposed fuse, and every one was a potential break. Pleasants had used the longer lengths in the buried portions, to minimize the number of splices there. At 3:15, Pleasants struck a match and lit the fuses, and the ignition sputtered and sparked toward the mouth of the tamp while the three men scurried in the opposite direction.

Out in the open air again, Pleasants and his team waited at the mine head and steeled themselves for the blast that had to be imminent. Pleasants kept climbing up the embankment above the mine head to stare impatiently at the Rebel fort, whose low dark hump emerged from the shadows as the sky began to lighten in the east. The minute hand of Pleasants's watch ticked past the half hour, and the screw of expectation took a twist . . . but still the silence held.

A miscalculation of five minutes in the burning of the fuse would not have been extraordinary. But then it was ten, and then it was fifteen minutes, and still dead silence, and the growing fear that all three fuses had gone dead. Most likely the fire had sputtered out at one of the many splices, or at a section made sodden by some new rain-fed spring or by the general dampness of the mine. If the fire had stopped before reaching the tamp, a man could go down and relight it. If it had stopped inside the tamp, they would have to dismantle the sandbag barrier to get at it— impossible to do in time for a morning attack.

The third possibility was that the fire was still fooling slowly along dampened fuse cord, and if a man went down to relight it, it would blow the powder and bury him body and soul under twenty feet of red clay.

So Pleasants held off until he was sure as a man could be that the fuse was dead. By then it was 4:15 A.M. and the sun was spoiling the night sky behind them. Harry Reese wanted the job of relighting the fuse: his proprietary feeling for the mine was as intense as Pleasants's. He lit the lamp in his cap and went down. Lieutenant Douty noticed Reese had forgotten to take extra fuse, in case he had to make a splice, so he grabbed a coil and ducked in after him.[34]

⸺✺⸺

General Burnside had shifted his headquarters at midnight, to the bombproof in the rear of Fort Morton. A line of horses was picketed nearby, for the use of staff officers, aides, and dispatch bearers. Operators sat by their telegraph keys at a long plank table, linked by separate lines to Warren's headquarters (a mile or two south) and to Meade at their old camp near the Shand house.

All around him Burnside could hear the shuffling of his troops filing up to the lines; he would have them all in position and ready to go right on schedule. He had brushed off Meade's suggestion that he postpone the attack till it was lighter. Meade had meddled enough. Burnside was going to keep to his schedule. It would have been strange if he had not left his headquarters and gone up to the battery to peer through the embrasure at Elliott's Salient, now a darker blot on dark ground, but soon—in ten minutes, more or less—it would erupt in a fireball of Burnside's making, and his battle would be on.

But the clock ticked on, the night paled, and the silent shape of the salient began to take on a solid, permanent look. At four o'clock he knew the wait was far too long. He summoned his aide, Major Van Buren, and told him to get down to Pleasants and see what the trouble was.

The movement of Willcox's brigades was painfully slow, four thousand armed men shuffling in an extended line along a deep and winding ditch whose walls and parapets rose well above their heads. By 4:00 A.M. Colonel Cutcheon of the 20th Michigan, at the head of Humphrey's brigade, had gotten only to the mouth of the southern covered way, the point where it debouched into the low ground of Taylor's Creek, a few hundred feet behind the main line. In the far bank, to the right of the covered way, a bombproof shelter had been dug. It was the size of an ordinary sitting room and had a table and chairs, and had seemingly been a regimental command post. Dr. O. C. Chubb, regimental surgeon of the 20th, commandeered the place for an aid station and had his assistants prepare the table for his use. Then he joined Cutcheon at the mouth of the covered way. From that point they could see in the growing light the dark streak of the Rebel line and the prominent bulge of the salient.[35]

Cutcheon checked his watch. It was after 4:00 A.M. Wasn't the explosion supposed to have gone off before this?

All in all, seventeen thousand infantry were waiting to make the assault: anxious in the predawn, dirty and unwashed, smelly, grouchy with sleeplessness, gut-griped from bad food and dirty water and fear. In Ledlie's close-packed line, the delay only screwed the tension tighter, adding to the men's sense that things were going wrong, proof that being put in this spot was the first of many deadly foul-ups to come. It was bad enough thinking the mine might blow you up with the Rebels—worse to realize that if it didn't blow up, you'd be charging forts with your bayonet again.

But seventeen-year-old Lieutenant Chase, with the 32nd Maine in Potter's division, took the delay with a teenager's careless good humor. He lay down in the brush of the creek bed just behind the front line, closed his eyes, and in a moment was fast asleep.[36]

⁓

At 4:15 A.M. Meade's anxiety kicked in. Time was passing; there was no sound from the front and no word either; the telegraph was silent. Meade's temper had a hair trigger and it was ready to fire. He told the telegraphers to wire Burnside, "Is there any difficulty in exploding the mine? It is now three quarters of an hour later than that fixed upon for exploding it."

The telegraph was silent. Line broken? Burnside away from his post?

Burnside hiding the fact that once again there had been a foul-up in his department? Meade snapped another question and set the telegraph clicking, "Is General Burnside at his headquarters? The commanding general is anxious to learn the cause of the delay."

Not a chirp from the telegraph. Wasn't anybody listening at Burnside's? It was 4:29 A.M. Meade had eight divisions concentrated for a stroke against a Rebel front weakened by the dispatch of reserves to the north side. They had labored hard to create this opportunity; they had to use it or lose it. "Major General Burnside: If the mine cannot be exploded, something else must be done, and at once. The commanding general is awaiting to hear from you before determining." If the mine was a fizzle, his assault would be desperate at best, head-on against fortifications. But worse yet would be to order the assault and have Burnside's mine blow up in the middle of it.

He waited six minutes by the clock and then telegraphed again: "The commanding general directs that, if your mine has failed, you make an assault at once, opening your batteries." The telegraph might never have been invented, for all the good it was doing. Meade's staff went about as if walking on eggshells. If the mine didn't blow up, their general surely would.[37]

In the depth of the mine, Reese found the break in the fuse at a splice some thirty feet from the tamp. He and Douty relit the triple fuse line, made sure it was burning strongly, and then began their four-hundred-foot scramble back to the open air. It was after 4:35 A.M. Pleasants sent Burnside his prediction that the mine would blow in ten or twelve minutes.

At Burnside's headquarters the telegraph was rattling off Meade's messages, each more demanding than the last, but Burnside would not answer them. His rationale for silence, at first, was that he did not know what had gone wrong, and would not until Major Van Buren returned. But after his aide brought the news about the fuse break, he clung to the idea that he need not answer until he knew something *definite:* that is, until he could tell Meade that the mine would explode according to plan. He could not bring himself to admit the possibility that it might not succeed.

When Pleasants reported the fuse relit, Burnside still did not respond. Perhaps he was afraid that something else might go wrong. The mine had to speak for him.

⌒

The 4th Division was roused in the pitch-dark of 3:00 A.M.—no drums or bugles that might alert the Rebels, just the sergeants and corporals going from tent to tent to rouse them with harsh whispers. They squatted by their tents in the hot darkness for a breakfast of hardtack crackers and raw salt pork, washed down with warm water or cold black coffee. Colonel Thomas and his staff dined apart but on the same dry, salty, greasy fare. The staff were Thomas's friends as well as his associates, especially Captain Marshall Dempcy and Lieutenant Christopher Pennell—the latter a young man, not yet twenty, "the only child of an old Massachusetts clergyman, and to me as Jonathan was to David." Thomas had a jar of cucumber pickles, which he shared round the circle. "They were gratefully accepted, for nothing cuts the fat of raw salt pork like a pickle." Troops were supposed to receive a regular issue of pickles, as a preventive for scurvy rather than a mere grease cutter, but the Colored troops received only one issue in their whole time of service. The pleasure that men took in that sharp, acidic tang was extraordinary—it stood out from the monotony and vileness of their normal diet. Colonel Bates of the 30th USCT would remember vividly, thirty years later, how delicious they were.[38]

Word of the change in plans was now passed to the company officers and filtered down from junior officers to the sergeants to the men. Captain Rickard of the 19th remembered, "We were terribly disappointed . . . officers and men." But whatever their role was to be, they had to prepare themselves to face the life-or-death matter of battle. Like their comrades throughout the army, the prospect made them reach for the consolation of religion and take thought for the families they'd left behind. In the 28th, man after man came up to Chaplain Garland White, asking the preacher to convey his last thoughts to loved ones, to tell his people he "died like a man," and "when pay-day comes, if it ever does come, send what money is due to my wife, and tell her to raise [our children] in the fear of the Lord."[39]

While Sigfried's troops were breakfasting, the brigade commander went round to his regimental commanders to give them personally the bad news he had received the previous night—and to square them away for the business at hand. He told Colonel Hall to assemble his 43rd regiment under arms at the entrance of the covered way, "ready to advance when I order you forward." To avoid accidents when the close-packed men jostled down the covered way, they did not fix bayonets, and their rifle-muskets were loaded but without setting the percussion caps. Hall gathered his officers and briefly repeated the orders. In keeping with the professional tone he sought to instill in his command, he made no emotional appeal: "Gentlemen, we have a little work to do this morning. I hope every man will do his duty. Good morning, gentlemen." The officers called their men into ranks, checked their equipment, marched them to the entrance of the covered way . . . and then ordered them at ease. Humphrey's brigade of Willcox's division was still backed up in the long zigzag trench.

While they waited, Lieutenant Shedd of brigade staff came by to repeat Sigfried's orders, "with unusual care, knowing that the Forty-third was leading the division." They were to move down the covered way "by the flank": the two lines in which the regiment formed would simply right-face and march down the covered way as a column of twos. In that formation they would pass out of the works and through the breach in the enemy lines. The formation would allow them to slip through narrow passages, like the covered way before them and some unknown but probably narrow breach in the trenches beyond.

As they got over the shock of their disappointment, they began to be concerned that something had gone wrong with the operation. The officers were all aware that the mine had been scheduled to explode at 3:30 or 3:45 A.M. It was now nearly five o'clock, and aside from the scuffle of boots and the rustle of clothing as their troops shifted about, the world was silent.

Then they felt "one or two slight motions of the earth, something like a heavy swell at sea," and heard "a dull heavy thud, not at all startling; it was a heavy, smothered sound, not nearly so distinct as a musket-shot."[40]

Part Four

~⚜~

THE BATTLE OF
THE CRATER

JULY 30, 1864

Chapter 10

Into the Breach

4:45–7:30 A.M.

A t approximately 4:45 A.M. the gunners on watch in Captain Richard Pegram's battery were sitting on the gun carriages or standing
about on the planking of the battery floor thinking about breakfast. The
sun rising behind the Yankee lines threw the shade of the parapet over
them, a temporary stay against the mounting heat. In the trenches to either side, the infantrymen of the 18th South Carolina were spaced out
along the trench line, one man every eight feet, some standing on the fire
step to draw a bead on the Yankee lines, others sitting on it leaning back
against the trench wall, catching a few winks.

Down in their bombproof Lieutenants Pursley and Jackson were just
getting to sleep after a duty shift.

The ground under them . . . bumped.

"The first jar I thought it was a boom had lit on my little boom-
proof," Pursley recalled, then Jackson "hollowed at me to get out" and
both jumped for the entry—

And in the next instant the earth cracked apart and let loose a terrible
uprush all afire in which dozens of lives blinked and disappeared, dismembered in the blast or strangled by the out-suck of air or hammered to
death by concussion or crushed by timbers or stifled in a monsoon downpour of dust. The 18th South Carolina was nearly obliterated along with
three companies of the 22nd; most of Pegram's gunners were killed and
their cannons were hurled skyward end over end.

Twenty feet below their boots, the fuses lit by Sergeant Reese had
touched off the troughs of gunpowder in the galleries, flashing simultane-

ous fire into the magazines and exploding four tons of black powder in the narrow confines of the mine. The blast hammered the containing walls, sending shock waves down against the impregnable planet and out into the immovable strata to every side, the blast able to release upward only, where a mere twenty feet of hard red clay lay between it and the sky.

The earth heaved to a shock so powerful that Captain Houghton of the 14th NYHA, sitting on a fire step in the Union line one hundred yards away, was "violently lifted to [his] feet," and saw through a loophole how "the earth along the enemy's lines opened, and fire and smoke shot upward." Colonel Cutcheon of the 20th Michigan, standing near the mouth of the south covered way two hundred yards from the salient, felt "a deep shock and tremor of the earth and a jar like an earthquake," and as he watched, there seemed to be "a heaving and a lifting of the [Rebel] fort and the hill on which it stood; then a monstrous tongue of flame shot fully two hundred feet into the air, followed by a vast volume of white smoke," like the blast from the mouth of a colossal cannon. Right through the flame and smoke, "a great spout or fountain of red earth rose to a great height, mingled with men and guns, timbers and planks, and every kind of debris, all ascending, spreading, whirling." General de Trobriand of Mott's II Corps division, watching from his trench line less than half a mile north, saw spring into the sky "an enormous mass . . . without form or shape, full of red flames, and carried on a bed of lightning flashes, . . . with a detonation of thunder." It bulged at the top and curled over like "an immense mushroom whose stem seemed to be of fire and its head of smoke."

The mushroom cloud peaked and lapsed, and collapsed earthward in a rain of earth, boulders, beams of wood, human bodies, and body parts "scattering and falling with great concussions to the earth once more." Two of Pegram's four cannons dropped out of the sky into no-man's-land, to lie on their backs with their broken wheels in the air. Great boulders of compacted clay, ranging in mass from the size of a privy to that of a small house, fell out of the huge cloud of dust and white powder smoke that cascaded out of the sky and rolled outward along the ground. With scientific detachment General de Trobriand noted that the white gun smoke, being lighter, tended to lift off while the dust drifted slowly down toward the earth.[1]

Under that cloud Ledlie's men in the front line were reeling from the eruption of a nightmare. The troops had been unprepared for the power

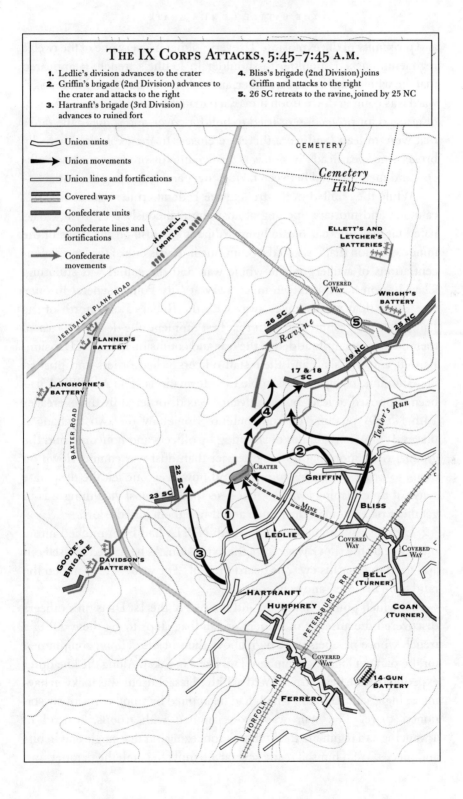

THE IX CORPS ATTACKS, 5:45–7:45 A.M.

1. Ledlie's division advances to the crater
2. Griffin's brigade (2nd Division) advances to the crater and attacks to the right
3. Hartranft's brigade (3rd Division) advances to ruined fort
4. Bliss's brigade (2nd Division) joins Griffin and attacks to the right
5. 26 SC retreats to the ravine, joined by 25 NC

Union units
Union movements
Union lines and fortifications
Covered ways
Confederate units
Confederate lines and fortifications
Confederate movements

CEMETERY

Cemetery Hill

ELLETT'S AND LETCHER'S BATTERIES

HASKELL (MORTARS)

COVERED WAY

WRIGHT'S BATTERY

JERUSALEM PLANK ROAD

26 SC

Ravine

25 NC

FLANNER'S BATTERY

17 & 18 SC

49 NC

Taylor's Run

LANGHORNE'S BATTERY

BAXTER ROAD

4

22 SC

2

23 SC

CRATER

GRIFFIN

1

MINE

BLISS

3

LEDLIE

COVERED WAY

COVERED WAY

GOODE'S BRIGADE

DAVIDSON'S BATTERY

BELL (TURNER)

COAN (TURNER)

HARTRANFT

HUMPHREY

PETERSBURG R.R.

14-GUN BATTERY

COVERED WAY

NORFOLK AND

FERRERO

and proximity of the explosion. To every soldier in every one of the twelve regiments packed shoulder-to-shoulder in Ledlie's trench, it appeared that the whole mass of earth, timber, and debris that had been blasted skyward was coming down upon him. Each man reflexively ducked, dodged, or cringed for protection or tried to bolt for cover, and some of the ranks that were to lead (and were therefore closest to the explosion) actually broke. The spearhead division was thrown into disorder as confused officers and men wavered between taking cover and launching their attack.[2]

While they milled in the trench, the Federal artillery cut loose, 144 cannons and mortars opening almost simultaneously onto their designated targets, the roar of the bombardment so close on the heels of the mine explosion that it seemed to continue it. It was one of the largest concentrations of artillery in the whole war, and the sound was stunning. Clara Barton heard it fifteen miles away at City Point. General Rooney Lee, more than twenty miles away with the Rebel cavalry north of the James, felt the ground shake. In that first moment, the deafening roar of their own guns simply added to the fear and confusion in the 1st Division. Bartlett and Marshall and their staff officers yelled orders and pushed men into line, trying to reassemble their formations. The 2nd PPHA had been supposed to lead, but its advance was disordered by the overeager 14th NYHA pushing in from behind. Somehow the two exchanged places. It took ten minutes of shouting by officers and noncoms, and the gradual realization that nothing heavier than dust was coming down on them, to bring the troops to order, and now everyone felt the desperate sense of time rushing away, so that it seemed the most vital thing was to get these people out of the trench and throw them into the fort.

Lieutenant Thompson of the 14th NYHA had been pitched into a mud hole by the shock wave from the explosion. As he hauled himself out and tried to clear his eyes, he heard the call "Forward!" He "scraped the mud from his eyes" and echoed the cry. . . .

At which point Thompson and the rest of the 1st Division's officers discovered the absence of ladders or sandbag steps to get them out of a trench whose parapets were high above their heads. Thompson jumped for the parapet logs and clambered up like a monkey. Along the line other expedients were being tried. Weld's 56th Massachusetts was lucky in having a single sandbag stair, which had been piled by troops previously stationed there. The stair was soon jammed with troops. Instead of advancing as a regiment, the 56th was squeezing out that single exit in bits and pieces. Weld himself made several attempts to climb the parapet, and was unable to get out. Some of the troops made steps by sticking the fixed bayonets on their rifles into the trench wall and bracing the rifle stock against a hip or on a shoulder. Those who got up first reached down to haul other men up beside them. That's what Captain Houghton of the 14th NYHA was engaged in when Colonel Marshall—standing below him in the trench—called up the order for Houghton to go forward. Houghton got hold of his color guard, hollered for his men to form on him, and as soon as he had gathered a bunch started across the field. To his right other clots and clumps of soldiers were also going forward, some following flags or officers with swords, some running at random. With the Rebel line in sight and no hostile fire, they saw clear victory and gave a shout so loud that officers in V Corps a half-mile away heard it over the roar of the cannonade.[3]

At Meade's headquarters a mile behind the front, General Grant was checking his watch, impatient at the delay, and "had just returned it to his pocket when suddenly there was a shock like that of an earthquake, accompanied by a dull, muffled roar" and a dark cloud rose into the sky. From this distance the sight was impressive rather than terrifying, informing the educated eyes of the staff that the explosion had been sizeable. They took one look at the spectacle and then jumped to the real business of the day, the management of a major assault that—if it continued to go as well as this—might ultimately involve the whole army.

After twenty minutes or so, Grant decided to ride over to Burnside's and see how things looked from that vantage point. He and his aide Horace Porter mounted their horses and jogged up the road toward the front. Then they swung south to pass through the reserve area to reach Burnside's headquarters behind Fort Morton.[4]

⚬⚬⚬

The earth jolt rocked Sergeant William Russell of the 26th Virginia, Wise's Brigade, where he stood on the fire step of his breastwork slightly more than one hundred yards to the south. In a Louisiana battery a hundred yards farther south, Lieutenant Henry Eugene Levy felt the earth "throb beneath our feet and, a moment after, as if a volcano had burst from the bowels of the land (200 yds to my left), men, spades, wheels, logs, vast boulders of earth and an indescribable debris obscured the rising sun." As he stared in horror, the Federal barrage opened, shell fire erupted all around, and Levy went down with a shrapnel wound. Watchers in Ransom's Brigade, two hundred yards to the north, could clearly distinguish one of the brass Napoléon cannons and the body of a man among the wreckage tumbling through the air, and then saw it all coming roaring down into the smoking crater below.[5]

⸙

The Confederate soldiers in the heart of the explosion saw nothing, were torn loose and thrown about or were overwhelmed by noise and the downfall of dust and debris. The blast blew Lieutenant Pursley out of the trench and into the air, "God only knows how high it sent me. I spread out my wings to see if I could fly but the first thing I knowed I was lying on top of the works." An artilleryman who had been standing by his gun, one foot up on the wheel hub, was also thrown skyward, but landed in a pit and was half-buried under a deluge of clay dust. Another man was hurled out into no-man's-land but was somehow unhurt. He managed to get up and scramble back to his own lines before the enemy advanced. Lieutenant Greer and Sergeant Hill of the 18th South Carolina never had a chance to get out of their bombproof: the shock brought the roof down around them and sealed the entry, and as soon as they realized they were not going to be crushed to death, they were overwhelmed by the horror of knowing themselves buried alive. Greer had a bayonet and began chopping and digging toward where the entry had been, while Hill pushed the loosened earth away. They had one canteen of water, it was blind dark, and the air they drank was suffocating with dust and liable to run out. The Lake brothers, a captain and a lieutenant, were in worse shape: buried one on top of the other, the lieutenant with a broken leg. Most of the 18th South Carolina, a third of the 22nd, three companies of the 23rd, and one company of the 17th were killed outright—278 men torn apart, suffocated, crushed.[6]

In the units of Elliott's Brigade immediately to the right and left, the men were "filled with consternation at the terrible calamity and awful destruction caused by this, to them, new mode of warfare. Some, partly stunned, and others who had been partly buried or tossed about by the explosion, came rushing down the line covered with earth and wild with fright." Lieutenant Moss of the 17th bolted out of his bombproof without boots or uniform coat and ran all the way down to Ransom's Brigade before he realized what he was doing, pulled himself together, and returned to his company. But the panic among Elliott's men was relatively short-lived. Colonel McMaster of the 17th quickly got out of his bombproof and rallied his troops. The 26th South Carolina, next in line to the north, was entirely unharmed and already manning the loops in the breastworks.

General Stephen Elliott had been asleep in a bombproof behind the position held by the 26th South Carolina, but he quickly recognized what had happened. Measures for dealing with a mine explosion on his front had been prepared by General Beauregard. Elliott's orders were to rally his men in the gorge line across the base of the salient, hold it against Federal assault, and mount a counterattack to retake the salient if it fell. He sent one aide to summon the colonels of the 17th, 18th, and 26th regiments and another to guard the entry to the long covered way toward which many of his men were fleeing. Elliott himself went down to the gorge line to rally troops, but there were almost none to be found. His frustration was extreme: there were not a Yankee in sight, he was standing on the very ground he was supposed to defend, but the men had run off. His judgment that his brigade was second-rate, and his officers worse than that, was confirmed.

Then he heard the Yankees cheer as they came charging through the dust cloud. He stormed off to the trenches north of the crater—he would build a force around the undamaged 26th regiment, move it into position, and counterattack.[7]

THE BREACH, 5:00–5:40 A.M.

The first wave of Ledlie's troops scrambled out of their trenches in small bunches whose separate elements immediately rushed to get across the deadly ground of no-man's-land, not pausing to form a disciplined battle line, not waiting for officers to direct them to the specific positions they were supposed to seize. The air was still thick with a choking fog of dry dust and bitter powder fumes that partially blinded the advancing troops, but also concealed them. Out beyond their flanks, Confederate infantry had begun to shoot into the cloud. The firing was blind, but Colonel Weld found it hot enough as the bullets kicked up dust around his feet.[8]

No-man's-land was littered with large clay boulders and two of Pegram's four brass Napoléon cannons, blown bodily out of the battery and dropped between the lines. The advance was partly blocked by the half-wrecked tangles of Union abatis (which Burnside had refused to clear) and by Confederate chevaux-de-frise—racks of sharpened stakes tied to each other by wire. Colonel Marshall and a detail cut the wires and swung the racks aside to let his men through. Behind them Bartlett's troops were advancing in the same disordered rush, Bartlett limping painfully on his cork leg across the broken ground. The soldiers were exhilarated now by the success of the mine, rushing so fast to catch their victory they would not wait to form but swarmed like iron filings to the magnetic center of the scene, the fuming heap of earth that had replaced the Rebel salient.

Colonel Marshall stopped at the base of the twelve-foot berm of thrown-out clay that surrounded the crater, and General Bartlett hobbled up to join him, grinning cheerfully as he plied his ivory-headed cane. The brigade commanders were bemused by the relatively easy completion of what they took to be their mission. Then they climbed the berm.

From the top they looked down into a huge sheer-sided crater, twenty-five to thirty feet deep, sixty or seventy feet across, and at least one hundred thirty feet wide, "filled with dust, great blocks of clay, guns, broken carriages, projecting timbers, and men buried in various ways." The nearly vertical walls were composed of jagged scarps and ledges of clay projecting through a covering of sandy topsoil and pulverized clay, which slipped and cascaded down around the men who skidded to the bottom on their heels and their butts. A ridge of solid clay (too steep to be walked on) ran across the pit from front to back, dividing the crater into two lobes, the northern or right-hand one larger than the left. The ridge probably marked the location of the main tunnel (where no powder had been set) and the pits the sites of the two side galleries. "The scene inside was horrible. Men were found half-buried; some dead, some alive, some with their legs kicking in the air, some with the arms only exposed, and some with every bone in their bodies apparently broken." Some soldiers were moved instinctively by the sight of those mangled and half-buried men, scrambled down and began digging them out. For others, this was simply the biggest rifle pit any of them had ever seen. If six feet of breastworks was good, thirty feet of hole had to be perfection. But for most, the draw of the crater was harder to explain. It was appalling and fascinating, and going down for a look-see seemed such a natural response that neither Bartlett nor Marshall attempted to check it—until they realized that the movement was out of hand.[9]

Bartlett's and Marshall's brigades did not take the crater; they mobbed it. The officers who went down into it to pull the men together found themselves in the situation of a man trying to shovel flies across a barnyard. Colonel Weld tried: "The men could not be got forward. It was a perfect mob, as far as any company or regimental organization was concerned, and that necessarily from the way we went forward," as individuals rather than as soldiers ranked shoulder-to-shoulder. Deprived of the power of belonging to the unit, "Each one felt as if he were to encounter the whole Confederate force alone and unsupported. The moral backing of an organized body of men, which each one would sustain by his companions on either side, was wanting." Soon enough Confederate rifle fire and canister from the distant guns began to sweep the top of the berm, and every man reflexively felt the need to find good cover and stay in it.[10]

Captain Houghton had kept his battalion of the 14th NYHA together and directed them to the Rebel trenches at the southern end of the crater. Here they found a portion of the salient still intact. (Apparently Pleasants had slightly miscalculated the alignment of his lateral galleries.) Their colors were the first planted on the position they called "the ruined fort." They captured several dazed Confederates and found two more of Pegram's brass twelve-pounders dismounted, overturned, and half-buried. At last the Heavies had a chance to do the work for which they had enlisted, defending a fort instead of charging it with bayonets. Houghton guessed there would be a magazine with powder and shot somewhere under the rubble. He sent a detail to ferret it out while he and his sergeant, Wesley Stanley, set their men to digging out and remounting the guns for use against the enemy.[11]

It was a proper thing to do in the absence of other orders, more useful than hunting for souvenirs and digging for johnnies in the crater. But it was not what Ledlie's men were supposed to be doing. The operational plan had called for the two brigades to pass the crater and storm Cemetery Hill. Ledlie had misguided Bartlett and Marshall by telling them their mission was simply to seize and hold the trenches around the crater so the Colored troops could pass through and attack the hill. But the execution of even that truncated assignment was compromised when Bartlett and Marshall lost control of their units.

Elements of their two brigades were mixed, but most of Marshall's troops had gone into the left lobe of the crater, and most of Bartlett's to the right, so down went the brigadiers to try to put their commands back together. As they understood it, their task was to solidify the lodgment they had made in the Confederate lines and widen the breach for the following divisions. Griffin's brigade of Potter's division had jumped off practically on the heels of Bartlett's trailing regiment, and the crescendo of rifle fire from the north meant Griffin's line was under fire from the unbroken Rebel entrenchments. But Willcox's men were still in the Union lines, unable to advance to protect the southern flank until Marshall's men could clear a space for them.[12]

The 14th NYHA would try. Captain Kilmer led his men against the breastwork of the gorge line trench that had been dug across the rear of the salient, thirty or forty yards back from the main line. A small body of Confederates made a stand, and as the Federal infantry climbed the barricade, the fighting was with bayonets and clubbed rifles. The Union troops took the cavalier, and Sergeant James S. Hill of Company C captured a Rebel battle flag, which he took back to General Ledlie as the seal of their triumph. But the gorge line was completely exposed to fire from Elliott's rallied infantry in the communication trenches behind the crater, and Kilmer was forced back to the ruined fort.

It also proved impossible to widen the breach by pushing down the trench line to the south. There were not as many lateral communication trenches here as there were to the north, but there were enough to shelter a substantial defending force. Two of Elliott's regiments, the 22nd and 23rd South Carolina, had rallied here and were soon joined by units from Wise's Virginia Brigade. Colonel Goode, who commanded that brigade, was prepared for the crisis. He pulled the 26th and 59th Virginia out of his front line (which was not being immediately assailed) and shifted them into positions on higher ground south of the crater. Together these units mustered upwards of seven hundred rifles, backed by artillery. Marshall had fewer than a thousand infantry available for an attack from this part of the line, not enough to drive so large a force from entrenched positions. Houghton's men took fire from Rebels in communication trenches behind the old main line, from infantry defending the farther end of the trench they occupied, and even from the Rebel picket line, which was now in the rear of Houghton's position. This not only pinned Houghton's and Kilmer's men in their fort, it also enfiladed the killing ground in front of the gorge line. If the breach was to be widened in this direction, Willcox's division would have to provide additional force.[13]

❧

On the northern flank of the crater, General Bartlett and Colonel Weld extricated the 56th Massachusetts from the mob, and Weld led them north into the opening of the breached trench line. From his position on the right of the crater, Weld could see an extension of the gorge line that slanted away from the crater to the northwest. Its raised parapet would have been an ideal defensive position, if its eastern face had not been exposed to fire from the Rebels holding out in and behind the main line. Believing that his division's task was to establish such a defensive position, Weld was determined to clear the Rebels from the main line. But the going was tough. There was maze of supporting and communication ditches behind the line that erupted with rifle fire as soon as Weld's men tried to advance.

The fire came from the 17th and the survivors of the 18th South Carolina. Captain Floyd of the 18th had been asleep in a trench to the north of the salient when the jolt of the mine woke him, and then threw him so violently to the ground that he lost consciousness. He came to, "covered up from head to foot with earth and debris," surrounded by the clay boulders and broken timbers that had somehow missed crushing him when they fell. "Tremendous firing and shouting . . . and the fierce, defiant yells of contending men, intermingled with the groans of the wounded and dying" told him the Yankee assault was under way. He raised up, saw the gap where Pegram's battery had been vaporized, and saw in the intervening trenches a hand-to-hand fight in progress between survivors of his regiment and Federal troops (Weld's) pressing up the trench line from the crater. Floyd rushed to join these fifty survivors, "bareheaded and look[ing] like we had just emerged from a clay hole."

A large number of Federals—Floyd thought as many as two hundred—charged and got in among them. "Swords flashed, and bayonets and the butts of rifles were freely used," a close hand-to-hand fight broken up when a Confederate mortar lobbed a shell into their midst, killing and wounding several men and "hurling the Confederates and Federals right and left." Floyd could see more bluecoats piling into the breach, so he ordered his men to fall back and take cover in a cross ditch about a hundred fifty feet back from the main line. They had to make a fighting retreat, "walking backward and firing as they retired, the officers using their revolvers and the men their guns." Half of the men never made it to the ditch; two officers were killed or mortally wounded, including the regimental adjutant shot through the lungs and Sergeant Berry shot through the head. Those that survived joined other troops that had rallied there, and held on, with orders to fire only when the enemy attempted to advance.[14]

Fire from this position, and others like it, brought Weld's advance to a halt. The original plan had envisioned a movement like Weld's sweeping the trenches clean by a classic flank attack, with part of the battle line in the trench and part behind and above it to outflank any traverses. But instead of a single line of trench, the works here were "complex and involuted, filled with pits, traverses, and bomb-proofs, forming a labyrinth as difficult of passage as the crater itself." Abstracted on a map, trenches seem to fill the coves and bulges and angles of the Confederate main line like cobwebs in a corner. Troops advancing at right angles to the main trench would shortly be faced with a communication trench or cross ditch angled across their advance, and infantry firing from its shelter. Squads of Union attackers might dash out into the open to flank stubborn defenders fighting behind traverses, only to be shot down by fire from communication trenches on their left. Moreover, the Confederates here were supported by the fire of eight or more cannons from the Wright, El-lett, and Letcher batteries, firing case shot and canister right over their heads into the advancing Federals. Weld's troops were driven to cover no more than twenty-five yards beyond the crater.

⁓

Powerful as it was, the mine had not proved as devastating as Burnside had expected. Pegram's battery and the regiment defending it had been annihilated, and Confederate troops had been killed or driven out of the trenches for twenty-five or thirty yards to the right and left of the crater. But the physical and moral effects of the blast stopped there. All around the attackers, enemy infantry had recovered from the shock of the blast, and rifle fire was coming in from three sides, grazing crisscross over the top of the crater berm. Federal troops on the scene heavily outnumbered the Confederates, but most of their force was not in a position where it could act effectively, whether as an assaulting column or as fire support for a charge. The crater was a barrier impassable to troops, whether advancing or retreating. The walls on the side facing the Confederates were too sheer to be climbed by a line of battle—so sheer that it would have been extremely difficult even to form a defensive line along the berm. Only at the northern and southern extremes of the crater, where it joined the half-buried trench line abandoned by the Rebels, was it feasible to scramble out. But these passages were narrow, and as other troops advanced across or through them—or stood in them to fire back at Confederate riflemen—they became gridlocked.

In Civil War engagements, it was generally the case that trench lines could not be successfully assaulted unless the attackers enjoyed a two- or three-to-one advantage in infantry, and superior artillery support. Led-lie's division sent fewer than four thousand men into action, and half of them were unable to advance or fire effectively because they were in the crater or blocked by troops packing the trenches ahead of them. Even in the first phase of the attack, when no Confederate reinforcements had yet been shifted to oppose them, they faced upwards of fifteen hundred

Confederate infantry, in covered positions, backed by a powerful artillery. And once they moved beyond the gorge line trench, they were subject to an infantry-artillery crossfire.[15]

Yet from Burnside's vantage point, it would have appeared that Federal artillery was dominating the battleground. General Hunt had 144 pieces in battery. "The firing from each piece [was] slow, deliberate, and careful, partaking of the nature of target practice," but the number of guns firing created a nearly continuous barrage that Hunt believed was very effective. Shell bursts flowered around all the Confederate artillery positions previously located by Hunt's observers—on Warren's front south of the mine, on the detached batteries up near the Plank Road, on the batteries on the near slope of Cemetery Hill. Lieutenant Bowley, watching from alongside Fort Morton, thought no one could survive such a bombardment: "the Rebel fortifications seemed to be ploughed through and through." As new positions were revealed, fire was shifted to suppress them, and secondary explosions indicated that caissons full of ammunition were being hit. But Wright's and Davidson's batteries, which were among the most destructive, were screened by the trees Burnside had failed to have cut down. And it was proving nearly impossible for Federal counter-battery fire to destroy the guns in Flanner's, Ellett's, or Letcher's batteries. Civil War artillery lacked the accuracy and penetrating power to destroy guns in properly designed emplacements.[16]

The striking power of Confederate artillery had not been impaired at all, and it was playing the dominant role in keeping the Federals at bay. Richard Pegram's battery had been destroyed by the mine, but only one other Confederate gun position had been affected by it, and that temporarily. Gunners in the one-gun battery south of the crater had panicked and run when the mine had gone off, but they had been quickly replaced. All around the rest of the arc, battery commanders recovered quickly from their initial surprise. They had been prepared for such an eventuality, their guns were properly positioned to defend the rear of Elliott's Salient, and they had laid in ample stocks of ammunition.

Colonel John Haskell commanded the artillery along the Plank Road, and Major James Coit the batteries on the ridge and the north end of the line. Coit had gone to sleep after inspecting Pegram's battery. The thump of the blast half-woke him, he felt as if he were "being rocked in a cradle," and then he came stark awake and looked out of his bombproof to see the fragments of Pegram's men and guns going up in flame and smoke. He knew immediately what had happened, and what needed to be done. Before the cloud of smoke and dust had settled onto the crater, he had run down to the site, ascertained the dimensions of the gap, and hustled north, through the labyrinth of trenches to where Wright's battery sat at the base of the sloping ridge that ran down from Cemetery Hill, backing the line held by Ransom's Brigade. This battery had been designed so that its guns could fire into no-man's-land or—by firing over Ransom's trenches—sweep the rear and flank of Elliott's Salient. The battery was well supplied with ammunition, and Coit ordered Wright to maintain a steady barrage of canister on any Federal troops advancing beyond the crater. Wright's fire interlocked with that from the Ellett and Letcher batteries midway up the slope toward Cemetery Hill, and dominated the ground west and north of the crater.

Haskell's batteries were ranged along the Plank Road and formed the center of the Confederate arc. Haskell had kept part of his command in reserve, in the deep ravine behind the Plank Road. When the mine blew, he ordered two batteries up the slope onto the road and placed them in some half-finished gun pits and a convenient dip in the road. With Flanner's and Langhorne's batteries already dug in at one end of his line, and eight mortars under Lamkin on the other, he had a solid row of guns facing the center of the Federal assault.[17]

The weakness of the position was the lack of infantry to defend the ground between the crater and the Plank Road. Artillery without infantry support is vulnerable to attack by skirmishing riflemen. Ransom on the north and Goode on the south pushed infantry toward the breach as soon as they could, along the shortest line—that is, along and just in the rear of the frontline trenches. But during the first hour after the explosion, nearly all the Confederate infantry strength was massed in the trenches left and right of the crater. All that stood between Ledlie's division and the guns on the Plank Road was a remnant of the 18th South Carolina that had fled to the lateral ravine. As Major Barnwell of Elliott's Brigade put it, "It must be artillery or nothing."[18]

Colonel Haskell was an amateur artilleryman, but a superb one. He had been a nineteen-year-old college student when the war began. In his first battle at Seven Pines in 1862 he had rallied troops under fire and led several infantry charges, had had his left arm nearly torn off by a shell, had tucked it into his uniform, and had walked off to the field hospital, where it was amputated. Now he masked the weakness of his position by seeing that his gunners had a steady supply of shells, case shot, and canister. The guns fired almost continuously, sweeping the ground in front of the breach and breaking up the halfhearted Federal advances. He also made effective use of his mortars. He found that their accuracy and ability to strike infantry under cover allowed them to prevent effective attacks from being mounted. To maximize their impact, he aggressively moved a two-mortar section under Lieutenant Eggleston down into the lateral ravine, from which it could more easily reach the crater and the adjoining trenches.[19]

But eventually he would need infantry. Haskell ran down the hill to find General Elliott, who was rallying his troops north of the crater, to beg some sharpshooters to keep Yankee riflemen from picking off his gunners. Elliott agreed to send help—but he had his own ideas for suppressing Yankee fire.

❧

After leaving the site of the crater, Elliott had found the 17th South Carolina, commanded by the despised Colonel McMaster, and the 26th commanded by Colonel Smith, preparing to defend the northern side of the breach. But Elliott was determined to fulfill his orders and redeem his own reputation and that of his brigade by counterattacking the Yankees and driving them from the salient. With some difficulty, Smith and McMaster thinned their firing line to pull an assault force together, and Elliott led them to a ditch that slanted back across the northwest side of the open flat behind the salient. He was furiously impatient with their slow movement—every minute made their task still more impossible. As soon as the 26th was in line, he "jumped up on the parapet . . . and, turning his side to the enemy as he faced the coming troops, was shot down by the foe not forty yards away." The few men who followed his lead were hit by heavy and continuous firing from the troops in and around the crater. K Company of the 57th Massachusetts had just been equipped with rapid-fire breech-loading Spencer rifles, and they had as much firepower as an average regiment. Elliott's men fell back with serious losses. Colonel Smith tried a second time but was wounded as soon as he started, and his men ducked back under cover as quickly as possible. The "attack" was scarcely noticed by the Federals, for whom the battle was becoming an extended firefight.

McMaster succeeded to the command and called off the assault, to Elliott's intense disgust: "Not a word from you," he snapped. "If you had obeyed orders this would never have happened." McMaster ignored the irrational complaint. There were more than a dozen Yankee battle flags flying from the berm of the crater; to charge them with the remnants of an understrength brigade was suicide.[20]

Elliott's combativeness had driven him into a tactical blunder, which might have proved costly. But he had also displayed some of the qualities that gave the Confederate officers on this battlefield a distinct edge over their Union counterparts: tenacity, determination, and the will to close with the enemy. McMaster was smart as well as combative. He left most of the 17th and the survivors of the 18th to hold on in the trenches north of the crater and prevent the Yankees from expanding the breach. He shifted the 26th and three companies of his own 17th South Carolina (about two hundred fifteen men) up the covered way into the lateral ravine, to fight a delaying action until the rest of the army could come to their aid. But between the ravine and the high ground occupied by Wise's Brigade there remained a gap of more than two hundred fifty yards, defended only by the guns of Flanner's battery firing from the Plank Road. So McMaster sent one runner to divisional headquarters to ask for reinforcements, and another to try to contact the 22nd and 23rd regiments, fighting on the south side of the crater.

He also sent a runner to Colonel McAfee, commanding Ransom's Brigade, apprising him of the situation and asking him to send what help he could. McAfee responded by spreading his regiments thinner and shifting strength to the south, to take over the frontage held by the 49th and 25th North Carolina and free them for action as a maneuverable reserve. But the initiative was still with the Union.[21]

Lieutenant Colonel Loring of Burnside's staff had accompanied Bartlett's advance into the northern lobe of the crater. After spending some time trying to help Bartlett reorganize his men, he concluded that the 1st Division was stalled. It had been forty minutes or more since the mine had exploded, and Ledlie's division was a jumbled mass jammed at the bottom of the crater and in the adjoining trenches. Loring did not know that Ledlie had ordered his brigadiers to make and hold a lodgment in the Rebel line instead of charging straight for Cemetery Hill. It seemed to him that they had been foiled by trying to pass through the crater, "an obstacle of fearful magnitude . . . which it was perfectly impossible for any military organization to pass over intact, even if not exposed to fire." He was also able to see the honeycomb of trenches that was balking Weld's attempt to push out to the right. Either the operational plan had to be adjusted or new troops had to be brought in. He scribbled a brief report and gave it to an aide with instructions to take it to Burnside's headquarters. Then he made his way back across no-man's-land to find General Ledlie and get him to reorganize his troops and move them forward.[22]

To Colonel Marshall it seemed the position Ledlie had ordered them to hold was untenable. Fire from Rebel infantry was steadily increasing, and artillery was now dropping shells on them. He turned to Major William Powell, the senior Regular on Ledlie's divisional staff, who was responsible for liaison with division headquarters. Although neither man knew that their real mission had been to seize Cemetery Hill, it was obvious that the only alternative to retreat was to carry the artillery positions on the high ground. But in their present state of disorganization they could not mount such a drive. Powell was ordered to find Ledlie and get him to provide the combination of reinforcement and reorganization that they needed to begin an attack.

Powell ran back down the slope from the crater to their old front line. No-man's-land was now a danger zone, with minié balls zipping overhead and the cannons in Davidson's batteries firing canister as regular as clockwork. After a short search Powell found Ledlie and some of his staff sheltering in an angle of the trench line. He explained the situation in the crater, the necessity of making an advance, and delivered Marshall's appeal for help. A decent man or a good officer would have taken Powell's information to Burnside with a request for reinforcement or for new orders, or gone to the front himself to see if the attack order could be executed. Ledlie did neither. His response was to "direct me to return at once and say to Colonel Marshall and General Bartlett that it was General Burnside's order that they move forward immediately." The order was meant to sound like the stern command of a determined soldier. In view of the information Powell had just delivered, it was utterly meaningless, a sign of Ledlie's incompetence and irresponsibility. Powell was enraged, but had no choice except to carry the order back to the front.

THE BREACH, 5:40–6:00 A.M.

In the crater, Marshall and Bartlett were mustering another assault to gain possession of the gorge line. If Burnside was watching from Fort Morton, it would have appeared to him that they were finally moving to complete their mission by driving toward Cemetery Hill. But their aim was simply to push the enemy back and establish a more defensible position, resting on the gorge line rather than the slippery slopes of the crater. They also wanted to make room for Hartranft's brigade, the lead element of Willcox's division, to get into the breach and join the 14th NYHA in pushing the Confederate defenders away to the south.

Hartranft was already on the scene. He arrived in Captain Houghton's little fort ahead of his brigade, and as his troops came across no-man's-land he called for "three cheers for the 14th!" Hartranft's orders called for him to pass through the breach and support the left flank of the assault on Cemetery Hill. But with Ledlie's division stalled in the breach, those orders could not be carried out. The only other maneuver available to him would have been to attack Goode's trench line from the front. If properly coordinated with the 14th NYHA, it might have pushed the Confederates back a bit. But Hartranft was leery of ordering a frontal attack on his own. That kind of decision required the judgment and authority of a division commander—but Willcox, like Ledlie, was back in the Union lines. So Hartranft's brigade had to huddle up under the parapet of the captured trenches, where they were exposed to fire from the infantry of Goode's command, and canister from Davidson's battery to the south. Hartranft would gradually work his men into the defensive perimeter south of the crater, but he never mustered a strong attack against Goode's position.[23]

In the southern lobe, Colonel Marshall sorted part of the 2nd PPHA and his two small infantry regiments (3rd Maryland and 179th New York) out of the mob. In the northern section, Bartlett pulled together elements of three Massachusetts regiments, the 29th, 57th, and 59th, to form a supporting line, but they couldn't get out of the crater because Weld's men were still in the side trenches. Led by Colonel Robinson of the 179th, Marshall's men climbed out of the crater where it was shallower, formed under fire, and made a rush for the cavalier. They got into it but couldn't stay. Like the 14th NYHA earlier, they were enfiladed by rifle fire from Elliott's troops south of the crater and from the trenches Weld had been unable to attack, and were under direct fire from the Confederate batteries to the north. Several companies of the 2nd PPHA took cover behind the "face" of the cavalier parapet, firing from the crouch, but most of the attackers turned and went running back to the crater.

In the meantime Powell had returned from his useless meeting with Ledlie. The orders he was bringing looked worse the closer he got. "[T]he firing on the crater was now incessant, and it was as heavy a fire of canister as was ever poured continuously upon a single objective point."

But shortly after he delivered Ledlie's orders, there was shouting from the northern side of the crater, and when Powell peered out of Houghton's fort, he saw a skirmish line of blue infantry sweep up over the berm and the broken trench, followed by a regiment in line of battle—the 9th New Hampshire and 31st Maine at the head of Griffin's brigade.

Powell's spirits revived. He thought that Ledlie might have passed his message to Burnside and Burny had sent Griffin's men to reinforce them or take the lead in a new assault. In fact, Griffin's brigade had drifted to that spot, driven by pressures and circumstances beyond the control of their officers.[24]

General Potter had prepared properly for his division's assault, building sandbag stairs so Simon Griffin's brigade could clear the trenches and rapidly form their line. Shortly after the mine exploded, Griffin's brigade was able to exit their trenches, remove obstacles, form a line of battle, and begin their advance. The plan called for them to follow on the heels of Bartlett's brigade and storm the unbroken trenches to the north of the breach. It was expected that the Confederates here would be stunned and demoralized by the mine explosion and by the eruption of Ledlie's battle line on their flank and rear, and that most if not all of the garrison would flee.[25]

Griffin's brigade was made up of regiments from Maine, New Hampshire, and Vermont—the kind of Yankees usually described as rock-ribbed. Three of his regiments (6th, 9th, and 11th New Hampshire) were veterans, but their ranks had been filled with raw replacements at the start of the campaign. The 31st and 32nd Maine and 17th Vermont had learned their trade during the campaign, at heavy cost. Every regiment in the brigade was reduced to no more than a third of its original strength. The veteran 2nd Maryland had recently been added to reinforce them, but it too was a shadow of its former self. However, their regimental commanders were competent men, and brigade commander Griffin was an excellent combat leader. To ensure good command control, he split the brigade into two elements, with Colonel White of the 31st Maine leading the advance while Griffin himself led the support.

Young Lieutenant James Chase of the 32nd Maine was stretched out in the brush, sleeping as only a teenager can sleep, when the explosion of the mine jolted him awake. He was disoriented, thought there had been an earthquake, and then saw the black cloud surging above the trees and realized what had happened. Colonel Wentworth got the regiment on its feet and led them out of the creek bed and into the trenches just vacated by the brigade's first line. They dashed past the entrance to the mine tunnel, which was now abandoned. As they climbed the sandbag stairs out of their trench, Chase saw the guns of a big battery to the south firing on the Rebels. The sight distracted him, his sword scabbard got tangled between his legs, and he fell headlong over the parapet. Another officer, coming up behind, began yelling at him, calling him a slacker, and Chase jumped up ready to punch it out with the fellow—then both came to their senses and ran to join the regimental line marching upslope toward the Rebel lines.[26]

Griffin's troops passed through some uncut brush into open ground and were hit by heavy volleys of rifle fire augmented by blasts of canister from a battery on the high ground behind the Rebel line. The lines in front of them were stronger than they had been the month before, when Potter's men had been unable to storm them. They were still fully manned by the 49th and 25th North Carolina of Ransom's Brigade, which had not been at all affected by the explosion of the mine. Nor were these troops concerned about their flank, which at that point was still protected by the 17th and 26th South Carolina. To evade the worst of their fire and continue the advance, Griffin's regiments edged away southward, toward the crater and the breach. Somehow the 6th New Hampshire got separated from the brigade and was left out in no-man's-land, under fire from the Ellett and Letcher batteries on Cemetery Hill and from riflemen in the trenches.

The lead regiment on Griffin's southern flank felt its way along till it hit a place where no rifles cracked, the ruined trenches just north of the breach. Free at last, the battle line gave a yell and dashed up and over the rubble and broken parapets. Griffin's line overlapped both the crater and the adjacent trench line. As it passed through the rubble, the 9th New Hampshire saw a Rebel soldier still buried to the chest in the dirt and gave him a cheer as they ran past. Sergeant Edward Parsons of the 9th New Hampshire planted his regiment's colors on the berm, took a bullet in the groin, and was carried off, bleeding to death. About half of the 31st Maine was sucked into the mob at the bottom of the crater, and part of the 32nd as well. Lieutenant Chase and his men lost their footing, tumbled, and rolled into crater. But Chase got to his feet; his men stuck with him, and their Colonel Wentworth came down and got them and they clambered up the slope into the mouth of the broken trench.[27]

Those of Griffin's troops who missed the crater blundered into Weld's positions with their bayonets fixed—men were hurt and units disrupted, but Weld and Colonel White straightened things out and joined forces to continue pushing the Rebels away from the breach. Weld's men continued working along the main trench line. White's troops pushed their way through and climbed over the backs of 1st Division troops who would not advance, to get into the open ground in the rear of the salient. Those who got through wheeled to the right to try to outflank the troops blocking Weld.[28]

The addition of Griffin's force made a difference. With more troops available, it became possible to outflank Rebel defensive positions and gain some ground. But the farther they advanced, the closer they got to the guns of Wright, Ellett, and Letcher, which could enfilade the ditches along which the Union troops were moving. Their drive was also thwarted by the difficulty of advancing in the labyrinth of communication trenches, traverses, gorge lines, and cross ditches behind the main Rebel line. As Federal units spread out in the channels of that Confederate delta, their advance lost weight and force, their units lost coherence.

The action was terribly confusing. Troops attempting to outflank a Rebel position might follow a promising trench line that took them behind the enemy position, only to find that the second line slanted away from the first, or failed to connect with it. Advancing units found themselves firing against Rebels to the north, while behind them other Rebels were still firing southward against troops advancing from the crater.

The tactics and weaponry of Civil War armies were unsuited to the task of clearing the kind of trench complex that confronted the Federal infantry north of the crater. Soldiers were trained to fight in line formation, which could not be maintained in ground crosshatched with trench lines. If they opened out and fought as skirmishers, with wide intervals between individuals, their firepower (with single-shot rifle-muskets) was drastically reduced. In 1918 or 1944, infantry in open order could lay heavy covering fire on an enemy trench with machine guns and semiautomatic rifles, and if a single infantry flanker could get into the trench, he could kill its defenders with an auto rifle or submachine gun. If he found himself on the opposite side of a wall or parapet from an enemy position, he could simply lob a grenade over the top and destroy the whole position. Hand grenades existed in 1864, but Civil War soldiers were not supplied with them or trained in their use.

The retreating Confederates were able to draw together as they pulled back. McMaster's men defended every traverse, and where none existed, they improvised barricades of broken timber and boxes. The Federals would dash up to these barriers, spread along the front, and then "jump over [to be] met with bayonet and clubbed musket. . . . Few battles could show more bayonet wounds than this." The remnant of McMaster's 17th South Carolina sacrificed themselves to delay White's advance. Company A, reduced to the strength of a squad, was overwhelmed by a rush of Federal infantry. Private Hoke, "refusing to surrender to a damned Yankee," swung his rifle butt to knock down four of the enemy before he was bayoneted. Company D found itself surrounded and was surrendered by the lieutenant commanding: twenty-seven men, sixteen of whom would die of scurvy in the Elmira POW camp.[29]

Colonel Wentworth led Chase and the rest of the 32nd Maine up over the berm, with bullets zinging the air around them, and a scattering of sodden thumps as men were hit. There was another of those cavalier trenches in front of them, slanting away from the main line. Colonel Wentworth led the 32nd Maine in the rush, his men storming over the low parapet. The fighting was up close and personal. Colonel Wentworth was shot twice, one close-range bullet going through his body to cripple the arm of a sergeant. They took the position but there was another trench beyond theirs, full of johnnies.[30]

Colonel Flemming's 49th North Carolina had rushed down the trench line in a column of twos and had filed into a communication trench facing south, and as soon as they were in position, they had leveled their muskets and opened a heavy fire on White's men, which had brought them to a halt. Flemming's men maintained a steady stream of bullets, with one line firing and a second loading muskets and passing them up, and details from other regiments maintaining a continuous chain of ammunition resupply. Flemming was killed by a bullet through the head, but his regiment held steady, Yankees and Rebels blazing away, heavy white powder smoke piling up above the trench in the still, hot air. With the 49th added to the survivors of Elliott's Brigade, and supporting artillery fire from the Ellett and Letcher batteries on the ridge, there was now a solid body of infantry blocking Griffin's drive.[31]

By 6:00 A.M. Griffin had gone about as far as he could. And although his troops were behind the Rebel's main line, they had not succeeded in forcing the Confederates to abandon their frontline trenches. This effectively limited the breach usable by advancing Federal troops to the crowded trenches fifty to seventy-five yards north of the crater.

Union Lines, 5:40–6:15 a.m.

Dr. Chubb, who had watched Hartranft's men go across, had to worm his way through the crowd to get back to the bombproof where he had his aid station. Shortly after he returned, General Ledlie appeared and stationed himself outside the entrance. Colonel Loring of the staff found him there, told him what was happening in the crater, and asked him to "see if he could not rectify" his division's situation. Dr. Chubb thought he heard Ledlie complain that he had not been properly supported, but missed Loring's response.

When Loring left to report to Burnside, Ledlie came inside the bombproof and took a seat. Chubb was curious about the state of the action, so he asked Ledlie if his division had been properly supported. Ledlie acknowledged that it had but said nothing further. Since Ledlie seemed unperturbed by the situation, Chubb returned to his own pressing business of tending the wounded.

Major Powell burst in shortly afterward. He had made a second dash across no-man's-land to seek Ledlie out and get his division commander to help break the logjam. He urged Ledlie to speak to Burnside, to get headquarters to stop piling troops into the breach, because "every man who got into the trenches . . . used them as a means of escape to the crater, and the enemy was reoccupying them as fast as our men left." If Burnside ordered attacks on the lines north and south of the breach, it might draw off Rebel strength. "All the satisfaction I received was an order to go back and tell the brigade commanders to get their men out and press forward to Cemetery Hill. This talk and these orders, coming from a commander sitting in a bombproof inside the Union lines, were disgusting." Powell told Ledlie that his orders could not possibly be obeyed, but no others were forthcoming. Powell returned to the crater.

It is possible that Ledlie was already drunk. That had been his pattern in earlier actions. At the crossing of the North Anna, strong drink had made him reckless, and during the June assaults on Petersburg he had gotten falling-down blackout drunk in the middle of the battle. Alcohol might account for the lack of cogency in Ledlie's response to Powell and his peculiar air of detachment from the battle raging a few yards away. But Ledlie was afraid of what was happening, of what was being demanded of him as a general on the field of battle, and with or without the anesthetic of whiskey, behind his affable exterior he had withdrawn into a protective shell, a psychological disconnection that made him emotionally and intellectually impervious to the increasingly desperate pleas of his officers.[32]

When Dr. Chubb looked up from his operating table, he saw Ledlie still sitting on the same stool, as if nothing out of the ordinary were going on. Outside the entry of the bombproof, Humphrey's troops were still waiting for orders to advance.[33]

⧖

The immobilization of Marshall's and Hartranft's brigades created a traffic jam that froze all movement on the southern axis of advance. Willcox's other brigade (under Humphrey) had to stay in the Union lines, its head on the line but its tail still in the covered way, with Sigfried's USCT troops queueing up behind them. At the rear of the covered way, Thomas's brigade was still "at ease," waiting their turn. At about 5:45 A.M. General Grant and Colonel Porter suddenly appeared on horseback. They had missed Burnside, who had left his headquarters and gone forward. Grant approached Thomas: why were his men not advancing? The colonel answered that his orders were to follow the brigade in front. But he and his men were ready: "Will you give me the order to go in now?" Thomas could have jumped the queue by avoiding the covered way entirely and advancing in the open.

Grant demurred. For the commanding general to interfere with an operation already under way might only derange things. The overlap between his authority and Meade's had caused a lot of confusion during the campaign, and Grant hoped to minimize it by vesting in Meade all authority for the tactical conduct of the battle. But what he had seen had made Grant uneasy. The battle was an hour old, and three of the five divisions deployed against the breach were still far to the rear. Porter and Grant continued their ride toward the front.[34]

Chapter 11

At Headquarters

5:40–7:50 A.M.

At his headquarters General Meade was brimful of justified frustration and concern. An hour had passed since the mine explosion and Burnside had made no report about the progress of the attack. If the program had been followed, Burnside's lead division should have been storming Cemetery Hill. But it was at least as probable that something had gone awry, that a disaster was in the making. Meade felt he could not go to the front to see for himself. He had to stay where the corps commanders could readily find him. He had hoped the telegraph would allow him to stay in contact with events at the front. But the telegraph was useless if his subordinates chose not to use it.

At 5:40 A.M. he could wait no longer and shot a message to Burnside: "What news from your assaulting column? Please report frequently."

Burnside answered almost instantly: "We have the enemy's first line and occupy the breach. I shall endeavor to push forward to the crest as rapidly as possible." The phrasing was ambiguous: an advance had been made, but why did Burnside have to "endeavor" to push forward?

At that moment Colonel Loring's orderly came galloping up the path from the front, carrying the message Loring had addressed to Burnside half an hour earlier. Under the stress of battle, the orderly had forgotten that Burnside had shifted his headquarters to Fort Morton and that Meade now occupied the old IX Corps headquarters near the Shand house. When Meade opened the dispatch, he learned that Ledlie's men occupied the crater, but (in the opinion of Burnside's own inspector general) "they could not be induced to advance." Burnside's attack was breaking down, and the man was trying to conceal the fact from headquarters! Meade's next telegram had the snap of anger in its phrasing: "The commanding general learns that your troops are halting at the works where the mine exploded. He directs that all your troops be pushed forward to the crest at once. Call on General Ord to move forward his troops at once." So little time had passed since Meade's first telegram that this last was also marked 5:40 A.M.[1]

Now the staff began to get the intelligence gathered from Confederates captured in the first rush, intelligence that indicated the Rebels did not have a fortified second line, none of the troops sent to north of the James had returned, and the troops manning the front line were retreating as Federal troops advanced. Beyond all reasonable expectation, Grant's strategy had worked perfectly to create the opportunity for a decisive victory. But that opportunity was being lost because Burnside's men were not reaching out to seize it. Time was slipping away.

At 6:00 A.M. Meade wired the new intelligence to Burnside, with the most urgent and emphatic order for an immediate and swift advance: "Our chance is now. Push your men forward at all hazards—white and black—and don't lose time in making formations, but rush for the crest."

General Meade's understanding of the state of his battle was out of phase with events. He was too far from the scene to see things for himself, and the telegraph was not providing him with the real-time intelligence he'd expected because Burnside's reports were infrequent, indefinite, and inaccurate. The reports Meade received just before 6:00 A.M., describing the Confederate forces as decimated and demoralized, were taken from prisoners captured an hour earlier, during the first helter-skelter rush of Bartlett's, Marshall's, and Griffin's brigades. His order to Burnside to push in all his men, "black and white," presumed that the way to Cemetery Hill was clear and Burnside's men were poised to take it. In fact his assault had been balked and his corps was gridlocked.

Assuming that conditions were ripe for a decisive stroke, Meade began planning operations to support and exploit Burnside's drive. Once IX Corps took up the advance, the Confederates would have to weaken the line on Warren's front. When that happened, V Corps could attack with advantage. Meade had already wired Warren, asking him to watch for an opportunity to attack: "How is it in your front? Are the enemy in force there, or weak? If there is apparently an opportunity to carry their works, take advantage of it and push forward with your troops." At 6:05 he shot a follow-up to Burnside wondering "what is going on on your left, and whether it would be an advantage for Warren's supporting force to go in at once." Although he had ordered Burnside to make use of Ord's troops, Meade would not wait for him to get around to doing it. He wired Ord directly: "The major general commanding directs that you at once move forward your corps rapidly to the crest of the hill, independently of General Burnside's troops, and make a lodgement there, reporting the result as soon as attained." He also told Hancock's II Corps and Wilson's cavalry division to prepare for movement.[2]

A short time later a note from Captain Sanders, Meade's liaison at IX Corps, informed him that Burnside had obeyed Meade's instruction and ordered his men to attack. Meade's confidence was further buoyed by Warren's responses to his earlier query. He confirmed that "the enemy has been running from his first line in front of General Burnside's right for some minutes." However, Warren was still only *watching* for an opportunity to advance, and he thought he saw evidence the enemy had a second line. Then at 6:20 A.M. he reported that what he had thought was a second line was actually Burnside's men massed in a captured entrenchment.[3]

That last report from Warren confirmed the intelligence of the POWs. It was time to bring V Corps and the cavalry into play, to complete the Confederate defeat. So at 6:30 A.M., Meade wired Warren to inform him that there were only three Confederate divisions south of the Appomattox, that the trenches were thinly manned and no reserves could be seen moving behind the Rebel lines, and that "the commanding general wishes, if it is practicable, that you make an attack." He also noted that Wilson's cavalry division, which had been poised to move around the Rebels' southern flank, had been ordered against the Weldon Railroad.

Meade had just begun to develop this new offensive combination when a telegraph message from Burnside negated the presumption on which it was based: "If General Warren's supporting force can be concentrated just now, ready to go in at the proper time, it would be well. I will designate to you when it ought to move. There is scarcely room for it now in our immediate front."

Meade exploded. The telegram made it plain that Burnside's troops were not advancing but still clogged the breach. Burnside had not carried out the order to rush the crest with everything and everyone—and yet he had the gall to tell Meade what to do about Warren! His response was a rebuke as well as a command:

Warren's force has been concentrated and ready to move since 3.30 a.m. . . . What is the delay in your column moving? Every minute is most precious, as the enemy undoubtedly are concentrating to meet you at the crest, and if you give them time enough you cannot expect to succeed. There is no object to be gained in occupying the enemy's line. It cannot be held. . . . The great point is to secure the crest at once, and at all hazards.

But clearly Burnside could not be depended upon to carry this through on his own. Meade therefore sent another wire suggesting Warren attack the enemy's extreme right flank, using whatever forces were at hand. If Burnside's attack had not caused Lee to weaken Warren's front, perhaps a demonstration against the flank would do it.

But Warren's response was ambiguous. Meade had asked him to undertake two different attacks, one in direct support of Burnside, the other a demonstration against the flank. Instead of executing either order, Warren raised questions about the operational specifics and also cast doubt on the estimate of enemy strength on which the orders were premised. Moreover, he still insisted that the enemy had a second line, although "We cannot make out what [it] is."[4]

Warren did not want to make any more frontal assaults. He had been dubious about this operation from the start and was incredulous at the early signs of success, and before he committed himself to action, he wanted to see for himself how the situation looked. So immediately after dictating his reply to Meade he left his headquarters and went to see Burnside at Fort Morton. For some reason his reply, marked as sent at 6:40 A.M., was not received by Meade until 7:30. Over the next hour Meade had no idea where Warren was or whether his prompting to attack had been received. Until Warren chose to reopen contact, V Corps was unavailable to Meade.

❧

General Burnside had been dilatory in reporting to Meade because he had spent only half his time in his headquarters. The rest he had spent up at the embrasures of the fourteen-gun battery, trying to see through the battle smoke and heat haze what was happening in the Rebel line. From that relatively low elevation, with shells bursting all over the terrain and banks of gun smoke here, there, and everywhere, he could get no clear sense of where his troops had gotten to—though it seemed clear they were not charging in line of battle up the slope to Cemetery Hill. It was not until Colonel Loring returned (between 5:30 and 5:40 A.M.) to report in person on affairs at the front that Burnside fully understood that his assault force was stuck with its head and shoulders in the breach, unable to advance. What (if anything) Loring said about Ledlie himself was not recorded, but he must have made it clear that the man was useless: Ledlie was not included in the orders Burnside subsequently issued to his division commanders.[5]

Neither knew about the miscarriage of Loring's earlier dispatch, and it did not much concern them: there were many reasons why couriers on a battlefield failed to deliver their messages.

While Burnside was trying to grapple with the crisis on his front, Meade's messages began rattling into the telegraphers, signs of a crisis in the rear. Burnside's first response—that he would "endeavor to push forward to the crest"—was a naïve attempt to fend off Meade's intervention while he got his attack restarted. The miscarriage of Loring's dispatch exposed the hollowness of that ploy and brought (at 6:00 A.M.) Meade's sharp response and his demand that IX Corps advance immediately to the crest at all hazards, with all troops, Black and White.

That order had no relation to the reality Burnside was facing. Meade seemed to think Burnside's troops were only one gallant rush away from crowning Cemetery Hill. Burnside knew it was impossible to advance against the hill until a passage had been forced through the impacted mass in the breach. But to confess as much would put his command of the field at risk, perhaps induce Meade to call off the attack and blame him for its failure.[6]

If Meade was out of touch with the real state of the fighting, the fault was Burnside's. He had neglected to keep Meade informed about the pace and extent of his original advance. He now compounded that problem by failing to give Meade a full and detailed accounting of the problems facing his offensive. It is possible that he did not fully appreciate the significance of the intelligence brought to him by Colonel Loring and other staff officers on the state of Ledlie's troops. Given his personality, it is also possible that he could not bring himself to accept evidence that his plans were falling apart and his troops could not or would not execute his commands. He certainly could not admit such a possibility to Meade. But whether he misconstrued the evidence or misrepresented it, the result was a crazy-making mismatch between orders and conditions.

In response to Meade's 6:00 A.M. telegram, Burnside dictated a new attack order to his chief of ordnance, addressed to General Potter, copies to Willcox and Ferrero: "The general commanding directs that you push forward at once and endeavor to gain the crest. Move forward with every available man." Captain Sanders was then able to telegraph Meade to confirm that his orders had been obeyed: "General Burnside says that he has given orders to all his division commanders to push everything in at once."[7]

No sooner had Burnside's order gone out than the telegraph began chattering again, with Meade's query about using V Corps to make a supporting attack. To a man in desperate straits, this would seem to have been the answer to a prayer. A coordinated attack by V Corps and Willcox's division against the Confederates south of the crater might perhaps have broken the attenuated lines held by Colquitt's and Goode's brigades. Warren was reluctant to make such an attack because it required a frontal assault against lines that (for all he knew) might be fully manned. Burnside may have shied from considering it for the same reason. But it was always difficult for Burnside to adjust or adapt his operations to changing circumstances—his instinctive response was to pile in more resources and bull his way through any obstacles. The narrow gate of the breach seemed to him the only possible route to a successful attack. And Warren could not help him there, because the jam-up in the breach would not even allow Burnside's own reserves to go forward. All Burnside could think to do now was order Potter and Willcox to press the attack along the lines laid down in his original orders. So he formulated a diplomatic statement, designed to keep Meade at a distance while preserving the privilege Meade had seemingly granted, of letting him direct Warren's use in the battle. At 6:20 A.M. he sent the telegram that would rouse Meade's wrath, in which he asked Meade to hold Warren's force in readiness to go in at a time Burnside would designate.[8]

Before any reply could be received, Burnside left his headquarters and went forward to try to get the advance moving and to try to save his battle before he had to contact Meade again. He went to the raised earthwork that overlooked the rear of the Horseshoe . . . and was shocked to see Grant and Porter clambering over the earthwork from no-man's-land.

⁓

After leaving Thomas's brigade, Grant and Porter had ridden forward, perhaps following the Baxter Road that ran alongside the covered way. They soon entered the danger zone, where men in the open could be hit by overshots from the fighting or sharpshooters in the trees behind the enemy line. At Porter's insistence they left their horses and went forward on foot across the railroad cut and the muddy banks of Taylor's Creek, into the area just behind the front line. It was full of shell holes and wrecked or abandoned equipment, and crowds of men were in constant movement across it—columns advancing to the attack, wounded being carried to the rear, ammunition bearers struggling forward with boxes of cartridges. Grant was dressed as usual, in the same uniform as any private soldier except for the shoulder straps with their three stars. No one recognized his rank, and Grant had to elbow his way through the crowd to get where he was going.

From the front line Grant could see some of the crowding around the breach, which confirmed his sense of the stultification of movement. He probably also saw some of Ledlie's men bolting back across no-man's-land—not enough to signify a rout, but an indication of the state of affairs. The battle plan had called for a sudden powerful surprise attack, a coup de main that would carry all key objectives before the Confederates could react. That much of the plan had clearly failed. Porter spied a group of officers in the advanced fieldwork about three hundred yards away, Burnside among them, recognizable by his height and the tall bell-crowned hat he wore. Grant wanted to confer with him, but the interior of the Horseshoe was too crowded with troops, too cut up by communication trenches for easy movement. So Grant climbed over the parapet of the frontline trench into no-man's-land and hurried along the face of the earthworks, heedless of the bullets singing all around them and the shell bursts chewing up the ground.

As Porter remembered it, Grant wasted no time giving Burnside his opinion that the opportunity for a decisive victory had already been lost and the attackers should be recalled. Burnside disagreed. He had just (in response to Meade's strident demand) renewed the orders for his division commanders to press the attack. If they could push forward enough to clear a path, he had ample reserves to exploit the breach. Grant thought Burnside was mistaken, but declined to intervene between Meade and his corps commander. The attack order to Burnside might have been part of some larger operational maneuver generated at Meade's headquarters. So Grant and Porter made their way back to where their horses were tethered, and then rode back to the Shand house.[9]

THE CONFEDERATE HIGH COMMAND RESPONDS,
5:00–7:00 A.M.

The Confederacy's frontline troops had responded quickly and effectively to the shock of the mine explosion, the massive artillery barrage, and the Union assault that had followed. Despite the disruption of their regimental organization, the first reflex of most squads and platoons was to hold and fight rather than retreat. Their efforts were effectively supported by regimental and brigade commanders, who had long anticipated such an attack and were familiar with the terrain they had to defend.

The higher command levels were slower to respond. Division commander Bushrod Johnson was awakened by the explosion, but when a storming column did not quickly emerge from the dust cloud over the crater, he concluded his front was holding well enough. Since he had not had any breakfast and was extremely hungry, he set his aides to rustling him up a decent meal.

Farther behind the front, the sound and shock of the explosion were muffled but loud enough to rouse Colonel Paul of General Beauregard's staff. He surmised that the long-awaited blow had fallen and went to wake Beauregard, who commanded this front. The general told him to take a look at the scene and then ride hard with his report to Lee's headquarters at Violet Bank over on the north side of the Appomattox. Beauregard himself rode out to the Gee house, on the Plank Road about seven hundred yards south of Cemetery Hill, from which he could overlook the battlefield. He may have stopped at Johnson's headquarters, but if he did, he left no wiser for it—Johnson had not yet seen the field.

Colonel Paul found Lee finishing breakfast. He too had heard the dull thump of the explosion and the suppressed roar of the barrage, but his chief concern had been the Richmond front, so he had been waiting to hear whether the firing signified a major attack or a diversion. The staff colonel left no doubt: the Yankees had staged a major assault, broken the line, and occupied the center of the works on Johnson's front.

Lee had known such an attack was possible, and had assumed the risk was acceptable when he'd sent Field's Division north of the river. But the Federal assault was heavier than he had expected. If they succeeded in driving a strong column through the breach they had already made, the defense of Petersburg would be broken. Lee ordered the instant return of Field's Division, but it could not reach Petersburg before evening, by which time the battle would probably have been won or lost. To seal the breach he would have to pull troops out of the lines north and south of the break and concentrate them for a counterattack. The maneuver would have to be conducted with the utmost speed, before the Federals could perceive the weakening of those lines.

That kind of celerity was possible because Lee had thought through the contingencies of defending his weakened front and had prepared key subordinates for their roles. His command system was far more fluid and flexible than Meade's, and although there were jealousies and conflicts among his officers, Lee's personality created an atmosphere of loyalty and trust. Lee immediately ordered his senior aide, Colonel Venable, to ride to General Mahone, commanding the division south of Bushrod Johnson. Mahone was to draw out two brigades, being careful to conceal the movement from the Federals on his front, and march as quickly as possible to Johnson's headquarters. In so doing, Lee was shortcutting his own chain of command. Orders should have gone from Lee to III Corps commander A. P. Hill, and from Hill to Mahone, with formal notification to Beauregard. But Lee acted with full confidence that Hill and Beauregard would understand and accept the necessity of his action.

Colonel Venable galloped up to Mahone's headquarters at the Branch house a few minutes after 6:00 A.M. to find Mahone prepared for action. The night before he had instructed his brigades to be ready to move at a moment's warning. Now he called out his own former command—the brigade of Virginia troops currently led by Colonel Weisiger—and Wright's Georgia Brigade, commanded by Lieutenant Colonel Hall in the absence of General Ambrose "Ranse" Wright, about fifteen hundred men in all. They slipped out of their places in the line by ones and twos and gathered in a cornfield just in the rear, where they could not be seen by the enemy. Three brigades would be left to cover Mahone's sector—Sanders's Alabama Brigade, Finnegan's Floridians, and Harris's Mississippians—with riflemen spread twenty paces apart.[10]

Weisiger's and Hall's brigades formed up and marched to a farmhouse on the Plank Road, where Mahone, Venable, and Weisiger waited in the shade of a peach orchard. Mahone rode out and halted the column, and ordered the men to drop knapsacks and blanket rolls, "which to the veteran plainly bespoke serious work . . . in the near future." They had two miles to march to reach the scene of the action, and the day was already stifling hot. Mahone turned to Venable and said "I can't send my brigades to Gen. Johnson—I will go with them myself." Venable, acting with Lee's authority, agreed. He knew Mahone's ability, while Johnson was an unknown. Venable then rode back to find Lee, who was gratified by Mahone's decision.[11]

Lee had ridden first to Hill's headquarters to find that the commander of III Corps had anticipated his orders—had ridden out to find Mahone and bring up whatever troops could be spared from his division. Lee and an aide rode south through Petersburg on Halifax Street, out to the valley of Lieutenant Run, a small stream that ran along the west side of the Plank Road. Mahone's men would come by the farm road that ran along the creek, because the slight elevation of the Plank Road would hide them from Federal observers. Lee rode far enough down the path to see that Mahone's brigades were on the way, then turned and rode up onto the Plank Road to assess the state of the front. Lee sat his horse on the open crest line, in plain sight, with Federal artillery shells booming to right and left in their attempt to suppress the fire from Flanner's battery. Lee asked his aide to count the Federal battle flags visible in the breach— he counted eleven, an indication that more than one division had broken through. However, they could also see that the Federal troops were not advancing, and the heavy drifts of gun smoke suggested that their own forces were holding on north and south of the crater.

Then they turned their horses and rode south to a more sheltered position, in the rear of Rives' Salient, a fortification that anchored the defense line south of the crater, where Colonel Venable and A. P. Hill rejoined them. As they conferred, the wounded from Wise's Brigade were starting to come back. Artilleryman Henry Levy stumbled by, clutching his wounded arm, and Lee spoke to him: "My friend, I hope you are not badly hurt." Levy felt he would gladly give his life for such a man.[12]

Young John Wise also saw Lee there, as he accompanied his father to the front. General Wise was in charge of the rear echelon in Petersburg, but "his feeling for his brigade was like that of a father for his children," and he had to see how they were doing under Colonel Goode's command. Father and son left their horses at the mouth of a covered way that led toward the front line. Young Wise was upset to see a fellow VMI graduate, Sergeant Major Suggs, wounded and "as bloody as a butcher's cleaver." Farther down the covered way they overtook a stretcher team carrying Captain Preston, who seemed to have been shot through the forehead above his left eye. The sight moved General Wise almost to tears: "Poor fellow . . . gallant and true to the last." (Preston survived— the wound was from a spent ball, which lodged in his skin.) But General Wise was gratified by the way Colonel Goode was handling the crisis. With the 26th and 59th Virginia supporting Elliott's 22nd and 23rd South Carolina, the Yankee drive south from the crater had been checked. Goode now had the equivalent of a small brigade firing into the southern flank of the Federal line, its own right flank fully protected by the trenches of their main line. Satisfied that Goode was taking care of his brigade, General Wise and his son returned to Petersburg, to rally the teamsters and clerks for a last-ditch defense of the city.[13]

The Breach, 7:00–7:30 a.m.: Griffin's Assault

Meade's 6:00 a.m. telegram had goaded Burnside to act, and at 6:30 he had sent orders to Potter and Willcox to "advance at once to the crest, without waiting for mutual support."[14]

Alone among Burnside's division commanders, Robert Potter was in close touch with the action on his front. His aides, among them Colonel Pleasants, had told him about the paralysis of Ledlie's division and the extreme difficulty with which Potter's lead brigade under Simon Griffin was clearing the trench labyrinth north of the breach. But Potter was also being bombarded with messages from Burnside, urging him to press harder and advance farther without suggesting how that might be done.

Pleasants was being driven to distraction by the torpor and confusion that were transforming his own brilliant technical coup into a humiliating mess. Orders were increasingly irrelevant to the situation; swift decisive action was imperative, but even when troops could be induced to move, they were like men wading through molasses. A colleague said of Pleasants "he was more like a crazy man that day, than one in possession of his senses." So much of himself, of his pride and his reputation, had been invested in this operation that its looming failure weighed equally as a disaster for his corps and a menace to his personality.[15]

The situation, seen without the illusions that bewildered Burnside and Meade, was maddening. Despite Potter's dispatches and the report made by Colonel Loring, Burnside persisted in believing that the troops massed in the breach were capable of gathering themselves for an assault on the hill, when in fact they could not even move out of the way of troops that *might* be able to mount one.

The breach was already so crowded that Bliss's brigade was still in the Union trenches and one of Griffin's regiments, the 6th New Hampshire, had been left out in no-man's-land. The 6th was being torn apart without being able to move or fire a shot in reply. The Rebels were shooting lengthwise down the column, from a projecting angle of their works. Shell fire from the Ellett and Letcher batteries on Cemetery Hill ripped through the pine grove on their right, showering them with kindling. The men lay flat and scraped the hard-packed clay with bayonets and tin cups in a pathetic effort to dig in. The heat rose to more than 100 degrees, and they drank their canteens dry. Captain Crossfield was cut in two by a shell as he lay on the ground: " 'Good-bye boys,'—and he was dead."[16]

Potter wrote to Burnside that sending more troops forward would be utterly useless, unless they were sent against some other point than the breach. Burnside never responded to that report. Instead he kept sending orders to "push the men forward as fast as could be done," with no suggestion as to how that might be done, "and this was, in substance, about all the orders that were received" by any of the division commanders.[17]

Potter would try his best to make the operation work. He recognized that Burnside's 6:30 A.M. order to "push for the crest" implied a critical change in Potter's mission. Instead of clearing the trenches north of the crater and supporting the right flank of Ledlie's advance, his division was now the spearhead. He and his brigadiers, essentially civilians in uniform, had to cope with the difficult tactical problem of changing front under fire. Griffin's brigade had been heavily engaged in the labyrinth for more than an hour. His men would have to disengage, reorient to the west, form a line of battle, and charge up an open slope swept by fire from Confederate artillery on the high ground, from infantry in the lateral ravine in front, and from infantry in the covered way on his flank. To prevent or reduce the enfilade fire from the right, Bliss's brigade would have to be brought forward to charge the entrenched Confederate positions along the base of the ridge running down from Cemetery Hill to the front line. Griffin protested that he could do nothing unless Ledlie's troops also advanced from the vicinity of the crater, and he was promised that the effort would be made.[18]

After his orders were given, Potter made one last try to get through to Burnside: "My division is about advancing again, but my opinion is that unless a very spirited attack is made to the right we shall not accomplish anything." He understood that Willcox's division was preparing to make a supporting attack to the left of the crater, but Potter insisted that the necessary front to assail was to the right, against the trenches held by Ransom's Brigade. That might at least distract the batteries of Ellett, Letcher, and Wright—otherwise their canister would enfilade any troops advancing toward the hill. But the only force concentrated to make such an attack was Turner's division of the Army of the James, and it was queued up back in the north covered way, waiting for Bliss's brigade to get out of its way.[19]

On Potter's order, Bliss got his brigade out of the trenches and formed his regiments in two wings for the advance. Bliss followed his brigade into action, thinking he could better control the movement of his two attack columns from behind the front, but in the confusion half of the 58th Massachusetts got lost, another regiment never got orders to move, and Bliss was separated from the command.

The rest of the brigade went on without him. The 51st New York and 2nd New York Mounted Rifles (dismounted) were on the right—they charged across no-man's-land, got into the rifle pits in front of the Rebel trenches north of the crater, and then worked their way into the main line, filtering through the survivors of Weld's and Griffin's earlier advance. On their left, the 45th Pennsylvania, 4th Rhode Island, and 58th Massachusetts crowded up to the breach—and stalled there, because of the heavy crowding close to the crater. The huge pit promised refuge to demoralized troops from Weld's and Griffin's commands, to wounded men seeking aid, and to details seeking water or ammunition for troops on the firing line. Bliss's troops gradually wormed their way forward, losing some of their companies that mistakenly turned into the crater.

Elements of Bliss's, Griffin's, and Bartlett's brigades were now mixed together, which complicated the command situation for Griffin's assault. The 45th Pennsylvania of Bliss's brigade, a little more than one hundred men commanded by Captain Theodore Gregg, had followed the 4th Rhode Island and 58th Massachusetts into the breach. Being last in line, they stuck near the crater, on the nominal boundary between the 1st Division and the 2nd. General Bartlett was desperately trying to round up troops for another attempt to advance out of the crater. He seized Gregg's men as the readiest to hand and ordered them to charge one of the batteries up near the Plank Road to the west. But Gregg was already under orders to make a charge to the north, with the rest of Bliss's brigade, to protect the right flank of Griffin's attack. After an exchange of messages among Griffin, Bliss, and Bartlett, it was agreed that the 45th would charge on the left of the line when Griffin advanced toward the Plank Road, with Bartlett's troops following, while the rest of Bliss's regiments would move north through the trenches behind Griffin's front and attack toward the north to capture or at least distract the Confederate artillery.[20]

While Griffin and Bliss were getting into position, firing broke out on the southern flank of the breach. General Willcox, commanding the 3rd Division, had also been goaded into attacking by Burnside's 6:30 A.M. order. But Willcox had dealt with the mismatch between orders and reality by interpreting the orders figuratively. Instead of recognizing (as Potter had done) that the task of storming the Plank Road had now passed to his command, he chose to regard the latest orders as merely an injunction to pursue more energetically his original assignment, which had been to protect the left of Ledlie's charging column. Willcox ordered Hartranft to push laterally down the Rebel main line to clear Ledlie's left flank, and told Humphrey to have his brigade ready to cross no-man's-land and join in. Hartranft's riflemen intensified their fire against Goode's Virginians and South Carolinians on their front, while the 27th Michigan on the left of Hartranft's line charged into the open ground between the Confederate main and picket lines hoping to get around Goode's flank. They ran into a murderous enfilade fire from the 23rd South Carolina, safely ensconced behind the main line trenches. The 27th tried to hold their ground but took heavy losses; their colonel was killed and the regiment fell back.[21]

But the rattle of gunfire generated by that attempt tricked Griffin into thinking Ledlie's men were attempting to advance, and he gave the order to attack.

Griffin had pulled as many men as he could find out of the labyrinth. The force that ultimately advanced on his order was drawn from the six regiments of his own brigade, the hundred men of Gregg's 45th Pennsylvania on their left, and some of Bartlett's men. All together, his force cannot have amounted to more than six hundred rifles. The regiments were all terribly understrength to begin with and had been reduced by those killed, wounded, captured, and demoralized in the earlier fighting. Griffin also had to leave a considerable number of troops facing the Rebels to the north, to hold the line until Bliss's attack got going.

Griffin's assault force had to form in the open flat behind the salient, under fire from the arc of artillery positions. Then it advanced up the open slope toward the Plank Road, taking fire from the lateral ravine in their front, which was held by some two hundred men of the 26th South Carolina and 25th North Carolina. They also took fire in the flank from Confederate infantry in the long covered way and the unassailed portions of the labyrinth. The right flank of Griffin's line recoiled from the enfilade; officers began to go down; the advancing troops plodded more slowly and reluctantly, like men walking into a furious rainstorm. . . . They reached that invisible line beyond which it was inconceivable to go, they wavered there, and then all at once everyone was going back, some walking slowly and firing, some running for the trenches.

Gregg's small regiment on the far left did not have to front the riflemen, and they kept going toward a battery (Flanner's) they could see up on the Plank Road crest line. But the guns were far enough away that they could carefully and deliberately fire canister into Gregg's line, until it too broke and officers and men came running back. Gregg, his colleague Captain Richards, and another officer jumped into the first trench they came to. In it was a lieutenant they knew, with half of his face shot away. They bandaged him as best they could and tried to pick their way through the maze back to the Union positions around the breach. As Richards rounded a corner, a Rebel major stepped out, pistol in hand, and demanded his surrender. Then Gregg turned the corner and reversed the balance. The major and two Rebel soldiers surrendered, and Gregg led the whole party back toward the crater—going warily, since they could not tell which parts of the maze were in enemy hands.

Griffin rallied his men and tried to mount another attack, accompanied by some troops Bartlett and Marshall had managed to pry out of the crater, but these moves were aborted almost as soon as they began.[22]

Behind Griffin, Bliss had formed four of his regiments behind the Rebel main line, the 4th Rhode Island and 58th Massachusetts on the left, the 51st New York and 2nd Mounted Rifles on the right. As Griffin's attack began, Bliss's regiments made their rush toward the wedge of entrenchments that backed the first salient north of the crater. Captain George Whitman led half the 51st into the fight. "As soon as the order was given to charge I jumped up on the breastworks and sung out for the men to follow me, and the way they tumbeled over them breastworks wasent Slow. Poor Cap Sims led the right wing in fine style, and just before we reached their works the Johnies skedadled." The attack by Bliss's regiments drove Colonel McMaster and the remnants of the 17th and 18th South Carolina into the salient north of the crater. But the attackers were stopped by the 49th North Carolina of Ransom's Brigade and canister from the Ellett and Letcher batteries that looked down on them from Cemetery Ridge. The 4th Rhode Island and 58th Massachusetts were ordered to charge those batteries, but the charge was misdirected, they wavered, and finally broke under heavy fire, and their elements drifted back into the trenches north of the crater. The fight was costly to both sides. McMaster's small command was hard hit, two entire companies wiped out—killed, wounded, or captured.

Bliss's troops had achieved one of the successes of the day, driving the Rebels back one hundred yards from the breach. But they could not reach or silence the artillery on the northern rim of the battlefield. Wright's battery kept blazing away—it would fire almost six hundred shells in the course of the action. Moreover, their advance into the labyrinth had not compelled the Confederates in the main line to retreat. There was still an infantry force manning that line, defended in front by unbroken abatis and chevaux-de-frise and protected in the rear by the maze of secondary entrenchments. Thus the breach through which Federal reinforcements had to pass was not much wider than it had been, and the gridlock around the crater was unrelieved.[23]

The troops of Potter's division sheltered in trenches and behind mounds of earth and held their gains west and north of the crater in a prolonged and intense firefight with McMaster's and McAfee's Confederates. To the men involved it seemed to go on for hours, biting cartridge paper and the bitter grit of gunpowder in waterless mouths, breathless heat, the sun. The men in the firing lines were losing heart and concentration. A captain in the 9th New Hampshire was accidentally shot by a careless private.

James Chase, the 32nd Maine's seventeen-year-old lieutenant, walked among his men where they sheltered behind a mound of earth. He had a line of shooters along the top, and another seated below, loading rifles and passing them up. He noticed the color guard huddling for shelter, the regiment's colors dipped to hide them. Reckless with the adolescent's sense of immortality, he grabbed the staff, climbed the mound, and planted it defiantly, bullets whipping around him as he jumped down. His captain wanted someone to go up and look through his glasses at the Rebel position up around the lateral ravine—he thought he had seen fresh infantry gathering there. Chase climbed up and saw troops moving down the covered way into the lateral ravine. He turned back to tell the captain.

At that moment he felt a heavy blow to the forehead above his left eye. He went out. When he came back, he was down behind the mound, his captain and the men bending over him. He could see them with his right eye, but his left eye was out and that whole side of his head felt numb. Shock left him oddly detached. Nothing hurt yet. He wanted to see himself. Whatever had happened to him had awed his comrades; they did whatever he asked! Someone held a steel shaving mirror where he could see: a .58 calibre minié bullet had hit him above the left eye; shattering the eyebrow ridge; tearing out his left eye, which hung by a nerve thread; smashing through his nose; and exiting at the inner corner of the right eye—which stared back out of the wreck of his face.

He wanted to know if he was going to die. "Yes, Chase," someone told him, "you have got a death shot." His captain appeared, and Chase bequeathed him his sword, to be given to his father. But the captain was not undone by the horror of the wound and told Chase it wasn't mortal. He washed the wound with water from a canteen and carefully picked bone fragments out of Chase's remaining eye. Then he detailed two men to make a blanket stretcher and carry Chase to the aid station in the covered way.[24]

BURNSIDE'S HEADQUARTERS, 7:00–7:50 A.M.

As Griffin's and Bliss's men were mustering for their supreme effort, Generals Warren and Ord arrived at Burnside's headquarters. Ord was there in response to the order, given by Meade at 6:00 A.M., that he was to advance "independently of General Burnside's troops." Soon after he arrived, a message came from General Turner, commander of his assault division: he found it impossible to move forward because Burnside's troops clogged the breach and had not entirely cleared the frontline trenches from which Ord's attack must take off. Ord sat down and wrote a dispatch to Meade, explaining that he could not obey the order to attack because Burnside's troops blocked the way. Coming on the heels of Loring's miscarried dispatch, Ord's message would convince Meade that Burnside's attack was hopelessly stalled. Burnside asked Ord not to send it, and assured him that he would soon get his troops moving. Ord was skeptical but gave Burnside some slack. Although he reported that General Turner's division could not get out into action because troops ahead of them were "unable to develop," he attributed the problem to the terrain.[25]

At the same time Warren had come to Burnside's HQ to make his own assessment of the chances for success and to clarify the question raised in the telegraphic exchanges among Burnside, Warren, and Meade as to who had the authority to order Warren's corps into action. Warren's bias was against making an assault. The horrible, incessant bloodletting of the overland campaign had convinced him that it was utterly futile to attack an entrenched enemy of any strength. He had never believed in the efficacy of the mine-assault combination: "I never saw sufficient good reasons why it should succeed. I never had confidence in its success. . . . I never should have planned it, I think." Although no sign of a fortified secondary line had been seen, Warren kept telling himself (as he would later tell the court of inquiry) "that is what the enemy had . . . or ought to have had if they did not." He also refused to credit the reports from Meade's HQ and the army signal stations that the Rebel reinforcements moving toward the breach were from Mahone's Division and that therefore the lines opposite V Corps were being weakened. Rather, he insisted those reinforcements were coming from north of the James, despite all evidence to the contrary.[26]

But if he distrusted the operation, he also did not want to bear the blame for aborting it. In his conversations with Burnside and his telegraphic exchanges with Meade, he systematically evaded every invitation that he act on his own discretion, whether it be to attack or to *refuse* to attack.

Burnside invited Warren to come with him for a closer inspection of the front. After they left Fort Morton, Meade's angry telegram arrived (the one sent at 6:40 A.M.), rebuking Burnside for his presumption with regard to Warren, and demanding Burnside attack "at once, and at all hazards." The temporary chief of staff, Julius White, did not know what to do with this message, so he did nothing—did not acknowledge its receipt or send a copy after Burnside and Warren.

The two generals took the north covered way to that part of the line Potter's division had held, now occupied by the 48th Pennsylvania, one of Bliss's regiments, and Turner's advance guard. They climbed a mound of earth behind their own main line and (as Burnside said) "reconnoitred the enemy's position until we were satisfied." They were in time to see the end of Griffin's attack, irregular clumps and lines of blue-coated infantry lurching up the slope behind their flags toward the smoke bank made by the riflemen in the lateral ravine, irresolute, ripped by canister, breaking up and coming back.

Burnside still thought he might succeed if Warren could do something about the fire coming from the batteries to the south of the breach. If Warren could carry those guns, then the troops around the ruined fort could push back the Rebels and widen the breach so Willcox's whole division could be brought through. He told Warren, "I think your plan would be to strike across by the fort which enfiladed our line." Warren parsed those words carefully: Burnside was suggesting, not ordering, Warren to attack. So Burnside had not been delegated authority to dispose of Warren's troops—and Warren was not about to act on a colleague's mere suggestion. He had already told Meade that the position Burnside wanted him to attack was beyond his power. He offered instead to "go back and explain to General Meade the circumstances, and, if possible, get him to come to the front and look for himself." If Meade did that, it would lift from their shoulders a responsibility that Warren did not want and that Burnside could no longer bear.[27]

Warren returned to his headquarters and at 7:50 A.M. telegraphed Meade to explain where he had been and to respond to his query whether Warren ought to attack. Warren endorsed Burnside's idea that it was necessary to attack the batteries south of the breach before making another attempt to storm the crest. But Warren did not offer to make the attack with his own troops, leaving it open for Meade to say whether Warren's or Burnside's men should undertake the attack. His chief point was that Meade should come to the front and take over: "I think it would pay you to go to General Burnside's position," from which he could telegraph orders to Warren as easily as from headquarters.[28]

Warren's idea had merit. From Burnside's HQ, Meade could have judged the state of the battle for himself. A conference on the spot among Meade, Burnside, Warren, and Ord might have clarified the possibilities for action, especially for a major intervention by V Corps—a move Meade had suggested in his 6:05 A.M. message almost two hours earlier.

⁓

In the meantime, Burnside had also returned to his headquarters, where—an hour after it was sent—he finally read Meade's angry response to his "diplomatic" proposal for the use of Warren's corps. All he could see in it was an accusation that his troops had, through recalcitrance or incompetence or a lack of energy and leadership on *his* part, failed in their assignment. What made it worse was his growing sense that imminent failure threatened an operation that was, start to finish, his property. His response at 7:20 A.M. was angrily defensive: "I am doing all in my power to push the troops forward and, if possible, we will carry the crest. It is hard work, but we hope to accomplish it. I am fully alive to the importance of it."[29]

But by now Meade was getting a clearer picture of conditions in the breach. Grant had returned and presumably communicated his own understanding of the situation. Meade was now convinced that Burnside had made a botch of things, and that he had been misrepresenting the facts to conceal the failure of his troops. So Meade's reply (at 7:30 A.M.) should have made the wires crackle: "What do you mean by hard work to take the crest? I understand not a man has advanced beyond the enemy's line which you occupied immediately after exploding the mine. Do you mean to say your officers and men will not obey your orders to advance? If not, what is the obstacle? I wish to know the truth and desire an immediate answer."[30]

Meade had, in effect, called Burnside a liar, as well as imputing cowardice or mutiny to his troops. It was an insult no gentleman could tolerate. Burnside's response was immediate, marked "About 7.35 am." He first defended his men: he did not mean to say "that my officers and men will not obey my orders to advance," only that it was "very hard to advance to the crest." It was not true that his men were still in the occupied line—most of Potter's division was beyond the crater, attacking toward the hill. But the chief matter was personal: "I have never in any report said anything different from what I conceived to be the truth; were it not insubordinate, I would say that the latter remark of your note was unofficerlike and ungentlemanly." But of course, Burnside's words *were* insubordinate. If redeeming his honor required him to break military protocol, so be it. In the Southern army, where the code of honor was taken more literally, a dispute of this kind might have been resolved by an "interview" at dawn, with seconds and surgeons in attendance. Duels were not unknown north of the Mason-Dixon Line, but the greater likelihood was a court-martial. With that in mind, Meade (7:40 A.M.) told Burnside to forward a written copy of his dispatch, so there would be no mistake about its wording.

Now Burnside was alert to the possibility that, if the attack failed, he might be not only blamed but brought up on charges. He therefore instructed his telegraphers to give him copies of all transmissions from Meade's headquarters, and from the other corps headquarters. This was possible because the lines to Warren's headquarters passed through Burnside's telegraph stations. But it was also against Meade's specific orders, which required telegraphers to give messages only to the officers to whom they were addressed.[31]

Meade seemed to recognize that the middle of a major battle was not the time for affairs of honor. At 8:00 A.M. he telegraphed again, telling Burnside that Captain Sanders had come to headquarters and clarified the situation. He now understood that Griffin had attempted to advance and had been checked. The question was, what to do next? Let Burnside report "the exact morale of your men"—that is, their ability to continue to fight—and try to make way for Ord's troops to join the battle on Burnside's right. He ignored Warren's request that he go to Burnside's position and assume effective command of the field.

Grant was present through all of this, but still chose not to intervene. If (as Porter recalled) his earlier visit to the front had convinced him that the attack had failed, it seems strange that he did not advise Meade to call it off and bring the troops back before heavier casualties were incurred. He may have held back in deference to the division of authority that was the basis of his working relationship with Meade. It was important to the morale and efficiency of the army command that he not undercut Meade's authority, especially at a time when Meade's political standing was dubious and his subordinates estranged. The only alternative would have been to replace Meade as commander of the Army of the Potomac, and there was no acceptable replacement at hand. However, the emotional tenor of the telegraphic exchange suggested a serious crisis at the front. Determined to see for himself what was happening, Grant quietly summoned Horace Porter and rode back toward Fort Morton, leaving Meade to direct the next phase of the action.[32]

But the time for maneuvers directed from headquarters had passed. The peremptory orders Meade had already issued were being obeyed, and the last units of Burnside's and Ord's commands were moving to the sound of the guns.

The Charge of the
Colored Division

7:00–8:30 A.M.

General Mahone rode ahead of his troops to confer with the generals on the scene and get a look at the action into which his men would be plunged. The command situation was a little complicated. Mahone was nominally part of A. P. Hill's III Corps of the Army of Northern Virginia but was serving with the forces of the Department of North Carolina and Southern Virginia, commanded by General Beauregard. He tried to check in with Hill first, but Hill was out looking for *him*. So he rode on to find Beauregard at Bushrod Johnson's headquarters, and explained the orders from General Lee that had brought him there. If Beauregard resented being bypassed, he did not show it. Instead he ordered Johnson to turn his troops over to Mahone and let him lead the counterattack. There seemed to be a general understanding that Johnson was not a good combat commander.

Mahone asked Johnson how much of his line the Yankees had managed to capture and how his forces were disposed. Johnson answered vaguely, thought the Yankees were somewhere around "the retrenched cavalier," a reference meaningless to Mahone. After pressing harder, Mahone got the estimate that about one hundred yards of trench had been seized. He asked Johnson to come with him to make an observation of the front, but Johnson declined.

Mahone left his horse at the mouth of the long covered way and walked down it till he came to the lateral ravine. Haskell's two mortars were positioned at the mouth of the ravine, looping shells at the Yankees, and the infantry of the 26th South Carolina and 25th North Carolina made a thin firing line along the low curving rim. Mahone bellied up and turned his glasses on the crater. What he saw was shocking: the Federals had seized far more than a hundred yards of Johnson's front. The crater alone, and the zone of debris around it, was nearly eighty yards across. The Federals appeared to have pushed some fifty yards to the south and a hundred yards to the north of the rim. Mahone counted eleven or twelve regimental flags planted on the crater berm, and from the banks of white powder smoke piling up among the trenches north of the crater, he judged there might be two or three divisions in the breach. On the other hand, the Yankees appeared disorganized. No advance from the crater seemed imminent. But if there had been, all there was to oppose it was the thin gray line here in the ravine and the unsupported batteries along the Plank Road. It was also apparent to Mahone that the two brigades he had brought with him would not be enough to ensure victory. He would need to call up Sanders's Alabama Brigade as well, though it would take several hours for the men to be extracted from their lines and brought into position. In the meantime he would do what he could with the force at hand.

Having assessed the terrain and the distribution of forces, Mahone hurried back up the covered way to meet his troops and give his brigadiers their instructions.[1]

UNION LINES, 7:00–7:30 A.M.

In and around the bombproof where Dr. Chubb had his aid station, traffic was getting heavier. Casualties kept coming through in bunches, pushing up the covered way past the troops of Humphrey's brigade, who had packed the covered way for an hour, ranked two abreast with bayonets fixed, waiting to advance. At 6:30 they had moved up with a yell, but when Chubb stepped outside, he saw they had stopped in the frontline trenches. Shortly after that, troops of the Colored division appeared in the entry of the bombproof, to stand and wait muttering together, voices lowered, accent undecipherable to Chubb but the tone jittery, eager, and nervous.

General Ferrero ducked into the bombproof and sat down to talk with General Ledlie. Soon after, a staff officer arrived with orders for Ferrero to "move his division through and charge down to the city." Ferrero said he would, "as soon as those troops [Willcox's] were out of the way." Since Willcox's men could not move until Ledlie's men cleared space south of the breach, Ledlie very obligingly sent an aide to the crater to

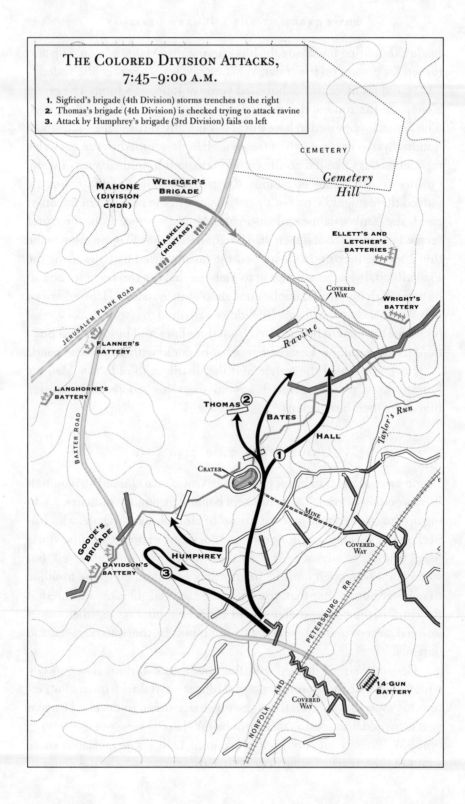

THE COLORED DIVISION ATTACKS,
7:45–9:00 A.M.

1. Sigfried's brigade (4th Division) storms trenches to the right
2. Thomas's brigade (4th Division) is checked trying to attack ravine
3. Attack by Humphrey's brigade (3rd Division) fails on left

CEMETERY

Cemetery Hill

MAHONE (DIVISION CMDR)

WEISIGER'S BRIGADE

HASKELL (MORTARS)

ELLETT'S AND LETCHER'S BATTERIES

COVERED WAY

WRIGHT'S BATTERY

JERUSALEM PLANK ROAD

FLANNER'S BATTERY

Ravine

LANGHORNE'S BATTERY

THOMAS ②

BATES

HALL

Taylor's Run

BAXTER ROAD

CRATER ①

MINE

COVERED WAY

GOODE'S BRIGADE

HUMPHREY

DAVIDSON'S BATTERY

③

PETERSBURG RR.

14-GUN BATTERY

NORFOLK AND

COVERED WAY

"order the troops out of the way, and see that it was done." The two generals remained seated, chatting, and the troops in the covered way still sweated and cursed in place.

Staff officers continued to appear at regular intervals, to repeat to Ferrero Burnside's order to advance. Burnside seemed to believe that repeating the same order at progressively higher volume would somehow produce a different result. Ledlie and Ferrero were of the same mind. Ledlie's answer to every new order to advance was "that he would do so as soon as 'those troops' were out of the way; and whenever General Ferrero made that answer, General Ledlie sent an aid[e] to order the troops out of the way, and see that it was done." Ferrero too seems to have been oddly disconnected from the events around him, as if he had never recovered from the shock of stepping off the boat from Washington into an operation already far advanced. What he made of Ledlie's behavior is beyond guessing. Perhaps he was grateful to find a colleague who was also keeping the crisis at a distance.

At some time between 7:00 and 7:30 A.M., Colonel Loring joined Ferrero and Ledlie in the bombproof. Loring had seen firsthand the gridlock in and around the crater, and like Potter he believed it was worse than useless for any more troops to try to move through the breach. If the attack was to be restarted, troops would have to strike at the unbroken trench lines north and/or south of the crater, in the hope that those garrisons had been weakened to reinforce the crater front. When yet another iteration of Burnside's attack order arrived, Loring intervened. "The order struck me as being so unfortunate that I took the liberty to countermand it on the spot." Ferrero had shown no great eagerness to get his troops into action. Now he professed to be worried about disobeying General Burnside's positive order to advance. Loring assured him that as a senior staff officer he had the authority to countermand the order. He would then go to inform Burnside of the true condition of the front, which (he believed) would persuade him to confirm the order calling off the attack.

Loring hurried to headquarters and made his case. The jam-up in the breach made it impossible for any troops to pass through without losing all organization, and "it was impossible to expect green troops to succeed where old troops had failed before them." The Blacks would not only fail in their own efforts, their intervention would disrupt the troops already defending the captured position.

But Burnside had just received Meade's most peremptory order to attack, had already been told to put in all his troops "white and black" and push for the crest, and he had no better idea of his own to offer. So he simply repeated his previous order and sent Loring back to the bombproof to deliver it.[2]

The order given to Ferrero was that his division was to carry the crest at all hazards, and that "if necessary" Ferrero was to lead them in person. Ferrero then instructed Sigfried to march his brigade "by the flank"—in effect, as a column of twos—until they had gotten through the crowded rear of the Horseshoe and the jam-up around the crater. Then Sigfried was to reform them either as a column or a line, at his own discretion, and "carry the crest." When Thomas brought his brigade up, Ferrero would order him in to support Sigfried on the left. Ferrero seemed to assume that with those instructions Sigfried could carry out Burnside's order, whether or not the division commander himself was able to catch up with the column.[3]

⊰≈⊱

The 4th Division had been in the covered way for an hour and a half, a long column of 4,300 soldiers lined up two abreast. They would squat in place for twenty or thirty minutes and then rise and shuffle forward, expectations rising, only to come to a standstill again. It was impossible to see out of the eight-foot depth of the covered way. The battle was an invisible mystery, an inexplicable rise and fall of percussive sound overhead. Then they had to squeeze together against the right-hand wall because the wounded had begun coming back. First there were small rushes of walking wounded and lightly wounded stretcher cases, some of them jaunty, high on the good fortune that had allowed them to escape from fighting: "I'm all right, boys! This is good for thirty days' sick leave!" Some called encouragement to the Black men waiting to advance, telling them "There's enough of you to eat 'em all up." A Black soldier is said to have replied that "we habn't got jis de bes' kind ob an appetite for 'em dis mornin." The numbers increased to a strong and steady stream, some walking hurt, some demoralized or panic-stricken, some carried bodily or on stretchers, bleeding from open wounds and missing limbs, some grimly silent and others screaming horribly, "moaning or bellowing like wild beasts." Thomas thought the effect on his troops was depressing. "There could be no greater strain on the nerves. . . . Unable to strike a blow, we were sickened with the contemplation of revolting death and mutilation."

Mixed in with the Union wounded were about fifty Confederate prisoners who has been dug out of the crater, some wounded, all of them thoroughly dusted with red clay. At the sight of the Black troops, some of them grabbed their guards and begged them "not to let the niggers bayonet them." One badly wounded soldier, borne on a tent-half, cried "For God's sake, boys, don't let the niggers kill me!" A corporal in Bowley's unit put a canteen to his lips and told him, "Don't be skeered. . . . We don't kill wounded men." Another prisoner, the wounded man's brother, showed his gratitude by giving the corporal two plugs of chewing tobacco.[4]

At 7:30 A.M. the Colored troops got the order to advance. Colonel Russell of the 28th turned to Garland White, the regiment's Black chaplain: "Brother White, good-bye. Take care of yourself—for today some must die, and if it be me, I hope our people will get the benefit of it."[5]

But instead of "one gallant rush," they had to forge their way against the heavy stream of wounded and demoralized men pressing back to the rear. Sigfried's brigade was in the lead, his column headed by the two regiments that had trained for the task of leading the charge, the Pennsylvanians of the 43rd under Colonel Seymour Hall and the Maryland 30th under Colonel Delevan Bates. Behind them came the 39th (Maryland, Colonel Ozora Stearns) and the Ohioans of the 27th (Colonel Charles Wright). The 43rd passed Chubb's bombproof and reached the mouth of the covered way. Ahead of them was an open area, crossed by the marshy banks of Taylor's Creek, and beyond that the Union main trench line. But the area between the creek and the trenches was crowded with the White troops of Humphrey's brigade, which had not yet advanced.[6]

Colonel Sigfried stopped Hall and carefully directed him to move behind Humphrey to the right till he reached the front of the Horseshoe, the sector from which Ledlie's men had jumped off. Ferrero would be waiting there to give him final instructions. Hall led his men across the open ground, crouching as they ran to avoid the overshots from the gunfight around the crater, breasting the gusts of wounded pushing to the rear. Ferrero and the division staff were gathered in the rear of the main trench line, waving to them. Ferrero cried " 'Here comes the Forty-third; let's give them three cheers,' took off his hat, waved it above his head, and led in the cheering." They piled into the frontline trench. Ferrero told Hall to take his men in on the right of the crater, and the brigade would follow.[7]

On Hall's order the men fixed bayonets "with a sharp rattling of steel," and the regiment began to clamber out of the deep trench—still largely devoid of ladders or sandbag steps. As a result the advancing column became attenuated, the first men over-rushing after their colonel while the next group was still being boosted up. Behind them Bates's 30th USCT was fixing bayonets and waiting its turn to go over the top.

Ferrero's headquarters party was now joined by General John Turner, commander of the division from the Army of the James that had been detailed to support the assault. His corps commander, General Ord, had directed him to join the attack more than an hour before, but Turner had been unable to move his troops forward—first because Bliss's men had still been in their lines and later because there seemed to be no room for his troops in the breach. Faced with a conflict between orders and possibilities, Turner decided to see for himself what was happening at the front, a proactive attitude all but unique among divisional commanders that day. With one aide he had made his way into the crater itself—the only division commander to do so—and recognized the impossibility of attacking through it. He had also seen no possibility of a successful attack against the Rebel trenches his division was facing, which were fully manned and fronted by unbroken obstacles. However, the sight of the Colored division going forward, and the possibility that an attack might open some space on the right of the crater, made him feel more optimistic about his chances. After a brief conference with Ferrero he left to organize his division's advance. One of his officers stayed to watch as Hall's men made their charge: "it is their first fight and we wonder if they will stand the shock."[8]

The 4th Division Attacks, 7:30–8:45 a.m.

The 43rd USCT led the charge across a no-man's-land that was now swept by the cross fire of infantry and artillery from Goode's front on the left and Ransom's on the right. As they got closer to the Rebel earthworks, the banging of rifle-muskets became a deafening roar, drowning out the nasty whine of bullets, and the air was dense with the sulfurous fumes of black powder. Shells passed overhead with a sound "like a great bird fluttering over the regiment." From beyond the enemy line they could hear the shouts of their own men and the cries of the enemy.

Hall led the rush up the slope to the crater—the pit below him, packed with men, was a horrible surprise, but he immediately saw the impossibility of trying to move troops through the crater or the clotted trenches near it. It seemed to him that the first tactical necessity was to widen the breach, and what prevented that was the presence of Confederate infantry in the salient that jutted out of the line north of the crater, and in the trenches around it. They were protected from frontal assault by thick abatis and chevaux-de-frise, but from his position Hall could see a narrow lane between the rear of the abatis and the outer slope of the entrenchments. He quickly devised a plan of attack, much like the one his regiment had been trained to execute. He formed the first company to arrive in a column of twos and led it into the gap and along the face of the Rebel trenches while his adjutant remained on the berm to point the way for the following companies. They went at the double-quick along the base of the enemy parapet, ducking under the loopholes when they saw them, so close that some officers and men were wounded by bayonets thrust at them through the loopholes, and others received powder burns from muskets fired just in front of their faces. Captain Wilkinson had his boot heel shot off, then his sword scabbard, and then a hank of hair.[9]

Hall led them forward for about two hundred yards, to the apex of the first salient north of the crater. Then he stopped and called out, "By the left flank, march." The double line of men faced left, men dropping here and there as the Rebels fired. Companies A and C (the color company) were at the right or northern end of the line and were hit hard by this rifle fire. Lieutenants Sherwood and Hogan had the men drop into the Rebel picket line for shelter—a risky maneuver with raw troops because once stopped, they might be hard to restart. But the two companies maintained their discipline. When Hall yelled "Charge," the two companies rose up and joined the rush, and "in that instant, with resistless valor, officers and men threw themselves over his works upon the enemy," the men clambering in at the loops or up the face of the parapet, boosted from behind by their comrades. Watching from the Union lines, the officer of Turner's command saw those "noble fellows . . . cross the field . . . under a withering fire, but still rush on regardless of fallen comrades, and the storm of pitiless lead . . . that pours upon them [from] three sides, and gain the works with a ringing cheer."[10]

After the cheer, the butchery. Hall's men broke into the trench using saber and pistol, bayonet and clubbed rifles. They overwhelmed the frontline defenders and attacked from the rear the Rebel troops who had been holding Bliss's men at bay. Dozens of Confederate infantrymen threw down their weapons, while others held their ground and fought desperately. Many slipped back into the trench maze to the west and north, and then turned to fight again.

Captain Wright, at the head of a company whose men had only been with the command a month, jumped the color guard of the 17th South Carolina with an empty pistol in his hand and captured a stand of battle flags. As soon as they saw that their captors were Blacks, the Rebel soldiers began "praying for him to protect them from the 'niggers.' " They had reason. The Black soldiers, carried away by the fury and terror of their first battle, and by the expectation that they must neither expect nor grant quarter, "killed numbers of the enemy in spite of the efforts of their officers to restrain them." The officers who had used Fort Pillow as a motivating symbol and "no quarter" as a battle cry now had to stop their men from acting on the symbolism.

Their efforts were strenuous and systematic. One captain shot a soldier who "in an agony of frenzy" killed a Rebel prisoner with his bayonet. Lieutenant Steele saw his company closing in on a batch of prisoners being marched to the rear and intervened because the men "in two minutes would have bayoneted the lot of them. It was a queer place for an argument, but I was met by cries that they would kill us, and had killed us wherever they could find us, and we were going to change the game." As he argued with his men, he kept pushing their muskets aside and standing in their way. The soldiers would not physically defy their officer, and the Rebels slipped away under guard. Steele understood their feeling, though he would not let them act on it: "There was a half determination on the part of a good many of the black soldiers to kill them as fast as they came to them. They were thinking of Fort Pillow, and small blame to them."[11]

Hall and his officers did get the killing stopped, and the Confederates began coming out of their bombproofs and traverses, holding their rifles aloft and waving pieces of white cloth in token of surrender. Hall counted two hundred prisoners, all South Carolinians. His men also captured the regimental colors of the 17th South Carolina, and recaptured national colors that had been lost by one of Weld's regiments earlier in the day. Hall sent flags and prisoners to the rear. The Rebel prisoners were used as stretcher bearers—those who stood upon "chivalry" and refused were compelled at the point of the bayonet.

Half of Hall's men were either killed or wounded, but he wanted the rest to get in position to complete their mission, which was to carry and hold Cemetery Hill. He sent Captain Wilkinson's company into trenches on the north side of the captured salient—the one originally held by the 25th North Carolina, some two hundred fifty yards north of the crater. Wilkinson's men would defend the flank and rear of the brigade when they made their charge for the hill. The regimental colors planted on the parapet here marked the extreme right flank of IX Corps' assault force. The rest of Hall's command pushed west through the trenches, toward the sound of the guns—which, to their surprise, belonged to their own brigade.[12]

Behind Hall's men, Bates's 30th USCT had crossed no-man's-land in a long column of fours, their bayoneted rifles held at "trail arms" to minimize accidents when they reached the crowded trenches around the breach. They were followed in the long queue by the 39th and 27th USCT. "We were not 10 yards away from the redoubt when there came the rushing, hurtling sound of grapeshot in close proximity." Canister fire killed men in sets of four and sometimes double sets. "The brains of the Color sergeant were spattered over the flag, but a stalwart Corporal seized the staff" and continued the charge.[13]

Bates led his regiment to the right of the berm and over the breastworks. As they rose above the sheltering bank of the earthwork, the roar and terror of the battle struck them in the face, "the incessant and terrible crash of musketry, the roar of the cannon, the continual zip, zip of bullets as they hiss by [them], interspersed with the agonizing screams of the wounded or the death-shrieks of comrades falling in dying convulsions right in the face of the living." They evidently had expected to be storming an enemy position, and some of the men who had disobeyed the order to leave muskets uncapped began firing. But they had jumped into the confused backwash of Griffin's failed attack, and the men they were shooting at were their own. An ugly friendly-fire fight was narrowly averted by Captain Hough of the 9th New Hampshire, who climbed up on a parapet and waved the national colors. The rear of the regiment went over the berm and into the northern end of the crater, coming suddenly face-to-face with General Bartlett and his staff, who "made frantic efforts to keep us out."[14]

Bates was at a loss as to which way to move. The hill that had been named as his objective was not strikingly higher than anything else on the skyline, the way ahead was blocked by other troops, and enemy fire was coming in from every angle. Major Van Buren of the staff was there, trying to organize Marshall's and Bartlett's men for a charge—and Bates's sudden arrival had thrown the effort into confusion. But Van Buren saw an opportunity to use these troops to eliminate the fire coming in from the north. He pointed out a white house on the Plank Road as Bates's ultimate objective. But he told Bates that before they could assail the hill they had to push back the Rebels who were crowding them in from the north. Bates would have to move to the right and attack the Rebels in the trenches below the ridge that ran down from the hill.

Van Buren returned to the crater to continue the labor of pulling out enough 1st Division troops to make up an assault force. When he looked back, he saw the Colored troops "jumping out . . . and striking off towards the right."[15]

Bates had gotten his men straightened out, and—since the trenches all around were crammed with men—had climbed up onto the main-line parapet and led his regiment in single file along the flattened top, followed by the 39th and more distantly by the 27th. Dashing along the parapet, then across the tops of the Rebel traverses and bombproofs, losing officers and men as they ran, they were able to pass behind and through Griffin's men and strike the breastworks that defended the rear of the salient the 43rd USCT was assailing from the front. The Confederate force here blended elements of Elliott's Brigade and the 49th North Carolina of Ransom's Brigade. Bates heard a Confederate officer yelling " 'Kill 'em!' 'Shoot 'em!' 'Kill the damned niggers!' " The sight of Black troops was a shocking surprise, carrying the force of mortal insult and realizing a Southerner's perennial nightmare. The firing rose to a pitch so intense that Lieutenant Bowley thought the air had become "a perfect rush and scream of lead."

But Bates had more men, and they were fresher than the Rebels and filled with the spirit of the bayonet. "Their usually black faces were an ashy color; the eyes set and glaring, the lips tightly drawn, showing the white teeth; the expression on every face was something terrible; it showed a determination to do or die." They piled into the trench. A Rebel officer urged a group of his men to "Rally, boys! Rally, and drive them back! They are nothing but niggers!" A North Carolina captain "saw the desperate hand to hand fight—saw the bayonets lock—the thrusts given—the rifles clubbed. . . . Maddened by the sight [of negroes] our men were nerved to fight in desperation." A Rebel major called out that they had all better die than "surrender to niggers." Bates's men answered with cries of "Fort Pillow!" and "No quarter!" Captain Floyd of the 18th South Carolina thought they had been overwhelmed by a whole division of "drunken negroes . . . [who] charged as though they were going to eat us up alive, yelling 'no quarters, remember Fort Pillow.' " Bowley saw Sergeant John Offer lower his bayonet and with a "wild shriek" charge right at the officer, followed by a dozen of his comrades. "The Sergeant's cap was off, and the 'plaits' of his hair stood up like little horses, and his frenzied manner made him grotesque and . . . most horrible-looking." Offer "drove his bayonet into the officer's breast, and bore him to the earth"—a Rebel infantryman ran at Offer with his musket reared back to club him with the butt, and was harpooned by a bayoneted musket hurled by Sergeant Dudley. The rest of the Rebels were killed with bayonets or musket butts, or forced to surrender.[16]

The 39th USCT came up to join them, and Sergeant Decatur Dorsey planted the flag of the 39th on the parapet. With the position taken, Black soldiers chased the Rebels into the network of little alleys that spread out into the labyrinth. Every one of these connecting trenches concealed a bombproof or hidey-hole where Confederate soldiers held out. Some would fight to the death rather than surrender to niggers; others came out praying "Lord have mercy on me and keep them damned niggers from killing me." The fighting was more ferocious than anything Bates had experienced as an officer in VI Corps. "It was the only battle I was ever in where it appeared to be just pure enjoyment to kill an opponent," Bates recounted, and he believed that the mutual hatred of Black men and White Southerners was at the bottom of it. Bates was shot five times, and at the height of the action a .58 calibre Enfield bullet ripped through his face from right cheekbone to left ear. His second in command was mortally wounded, and two of his senior captains were killed.[17]

The victory was clinched when the 43rd swept in from the other side of the Rebel position. Without prior planning, Hall and Bates had carried out a perfect pincers movement, with Hall attacking the salient from the front while Bates hit the flank and rear. The two were experienced combat officers who had had the intelligence to recognize where the Confederate line was vulnerable to attack and the initiative to act decisively on that recognition. They had succeeded because their troops were well-prepared, had confidence in their commanders, and were themselves eager to close with the enemy.[18]

That eagerness was due in part to the indoctrination that had convinced them that theirs had to be a fight to the death, with quarter neither asked nor given. Filled with awareness of their own commitment to do or die, and exhilarated by the emotions of a well-managed charge, they believed in the power of their bayonets to overawe the enemy and they "confidently expected that the Rebs, would not stand the cold steel, and so it proved." In this case they benefited from the expectation that any battlefield confrontation between the races would inevitably produce massacre. But the balance of terror could shift if Confederate attackers should gain the upper hand.[19]

The fighting was brief but intense. The 17th and 18th South Carolina and the 49th North Carolina, who had held off every prior attack in this area, were (as McMaster admitted) "driven by the charge of a negro brigade." Most of McMaster's survivors retreated into the covered way and took shelter there and in the lateral ravine. The 49th North Carolina were pushed back into the web of trenches that filled the angle where the long covered way met the main line, where they formed a solid defense in front of Wright's battery.

Sigfried's units also suffered serious losses. All four of the attacking regiments had had their ranks disorganized by the process of passing through the troops in and around the breach. They had been forced to move "by the flank," and even single file, in a long column of twos whose continuity had been continually broken by physical obstacles and the cross movements of other units. A number of men had gotten separated in the maze of trenches, and some of these had inevitably drifted into the crater. To reach their position the units had had to march across the open ground that was subject to a heavy cross fire of infantry and artillery, and they had taken significant losses in doing so. Even out here on the flank of the advance, congestion was a problem: the 27th USCT was unable to squeeze into the front line, and remained back in the trenches close to the main line.[20]

The attack by Sigfried's brigade gave the Union army control of the front for some two hundred yards north of the crater, and cleared enough of the labyrinth behind it to relieve their right flank from rifle fire. With the 30th, 39th, and 43rd in position fronting the lateral ravine, and the 27th behind them as a reserve, Sigfried's brigade was seemingly positioned to make another advance against the lateral ravine and the high ground beyond. But the troops were disorganized by the fighting and by their passage through the trenches. Their position was exposed to a "terrible fire" that came from the infantry and artillery on the ridge that overlooked their right and from the infantry in the lateral ravine in front. The 43rd was in an especially vulnerable position, holding the extreme right of the Union line. Many men were wounded, and others had to leave the firing line to tend them or to guard the prisoners. Others became separated from their companies while pursuing Rebel fugitives into the tangles of the trench complex. There was a natural letdown after the victory, a tendency simply to take cover and seek some respite from danger, to recover from the shock of battle, to savor the sense of having passed a great test. It had all taken less than half an hour.[21]

Sigfried's three advanced regiments had already lost something like half of their original strength, either to combat or the friction of pushing their way through the White troops ahead of them. The loss among officers was particularly severe, and it was about to get worse. When Colonel Hall climbed up onto a parapet to inspect the ground over which he expected to charge, he was immediately hit by a bullet that shattered the bone in his right arm just below the shoulder. A soldier used Hall's handkerchief to make a tourniquet and led the colonel back through the trenches to the crater and back to the Union lines. As they were crossing, Hall had an altercation with an unnamed colonel who tried to snatch the captured flags and prisoners (and the credit) from the 43rd's guard detail. That was the last service he was able to do his regiment: his arm would be amputated that afternoon. Colonels Hall and Bates had been chosen to lead the assault because they were considered the best combat commanders in the division. Both were now out of action.

There was a brief lull. Lieutenant Proctor of the 30th explored a bombproof to satisfy his "Yankee" curiosity about what the johnnies had had for breakfast—found and enjoyed a plate of corn cakes. When he came outside, he heard a Rebel officer call out, "Stop firing!" Proctor found the ensuing quiet ominous and told his men to load their guns and stand ready. One of his soldiers pointed to a body lying in the trench and said, "That man ain't dead; shall I kill him?" When Proctor told him to let the fellow live, "the supposed dead man rose up and made a very pathetic appeal for his life." He said he was from South Carolina but had always been opposed to the war and had been conscripted to serve. Proctor sent him to the rear.[22]

❧

Thomas's brigade also went through the laborious process of boosting men over the breastworks and getting them started for the breach. The delay was significant: Thomas's lead regiment was half an hour behind Hall's 43rd USCT. Ferrero's orders were for Thomas to pass through the breach "by the flank" and reform on Sigfried's left. The New Yorkers of the 31st USCT led, commanded by Colonel W.E.W. Ross. They were followed by the 19th, the Maryland outfit originally commanded by Thomas himself, now led by Lieutenant Colonel Perkins; the Baltimore/Washington "hard cases" of the 23rd (Colonel Cleaveland Campbell); six companies of the incompletely recruited 28th, the Indiana regiment led by Lieutenant Colonel Charles S. Russell; and the Illinois 29th, commanded by Colonel Bross in his splendid full-dress uniform and Burnside whiskers. As they were going forward, Hall's stretcher bearers were bringing him back to the lines. He called encouragement to the 19th as they went past him: "Go in, boys; there is plenty there for all of you."[23]

Ferrero followed them part of the way across—then turned and came back. His orders did not *require* him to go in with his troops. It was barely twenty-four hours since he had returned from Washington. He seems not to have known what to do with himself, so he went back to the bombproof and rejoined General Ledlie.

Thomas led his brigade across no-man's-land, running straight for the berm of the crater. Sergeant Harry Reese was watching them from his position in front of the mine—like Pleasants, consumed with frustration and anger at the incompetence of the assault.

> If I had known what a blunder was going to be made in the assault
> . . . I never would have gone into [the mine] to relight the fuse. . . .
> It made me still more furious to see a division of Colored soldiers
> rushed into the jaws of death with no prospect of success; but they
> went in cheering as though they didn't mind it, and a great many of
> them never came back.

General Potter was also watching from a position on the right of the Horseshoe. He too was impressed by their good order, but that did not alter his view that to jam more troops into the battle on this part of the front would simply compound the confusion. He had just seen Griffin's assault repulsed and had no intention of obeying yet another order to "attack at all hazards." He was going to Burnside's headquarters to ask him personally "not to send any more men there."[24]

But in the crater Major Van Buren still had hopes of mounting an assault, and he was gratified to see Thomas's men as "they came on in good style, under a sharp fire, . . . much broken and disordered by the unfavorable ground."[25]

Thomas and the brigade staff led the way up onto the berm, and they too were stunned by their first sight of the crater. No troops could have hoped to pass through at this point. Thomas shifted their direction to the north, to the area where Bates had crossed the line. The crowding and confusion there had gotten worse. Thomas's double column had to squeeze down to single file and march by the flank, pushing and shifting and wangling their way through. Their organization was deranged; individuals and squads went astray in the trenches or brushed too close to the crater and were drawn in. Colonel Joseph Barnes of the 29th Massachusetts saw them "pouring through the opening down into the crater" in some numbers. Still, Thomas's officers did a remarkably good job of keeping their men together, and Major Van Buren saw them go "right over the tops of the bomb-proofs, and over the men of the first division" advancing despite fire that was coming from guns near the Plank Road and up on the ridge to the right, as well as from mortars in a position he could not see (in fact, the lateral ravine only some two hundred yards away).[26]

Thomas led his raveled files to the right, looking for Sigfried's troops, whose advance he was supposed to support. Instead he found a line of rifle pits a few hundred feet west of the main line, and jumped at the opportunity they offered to shelter and reorganize for a further assault toward the lateral ravine. The 31st and 23rd regiments took serious casualties as they rushed into the position, and found the pits were useless for defense—too exposed to offer much shelter, and "entirely occupied by dead and dying Rebel troops, and our own." They dug frantically to connect the pits and make a shallow trench protected by a low parapet.

The rear of Thomas's long thin column was broken up by crosscurrents among the White troops through whom they had to pass. Lieutenant Beecham and his platoon of the 23rd went left while the rest of the regiment went right. The 28th and 29th regiments also lost contact with the rest of the brigade as they passed close by the crater. They strayed to the left and a number of their men drifted into the pit. One of Bross's file closers in the 29th, a "massively built [sergeant] stripped to the waist," caught one of his men trying to duck into the crater—grabbed him and threw him over the berm facing the enemy with the words, "None ob yo' d—n skulkin'." Bross led both regiments to shelter on the reverse of the cavalier that ran across the face of the crater that faced the enemy. Confederate riflemen hit them as they ran, concentrating fire on the color-bearers. Corporals Isaac Stevens and Frederick Bailey were killed—Stevens was free and a bachelor, Bailey a former slave and the father of a young child— but Corporal Brown planted the colors on the parapet and the two regiments took cover. The 19th USCT was unable to get all the way forward, and there was no room for it behind the cavalier. The regiment took shelter or attempted to dig in close to the northern end of the crater.[27]

Thomas's position was about seventy-five yards northwest of the crater, facing uphill toward the lateral ravine, from which came a steady stream of infantry fire. He had not been able to connect with Sigfried—the troops on his right were the defeated elements of Weld's and Griffin's commands. He had lost touch with the 28th and 29th, which were not yet in position behind the cavalier. Thomas believed the responsibility to carry the crest now devolved on him, and as soon as the 31st and 23rd reached the rifle pit line, he tried to form them for an attack. He sent his orderlies, carrying the brigade's guidon flags, to mark the center and flanks of his line, and then ordered the charge. But as soon as his troops began the assault, the Confederates in the ravine hit them with heavy and continuous rifle fire, supported by shell fire from Flanner's guns on the Plank Road and canister from the ridge. Colonel Ross of the 31st was shot and killed; his second in command, Captain Wright, was killed as he bent over his colonel; dozens of noncoms and enlisted men were hit; and the third ranking officer was also killed, leaving the regiment without its senior commanders. The 23rd lost fewer officers, but its enlisted ranks were cut up. The attack fell apart before it got well started, and the soldiers went to ground where they were.

Thomas's beloved comrade, Lieutenant Christopher Pennell, tried to inspire them to rise and try again. He took one of the brigade guidons from a wounded orderly. Holding the staff with its green pennant in his left hand and drawing his sword with his right, he stood up and began to run along the front of the line, "trying to call out the men along the whole line of the parapet." It was a deliberately sacrificial gesture, so astonishing in its display of courage that the White troops in Weld's command stopped firing, and some "were shot because, spell-bound, they forgot their own shelter in watching this superb boy." In other battles, enemy soldiers had been known to hold their fire in tribute to such displays of individual courage. Not here. "In a moment, a musketry fire was focused upon him, whirling him round and round several times before he fell." The Black troops of the 31st who rose to join him as he ran along the line were "mowed down like grass." The men clung to the earth, afraid to rise up, as if an iron lid had been slammed down over their heads. Behind Thomas's position, Major Rockwell jumped up on the parapet and tried to lead the 19th USCT forward in support. He was instantly shot down "and fell back dead, with a cheer on his lips."

Thomas was profoundly shocked by Pennell's death and the decimation of his command. Pennell's body was not recoverable: "He was doubtless literally shot to pieces, for the leaden hail poured for a long time almost incessantly about that spot, killing the wounded and mutilating the dead." The rifle pit line was too exposed for defense. Thomas called for his men to retreat, and they turned and dashed back to take cover in the nearest section of entrenchments. Of all the officers who had stood up to join the charge, only Thomas and his aide, Captain Dempcy, had survived unhurt.[28]

But Major Van Buren was still working hard to make IX Corps' attack succeed. He had been running up and down the line, trying to organize a coordinated advance all across the front. He now believed he had the necessary elements in hand. He had conferred with Marshall on the left, who'd promised to muster an assault out of the vicinity of the crater, and then with Sigfried on the far right. He found Thomas with his troops, hugging the ground under direct fire from the lateral ravine in front and enfilade from the artillery on the right above the long covered way. Thomas agreed to make the assault but gave Van Buren a message for General Burnside: "Unless a movement was made to the right, to stop the enfilading fire, not a man could live to reach the crest." Notwithstanding, Thomas would attempt to carry out his present orders by attempting another attack in ten minutes, coordinated with Sigfried on the far right and the White troops (Griffin's) between them. It was approximately 8:30 A.M. The attack had been under way for more than three and a half hours.[29]

By coincidence more than by direction, something like a coordinated assault was finally taking shape across the Union front. On the presumption that the charge of the Colored division was the start of a general advance, Turner ordered brigade commander Colonel Bell to move out of the Union lines and cover its flank by passing through the captured line to the right of the crater. Colonel Coan, commanding Turner's other brigade, was ordered to threaten an attack on the trenches well to the right of the breach, to divert fire from Bell. Coan got as far as the belt of trees, and most of his brigade took shelter there, maintaining a sharp fire on the enemy. One regiment, the 97th Pennsylvania, managed make a small lodgment in the Rebel line about halfway between the crater and Wright's battery. Bell's brigade reached the Rebel lines to the right of the crater, only to find the way forward still blocked by the congestion in the trenches. The brigade's formation was partly sheltered by the captured breastworks, but they were hit by canister from the one-gun battery to the south and by intermittent rifle fire from the flanks. Their casualties accumulated slowly.[30]

Back at army headquarters, Meade had received some very promising reports about the initial attack of Sigfried's brigade, and at 8:45 A.M. he finally gave General Warren the order to "go in with Burnside, taking the two-gun battery" south of the breach. But Warren did not instantly obey. Rather, he spent the next half hour studying the enemy positions and a new Federal attack by Humphrey's brigade of Willcox's division.

Colonel Cutcheon and the 20th Michigan, Humphrey's brigade, were still in the Union lines when the last of Thomas's regiments rushed past their rear heading for the jump-off from the Union front line. "As soon as the last regiment of the colored division had passed out [of the lines], the order came, 'Forward, Second Brigade!' " Willcox intended their assault to silence the artillery firing into the breach from Davidson's one-gun battery. Colonel DeLand of the sharpshooters stood on the parapet, trying to get some sense of the terrain his men would have to cross, when a Confederate shell exploded in the soft earth below the trench face. The blast of dirt and gravel "skinned" one whiskered cheek and part of his scalp. Shocked and bleeding heavily, he was led to the rear by an orderly sergeant while Captain Elmer Dicey, the ranking officer, led the regiment forward.[31]

The 2nd Michigan led the way over the breastworks, followed by Cutcheon's 20th Michigan and the 1st Michigan Sharpshooters. None of the three mustered more than one hundred fifty men, and the 20th had only one hundred fifteen "guns in line." As they ran forward, dodging shell fire and skirting the shell holes and debris that littered the field, the three regiments became somewhat mixed. The abatis in front of the enemy's line had not been cleared, and as the Michigan troops grappled with it, they were hit with canister from the two-gun battery on Goode's front, which killed or wounded dozens of men. They broke through the obstacles but then had to run across two hundred yards of open ground, under heavy fire from Davidson's guns and the rifles of Goode's Virginians. Their objective was the section of Rebel trench south of the "abandoned fort"—the unexploded half of Pegram's battery that had been captured by the 14th NYHA at the beginning of the battle. Hartranft's brigade of their division was somewhere on the other side of the fort, holding on after the failure of their last advance. But the Michigan regiments got support from the two wrecked cannons in the fort, which had now been restored and were being manned by Sergeant Wesley Stanley and a pickup squad from the 14th and Hartranft's brigade.

The Sharpshooters took the lead after they passed the abatis, and they got in under the parapet of the Rebel picket line some seventy-five yards south of the crater. When the 2nd came up, the two regiments went up and over—there were twenty Rebels in the position, and they surrendered immediately. On their left, Cutcheon's 20th Michigan followed suit, and captured another thirty men. A Rebel lieutenant who tried to run away to avoid surrender was hit by a bullet from his own side—for as soon as the Michigan troops got into the position, it was swept by fire from Confederates in the main line. The Rebel wounded begged to be sent to the rear, but Cutcheon found that he could not move his own wounded because of the intense fire.

Now Humphrey sent his other four regiments forward on the left of the Michiganders to storm the one-gun battery, which was the keystone of the Confederate defenses.

Confederate Colonel Goode had been begging his division commander, Bushrod Johnson, to send him some help and to come see for himself the state of things. But Johnson remained in his headquarters, enjoying his breakfast, and his responses showed the same incomprehension of real conditions that made Burnside's and Ledlie's orders appear so absurd—except that where Burnside kept demanding that his troops attack at all hazards, Johnson wanted Goode to hold at all hazards. It did not help Goode's state of mind that Johnson's dispatch assumed the position Goode was defending was several hundred yards away from the one he actually held.[32]

Colonel Goode had only one infantry regiment, the 46th Virginia, to meet Humphrey's second attack. Two other Virginia regiments, and the 22nd and 23rd South Carolina of Elliott's Brigade, were deployed to confront Hartranft's and Marshall's troops on the southern side of the crater. To meet this new threat, Colonel Goode ordered most of these troops to shift their fire. As Humphrey's second wave advanced, they were hit by rifle and artillery fire from the front and by oblique fire from the Virginians and South Carolinians. The regiments in this advance were also seriously understrength. The lead regiment, the 46th New York, was staggered by the concentrated fire of canister and minié bullets and then broke and ran, carrying the other three with it.

The left wing of Van Buren's would-be offensive had shot its bolt, and there was now no organized reserve for the left of Burnside's line. But Van

Buren persisted in his efforts to organize a coordinated assault, to be led by Thomas's USCT units and supported by rallied elements of Marshall's, Bartlett's, Griffin's, and Sigfried's brigades. But they would face an enemy who had been strongly reinforced.

Mahone Prepares to Counterattack, 8:15–9:30 a.m.

The first of Mahone's two brigades had finally arrived at the mouth of the long covered way. Sergeant George Bernard of Company E, 12th Virginia, saw his brigade commander, Colonel Weisiger, conferring with Mahone as they stood by their horses. "For the first time that day, a line of infantry was between our guns [on the Plank Road] and the enemy." To young John Wise, Mahone's men looked "weather-worn and ragged" but also war-hardened, lean, and as "agile as cats." General Lee expressed his relief that Mahone's men were at last on the ground.[33]

Mahone preceded his men down the covered way. Near the junction with the lateral ravine he met a fugitive from McMaster's command, which had just been overrun by Hall and Bates. He tried to stop the man to find out what had happened, but the soldier just blurted, "Hell is busted back thar," and kept going. Mahone went on up the ravine to a low knoll, at the point where another ravine cut in from the west. From this higher ground he could see how the Federal force in and around the crater had increased in just the last twenty or thirty minutes. There looked to be eight thousand men or more, and they held a position three hundred yards wide. His two brigades mustered no more than fifteen hundred rifles, and even with the aid of the troops that had been holding the Federals back all morning, he would be outnumbered. If he expected to drive the Yankees out of the breach, he would need more fresh troops. Before forming his attack, he sent an aide to bring up another of his brigades—the Alabamans commanded by General Sanders.[34]

His men ducked through the tunnel under the Plank Road and trotted single and double file down the covered way to the junction of the ravine, where Haskell's mortars were planted. The brigade sharpshooters led the column, followed by the 6th, 16th, 61st, 41st, and 12th Virginia—perhaps eight hundred men, the 61st the largest unit with about two hundred. As they came down the covered way, they met more fugitives from the fighting below. As Colonel Stewart of the 61st remembered it, when the Virginians began "ridiculing them for going to the rear, . . . one of them remarked: 'Ay, boys, you have hot work ahead—they are negroes, and show no quarter.' This was the first intimation that we had to fight negro troops." The news "seemed to infuse the little band with impetuous daring, as they pressed onward to the fray. Our comrades had been slaughtered in a most inhuman and brutal manner, and slaves were trampling over and mangling their bleeding corpses. Revenge must have fired every heart and strung every arm with nerves of steel for the herculean task of blood." Meade Bernard of the 12th Virginia also remembered meeting fugitives from Elliott's Brigade, one of whom told the Virginians to "show them no quarter, boys, they raised the black flag on us and showed us none." However, Bernard had only "an indistinct recollection that 'this same soldier informed us that a large portion of the enemy . . . were negroes.' " Neither Major Etheredge of the 41st nor Sergeant George Bernard of the 12th remembered hearing that the Yankees had shown no quarter, and Bernard did not discover that there were Black troops on the field until he engaged them face-to-face.[35]

The Virginians "flanked right" and filed up into the ravine. Mahone ordered the men to lie down. All orders were given in an undertone so that their presence would not be suspected. Muskets were ordered to be loaded, but without the percussion caps set—so the men would close with the enemy rather than stop to fire. Colonel Rogers of the 6th was impressed by the order "No shot is to be fired until after the men are in the broken trenches. . . . Let your men understand that it is only forward, and with cold steel." There had to be no doubt in the soldiers' minds that they would close with the enemy. As the orders were passed down, officers in each company spoke to their men, using whatever rhetoric and tone had proved to be most effective in instilling fighting spirit in their neighbors and kinfolk. Some units "distinctly heard the command: 'Fix bayonets and no quarters.' " In Bernard's company, Captain Jones spoke "with great coolness of manner: 'Men, you are called upon to charge and recapture our works, now in the hands of the enemy. They are only one hundred yards distant. The enemy can fire but one volley before the works are reached. At the command . . . every man is expected to rise and move forward at the double-quick and with a yell. Every man is expected to do his duty.' " Bernard was lying next to his young friend Emmet Butts, a fellow lawyer. There was a superstition to the effect that a man was safest in battle if he stayed in his appointed spot in line, and for some reason Bernard felt the need to defy it. So he proposed that he and Butts trade places, and Butts agreed "with a smile."[36]

At some point they were reinforced by the 61st North Carolina, the only troops General Hoke could spare from the northern section of the front. Mahone had wanted the Georgia Brigade to file past the Virginians and form on their right, but the Georgians were just now coming down the covered way, and a glance down the hill told Mahone and Colonel Rogers that the enemy were preparing to charge.

Mahone would not wait. He had Weisiger's Brigade in line and the 26th South Carolina and 25th North Carolina as a reserve. If nothing else, he would make a spoiling attack, striking the Yankee advance before it gathered momentum and its disparate elements pulled together. As he turned to give the order, the artillery on the Plank Road opened a concentrated fire on the troops assembling in front of the crater.

Mahone's Counterattack

9:00–11:00 A.M.

Colonel Thomas never received a response to the urgent request for support he had sent to General Ferrero. What came back was an order that exposed Ferrero's utter incomprehension of the disaster in which his troops were immersed: "Colonels Sigfried and Thomas, if you have not already done so, you will immediately proceed to take the crest in your front." Did the man actually suppose they had already stormed Cemetery Hill? But Thomas would obey the order.

Four groups of units would participate in the assault. The 28th and 29th USCT would lead the left-most group, attacking from the cavalier line, hoping to be supported by rallied elements of Marshall's and Bartlett's brigades. Thomas's 23rd and 31st USCT would be on their right, attacking out of the trench complex north of the crater. On Thomas's right, Griffin would rally his troops for another try at storming the lateral ravine, with Sigfried's brigade advancing to protect their right flank. Since these groups were not in immediate contact with one another, the advance by Thomas's troops would be the signal for the assault.

In each of these sectors, officers had a difficult time reorganizing their troops. All of the units tapped for the assault had suffered serious losses, especially in officers, and all had been disorganized by their entanglement in the crowded trenches around the crater. The two regiments under Thomas's immediate command had retreated into trenches already occupied by the survivors of the earlier attacks by Weld and Griffin. The 31st was shattered by the losses suffered in the last attempt to charge, so Thomas had to sort out and concentrate the companies of the 23rd to make up his attack force. But the 23rd had also lost a lot of officers and men, and part of this regiment (with Lieutenant Beecham) had attached itself to Colonel Bross and the 29th.

On Thomas's left the 28th and 29th USCT held the gorge line that covered the front of the crater facing the enemy, the 29th under Bross right up on the line and the 28th sheltering in rifle pits behind them. They were perhaps fifty yards more advanced than the 23rd of Thomas's command. These regiments had also gotten their ranks tangled in the advance, had suffered serious losses among junior officers, and in seizing their line had mixed with White units already in place. Their position was not ideally suited to making a charge: they were behind the cavalier parapet of the gorge line, and the trench was on the opposite side. To begin the charge they had to mount the parapet, jump the trench, form up, and then rush the hill. Colonel Russell of the 28th was not sanguine about their prospects. "The troops were very much dispirited," and packed together "just as thick as they could possibly stick."[1]

In the ruined fort, behind and to the left of Bross and Russell, Colonel Marshall and his officers were trying to pull enough troops out of the crater and the fort to give weight to Thomas's attack. Captain Kilmer of the 14th NYHA had been encouraged by the sight of Thomas's men advancing across no-man's-land "in splendid order," and he was able to rally some of his men with the promise that this reinforcement would turn the tide. But he could not overcome the inertia produced by hours of disorganization and discouragement, and the habits inculcated by weeks of trench warfare, which made the men unwilling to leave the shelter they had found. Moreover, some of his troops "declared that they would never follow 'niggers' or be caught in their company, and started back to our own lines." They were held to duty at gunpoint, but there was no hope of inducing them to charge.[2]

The survivors of Griffin's brigade held the trenches on Thomas's right. Their losses had been extremely heavy and their morale severely weakened by the failure of their earlier assaults. When they'd retreated into the trench labyrinth, their regimental organizations had been broken up, and they had become intermixed with the 1st Division troops that had hunkered down in the trenches north of the crater. It was a remarkable achievement for Griffin and his officers to rally some hundreds of them for yet another attack, but these soldiers had already tested the Rebel positions and found them too strong to be carried. Faced with strong resistance, they would back off rather than try to close with the enemy.

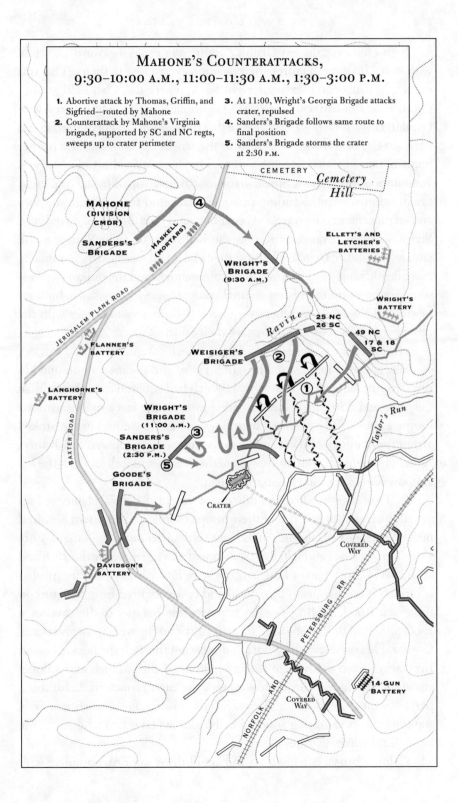

MAHONE'S COUNTERATTACKS,
9:30–10:00 A.M., 11:00–11:30 A.M., 1:30–3:00 P.M.

1. Abortive attack by Thomas, Griffin, and Sigfried—routed by Mahone

2. Counterattack by Mahone's Virginia brigade, supported by SC and NC regts, sweeps up to crater perimeter

3. At 11:00, Wright's Georgia Brigade attacks crater, repulsed

4. Sanders's Brigade follows same route to final position

5. Sanders's Brigade storms the crater at 2:30 P.M.

CEMETERY

Cemetery Hill

MAHONE (DIVISION CMDR)

SANDERS'S BRIGADE

HASKELL (MORTARS)

WRIGHT'S BRIGADE (9:30 A.M.)

ELLETT'S AND LETCHER'S BATTERIES

WRIGHT'S BATTERY

Ravine

25 NC 26 SC

49 NC 17 & 18 SC

JERUSALEM PLANK ROAD

FLANNER'S BATTERY

WEISIGER'S BRIGADE

LANGHORNE'S BATTERY

Taylor's Run

BAXTER ROAD

WRIGHT'S BRIGADE (11:00 A.M.)

SANDERS'S BRIGADE (2:30 P.M.)

GOODE'S BRIGADE

CRATER

DAVIDSON'S BATTERY

COVERED WAY

PETERSBURG RR

NORFOLK AND

COVERED WAY

14-GUN BATTERY

Sigfried's brigade, on Griffin's right, was in an awkward position, with Rebel infantry in entrenched positions very close to theirs. This was especially true on the extreme right flank, where the 43rd held strongpoints nose to nose with the North Carolinians in the long covered way. Captain Horace Burr was "very sure that the right of the Forty-third could have shaken hands with the Rebs in the works beyond, had the proper frame of mind existed on both sides." They were also short of water and ammunition. Lieutenant Steele made four round-trips through the cross fire in no-man's-land, sending prisoners back and trying to get supplies and replacements forward.[3] Casualties and confusion had reduced Sigfried's three advanced regiments to half strength. (The 27th was still jammed up in the trenches behind them.) All had lost heavily in officers, and the 30th and 43rd had lost their commanders and the ranking successors. Sigfried ordered his regimental commanders to reorganize for a renewal of the assault, and then went back to the crater to confer with the other brigadiers about coordinating their efforts.

His men were scattered through the trench complex they had carried, so the regimental flags were brought forward and the men summoned to rally around them. The 39th USCT, which had suffered fewer losses than the 30th and 43rd, probably provided most of the force that assembled for the advance. They formed their lines as best they could in the broken ground, still under canister fire from the ridge, and prepared to advance. At that moment Lieutenant Bowley of the 30th heard a cheer from the left and saw Thomas's men begin their rush.[4]

In Thomas's position the officers of the 23rd USCT clambered up out of the trenches and called their troops to follow. About two hundred men, White and Black intermixed, got to their feet to follow them. Fifty yards to their front and left, their movement was mirrored by the 28th and 29th USCT. Both parts of the brigade were hit by heavy rifle fire (probably from Goode's units to the south) and case shot fired from the guns on the Plank Road. As Bross's men mounted the parapet of the cavalier, a shot splintered the flagstaff and tore up Corporal Brown's wrist and hand. Corporal Maxon lifted the colors and was shot through the neck. Captain Brockway seized the broken staff and mounted the parapet, and a bullet smashed his ankle. The 29th wavered, the men crouching behind the parapet—they could see and hear all too clearly the consequences of standing up, "the grating sound a ball makes when it hits a bone . . . the heavy thud when it strikes flesh."

Colonel Bross, conspicuous in his full-dress uniform complete with yellow sash, grabbed the colors and hopped up onto the parapet of the cavalier. "The man who saves these colors shall be promoted," he cried. The regiment rose to his call. He turned and jumped over the ditch on the far side, and as he did, a bullet thumped hard into his body. "Oh Lord!" he cried, and as the troops rushed past him, he called out, "Forward, my brave boys." The flag was taken from his hand by the seventh man to carry it that day. Neither flag nor bearer returned. Of 400 men who had followed Bross into the battle, only 128 came back.[5]

Behind Bross, Russell and his officers called for the 28th to charge. As they mounted the parapet, the color-bearer, Sergeant Thomas Hayes, had his right arm nearly torn off by shrapnel or a canister ball. He fell backward into the trench, and his left leg was impaled by the bayonet of an abandoned rifle jammed in the ground. Other officers and men were shot down, among them Captain Hackheiser—the German immigrant who had written to his fiancée, Miss Kinder, about the gratification he felt serving his adopted country and working with former slaves. Russell thought no more than two hundred men out of both regiments were behind him. Other units along the line saw the Black regiments start forward and moved to join them. Some of the men Marshall and Kilmer had gathered tried to advance on Thomas's left, and Griffin's men rose to join them on the right. That was the signal for Sigfried's troops, who also started forward.

But the advancing lines had none of the solidity and solidarity necessary for a successful attack. Units were too widely separated to take heart from one another's presence, let alone to offer support.[6]

❧

General Mahone, up in the lateral ravine, had a comprehensive view of the Federal advance. He could see their units were thin, widely spaced, and wavering as shell fire began to flower among them. Mahone and Colonel Rogers of the 6th Virginia saw a Union colonel—almost certainly Bross—standing on a parapet encouraging his men. They saw him "seize his colors and spring over the protecting ditch, and by every gesticulation showed the way to the front—and perhaps to victory." Some of the troops behind Mahone, seeing the enemy forming for the attack, fired without orders—a scattering volley, yet it seemed to make the Yankees waver.[7]

The time to hit the Yankees was before their attack could gather itself together and build momentum. Mahone's men would have the advantage of surprise, rising out of the concealment of the ravine, and they would be charging downhill. His men were fresh and their morale was high. Mahone gave the order to charge, instantly echoed by Weisiger, and eight hundred men rose to their feet, formed their double line of battle, and stepped in unison forward up and over the rounded rim of the ravine. In two more steps they were moving downhill at the double-quick, bayoneted rifles at port arms, and they let loose the stretched-out falsetto howl known as the Rebel yell. Overhead the supporting barrage homed in on the core of the Federal position, the lines around the crater.

Sergeant Bernard of the 12th Virginia was at the extreme left of the brigade line. "Just as we were well over the brow of the hill, I cast my eyes to the right, and I will ever carry a vivid impression of the rapid, but steady and beautiful, movement of the advancing line of some 800 men . . . their five battle-flags . . . floating in the bright sun-light of that July morning." But Bernard was dismayed to see that Captain Jones had lied about the hundred yards—it was nearer to two hundred fifty to the Yankee lines, enough to give the enemy time for three volleys at least.

As the attack developed, the battle line of Weisiger's Brigade stretched out to the right, as the sharpshooters led the 6th and 16th Virginia on an oblique against the crater and Thomas's advancing troops. The other three regiments charged toward Thomas's and Griffin's troops, the 61st on the right, the 41st in the center, and the 12th on the left. Just behind them the 26th South Carolina and 25th North Carolina joined the advance, moving toward Sigfried's position. The South Carolina troops and the 49th North Carolina holding the trenches on the right flank intensified their fire when they saw the Virginians advance, and then joined the attack, driving in on Sigfried's and Bliss's troops from the north.[8]

THE FEDERALS BREAK

The fighting turned in a flash, a reversal so sudden it seemed instantaneous. To Lieutenants Bowley and Silverwood, watching from Siegfried's position, it seemed to take only three minutes from the moment Thomas's and Griffin's men stepped off until the sudden outcry of "The Johnnies are charging! Here they come!" Silverwood saw the rebels "rise out of ground" in line of battle and rush down on Thomas and Griffin. In the next moment the advance dissolved into a disordered rush of men, Black and White, running for the rear.[9]

The Union troops were not skulkers or slackers. These were the men who, in spite of all obstacles, had pressed to the front and continued striving to drive home a costly and difficult attack. They were still willing to try, but by now they had seen too much of the effectiveness of enemy fire on the ground in front of them. They were probably right up against that invisible deadline beyond which not even the bravest man could be expected to go—when Mahone's battle line, two hundred yards long, rose up suddenly out of the ravine, lowered its bayonets like the teeth of some monstrous harrow, and began marching down the hill toward them at an accelerating mechanical cadence. They could see the whole of the Rebel line, which reached well beyond the flanks of their own units and was more cohesive.

Thomas's units were the most advanced, and were therefore the first to be assailed and the first to break. Lieutenant Bowley saw Thomas's men "coming back faster than [they] went over," and beyond them White troops of the 14th NYHA "stampeding for the Crater like a flock of sheep." The part of Griffin's brigade that had tried to advance with Thomas also broke, "a panic commenced [and] black and white troops came running back together."[10]

The different elements of the Federal attack force had never managed to join together. When they broke, each element turned and ran for its starting point as the likeliest place to find cover, and Mahone's regiments divided up in pursuit. Three major streams of retreat developed, and three corresponding lines of pursuit and attack. On the Federal left, the 28th and 29th USCT and the White troops advancing with them broke back through the ruined fort and into or around the crater, pursued by Mahone's sharpshooter battalion and the 6th and 16th Virginia. In the center, Thomas's and Griffin's units sought shelter in the trenches north of the crater, where they were assailed in front by the 61st and 41st Virginia and hit from the flank by the 12th Virginia, which found an undefended gap between Griffin's and Sigfried's units. On the right Sigfried's brigade was attacked from the front by the 26th South Carolina and 25th North Carolina out of the lateral ravine, and by the elements of Elliott's and Ransom's brigades that had hung on in the trenches to their right. These same elements also attacked the defensive positions held by the survivors of Bliss's brigade behind Sigfried's right. In the chaotic and bloody fighting that followed, the Confederates succeeded in retaking most of the trench line north of the crater, by killing, capturing, or driving out the defending units. But Federal troops were able to hold on and rally in the ruined fort and the trenches around the crater and stop Mahone's counterattack short of its goal.

To make sense of this complex action we have to follow the sequence of events in each of these streams, starting on the left with the troops that had advanced from the ruined fort and the cavalier line in front of the crater.

The troops that had charged with Bross and Russell had been hit hard by rifle and shell fire as soon as they'd attempted to go forward. Bross and many of the officers had been killed or wounded, and several color-bearers had been shot down before Mahone's men suddenly emerged from the lateral ravine. When the Virginians' battle line swept down toward them at the quickstep, the Union troops broke and ran back the way they had come. However, not all were routed. A group of Black troops from different units, without officers, rallied behind the cavalier parapet and fired back at the advancing Confederates. They held out for ten or fifteen minutes, loading and firing as fast as they could, checking the advance of the 6th and 16th Virginia and forcing Mahone's sharpshooters (who led the right of his line) to take cover and fire back. The riflemen were able to work around and hit them from the side, and in the end the Blacks "were nearly all shot away." Lieutenant Beecham was less fortunate. He took his stand behind an earthwork, and "a few of my colored boys, who knew no better, stayed with me, and we all got it in the neck, or where it answered the same purpose." Mahone's men swarmed over the parapet before Beecham's group could fire a volley, Beecham's first sergeant shot the Rebel color-bearer, and in the next moment the sergeant was shot dead. Beecham was hit and rolled into a bombproof to hide as the Confederates swept over and through his position, killing the men who manned it.[11]

Most of the 28th and 29th USCT were driven back to the crater, and individuals sought shelter in the trenches just north of it, in the crater itself, and in the ruined fort. The 19th USCT had wedged itself into the line to the right of the crater and stuck there, "unable to strike a blow, but receiv[ing] heavy losses" from the barrage laid down in support of Mahone's advance. The eruption of retreating troops split the regiment, driving about one hundred officers and men into the crater and the rest back across no-man's-land. Sigfried, who had gone to the crater to confer with his fellow commanders, did not know the charge had been broken until a White color-bearer with his colors dashed through the position, followed by dozens of soldiers, White and Black, fleeing to the rear. Sigfried was unable to get through the rout to rejoin his own command and so eventually made his way back to the Union lines.

On the left of the crater the USCT fugitives were mixed with demoralized elements of the 14th NYHA and 2nd PPHA of Ledlie's division as they swept into the ruined fort, which was defended by Hartranft's brigade and part of the 14th NYHA. Colonel Marshall, commander of Ledlie's 2nd Brigade, tried to stop the rout but was swept out into no-man's-land. Rather than follow these fugitives to safety, he made his way back and resumed command of his brigade.

Hartranft did his best to hold on to the ruined fort, the only possible anchor for a defensive position. The three Michigan regiments of Humphrey's brigade were still holding the captured rifle pits and trenches south of the fort. Hartranft ordered the 20th Michigan—the most distant of the three—to retreat into the fort and form a cordon to check the stampede of troops through that part of the line. Colonel Cutcheon complied, with fewer than one hundred men: "It was the most fearful panic I ever saw or imagined . . . fearful, sickening, *shameful, shameful,*" White troops and Black mixed together in abject flight. But the rout passed through the fort, and the Michiganders stepped up to the embrasures alongside Sergeant Stanley's restored cannons to add their strength to the defense. Cutcheon's men were now thoroughly mixed in with Hartranft's and Marshall's, fighting as individuals not as an organized force.[12]

Meanwhile a lone Black rifleman, who had been on the far left of Bross's advance, kept on up the slope after the rest of the line had peeled away. Somehow in the smoke and confusion the right of Mahone's advance swept past him, and then there was nothing in front of him but Flanner's battery up on the Plank Road. Even if it had occurred to the gunners that the man marching toward them was an enemy, they would hardly have wasted a shell on him. The man kept on, crossed the Plank Road in the space between the gun positions, and marched on into Petersburg, where he was finally surrounded and captured. He was never asked to explain his actions. Perhaps he just wanted to show that the Colored division could have done the job if it had been allowed to.[13]

❦

The central stream of the retreat flooded into the section of captured trenches between the crater and the salient captured earlier by Sigfried's brigade. Here too individuals and small groups of soldiers (Black and White) stopped behind the nearest cover and turned to fire back at the enemy. They barely had time to fire once before the Confederates were on top of them, crying "No quarter!" as they plied their bayonets. The 61st and 41st Virginia burst through a thin line of Black infantry, elated by the thought that Negroes "could not stand the Rebel yell and cold steel."[14]

In many places it was possible for troops to escape through the trench complex back to and through the main line, all the way back to the Union lines. Some may have run over the tops of the bombproofs, traverses, and parapets. In other places the trenches in front of them were cleared by troops that had seen the rout and decided to head for home. Thomas was carried out beyond the main line but managed to rally a number of his men as they passed out of the Rebel trenches, and they took cover with the 97th Pennsylvania, the regiment from Coan's brigade (Turner's division) that had made a lodgment in the Confederate picket line about one hundred yards north of the crater.[15]

But for most of the men who fled Mahone's advance, the trench labyrinth proved a trap. It was ill-suited for rallying. Soldiers jumped into it by platoons and squads, and found themselves in a crook or corner, cut off from other units by the twists and turns of the trenches. It was easy to become disoriented, to lose the sense that told you which way was home and which toward the enemy. Some of the trenches were already filled with the troops that had been repulsed in the earlier attacks led by Weld and Griffin. The routed troops piled in on top of them, wounding some with their bayonets, destroying whatever organization had remained. To a man in the 9th New Hampshire it seemed that the Negroes jumped into the midst of his regiment, reducing them to "a mass of worms crawling over each other."

For the Black units the difficulties were compounded. Because they had pressed the attack so strongly, they had lost heavily in officers and senior noncoms. They had no experience of being rallied after a defeat, had not learned that it was possible, let alone how to do it. They also were psychologically burdened by the presumption that for them the only choices were victory or death—and now victory was impossible. As Mahone's men came on, Lieutenant Kenfield (17th Vermont) heard their officers ordering their men to "save the white men but kill the damn niggers." In the desperate confusion some White Yankees became as murderously enraged against their Black comrades as they were against the rebels. Private Barnes (9th New Hampshire) heard one of his comrades yell, "Give the black devils a dose, and then take the bayonet to the rebels."[16]

Fighting in the labyrinth was face-to-face, as enemies turned blind corners and blundered into one another. Private Holland of the 41st Virginia was shot in the breast, bayoneted in the mouth, and had two teeth knocked out by a swung rifle butt. Captain Hunt of the 31st Maine shot a Rebel with his pistol at so close a range that the bullet went through and killed another soldier. Private Putnam Stith of the 12th Virginia rounded a bend in the trench and blundered into an appalling confrontation—one of his comrades down and "a negro who had the most fiendish countenance I had ever seen" was standing over him, the muzzle of his rifle against the comrade's head. Everything happened in an instant that somehow seemed to take forever. Stith drew his rifle back and swung the butt at the Negro's head. He had time to note that "there was a malicious grin on [the Negro's] face," time to wonder why the Negro had not already swung his rifle around and shot him, before his gun butt slammed into the soldier's head and put him down. "I will state here that several times in my dreams in the twenty odd years that have elapsed since the battle of the Crater I have seen this same negro with the same horrible countenance."[17]

Colonel Weld of the 56th Massachusetts (Bartlett's brigade) was cut off when his own regiment pulled out, and was carried by the momentum of the retreating troops into a trench where White troops and Black "were packed in there like sardines in a box. I literally could not raise my arms from my side." Nor could he see over the top of the trench in which he was stuck. He had time enough to appreciate the horror of his situation. "Men fell dead in heaps, and human gore . . . made the very earth mire beneath the feet. . . . It was a perfect pandemonium." Then he heard Confederate soldiers yelling and looked up to see a battle flag on the parapet just above his head—then "muskets were pointed over the parapet, and discharged into the confused mass of our men below, who could do nothing in defense." The 41st and 61st Virginia, with part of the 12th, had charged up to the lip of the trench, from where they could shoot Yankees like hogs in a pen.[18]

At almost the same moment, the Federal position was attacked from the flank by elements of the 12th Virginia that came pouring down the trench lines from the north. Most of the 12th struck a gap between Sigfried's and Griffin's lines. Sergeant Bernard never saw a live enemy until he entered one of the little ditches that opened into the trench complex. A Black soldier suddenly rose up in front of him, "the first colored soldier I ever saw, and this was my first knowledge of the fact that negro troops were before us." Far from feeling murderous rage, Bernard was glad to let the Negro surrender so Bernard could keep moving on. Bernard blundered through the trenches, turned a corner—and saw only thirty feet ahead of him a trench jam-packed with soldiers. He had struck the flank of the line held by Weld and Griffin, and his unit was positioned to pour fire down the length of the trench, killing half a dozen with every bullet. But again he held his fire, because "I regarded these also as practically our prisoners."[19]

Etheredge's and Stewart's men did not share Bernard's scruples. They fired down into the packed trench and could hardly miss a shot. Federal officers and men yelled surrender, but it wasn't easy to get the shooting stopped.[20]

Lieutenant Kenfield took off his sword and stuck it into the side of the pit in which he was sheltering. He took out his gold pocket watch and chain and hid them in his boot—a prisoner would need items of value to trade. The Rebels swarmed around him, took his hat and revolver, and hustled him to the rear. As he went, he saw Mahone's soldiers "run their bayonets through many a colored man showing him no mercy. I often think of this scene and a cold shudder goes through me as I think of how those poor colored men were butchered in cold blood." Black troops tried to surrender, "but were not allowed to do so." Sergeant Bernard of the 12th Virginia was also sickened by the killing of wounded and unarmed Blacks, most of which occurred during the first ten minutes after the surrender. "The whole floor of the trench was strewn with the dead bodies of negroes, in some places in such numbers that it was difficult to make one's way along the trench without stepping on them."[21]

Weld was cornered in a bombproof along with a Black soldier. Rebels standing only eight feet away called out, " 'Shoot the nigger, but don't kill the white man'; and the negro was promptly shot down at my side." Weld surrendered, and the Confederates stole his haversack and other belongings. One took his hat and clapped a shabby substitute onto his head like a man snuffing a candle. With other prisoners Weld was led over the parapet to the rear, across ground swept by the fire of his own army. A Black soldier was trudging along ahead of him. In rapid succession a Rebel soldier rushed up to the man and shot him through the body, another stepped in and shot him again, and then another shot him, and "he dropped dead at the third shot. It was altogether the most miserable and meanest experience I ever had in my life."[22]

It took the Confederates a considerable time to break into the Federal positions and force the surrenders of the units trapped there. It also took time to work through the labyrinth of ditches leading back to their original main line, and pockets of resistance had to be mopped up along the way. Until that process was completed, Federal troops at the northern end of the line were able to retreat toward the crater down the trenches of the

Rebel's original front line. That was the route followed by elements of Sigfried's brigade that were not ready to give up.

⤚⧽

Sigfried's brigade, on the far right of the Union line, was caught in an awkward position by Mahone's counterattack. Three regiments held the lines facing north and west. Elements of Bliss's brigade, including the 51st New York, held the right flank and faced north. They were threatened by infantry on the front and the flank, and were also exposed to interlocking fire from the Ellett and Letcher batteries on the ridge and Wright's battery on the main line. An attacking force built around the 39th USCT had been culled from the troops holding the lines and had just begun its advance when the Rebels rose out of the ground and swept down on Thomas and Griffin. In the next instant the positions held by Sigfried's men were crisscrossed by fire from the 49th North Carolina and the remnant of the 17th South Carolina that had been holding the trenches on their right, and from the 25th North Carolina and 26th South Carolina advancing down the covered way from the lateral ravine.[23]

Sigfried's position was not in the direct path of Weisiger's attack, so the officers had a brief interval in which to realign their men and open fire. But their own forward momentum was stopped, and they were being hit by heavy fire from two directions. A cry went up: "The white troops are breaking! Close in to the left!" They tried to close up with Griffin's retreating line, and for a few minutes the Black troops held their line as they moved backward and to the left, step by step, firing as they retreated.[24]

The Confederates on the northern side of the field saw the powerful onset of Mahone's troops sweeping downhill, saw Griffin's men break and Sigfried's men stumbling backward. The Confederate officers recognized the turn of the action and called their men up to seize the victory. The 49th North Carolina and the remnant of the 17th South Carolina made a rush from the flank as the 26th South Carolina and 25th North Carolina attacked from the front. "The enemy charged with a yell and poured a volley into their very faces. Instantly the whole body broke" and ran for the trenches, some in a panic, but many just looking for a place to make a stand. Officers and color-bearers tried to rally knots of men—the 43rd lost four captains and six lieutenants in short order. Black NCOs stepped in to take command; the color-bearers were shot and replaced. Captain Seagrave and a small group of Blacks refused to surrender. Seagrave with his knee shattered by a bullet emptied his pistol and slashed out with his sword, killing or wounding six men before the Rebels swarmed in, killed his men, and bayoneted and clubbed him down with musket butts.[25]

Lieutenant Silverwood saw the Rebels closing in and took responsibility for saving the colors of the 43rd. He acted as rear guard for the color party, keeping the Rebels off with his revolver as they dodged through the trenches to the main line. The color guard dropped over the parapet into no-man's-land, but when Silverwood sprang onto it to follow, he was hit by a combination of live and spent bullets that knocked his sword out of his hand and broke three of his ribs. He tried to rally the men in a ravine just outside the works, but the blows of the spent bullets had damaged his lungs, and he collapsed, bleeding from mouth and nose. Color Sergeant Decatur Dorsey similarly led a contingent that fought off Rebel pursuers and saved the flag of the 39th USCT, for which he would win the Medal of Honor.[26]

The 51st New York and the remnants of Bliss's brigade were also driven from the trenches they held on the northern flank of Sigfried's position. Captain Samuel Sims jumped up onto the breastworks, exhorting his troops to make a stand, and was shot down by Sergeant LaMott of the 17th South Carolina. An admiring Confederate officer thought Sims's conduct "as heroic as ever illustrated on any battlefield." But the gesture was useless. The 51st gave way. Captain George Whitman inherited the command and tried to halt the retreat at the Rebel's main line, but the men refused to stop until they had regained the Union lines.[27]

Lieutenants Williams and Hand of the 43rd were with the companies holding Sigfried's extreme right flank, and they held out for some time after the main position fell, bypassed by the assault. Hand thought it might have been as late as 11:00, though it was probably closer to 10:00 A.M. when the Confederates broke into their position, "finishing or capturing the few left." A Rebel soldier pinned Hand to the ground with a bayonet thrust but an officer stopped his assailant from killing him. There were a number of Black soldiers isolated in rifle pits and bombproofs, and the Confederates routed them out, killing most of them. Colonel William Pegram saw a Black soldier fighting with one of the Confederates. The man was surrounded and forced to surrender. When a Confederate told the Negro he was going to kill him, the Black man snatched up his musket again and fought desperately until another soldier shot him dead.[28]

The soldiers who fled or retreated from Sigfried's position followed three different routes. Some units, whose officers retained control, retreated down the trench line toward the crater, where it seemed possible to make a longer stand. Other fugitives from the 30th, 39th, and 43rd chanced on the section of Rebel line held by their own 27th USCT, and rallied there. The Ohioans had been stuck in the trenches to the rear of the advance, unable to move up through the press of bodies. The Confederate attack swept past their position as it headed for the crater. Lieutenant Colonel Charles Wright held his position briefly, fending off probing attacks by Ransom's Brigade. But they were completely isolated and in danger of being cut off. Luckily there was a shallow ravine that ran from their position into the belt of trees in no-man's-land. Wright's men filed into it and made their way back to their lines in good order, with relatively few casualties.[29]

However, most of the routed troops from the brigades of Bliss, Sigfried, and Griffin fled through the labyrinth and broke across the main line along a section of trench one hundred to one hundred fifty yards from the crater. Their flight led to the collapse of the whole right wing, reserves as well as assault force. Just on the other side of the breastworks was Bell's brigade of Turner's division—technically a part of X Corps, though serving this day with Ord's XVIII Corps. Turner had sent them forward to support the Colored division's attack, but they had been unable to get into the crowded trenches, and had remained in an exposed position outside the Confederate lines, taking casualties without being able to advance, retreat, or return fire. Now the fugitives swept down on them like a rock slide, and "in less than ten seconds that line had vanished and there was no more Tenth Corps in that neighborhood." General Turner was outraged by the stampede, and blamed it all on the Colored troops, who "for some unaccountable reason . . . were seized with a panic and came rushing back to our lines."[30]

The rout of Bell's brigade eliminated any hope of mounting a new attack on the north side of the crater. Coan's brigade held its position for a time, providing some cover for the troops fleeing across no-man's-land, but it soon withdrew to the Union lines. The 6th New Hampshire of Griffin's brigade had also been left out in no-man's-land, guarding a nonexistent flank under a steady cross fire. Once the trenches north of the crater were abandoned, the North Carolina troops facing them intensified their fire. The 6th New Hampshire had to retreat under the gun, and Sergeant Major Cohn was badly wounded running orders up and down the line. (He would win his second Medal of Honor for his work.)[31]

General Potter had just found Burnside and Ord in the fourteen-gun battery, peering through an embrasure trying to discern what was happening in the haze and smoke. He had come to deliver in person the message that it was worse than useless to keep sending troops into the breach, and had barely opened his mouth to speak when he heard a confusion of firing, shouts, and cries. When he turned to look, he saw "that this division of colored troops had given way and was coming back." Without completing a sentence, Potter turned and ran to look after his division. He reached the front line in time to meet the wreckage of his two brigades as they spilled across no-man's-land and piled into and ran over the trenches they had left three or four hours before.[32]

The fleeing troops poured back over the Union breastworks. Some rallied in the old front line, among them Lieutenant Proctor and some of the 30th USCT. Now that he was safe, shame and rage overcame him: "I was literally insane over our defeat, and walked along slowly, watching the Tenth Corps and our men put in their minutes, swearing like a sea cook." Then "a cannon shot disemboweled a young soldier a few feet in front, and the demoralization seized me, and I rushed for cover." Most of the fugitives kept going, back through the two covered ways and over the open ground alongside, never stopping till they were safely behind Fort Morton. General Ord tried to stop them, and was knocked flat by the rush.[33]

In the bombproof by the mouth of the south covered way, Dr. Chubb and his colleague Dr. Smith were tending to the wounded when they heard the cries and saw the rout go past the entryway. Generals Ledlie and Ferrero stepped in out of the clamor and rush, and "General Ledlie asked me for stimulants, and said he had the malaria, and was struck by a spent ball. He inquired for General Bartlett, as he wanted to turn over the command to him and go to the rear." An aide told him, without apparent sarcasm, that Bartlett was in the crater, from which he had been sending reports since 5:00 A.M. Smith gave Ledlie rum and whiskey, and Ferrero asked for some as well. He too confessed that he was exhausted, but after getting his stimulants, he went back out to the front line. Ledlie remained in the bombproof for another half hour, and then went to the rear.

Not all of Sigfried's and Griffin's defeated troops took the direct route back to their own lines. A second stream of retreat led along the trench lines toward the crater. Many of those who took this route simply preferred the shelter of the trenches to running the gauntlet of fire across no-man's-land. But many were still under command and were trying to get back to the crater and the ruined fort to rally and make another stand. Lieutenant Warson led a contingent from the 43rd USCT out of the Confederate main line and then turned toward the crater, moving between the main-line parapet and the Rebels' abandoned picket line. About one hundred yards from the crater they found the 97th Pennsylvania holding out in an angle of the picket line, along with Colonel Thomas and some troops from his brigade. Warson and his men attached themselves to Thomas's command and dug in.[34]

Lieutenant Bowley of the 30th USCT gathered a number of soldiers from his regiment who wanted to stay and fight, and he led them through the traverses toward the crater with "the Johnnies not 20 yards behind us." They were halfway there, passing behind the trenches in which Stewart's and Etheredge's regiments had trapped Weld's troops, when a section of Confederates fired at them from behind a bombproof. Bowley heard a piercing scream from the rear—the corporal carrying the regimental flag had been shot dead, the blue flag with its eagle insignia and regimental number was on the ground, and pursuing Confederates were running up to seize it. "Big Bob" Bowen of Company H turned and charged the Rebels, hurling his bayoneted musket ahead of him like a spear. The Rebels ducked, Bowen snatched up the flag, "sprang like a deer over the breastwork and ran for the Union line." This was heroism, not flight—to save the flag from capture was a moral imperative—and it also distracted the pursuers, who blazed away at the flag bearer while Bowley and the rest crouched and dodged their way the last hundred yards to the crater.

Ahead of them Bowley saw General Bartlett standing erect among the bullets, shouting encouragement to his firing line. Bowley's men covered the last few yards on the run, and just as Bowley reached the edge of the crater, he turned to look back and caught a brief glimpse of the pursuing Confederates bayoneting the wounded men who had been shot down at his heels. He jumped the berm and landed in the shallow north end of the crater. His men were the last of the defeated troops to reach the crater by way of the trenches and traverses.[35]

They had found a precarious shelter. Routed troops were still rushing through the position in bunches, heedless of everything but the necessity of getting back to their lines, carrying away with them many of the troops who had been defending the trenches just north of the crater. Black soldiers seemed to predominate on the northern, or right, side of the crater, a crossroads of the retreat paths for Thomas's and Sigfried's units. Officers and color-bearers from a number of different regiments rallied the Black troops in the rifle pits and trenches and got them firing back at the advancing Confederates, but Bowley thought there were no more than seven hundred defenders in this part of the line.[36]

There was a sudden upsurge of firing, and Mahone's Confederates came charging out of the smoke. A major from one of the USCT regiments planted his colors on the crest of the berm, and the Black troops with him opened a heavy fire on the Rebels charging the face of the crater and the ruined fort. Lieutenant Kibby of the 4th Rhode Island (Bliss's brigade) walked along Bowley's line helping him steady the men, saying "Shoot low, boys, shoot low" and setting an example with his revolver. In contrast, another officer cringed against the crater wall, "wildly waving his sword and shrieking . . . 'Drive them back! You must drive them back! We'll all be killed if they capture us in here with the negroes!' "[37]

The troops attacking this end of the line were Mahone's sharpshooters and the 6th and 16th Virginia. These outfits had charged obliquely down from the ravine, and so had a longer march across open ground than the rest of the brigade. They had been checked at the cavalier trench when Bross's and Russell's men had made their brief stand, and when they moved against the crater, they were hit with heavy fire from Union soldiers along the berm and from the two captured cannons, restored by Sergeant Stanley, firing out of the ruined fort. The sharpshooters caught the brunt of it, but the other two regiments were decimated as well. Colonel Weisiger was wounded leading the attack and carried off the field. Colonel Rogers of the 6th Virginia took over and led a desperate charge that carried some of his troops into some trenches just north of the crater, where the fighting was up close, with bayonets and clubbed rifles. The Federal units were all intermixed. The 21st Massachusetts, one of Ledlie's regiments, lost its colors, and Sergeant Wilkins of the 9th New Hampshire, a survivor of Griffin's failed attack, recovered them in a hand-to-hand grapple. A big Rebel officer got Captain Gregg of the 45th Pennsylvania by the throat, put a pistol to his head, and demanded his surrender. Gregg somehow broke free, got the Rebel's pistol, and killed him with it—just as Sergeant Bacon shot the Rebel soldier who was trying to skewer Gregg from behind with his bayonet. Corporal Hogan killed the color-bearer and captured the flag of the 6th Virginia, and Colonel Rogers was cut off and taken prisoner by an isolated squad. But the Federals were driven out of the position and Gregg led the survivors back toward the crater, protected by Blacks who "kept up a heavy fire of musketry on the advancing enemy, compelling them to take shelter."[38]

While Rogers's troops had been attacking near the crater, the other three regiments of Weisiger's Brigade were finishing the mop-up of hold-outs and the removal of captured Yankees from the trenches to the north. Led by Colonel Stewart and Major Etheredge, the regiments had begun to push south through the trenches toward the crater. Word of the capture of Rogers and the repulse of his attack goaded them to action. Some elements continued to push through the trenches, colliding with knots of Yankees in sudden close combat. They pushed the Federals back till they could see the crater smoking like a volcano with the constant musketry. Others were organized to dash across the open ground to take the defensive lines by storm. Major Etheredge of the 41st Virginia thought that half the brigade was shot down trying to get to the positions held by the Yankees. He led his men over the breastworks and into the ditch. Their muskets were uncapped, so they fought with bayonets and gun butts—"drive the bayonet into one man, pull it out, turn the butt and knock the brains out of another, and so on until the ditch ran with the blood of the dead and dying." Etheredge and Stewart had to detail men to pile the corpses out of the way—they were thick enough to impede troop movement. Closer to the crater Captain Broadbent of the sharpshooters led a charge that rescued Colonel Rogers after a hand-to-hand struggle, but the Yankees countercharged, killed Broadbent, and drove his troops back. The sharpshooter company of Weisiger's Brigade was annihilated. Of a hundred men who began the action, all but six were killed or wounded.[39]

Meanwhile Sergeant George Bernard led his squad through the backwash of Etheredge's and Stewart's assault, through trenches where stray Yankees were still being mopped up. Close to the crater the squad saw a bunch of Black soldiers being pursued by Confederate soldiers, who shot at them and beat them with rifle butts. One of the Blacks ran toward Bernard as a Confederate soldier drew a bead on him from behind and shot him dead—so intent on killing the Negro that he was careless whether the bullet went through or by him and hit Bernard. "A minute later I witnessed another deed that made my blood run cold." A Black soldier with a sergeant's chevrons on his sleeve was "begging for his life" as two Confederate soldiers stood over him, one "striking the poor wretch with a steel ramrod" while the other shifted around as if looking for an angle, and then shot him in the hip at point-blank range. The soldier "clapped his hand" to the wound and continued begging for his life. "The man with the ramrod continued to strike the negro . . . whilst the fellow with the gun deliberately re-loaded it, and placed the muzzle close against the stomach of the poor negro, fired, at which the latter fell limp and lifeless." The sight revolted Bernard and the men with him. "It was a brutal, horrible act, and those of us who witnessed it from . . . a few feet away, could but exclaim: 'That is too bad! It is shocking!' "

He rejoined his regiment, which was holding a shallow communication trench and exchanging rifle fire with Federal troops on the northwest side of the crater. Here he learned that his friend Emmet Butts, who had dared fate by switching places in line with Bernard, had been killed by a shot through the forehead.[40]

General Mahone had remained in the lateral ravine, where he could follow the ebb and flow of the action. His Virginians and the North and South Carolina troops had cleared the trenches north of the crater and driven the Federals back into the original breach, but he saw Weisiger's men recoiling from the crater and the ruined fort. Despite that check, Mahone thought he had the Yankees on the run and that a follow-up attack would finish the job.

The Georgia Brigade had arrived in the lateral ravine just after Weisiger's troops had made their charge. There were about seven hundred men in four regiments, the 3rd, 22nd, 48th, and 64th Georgia. Officially it was Wright's Brigade, named for its famous commander, Ambrose "Ranse" Wright, but with Wright on medical leave it was commanded by Colonel Hall. Mahone told Hall to move out of the ravine to the south onto the open slope below the guns of Flanner's battery on the Plank Road and then wheel and attack toward the south side of the crater. The Georgians' advance was to be supported by Weisiger's men, firing from sheltered positions in an arc that covered the northwest quadrant of the Federal position. They leveled a devastating fire on the crater, aided by the large number of rifles and cartridge boxes they had captured. While one man fired, another loaded the next rifle and passed it up, so that the fire was nearly constant.

To provide the Georgians with additional support, and to put more pressure on the Federals, Mahone asked Colonel Haskell to bring additional mortars close to the crater. Haskell went to scout out a good position, his empty left sleeve pinned up to the shoulder, a borrowed pistol in his right hand. He turned the corner of a trench and came face-to-face with a Federal officer and a squad of Black troops. Haskell fired first, killing the officer, and his call brought Confederate infantry, who killed all the Blacks. Now with an escort he continued to scout out mortar emplacements in rifle pits a stone's throw from the crater. Then he went back for his light mortars, known as "eprouvettes" by the officers and "dog-mortars" by the enlisted men. But they did not arrive in time to support Hall's attack.[41]

The Federal troops who had rallied around the crater were not entirely demoralized. They were in well-protected positions with plenty of ammunition. Two strongpoints anchored their line. On the right there was a strong force of riflemen, mainly Blacks, on the berm and in the trenches just north of the crater, the men packed together as close as possible. They gave as good as they got in the firefight with Weisiger's men. The weakest part of the line was the middle portion, the crater itself. In front of it was a thin line of men from every one of Ledlie's regiments and some of Thomas's, sheltering in ditches and shell holes. Behind them another line of riflemen clung precariously to the crater berm, many of them kicking their heels over empty space and the thirty-foot drop to the crater floor. The strongest position was the ruined fort on the southern flank, and the trenches alongside it. The two restored artillery pieces were manned by Sergeant Stanley and his pickup gun crews from the 14th NYHA, now joined by Captain Rickard and a contingent of the 19th USCT. The riflemen were from every regiment of Marshall's and Hartranft's brigades, plus Cutcheon's 20th Michigan. Hartranft reinforced them by bringing the 2nd Michigan and the 1st Michigan Sharpshooters into the fort, abandoning the positions they had captured south of the fort.

The Georgians formed their line and began their charge with gusto, and ran right into the interlocking fire of riflemen in the two strongpoints and blasts of canister from Stanley's guns. Soldiers marching shoulder-to-shoulder could hear the bones crack as the shots came home, their lines withered, and men fell "like autumn leaves." They rallied and made a second attempt, but the Federals shot them up again, and the infantry gave up and took shelter in scattered emplacements west of the crater. In two abortive charges the Georgians had lost as many men as Weisiger had lost cleaning out the trench lines hand-to-hand. According to the official tally,

Mahone's two brigades lost five hundred of the fourteen hundred men they had taken into action. But many more men were missing, lost in the trench maze, or sent to the rear to guard prisoners, or skulking to escape danger. Officers on the scene believed the two brigades had lost fully half their strength.[42]

The concentration of firepower Hartranft had gathered on the left had stopped Mahone's counterattack cold. But the success had an unfortunate side effect. General Warren had been studying their position for half an hour, hesitating to obey Meade's order that he attack in support of Burnside. When the Michigan troops pulled back to the ruined fort, Goode's Virginians reoccupied the position and moved up to within pistol shot of the fort. When Warren saw Rebel flags go up, he telegraphed Meade that an attack on the battery was no longer feasible. "I am . . . no more able to take the battery now than I was this time yesterday. All our advantages are lost."[43]

"They Fought Like Bulldogs, and Died Like Soldiers"

LAST STAND IN THE CRATER, 8:45 A.M.–2:30 P.M.

General Meade was utterly out of touch with events. He had received no communications from Burnside since 8:00 A.M. The last message from the front had come from Grant's aide, Colonel Comstock, who had reported from Warren's position that a brigade of troops (probably Sigfried's) was advancing to the right along the enemy's line. That suggested Burnside was pressing his commanders to advance their troops as ordered. Then at 8:45, Meade received word of a stunning success: Captain Sanders telegraphed from Burnside's headquarters that the White troops had succeeded in turning a captured artillery piece on the enemy, and that the Colored division had scored a triumph, capturing prisoners and a set of Confederate battle flags. Reports by word of mouth suggested that the Blacks had captured as many as four colors and hundreds of Confederate troops. On that news, Meade immediately telegraphed Warren to "go in with Burnside, taking the two-gun battery." He also told Warren the cavalry were moving up on his left, to protect his flank and, in the event of success, to strike the enemy's southern flank.

Fifteen minutes after those orders were given, a new telegram arrived from Captain Sanders that turned Meade's picture of the situation inside out: "The attack made on the right of the mine has been repulsed. A great many men are coming to the rear." Sanders was at Fort Morton and could see the unmistakable evidence of defeat as Bell's brigade and the fugitives of Ferrero's and Potter's divisions swamped the front line and reversed the flow of supplies down the covered way like a high tide stemming the current of a stream. On the heels of Sanders's message came a telegram from Burnside that confirmed Sanders's report but made one last bid to have Warren save the day: "Many of the ninth and eighteenth corps are retiring before the enemy. I think now is the time to put in the fifth corps promptly."

That the outcome had been a defeat was confirmed by Warren's telegram at 9:15 A.M., reporting the loss of the captured trenches south of the crater and stating his belief that an attack by his corps now would be useless. Confirmation also came from Grant himself. His second trip to the front had not taken him as far forward as the first, but he too had seen enough to know that the attack was beyond recovery. At 9:30 A.M. Meade wired Burnside: "The major general commanding has heard that the result of your attack had been a repulse, and directs that if, in your judgment, nothing further can be effected, that you withdraw to your own line, taking every precaution to get the men back safely."

Additional messages from Warren and Colonel Comstock of Grant's staff suggested that only a small Union force remained in the crater perimeter, and that the Confederates were containing rather than attacking it. That information led Meade (at 9:45 A.M.) to make the order to withdraw definitive rather than discretionary. The withdrawal order also went to Ord, and both Hancock and Warren were ordered to cease offensive operations. At 10:00 A.M. Meade modified Burnside's orders slightly, giving him permission to postpone his withdrawal till nighttime if that would provide greater safety. The great point now was to get the troops back without incurring heavy casualties.[1]

BURNSIDE AND MEADE, 8:45–10:30 A.M.

Burnside still clung to the belief that an attack by Warren would clear the bottleneck. He had earlier received two messages from Captain J. C. Paine, an observer in a signal station to the south, reporting the movement of strong Confederate forces (Mahone's three brigades) from the southern end of the line toward Cemetery Hill. Burnside therefore believed that the Confederate lines opposite Warren's front were weakened and vulnerable to attack. Some historians of the battle have agreed with that assessment. However, the weakened portion of the Confederate line was the refused southern flank, several miles distant from the Union lines. An attack against it could not have been mounted in a timely way. Warren had only one division in that sector, its troops spread to cover lines vacated by the troops that had been concentrated to support Burnside. The trenches immediately in front of this latter force were still strongly manned by the brigades of Colquitt, Goode, and Harris. Sanders's Alabama Brigade, then in transit to join Mahone, might also have been in position to respond as a reserve. The remnant of IX Corps still in the breach was utterly unable to cooperate with such an attack or to make use of any success it might have. It was too late for an attack by V Corps to produce a victory.

What an attack by V Corps might have done was provide cover for the withdrawal of the troops in the crater perimeter. But Burnside would not admit such a pullout was necessary. Accompanied by General Ord, he mounted up and rode to Meade's headquarters, livid with rage and frustration, to get the order to withdraw reversed. His personal and professional reputation was invested in this operation, and he had risked a court-martial by his way of conducting it. Now the last chance of making it work was being snatched away. Emotion reinforced the rigidity of mind that made it so hard for him to make adjustments in an operation already launched, so impossible to fold his cards and leave his lost money on the table. Burnside believed that Meade had to be overwhelmed by rhetoric and compelled to give him the resources to renew the attack.

His appearance at Meade's headquarters began as an unwelcome surprise and soon became an ugly confrontation. Burnside, "much flushed, walked up to General Meade and used extremely insubordinate language," asserting that if his men were allowed to remain where they were, they could carry the crest before dark. Meade held his temper and asked *how* Burnside proposed to take the crest, when his men had been at it "from half past five in the morning, and not only had they not taken it, but [had been] driven out of the works they were occupying." To clinch his argument, Meade turned to Ord: did *he* think there was a chance the crest could be carried? Ord said he did not. Meade turned to Grant, who agreed it was time to withdraw. Meade then formally gave Burnside a peremptory order to withdraw. When Burnside protested that the cross fire between the lines was extremely heavy, Meade granted him discretion to wait until dark.

Even then, Burnside refused to let it go. As he and Ord left the headquarters tent, he remarked that there were fifteen thousand troops in and around the crater, and it would be "strange if you cannot do something with them." Ord may have felt the words implied a lack of combativeness on his part. He raised his arms and asked, "If you are held by the throat . . . how can you do anything?"[2]

Burnside used Meade's telegraphers to transmit the withdrawal order to Julius White, his acting chief of staff. White recommended that the troops hold their position and that the front lines be extended to reach them—an absurdly impractical suggestion. Burnside answered: "I have no discretion in the matter. The order is peremptory to withdraw. It may be best to intrench where we are for the present, but we must withdraw as soon as practicable and prudent." White was to transmit that order to the division commanders, instructing the officers on the line to consult with one another and develop a plan for withdrawal. Then Burnside re-mounted for the slow ride back to Fort Morton.[3]

Behind him, Grant and his staff were mounting up, while Meade's people were packing papers and equipment for the return to their own headquarters. By 10:30 A.M. the Shand house headquarters would be empty.

Perhaps Meade assumed that there would be no great difficulty about getting the troops out with minimal losses. He did not know the extent of demoralization and disorganization in IX Corps, in part because Burnside refused to recognize or report it. Still, given all that had occurred, it is almost incomprehensible that he should have closed shop and ridden off, as if to say, *What could go wrong with Burnside in charge?*

⌘

In his anger and his intense desire to recover the authority to continue the attack, Burnside had not given intelligent consideration to the problem of the withdrawal. He did mention the cross fire across the line of retreat but said nothing about the demoralized condition of his troops—perhaps because he still hoped Meade would let them try another attack. With Rebels holding positions within fifty yards of the crater on either side, there was not a single square foot of ground between the lines that was not subject to cross fire from rifle-muskets at close range. That same ground was also swept by canister fire from batteries at both ends of the Confederate line. Withdrawal would be extremely costly unless that flanking fire was sup-pressed by artillery or distracted by diversionary attacks. Burnside's in-fantry was incapable of further offensive action, so the diversionary maneuvers had to be made by troops not under Burnside's command, from V Corps and one of Ord's reserve divisions that had not yet been in action. But Meade had already ordered the other corps to stand down and had not delegated to Burnside the authority to bring them into play.

Burnside's ideas for the withdrawal envisioned either retreat under cover of darkness or the digging of a covered way across no-man's-land, through which the troops could withdraw in safety. Both plans required the troops in the crater to hold out until nightfall, which showed that Burnside did not grasp their actual condition, despite the reports of Loring, Van Buren, Potter, and others. He also fobbed off the task of developing a plan of withdrawal onto the officers in the breach. These men had been cut off from regular contact with headquarters for hours. They could offer useful advice on what support might be needed for a withdrawal but could hardly make practical plans, since they had no knowledge of what force might actually be available to help them. Nor could they truly consult the division or corps headquarters, or be consulted by them. Couriers carrying messages to and from them had to run a gauntlet of fire that diminished their chances of arriving at all, let alone in time.[4]

The only measure taken by Burnside after his return from Meade was to order General Ferrero to have his troops begin digging a covered way out toward the crater. It is revealing that in IX Corps this laborious and essentially hopeless task was assigned to Blacks who had just been in action, rather than to any of the White regiments that had remained in reserve. Similar orders also went to a White unit in Ord's command that had not been engaged. The exercise was utterly pointless: even without the Confederate cross fire, a covered way of that length could not have been dug in less than two days.[5]

THE PERIMETER, 10:00 A.M.–12:30 P.M.

After the repulse of Mahone's assault, there was a lull of sorts. In and around the crater perimeter, troops on both sides were reorganizing after the confusion of charge and retreat. The Confederates had their own wounded and a large number of prisoners to send to the rear. Rebel soldiers scoured the recaptured trenches, and in one of them found Lieutenant Beecham. He had lain there completely prostrated by shock and exhaustion, made feverish by the terrible heat, suffering a degree of thirst that seemed unendurably painful. It took him a while to realize his wounds were not serious. Then a straggling Confederate happened along, took him prisoner, stole his belt, and marched him to the rear.[6]

The Federal perimeter centering on the crater was an ellipse perhaps one hundred yards across and forty deep. Most of the position was the crater itself, a sheer-sided pit twenty-five to thirty feet deep, sixty or seventy feet wide and at least one hundred thirty feet long. The one advantage of a perimeter defense is that it allows troops to be shifted along interior lines to meet emerging threats. But the crater was impassable, and its central position effectively split the defense into three independent sectors: the ruined fort on the left (or southern) flank; the west-facing berm of the crater in the center; and a section of trench just north of the crater on the right. No exact count was made of the men in the perimeter, but three thousand would be a reasonable estimate. Not all of these were defenders. Although a thousand men were packed into the crater, none could participate in the defense. Aside from the fact that some of these were wounded, and some too demoralized to fight, the crater was too deep and steep-sided to permit those at the bottom to fire against an advancing enemy.[7]

In addition to the crater perimeter, an angle of the Confederate picket line about one hundred yards beyond the northern rim of the crater was still held by the 97th Pennsylvania. They were the only regiment of Turner's division to make a lodgment in the enemy lines, and they stayed when the rest of the division fell back. Colonel Thomas had joined them with a number of men from his brigade, and a contingent of the 43rd USCT under Lieutenant Warson also rallied there. As long as they held out, they prevented the North Carolinians of Ransom's Brigade from bringing the rear of the crater under fire (which would make escape more costly). But they were isolated and low on ammunition.[8]

General Hartranft assumed overall command in the perimeter, although the compartmentalization of the position left Bartlett effectively in charge of the northern sector. Hartranft set up headquarters in an improvised bombproof and reviewed the state of his command. The strongest part of the perimeter was the ruined fort at the south end, with its two remounted cannons and a few hundred riflemen. They included the 14th NYHA, led by Captain Houghton and Captain Kilmer, and Captain Rickard's contingent of the 19th USCT. Most of Hartranft's own brigade was there, as were the Michigan regiments of Humphrey's brigade, reduced to about two hundred rifles. The center of the position was the weak point. It consisted of the hundred-fifty-foot-long berm of the crater, where a single thin line of riflemen had to maintain a precarious toehold on the sliding sand and clay while they plied ramrods and pulled triggers. Colonel Marshall commanded in and around the southern lobe of the crater and General Bartlett commanded the north, but the men lining the berm represented nearly every brigade in IX Corps.

Bartlett appointed Captain Gregg of the 45th Pennsylvania brigade officer of the day and ordered him to pull the northern half of the defense together. Gregg thought they ought to go back to their own works, but Bartlett believed they would be slaughtered if they tried. He intended to hold the fort to the end and was confident that the army would make another attack north of their position to cover their retreat. In the meantime Gregg was to see to it that every man did his duty, and to report the name of any officer who failed to rally his men.

Gregg planted his regiment's flag on a high point of the berm to tell their comrades back in the lines they were holding on. Then he went through the northern lobe of the crater with one of Bartlett's aides trying to get men up on the firing line. But the only soldiers willing to follow him were twenty-five or thirty Blacks, who posted themselves along the berm and in a small earthwork just in front of it. Lieutenant Bowley exaggerated only slightly when he claimed "that from noon until the capture of the Crater, two hours later, the firing was kept up almost wholly by the colored troops." His opinion was confirmed by Sergeant Bernard of the 12th Virginia, whose unit faced this part of the perimeter: "From this time on the fire was kept up, mainly, by the colored troops and the officers handling muskets."[9]

The Confederates held an arc of protected positions that ran from the original main line on the north, around the rear of the crater, and back to the main line on the south, their distance from the crater varying from as few as twenty-five to as many as one hundred yards. The southern wing of the position was still held by Goode's Virginians and the 22nd and 23rd South Carolina. In the center, Mahone's two brigades held the lateral ravine and a discontinuous series of rifle pits and support trenches that covered the whole front of the crater. Mahone's left connected with the clutch of North and South Carolina regiments that had first defended and then recaptured the labyrinth. Mahone did not want to press the issue until Sanders's Alabama Brigade arrived. In the meantime he sent back for a resupply of ammunition and tried (with limited success) to establish communication with Goode's command on the south and McAfee's North Carolinians on the north, to concert the final assault. But even without consultation, each commander understood that his troops needed to hold their ground and maintain fire to keep the Yankees pinned down in the breach. To increase the pressure on the Federals, Mahone also asked for heavier fire from Haskell's mortar batteries in the lateral ravine, up on the Plank Road, and in the rifle pits close to the crater. The crater itself was so deep that cannon fire from the Plank Road could not reach troops sheltering at the bottom.[10]

As ammunition arrived and organization was restored, the Rebels started firing. The Federals answered, and the crescendo of sound marked the start of a new firefight. Volleys and single shots blended together, sometimes like a ripping or tearing of heavy cloth, the rattling of sheet iron, or corn popping. Bullets whipped by with "a most villainous greasy slide through the air," some passing with a short sharp " 'clit' like striking a cabbage leaf with a whiplash, others . . . with a sort of screech, very much as you would get by treading on a cat's tail." Civil War Enfields and rifle-muskets fired a conical lead bullet at a relatively low muzzle velocity, which caused the bullets to tumble through the air "singing, awhew, awhew, awhew, which would provoke a laugh from the veteran." But what they did on impact was not funny: the soft lead partly hollow bullet expanded or fragmented when it hit, and its tumbling trajectory continued through the human body, smashing bones and bouncing off them to tear up the internal organs. The wounds they made were terrible, and even if not immediately fatal, in the absence of antibiotics or strong antiseptics, the wounds were extremely liable to gangrenous infection.[11]

The Confederate advanced positions were only twenty-five to fifty yards away from the crater, and some riflemen worked their way into point-blank range, so the exchange of fire was murderous to both sides.

On the north side of the crater, the Black troops rallied by Gregg "behaved nobly, keeping up a continual fire of musketry, thereby holding the Rebels on the right of the fort at bay and keeping them from entering it." One Black soldier crawled up atop a stack of dead bodies in front of the line and opened fire on the Confederates. Rebel riflemen picked him out and concentrated their fire. While loading he was shot in the face, but he fired, and while reloading he was shot again in the back of the head, and then hit by a third shot that brought him down. Another Black rifleman spread encouragement along the line by cheering his shots—" 'I'se done killed one,' and a moment after, 'Glory! I'se done got another.' " He too was killed by a head shot when he exposed himself for a moment.[12]

Sergeant James Lathe and Private Henry Ford of the 9th New Hampshire killed more than a dozen men between them, firing at distances so close they could hardly miss—hardly more than the width of a tavern's common room. Lathe had always been a good soldier, had in fact commanded his company in this battle, though he was one of those who would willingly join in volley fire but had qualms about deliberate killing. The hours-long fighting had sent him into a kind of battle frenzy in which he killed six men at close range and cheered every shot. Later he would feel the need to justify himself: "I make no claim to having killed a man until I was cornered in that infernal den, where I had no hope of getting out alive; then I did as I saw some others do—worked for all I was worth." Finally a Confederate bullet ripped off two fingers and half of his shooting hand, an exceptionally painful wound that made him cry out. Lieutenant Sampson of his regiment bound up the wound with his handkerchief and sent Lathe to run the gauntlet through no-man's-land back to the lines. When Sampson tried it himself a bit later, the cross fire was worse and he was killed.[13]

On the south the Michigan Sharpshooters, and especially the Native American company, used deliberately aimed fire to make Goode's Confederates keep their heads down. They refused to fire wasteful volleys, but "if a Johnny showed himself he was their game." They were wise to waste no bullets: ammunition was running low. Hartranft sent runners back to his division commander, Willcox, who had had the foresight to gather a supply of wooden cases filled with cartridge tins and pile them close to the front. The 51st Pennsylvania was broken up into four-man delivery details. Each foursome made a pile of cartridge tins in the middle of a shelter half, grabbed the corners, and ran the load across no-man's-land. This improvised supply chain delivered ten thousand rounds at the cost of six casualties. But the difficulty of passing men or supplies through the crater prevented the wider distribution of this windfall. Only one shelter-half load made it to the north lobe. Captain Gregg's Black volunteers had to ransack the pockets and pouches of the dead and wounded. They managed to accumulate several hundred rounds, but the constant firing exhausted this supply as well. Several men tried to make the run back to their own lines to get more ammunition, but to exit the crater at this end they had to climb up the berm. When they did, Rebel sharpshooters killed them.[14]

Out in front of the crater Confederate units were also taking losses and feeling the strain of unremitting combat. The South and North Carolina regiments had been fighting since 5:00 A.M. and had taken heavy losses. Mahone's two brigades had lost half their combat strength. The troops were on the edge of a kind of hysteria. In the 12th Virginia, two soldiers (neighbors from Petersburg) nearly came to blows when one asked the other why he wasn't up on the firing step shooting at the enemy—an imputation of cowardice the second man was honor-bound to resent in a way that might have turned ugly—except that at that moment a third fellow townsman fell shot through the head and the two brawlers shifted their resentment back to the Yankees.[15]

The Confederates now brought their artillery back into play, with replenished stocks of canister and case shot. Their fire swept low across the top of the berm, and now and again shells would chew up a chunk of it, killing and dismembering the men in the firing line. Wright's battery found that it could fire directly into the open north end of the crater, into crowds of men so densely packed that every canister blast could kill or hurt a dozen men. Every explosion from the battery was followed by the instantaneous whizz of the shot and the staccato thuds of impacts, combined with the nauseating dull crack of a bone break muffled by flesh. Soldiers screamed as body parts that were torn from their comrades became projectiles, or a man might be "dashed in the face with a hot steaming mass of something horrible that covered his eyes and filled his mouth . . . a mass of brains, skull, hair and blood" from a comrade decapitated by flying metal.[16]

Bartlett called for men to build a breastwork across the gap—a deadly job that would put them squarely in front of every blast. The only volunteers were Black troops. They tried rolling some of the more manageable clay boulders into the gap, but the canister blew the boulders apart. Someone called out for them to "put in the dead men." So dozens of corpses, White and Black, Union and Confederate, were rolled or thrown into the gap. Human bodies thickly stacked were better than packed clay against canister, but repeated blasts eventually tore the bodies into chunks too small to be useful. So behind that shelter the Blacks dug out and packed in earth and shattered timbers to make a more conventional breastwork.

The riflemen up on the berm were also using the dead, making headlogs of them by laying their bodies crosswise atop the berm and scraping out loopholes underneath.[17]

But no barrier could protect the troops from Confederate mortars, which began bombarding the Union positions at about 11:00 A.M. There were eight firing from the battery up on the Plank Road, less than six hundred yards away, and two firing out of the lateral ravine only two hundred yards away—and Haskell may have managed to bring additional mortars forward. The shells went up in a high looping trajectory and dropped straight down into the crater. Measured by its outside dimensions, the area of the crater was some 1,850 square yards, but the bottom of the pit, in which the soldiers stood or crouched, was smaller. The central ridge filled some of it, the floor was strewn with boulders and wreckage, and there were dead and wounded men lying on the ground. When the bombardment began, there were probably no fewer than nine hundred and as many as eleven hundred men in the crater itself: men wounded or demoralized, Confederate prisoners, soldiers unable to squeeze into the firing line. Each man had something less than two square yards of space to stand in; every man lying down used more than that.

Now Colonel Haskell's mortar shells came dropping into that crowd, and with men packed in so tightly, nearly every explosion chewed its human meat. The mortars were close enough for troops to hear the distinctive *thump* when they fired, and the men could see the smoke trail of the shells as they soared into hard blue sky. The men would wait for the drop, make a guess where it would hit, and try to scramble out of the way, banging into men who had guessed differently. Some escaped; some didn't. Sometimes the shells were duds or they burst in holes or in piles of bodies that muffled the blast and ate the shrapnel. Private Ben McAlwee of the 3rd Maryland picked up a shell whose fuse still burned and threw it back over the parapet at the Rebels. But the toll of dead mounted steadily, and for most of the men in the crater, terror of the shells replaced every other thought. As Lieutenant Bowley watched, the major of a Maine regiment was struck by a shell that instantly exploded, blowing his head to fragments and dropping his body to hang upside down over the edge of the crater like a slaughtered animal, his blood pouring down the wall "as from an overturned bucket. I never supposed that a human being could hold so much blood."[18]

Another shell exploded close to General Bartlett, killing a soldier beside him and hurling a chunk of clay crack into his cork leg, throwing him to the ground. Officers and men rushed to his aid: "Oh, no! . . . It's only my cork leg that's shattered!" They moved him to a relatively safer spot, close to the front wall, where he could give orders sitting down.[19]

Men were also felled, and some killed, by the terrible heat in the crater. The heat had been building up across the region since the last thunderstorms on July 21, so that even at night the air was stifling. Now it was noon and the sun that had been ferocious all morning was pounding straight down into the crater, baking the clay walls and floor of the pit. The air at the bottom was oven-hot and full of the dust coughed up by shells and scraped by moving feet. "The midsummer sun caused waves of moisture produced by the exhalation from this mass [of men] to rise above the crater," like steam from a simmering pot. Heatstroke and heat exhaustion took their toll, but thirst was the overwhelming agony. Most soldiers had gone into the fight with one canteen of water, which had long since been drained. "Wounded men died there piteously begging for water, and soldiers extended their tongues to dampen their parched lips until their tongues seemed to hang from their mouths." Exhausted and demoralized soldiers sat slumped against the walls, deaf to the pleas of officers that they return to the line.[20]

The artillery in the ruined fort was also dying of thirst. There was no water to swab the barrels after firing, and the buildup of powder residue increased the danger that a gun might blow itself up. A volunteer asked Colonel Griffin for permission to take a load of canteens, run back to their lines to fill them, and bring them back. Griffin believed it was suicidal but gave his permission. The man dodged away, and Griffin thought that if he made it across, he'd probably stay where he was rather than come back. But to his astonishment the man returned, dodging more slowly with his garlands of sloshing canteens, some of which were punctured and drained by Rebel bullets. After that several more volunteers stepped up, and once again Griffin was surprised and gratified to see each of them return to their beleaguered outpost. One of these men was shot and killed just outside the position. Another soldier dashed out to grab the vital canteens and bring them home. He took a bullet of his own but got back over the parapet.

In the northern section of the crater Gregg called for volunteers to bring water back from their own lines. Again it was the Black troops who came forward. Most who tried it were shot as they tried to climb out of the works, but a few managed to run the gauntlet and return with full canteens. To enable these supplies to circulate throughout the position, Bartlett ordered the cutting of a "traverse" or tunnel through the central ridge that bisected the crater. "After much exertion [Gregg] succeeded in getting a few negroes to undertake the work."[21]

"It Will Be Impossible to Withdraw These Men. . . .": 12:30–2:00 P.M.

Back in the ruined fort, Hartranft and Griffin finally received the order General Burnside had sent nearly two hours before: the troops were to be withdrawn and the officers in the breach were to consult and concert a plan for evacuating the position. They sent a runner to Bartlett to get his opinion, and in short order they had it. "It will be impossible to withdraw these men, who are a rabble without officers, before dark, and not even then in good order. Please let me know what your plans are." His reply was marked 12:40 P.M., eight hours after the mine had exploded.

Hartranft had already reached the same conclusion. Prolonged defense of the position was impossible, and the troops were too disorganized to withdraw without substantial support. His dispatch to headquarters echoed Bartlett: "The men here are a rabble. . . . They are suffering very much from [want of] water, and the troops cannot well be organized." He asked for diversionary attacks by infantry to the right and left of the breach, and strong artillery support. Griffin endorsed his recommendations, and a courier set out to carry the dispatch back to Burnside, dodging bullets across no-man's-land. Hartranft had no way of knowing that the V and XVIII Corps were no longer available, that the only infantry in position to attack was IX Corps, whose units had been wrecked by the day's fighting. Artillery was available, but there was no reason to think that the guns that had failed to suppress Confederate fire for the last eight hours would succeed in the next sixty minutes. Still, their plan was the most practical solution to the problem of withdrawal. It was too bad that Burnside did not get the message until it was too late.[22]

At some point the men in the perimeter noticed the efforts being made to dig a covered way across no-man's-land from the Union lines. At various points the trapped soldiers tried to dig back to meet them halfway. They had to scrape at the clay with hands and bayonets—engineer troops were supposed to have been sent with the storming party, but there were neither engineers nor shovels in the crater. These projects had no chance of succeeding. Nevertheless, Hartranft asked the men making water or ammunition runs to bring shovels on their next trip.[23]

Within the perimeter things became more desperate from moment to moment. Enemy troops pressed in more closely on three sides, filling the traverses to within point-blank range. They were close enough to throw bayoneted rifles like javelins over the top of the berm and into the crater. Their gunfire homed in on every gap in the earthworks, every loophole along the berm. The soldiers would block these with blouses, knapsacks, blankets, anything they could lay their hands on, but the killing and wounding went on. Rebel marksmen concentrated fire on the embrasures for the two captured artillery pieces and killed several of the men serving them, including Sergeant Wesley Stanley, whose achievement in restoring the guns and manning them under fire would earn him the Medal of Honor.[24]

Officers made an effort to organize troops at the bottom of the crater to reload weapons and pass them up to the riflemen on the rim. A chain of men could pass rifles up to the central ridge, and from there they could be passed along the berm. Sergeant Burnham of the 9th New Hampshire used three or four different rifles to fire about two hundred rounds over a period of about two hours. But the process was painfully slow, and fell apart every time a mortar shell came looping in, sending the men diving for cover. Along most of the firing line, soldiers loaded and fired on their own. In the northern lobe, the cartridges scavenged from the dead and wounded were running low. The Spencer repeating rifles of the 57th Massachusetts Company K were silent for lack of ammunition. The regiment itself was reduced to fewer than a hundred men, equivalent to an understrength company. Back in June, Privates Park and Murray had jokingly requested a transfer to the navy to escape trench duty. Now Murray was dead and Park was seriously wounded and certain to be left as a prisoner to the enemy. (He would die in a prison camp.)[25]

The line along the berm was extremely tenuous. It was about one hundred seventy feet long, and along most of that length it was only possible to deploy one rifleman every three feet. This meant that the longest section of the perimeter could be manned by no more than fifty or sixty riflemen at a time. Once the ammunition for Company K's Spencer repeaters was exhausted, the maximum firepower this sector could bring to bear on an attack amounted to one sixty-shot volley. Riflemen clung to the sliding inner wall of the berm by their elbows, bellies, and toes, aiming and firing through loopholes that might have a dead body for a head log. Then they would roll sideways to lie on their backs, kicking their heels into the clay to keep from sliding over into the pit, and in that position— looking up into the unrelenting sun—they would tear the paper cartridge with their teeth (with lips cracked from heat and unslakable thirst), thumb it into the barrel, ram it home with the ramrod, set a new percussion cap, and then roll back to the loophole for another shot. If a sharpshooter had a bead on the hole, they would roll right into a head shot that would slide them dead over the edge and down into the pit.

Conditions in the crater were intolerable. At 1:00 P.M. the intense heat and glare of the sun poured straight down into the pit. Dead and wounded men were strewn all over the bottom and up the sides of the crater. The headless body of the Maine major still hung upside down on the wall, now completely drained—his blood had flushed down the clay wall, painting it a blackening red. The clay floor of the crater was baked hard by the sun and it held the blood in pools that dried slowly. Parts of dismembered bodies were scattered everywhere, abuzz with flies, and the stagnant ovenlike air was thick with a horrible stench from bodies and parts of bodies that had been rotting in the heat for eight hours, and from human shit—it was impossible to make or use latrines or sinks, and diarrhea was chronic in both armies.[26]

A thin but steady stream of men continued to run out of the breach and back to the Union lines. However, these now tended to be men acting deliberately and with the permission of their commanders, rather than fugitives fleeing in panic. The cross fire in no-man's-land was now so severe that demoralized soldiers preferred the immediate safety of the trenches. Captain Houghton of the 14th NYHA got Colonel Marshall's permission to lead his company back, but only one man (his orderly) was willing to risk the run. No-man's-land was "so thickly strewn with killed and wounded, that one disposed to be so inhuman might have reached the works without stepping on the ground." The two men took off at a dodging run that ended in a leap into the Union picket line. Houghton took charge there and directed the men's fire to the left of the breach in an attempt to provide some cover for other men making the run.[27]

In their isolated position north of the crater, the officers and men of the 97th Pennsylvania also decided it was time to leave. The Rebels were pressing them more closely; a final attack seemed to be imminent, and it would surely wipe them out. Colonel Thomas and his Black troops pulled out with them. Lieutenant Warson claimed that his contingent from the 43rd USCT were the last to leave the enemy's works. They made the dash successfully, but the loss of their position allowed the Rebels to tighten the barrier of cross fire across the rear of the crater.[28]

In Hartranft's command post, desperation was mounting. It was apparent the Rebels were concentrating for a final attack, and it was obvious the troops would not be able to stop it when it came. Their numbers were too few, their morale too low, and the Rebels had very little open ground to cover before they reached the earthworks. The barrels of the two captured cannons were so foul that the guns were liable to blow up or become unusable at any moment. The sense of impending doom was reinforced by the mournful drone of the Native American sharpshooters: four of them had been mortally wounded, and "clustering together [their comrades] pulled their blouses over their faces and chanted a death song."[29]

Hartranft now suggested that Colonel Cutcheon of the 20th Michigan make the run back to the lines. As a regimental commander he might have greater authority pushing their requests for water and ammunition, and for fire support to cover their retreat. Cutcheon agreed, and he survived the dash across no-man's-land—but there were no commanding officers in the section of the lines he reached. He finally collared an aide to

General Burnside and had him deliver Hartranft's request. Cutcheon then went looking for Willcox in the bombproof where Dr. Chubb had set up his aid station. Once there, he nearly collapsed from exhaustion and dehydration but went out again to seek his division commander. From the front line he saw the three Michigan battle flags still flying over the fort. Just then he heard the musketry rise to a frenzied pitch—the Rebels were attacking again, too soon for Burnside to have acted on Hartranft's last message.[30]

The Last Stand, 2:00–3:00 p.m.

It was after 1:00 p.m. when the head of General Sanders's Alabama Brigade entered the covered way. John Caldwell Calhoun Sanders was only twenty-four. He had enlisted out of the University of Alabama, had won election as company captain, and had been promoted to higher command for his gallant and effective service in combat. He had won a brigadier general's star at Spotsylvania leading the counterattack that had halted Hancock's powerful assault.[31]

Mahone met him up by the Plank Road and gave him his instructions. The Federals in the breach probably outnumbered the troops available for an attack. There were only 632 riflemen in Sanders's Brigade, and they would have to attack in the open, across the same ground where the Georgians had been so badly shot up. They would get fire support from the rest of the forces around the perimeter, but not all of those troops could immediately join the assault. The units from Goode's, Elliott's, and Ransom's brigades had been fighting for seven hours, and most of the survivors were probably played out. Weisiger's Virginia Brigade and Hall's Georgians would pitch in, but they had lost heavily in their earlier assaults—they might add eight hundred or so to the attack. Yet Mahone believed it was imperative the Yankees be driven out and the breach closed. He had no way of knowing that Meade had called off the offensive, and naturally presumed that if Federal troops held on to the breach, another, more powerful attack might well be forthcoming.

So he told Sanders that the safety of Petersburg and the survival of this part of the army depended on his success. The Federals in the breach were demoralized by defeat and the steady bombardment of the mortar and artillery batteries, and Mahone's earlier success convinced him they would break if they were hit hard. He wanted Sanders to attack with determination, but also with intelligence. The key to the position was the unwrecked half of what had been Pegram's battery. It was well fortified and heavily manned with riflemen, and its two cannons could blast canister across the whole battlefront. Once it was taken, the rest of the position would be untenable. Sanders was to follow the lateral ravine to its southern extremity and then have his men crawl as close to the Federal line as possible, taking advantage of the ground and the hanging banks of dust and gun smoke. Their attack should start within two hundred yards of the Union line. On the signal they were to rise up in unison and advance in a stooping posture, with bayonets fixed, and neither yell nor fire their weapons until fired on by the infantry in the fort. Then they would have to charge at the double-quick over the remaining distance. Once they were up to the earthwork of the fort and the crater's berm, they would be safe from Federal artillery and could close with the defenders. Their own artillery would fire in advance of their charge. The infantry units ringing the perimeter would support them with rifle fire and then pitch in once they had closed with the enemy.[32]

As the Alabamans moved up, a refugee from one of Elliott's regiments asked if he could come with them. He had been blown up by the mine and wanted a chance to get even. Captain Featherston of the 9th Alabama asked how high he'd been blown: "I don't know, but as I was going up I met the company commissary officer coming down, and he said: 'I will try to have breakfast ready by the time you get down.' " However, this man said nothing about Black soldiers refusing to grant quarter. Featherston was therefore astonished when he saw among the Union POWs "a large number of negroes, as black as the ace of spades, with cartridge boxes on and in every sense of the word equipped as soldiers."[33]

As the brigade started down the covered way, Mahone tried to give their fighting spirit that extra edge by telling them General Lee would be watching their charge. As this word spread down the line, it got twisted into the notion that Lee was planning to lead the charge, which led an Alabama soldier to declare he would tie Lee to a sapling to prevent it, and then charge all hell. To other passing troops Mahone said "that negro troops were in possession of the Crater and had come in yelling 'No quarter for the Rebels!' He did not say, 'Show no quarter,' but [we] decided that point."[34]

The brigade crawled out to a position nearly opposite the ruined fort. The men lay flat while their artillery bombarded the crater and the lines beyond, hoping to draw the Federals' fire away from the infantry attack. The ploy failed, and the Confederate guns ceased firing. The Alabamans got to their feet and advanced at the quick-step, bayonets leveled. The smoke blew away and Featherston saw the "grand and cruel spectacle" of his brigade's double line of battle advancing over open ground under the eyes of two armies. A hundred yards from the earthworks they saw the sunlight flash along a row of leveled gun barrels, bayonets seeming as thick as the bristles of a porcupine. The Alabamans were hit by a storm of rifle fire and canister just as Sanders's call to charge was echoed down the line, and the brigade ran forward with a yell. On their right, Goode's Virginians and South Carolinians added their fire from the flank, and on the left Mahone's Virginia and Georgia brigades and McAfee's North Carolinians rose to join the assault.[35]

In the ruined fort Hartranft and Griffin watched the Confederate onset. No word had come back as to whether or not their comrades had prepared the supporting attacks and fires they had requested. They therefore ordered an immediate retreat. A rear guard would stay to check the assault, but everyone else should prepare to run for it. Word went by runner to Marshall in the south lobe of the crater, and through the passage to Bartlett in the north. But Bartlett already knew what was coming. He told Captain Gregg that the captured works were going to be abandoned and that he should get out while there was time. Bartlett, with his one leg, had no choice but to remain. Gregg gathered up his color-bearer and as many men of his own regiment as he could lay hands on and led them out the back of the fort and into the cross fire that swept no-man's-land. When they reached their lines, Gregg collapsed from exhaustion.[36]

Behind them the Alabamans' line ran straight at the ruined fort, bleeding men to rifle fire, and got under the parapet where neither bullets nor shell fire could reach them. At almost the same moment the northern face and flank of the crater were assailed by elements of Mahone's Virginia and Georgia brigades, together with parts of the 25th and 49th North Carolina.

In the northern lobe of the crater Bartlett heard someone yell, "Here they come!" and asked his men to lift him up so he could see over the railroad tie that served as a head log. The instant his head appeared, a bullet creased his scalp, stunning him. His men laid him on the ground.

Up above them the Virginians, Georgians, and Carolinians charged with a yell. Though they had started after the Alabamans, their advance was faster and less costly because they had less ground to cover and did not have to face the fire of the two cannons and massed infantry that had held the ruined fort. Lieutenant Bowley believed that if the White troops here had remained in the firing line, they could have damaged the attackers heavily—they had jumped off from trenches no more than ten feet from the outer line. But there was only a thin line of Black troops in a half-trench in front of the crater, their last cartridges were spent, and they were swarmed under by the Confederate assault. Then there was only the thin line of widely spaced riflemen along the berm, who barely had time for one volley before the Confederates were right up against them.

Along the front of the ruined fort and the berm of the crater Union and Confederate infantry were now holding opposite sides of an embankment some six feet thick, with the Alabamans fronting the fort and the southern lobe of the crater and the rest of the Confederates ringing the northern lobe. In order to use their rifles, men had to expose themselves by jumping up onto the parapet. Those individuals who tried it were shot down. "There was quite a number of abandoned muskets, with bayonets on them, lying on the ground around the fort. Our men began pitching them over the embankment, bayonets foremost, trying to harpoon the men inside, and both sides threw over cannon balls and fragments of shells and earth, which by the impact of the explosion had been pressed as hard as brick."[37]

The men on either side could clearly hear each other's orders, battle cries, threats, and curses, many of the latter directed at "niggers." Soldiers on both sides were primed with the expectation that when Rebels and armed Blacks came together, neither could expect mercy. Many of the Federal troops defending the crater had heard Mahone's men chanting "Spare the white man, kill the nigger!" during the Rebels' first counterattack. Confederate troops had heard the rumor that Sigfried's men had shown no quarter during their morning attack, and some had heard their officers' orders (explicit or implied) to show no quarter in this assault.[38]

The White troops in the northern lobe of the crater were thoroughly demoralized, they expected the Rebels to come pouring over the top at any moment, and "the cry was raised that we would all be killed if we were captured among the negroes." Down at the bottom there was intense confusion, terror, and violence, with large numbers of men cowering helplessly while others continued to hold their ground, firing and reloading. And in the middle of all that, here and there a White soldier shot or bayoneted or gun-butted a Black soldier who was trying to share his shelter or flee past him, or small groups of Whites turned on and mobbed Blacks fighting nearby, crying out whatever words they knew that might tell the Rebels they shared their disgust, never wanted this comradeship with niggers, asked only to be allowed to surrender. Their fear of being murdered was real, but it doesn't sufficiently explain the outbreak of a race riot among troops of the same army in the midst of a battle. Northern Whites were able to kill Black men wearing their uniform because they too believed that the uniform, the flag, and the nation belonged to the White man, and that the Black man's presence in their midst as comrades was an insult to their dignity as White men. As Lieutenant Emery of the 9th New Hampshire told a reporter, "the men was bound not to be taken prisoner among them niggers." The same thing was happening in the southern lobe of the crater. Captain Kilmer of the 14th NYHA testified that White Federal soldiers "bayoneted blacks who fell back into the crater. This was in order to preserve the whites from Confederate vengeance. Men boasted in my presence that blacks had been thus disposed of, particularly when the Confederates came up."[39]

Down in the pit Lieutenant Bowley distinctly heard Major Etheredge of the 41st Virginia order his men to rise up, fire a volley, and charge. General Bartlett had recovered from the blow to his head, and recognized that to prolong the battle was simply to invite a massacre, but in all that sound and fury he could not at first be heard by the Confederates. But the cry of surrender spread among the troops in the crater, and Etheredge's men finally heard it and slackened their fire. Even then some men kept firing out of the pit, and many of the Blacks refused to stop fighting, believing they would be shown no quarter. Private Bird of the 12th Virginia gave them the accolade: "They fought like bulldogs, and died like soldiers."[40]

Finally a call went echoing up from the bottom and passed back through the ranks, "the Yanks have surrendered," and Confederate troops came skidding down the wall and clambering over the corpse barricade into the crater. Ransom's men had declared their intention to take no Negro prisoners before the fighting at Plymouth, and now they were maddened by the long day's fight and by their memory of the morning's combat, in which Sigfried's men had stormed their positions crying "Fort Pillow!" and "No quarter!" The first men down "plunged their bayonets into the colored wounded lying there." Private William Day of the 49th North Carolina recalled that they spared White men as they could, but Blacks who tried to surrender were answered, "No quarter this morning, no quarter now." Private Day remembered how "negro skulls cracked under the blows [of musket-butts] like eggshells." Major Love of the 25th North Carolina wrote, "such Slaughter I have not witnessed upon any battle field any where. Their men were principally negroes and we shot them down untill we got near enough and then run them through with the

Bayonet. . . . We was not very particular whether we captured or killed them." Colonel John Haskell observed, "Our men, who were always made wild by having negroes sent against them . . . were utterly frenzied with rage. Nothing in the war could have exceeded the horrors that followed. No quarter was given, and for what seemed a long time, fearful butchery was carried on." Though he did no killing, Haskell's coat became so sodden with blood that he threw it away in disgust.

Some Blacks bolted for one of those abortive covered ways, where they were cornered, but many picked up weapons and made a rush at the Confederates with bayonets and clubbed rifles. The Rebels actually gave way, and the surrender hung in the balance. But Major Etheredge restored order by gathering his men back against the crater wall and calling out that if the Blacks surrendered, they would be treated as POWs. Union officers added their voices in assurance, Confederate officers checked the killings, and the Blacks put down their guns. The prisoners were disarmed, robbed of various items of value, and put under guard for the march to the rear. Several were killed by Federal artillery as they staggered up the slope.[41]

Back in the crater, a Confederate officer detailed a couple of Black soldiers to carry General Bartlett to the rear. Bartlett protested, and two White soldiers were given the task. All of the Black soldiers who were ambulatory were marched to the rear. Many of those too badly wounded to move or be moved were killed by bayonets or musket-butts. To Private Day it seemed that the ground was "covered with broken-headed negroes."[42]

✦

At the southern end of the perimeter, in the ruined fort, Hartranft ordered the remaining troops to make a run for their lines. Almost simultaneously with that order, Sanders's Brigade made its final move.

The 9th Alabama's Colonel J. H. King, perhaps on Sanders's orders, told his men to stick their hats on their bayonets and hold them up to draw fire. The hats went up and were shot to pieces, and on that cue King ordered his men up and over the embankment. Captain Featherston and Sergeant McWilliams led their company up. McWilliams opened his mouth to shout and took a bullet that blew out the back of his head without bruising his lips, and in the next moment Union and Confederate soldiers were fighting hand-to-hand, braining each other with gun butts and stabbing with bayonets, each side driven to desperation by its belief that the presence of Blacks guaranteed a war without mercy.[43]

The three Michigan regiments retained a degree of organization.

Most survivors of the 2nd and 27th made a concerted push to get out of the fort, while a rear guard sacrificed themselves to hold back the assault. The color-bearer of the 2nd tried to save his regiment's flag by hurling it "like a javelin toward the Union lines," but he was killed and the flag was picked up by the Confederates. The Sharpshooters stayed the longest. Privates Thatcher, Scott, and Haight were the last to leave, backing out of the fort with their faces toward the enemy, still firing aimed shots and reloading while their comrades made their escape. Thatcher was wounded and left behind; Scott ran for it. Sidney Haight fired his last shot and a Rebel officer came running at him, waving a sword and demanding his surrender. Haight waited for him, parried the sword swing, and stuck the officer in the body with his bayonet. Then he dropped the rifle and ran for his own lines, the last free man to leave the crater.[44]

Sanders's six hundred stormed the fort and swarmed up onto the berm of the crater, killed the few riflemen manning the rim, and glared down into the bottom of the pit. Captain Vance was one of the first to stand on top, and he was immediately shot in the leg by a Black soldier below him in the pit. Vance fell forward and landed on the Black man, and the two wrestled on the ground, the Black man trying to stab Vance with a knife. In Vance's memory, the revulsion he felt at this physical intimacy with a Negro was more vivid than his sense of a life-or-death grapple: "I had to inhale an odor equalled only by the skunk." After an intolerable interval several of his men dropped down, "plunged their bayonets through the negro's body," and finished him off by smashing his head with a rifle butt. As they handed Vance up to the litter bearers, he clung to the knife he had finally wrested from the Black man's hand.[45]

The Alabamans as a group did not make the mistake of charging into the crater but stayed up on the rim, where the Federals could not reach them and they could shoot Yankees with impunity. With both the fort and the northern half of the crater in Confederate control, the Federals in the southern lobe now cried their willingness to surrender. But here too the general confusion and the "no quarter" presumption complicated matters. Soldiers who surrendered to one officer were shot by soldiers not aware of their agreement. Believing they would be killed in any case, some Federals urged one another to die fighting. Finally the adjutant of the 8th Alabama yelled, "Why in hell don't you fellows surrender?" and a Union colonel answered "Why in the hell don't you let us?" Lieutenant Kibby of the 4th Rhode Island waved a white handkerchief on his sword, and the troops in the crater began to lay their rifles down.

Confederate troops slid down into the crater to disarm the prisoners and look for their own wounded. "The slaughter was fearful. The dead were piled on each other. In one part of the fort I counted eight bodies deep. There were but few wounded compared with the killed." At the bottom of the crater Private Andrews of the 23rd South Carolina found two men, one Confederate and the other Black, "on their knees, with their guns clenched in their hands, their bayonets thrust through [the other's] bod[y] . . . their backs against a clay wall, both stiff in death." For the Alabamans, "This was the first time we had met negro troops, and the men were enraged at them for being there and at the whites for having them there." Like the Virginians and North Carolinians in the northern section of the crater, they began killing the Black wounded. Their emotions were exacerbated by Federal artillery fire, which was now leveled on the area in and around the crater as well as on the Confederate batteries and the ground over which Mahone's brigades had attacked.[46]

The potential for another Fort Pillow massacre was real. The situation was fluid and explosive, the self-control of the Confederate troops and the authority of their officers balanced on a knife edge. Some men were carried away by murderous rage, but others (like Sergeant Bernard earlier in the day) were appalled by the cruelty of their own comrades. Private Dorsey Binyon of the 48th Georgia regretted that "some few negroes went to the rear as we could not kill them as fast as they past us." On the other hand Noble Brooks, another Georgia private, was deeply upset: "Oh! the depravity of the human heart; that would cause men to cry out 'no quarter' in battle, or not show any when asked for." Officers displayed a similar range of responses. Etheredge wanted to stop the massacre, for reasons both moral and practical—the Yankees would keep fighting if quarter were not granted. On the other hand, Major Love clearly did not care what his North Carolinians did about killing Negroes, and other officers vented their rage by killing prisoners, or encouraging or allowing their men to do so. Among Sanders's men, one lieutenant found the killing *"heart sickening"* and tried to check it. On the other hand, Captain Featherston apologized to his wife for having taken the Negroes prisoner instead of killing them: "All that we had not killed surrendered, and I must say we took some of the negroes prisoners. But we will not be held culpable for this when it is considered the numbers we had already slain."[47]

The animus was almost as strong against White officers leading Black troops. They had been proscribed as criminals by Confederate law, and military policy sanctioned their treatment as felons. Many of the USCT officers in the crater tore off the green cap badge that identified them with IX Corps' 4th Division, and when their captors lined them up among the corpses at the bottom of the crater, many claimed to be serving in White outfits. Lieutenant Lemuel Dobbs was outraged by their defeat, by the murder of his wounded men, and by the abjection of his fellow officers, and when the Rebels got to him, he chose defiance over compliance: "I am Lieutenant Lemuel D. Dobbs, Nineteenth Niggers, by ---!" Luckily the officer dealing with him admired his courage more than he detested his service—Dobbs was spared, and even accorded a measure of respect during the first moments of his captivity. In general, though they were menaced and insulted, "Colored officers" who managed to surrender were not murdered.[48]

As the heat of battle waned, the killing became more desultory. Private Bird of the 12th Virginia recalled that in the relative quiet it was possible to hear the calls of "some poor wounded wretch" hiding in some crevice of the position, who "begg[ed] for water and [was] quieted by a bayonet thrust." Officers regained control of their men and got them to focus on the essential task of manning the shattered line they had recaptured.[49]

In the end the killing in the crater was stopped, and a large number of Black soldiers went to the rear as prisoners. Although some Federal officers, such as Bowley, thought all wounded Blacks had been killed, many were taken from the crater, perhaps carried by their comrades. But a different kind of killing, not attributable to the heat of battle, went on in the rear. As the prisoners were marched back, they ran into odd groups of Confederate soldiers, passing into or out of the fighting, or doing guard or fatigue duty in the rear, and many of these meetings resulted in Black POWs being killed out of hand. Although General Mahone had ordered the men to show no quarter to their enemies, he tried to check the killing of prisoners being marched to the rear. These killings made Porter Alexander slightly queasy, morally speaking: "Some of the Negro prisoners . . . were afterwards shot by others, & there was, without doubt, a great deal of unnecessary killing of them." But Lieutenant Colonel William Pegram put his qualms aside: "It seems cruel to murder them in cold blood, but I think the men who did it had very good cause for doing so." He was prepared to advocate the murder of all captured Blacks as perfectly proper, and necessary "as a matter of policy," because it clarified the racial basis of the Southern struggle for independence. He took satisfaction in the belief that fewer than half of the Blacks who surrendered on the field "ever reached the rear. . . . You could see them lying dead all along the route."[50]

As the fury of battle passed, a more humane response became possible—so long as captured Blacks adopted the traditional manners of servility. Colonel Frank Huger of Mahone's Division recognized among the dying the Black barber who used to shave him when he lived in Norfolk. The barber begged "Mass Frank" for some "old greasy water"—didn't think he deserved and wasn't asking for any nice cool water. Huger gave him a cupful. Colonel Stewart of the 61st Virginia gave his protection to "one old cornfield chap [who] exclaimed, 'My God, massa, I never pinted a gun at a white man in my life; dem nasty, stinking Yankees fotch us here, and we didn't want to come fus!" John Haskell took under his protection a Black soldier who had tried and failed to kill him, because the man fell to his knees and "threw up his hands and in true, 'rice-field Gullah' begged his life." The man also claimed that he had been forced "into the Yankee army against his will."[51]

Yet there were men whose responses were simply human and humane. George Bernard was one such man, and a private in the 61st Virginia was another. He was at a frontline loophole late in the afternoon. In front of him were hundreds of wounded men lying out in no-man's-land, mutilated and bleeding, with that merciless sun glaring down through the heavy air. The firing was still hot, and though there were dozens of voices crying, yelling, or screaming for water, any man who tried to help them was in danger of being shot. Below his loophole was a Black soldier whose legs had been blown off by a shell. He had made a shelter to protect himself from the unrelenting glare of the sun by jamming three bayoneted muskets into the ground and draping a tent cloth between them. He was so parched with heat and loss of blood that his need for water was stronger than the pain, and he kept pleading for water. The Confederate waited for a lull in the firing, filled a cup with water, and reached it through the loophole, pushing it closer with a stick or musket barrel. While doing that he was exposed to any sharpshooter with a bead on his loop.

The Black man drank the water immediately, but he had probably been wounded in the belly as well, because he "commenced to froth at the mouth, dying in a very short time."[52]

Chapter 15

Flag of Truce

JULY 30–AUGUST 1, 1864

T he Battle of the Crater was over, but the fighting continued. Commanders on both sides had reason to fear attack, and kept their infantry and artillery firing as a deterrent. Burnside's corps had been decimated and disorganized, and its front seemed vulnerable. Warren was worried about the open southern flank. On the Confederate side Mahone had recovered the original line but only by a razor-thin margin. Elliott's Brigade was virtually wiped out, and the front was held by five brigades that had all suffered heavily in the fighting. The lines to the south were held by the thin cordon of troops Mahone had left behind. There were still no reserves, and there would be none until Field's Division returned from Richmond that evening.

The firing was less intense but still severe, and it effectively pinned the troops in their trenches just as it had before the battle. The difference now was that there were two or three hundred wounded lying between the lines, and firing made it impossible to bring them in or relieve their distress. Even in the rear of the Confederate line, the rain of shells and bullets was so heavy that the wounded and dead in the crater and adjoining trenches could not be removed. In the crater itself riflemen had to stand on dead bodies to man their loopholes until a fire step could be hacked out of the steep eastern wall. A few men were spared to stack bodies out of the way and search the crater for survivors of the explosion. Buzzing clouds of flies swarmed over the bodies, the parts of bodies, and the places where blood pooled on the clay, and persecuted the men who labored in the pit.[1]

On the Union side, Burnside was forced to confront the true dimensions of the disaster to his corps. The usually reliable Robert Potter reported his division as "nearly annihilated." Potter's estimate of losses would diminish as, by ones and twos, soldiers returned who had been separated from their units by the rout. But for the next day and a half it was clearly beyond the division's strength to cover the trench line they had manned before. The loss of field officers was catastrophic: in Griffin's brigade alone all seven of the acting colonels had been shot.

Ledlie's division was utterly disorganized, its two brigadiers captured and its commander disgraced. Ferrero's division was also disorganized, having been split during its advance and fragmented in the mad scramble of the retreat. It had also suffered the heaviest casualties of any Union division. Of the estimated 4,300 officers and men it took into action, more than two hundred were killed or mortally wounded, seven hundred wounded, and more than four hundred missing. These losses amounted to 31 percent of the division, and those regiments that had been most intensely engaged lost 40 percent. Willcox's situation was not quite as critical. He had in hand the four regiments of Humphrey's brigade that had broken before closing with the enemy, and had therefore suffered fewer losses. Even so, half of his division was disorganized, and 20 percent of his men had been lost. All together, a quarter of IX Corps was killed, wounded, or missing, and half of the remainder could not immediately return to the line.

Potter and Willcox also reported that many wounded were still lying between the lines. The situation called for a cessation of hostilities so they could be brought in. But Burnside was wholly occupied with the problem of reorganizing his broken troops and strengthening his vulnerable line. He was also distraught. He had staked everything on the success of this operation—only that morning he had had his orderlies prepare to move headquarters into Petersburg!—which now had ended in ignominious defeat. He could not blame himself for the outcome, and though he must have felt betrayed by Ledlie, he could not condemn him without raising questions about why and how he'd gotten his assignment. The one betrayal he could afford to resent was Meade's—Meade who had mocked and thwarted the mine idea from the start, arbitrarily set aside the plan to use Ferrero's division as the spearhead, refused to let him use Warren's troops, insulted his honor in a telegraphic message certain to become public knowledge, and finally abandoned him to the task of withdrawing the troops without aid from the rest of the army.[2]

So when a message from Meade arrived at 4:40 P.M. asking whether he still held the crater and planned to withdraw at night, Burnside angrily crumpled it and threw it away. To a staff officer, he said he "would not answer such a message; that if General Meade felt disposed to cease offensive operations on the right and left; and leave us to get out of the crater as best we could, and had taken so little interest in the matter as to not know . . . we had been driven from the crater before two o'clock, I certainly would not give him the information."

Meade's ignorance was not feigned. He had left his tactical headquarters before eleven o'clock, and Grant had left even earlier. At that time they knew that IX Corps had been defeated and partially disorganized, but they had no reason to think the losses catastrophic. Burnside's troops still held the breach, and as far as Meade knew it was possible for them to hold it until nightfall. Ord and Warren were busy shifting troops to bolster the defense. No one but Burnside knew all that had happened, and Burnside made no report.

In venting his spite against Meade, Burnside ignored the substance of the wire, which was to suggest that Burnside begin preliminary discussions for a truce. It was important to act promptly, because General Beauregard had a history of refusing such proposals. Burnside's petulance would delay the truce and the delivery of aid to the wounded lying between the lines.[3]

Meade did not follow up his wire until later that evening, because he had other concerns. Grant was already thinking of ways to develop the next offensive operation out of the conditions created by the day's repulse. It was his characteristic response to every battle, whether successful or not. At 2:15 P.M., while the killing in the crater was at its climax, he had telegraphed Meade to suggest an immediate movement by cavalry and infantry against the Weldon Railroad. Lee's reserves had not yet returned, his south flank had been weakened by Mahone's move against the crater; now was the time to strike. They should at least cut the Weldon, and if they moved quickly, Grant even thought "we may yet take Petersburg." Grant left it to Meade to plan the operation. He had just learned that President Lincoln would be arriving the next morning for a conference, which would probably concern their disagreement over how to handle the continuing threat posed by Early's command. If it did nothing else, a strike at the Weldon would prevent Lee from sending a substantial reinforcement to the Shenandoah. (That very day Early's cavalry had recrossed the Potomac and burned the city of Chambersburg, Pennsylvania.) Whatever thought Meade might have given to that proposal had to be reversed when, at 4:00 P.M., a signal station reported that Lee's reserve divisions were crossing to the south side "in a continuous stream." Grant now warned Meade that Lee might attempt a preemptive assault of his own.

In the midst of these shifting directives from Grant, Meade received a report from Ord that gave the first indication of how bad things were with IX Corps. So at 7:40 P.M. Meade sent another curt demand for information—which Burnside also tore up. But Meade pressed his inquiries elsewhere and by 8:30 P.M. could tell Grant that unofficial reports indicated that the enemy had retaken the breach, along with "a number of prisoners, including Brigadier-General Bartlett." He relayed a report from Ord that there were many wounded lying between the lines and asked Grant's permission to call for a truce. Grant gave his okay and then left for Fort Monroe and his meeting with Lincoln. Meade then sent a last telegram to Burnside at 10:35 P.M. asking whether he had any wounded left on the field and reminding him that he had not replied to Meade's earlier dispatches. He did not renew the suggestion of a truce, although there was no reason to delay it now that the idea of attacking the Weldon Railroad had been abandoned. Then Meade went to bed.[4]

THE WOUNDED: 2:00 P.M. TO EVENING, JULY 30, 1864

All during the long hot day of fighting, on both sides of the line, there had been a steady draining away of wounded men walking or being carried to aid stations. These were the fortunate ones. Many of the wounded had to lie where they fell, because of the intense rifle and artillery fire that reached even the rear areas in this sector. Men huddled with their pain or bled to death in bombproofs and out-of-the-way angles of trench, or lay in the open under the broiling sun as bullets zipped overhead or bit the ground around them. Estimates of the number of wounded left on the field vary from fewer than one hundred (Burnside's self-serving guess) to more than seven hundred. A more systematic tally, made during the truce, suggests that more than two hundred Federal soldiers were left wounded on the field, along with a smaller number of Confederates.[5]

The wounded who made it to the aid stations often waited hours to have their wounds tended by the few overworked surgeons. This was not the largest or bloodiest battle of the war, but on the Union side a high number of casualties was concentrated in a single corps. As one surgeon described the experience: "I am not much out of the sounds of the wounded from morning till night. My hands are constantly steaped in blood . . . so much that the nails are soft and tender." Bullets were extracted, arms and legs amputated, in the most unsanitary conditions, with inadequate antiseptics and, often, no anesthesia. "We operated in blood-stained and often pus-stained coats . . . used undisinfected instruments from undisinfected plush-lined cases, and still worse, used marine sponges which had been used in prior pus cases and been only washed in tap water. . . . The silk with which we sewed up wounds was undisinfected. If there was any difficulty threading the needle we moistened it with . . . bacteria-laden saliva." Flies swarmed over the wounds, maddening and frightening, laying eggs that rather quickly turned into maggots. A wounded man from the 45th Pennsylvania remembered pulling a handful of the squirming creatures out of the wound in his back. Despite the disgust they inspired, the maggots could actually help forestall gangrene, since they ate only necrotic flesh.[6]

The only relief for postoperative pain was laudanum, which was not dispensed liberally. The wounds made by minié bullets were complex, and since antibiotics were nonexistent, death by gangrenous infection was a frequent outcome for abdominal wounds and bullet-broken arm and leg bones—which is why amputation was a standard treatment. Surgeons cut away the smashed fingers of Sergeant Lathe's right hand, and the bones through the middle of his palm as well, leaving him with a sort of lobster claw. But he was glad to be alive (lockjaw would nearly kill him), and he joshed his wife that they had left him "the worst-looking *Paw* you ever saw. It will look like a meat fork." He had seen much worse at the field hospital: dozens of men lying on the ground, on benches or tables, "wounded in every conceivable way, from cannon and shell wounds, and burns from exploding shells, with bowels torn out and bodies gashed and mangled from bayonet thrusts, or with heads and faces smashed almost beyond recognition by blows from a musket-breech, though by far the greater part . . . were made by the deadly Minie balls." His brother, who served with him, came by after the operation and brought him fresh clothes. The ones he had worn from the battlefield were "soaked with blood from my own wound and covered with scraps of flesh, brains, and everything else that could fly from men that had been torn to pieces by shot and shell." Of the twenty-three men Lathe had led into the battle, only four were left.[7]

James Chase, the seventeen-year-old Maine lieutenant who had been shot in the face, was left in the shade of the pines outside the aid station for hours, the whole left side of his face swelling and throbbing, the pain building up in his shattered cheek and eye socket. His left eye was out of the socket, and he could no longer see out of the right. Eventually the wound was washed and rebandaged by a surgeon (who must have removed the extruded eye), and Chase was put in an ambulance with several other wounded for the ride to the train. The jouncing of the ambulance caused such pain in his wounds that he finally gave up his soldier's stolidity and shrieked.

After treatment at IX Corps' aid stations, the wounded were piled on flatcars, and the military railroad carried them to the army hospital at City Point. This was a large and (for the time) well-maintained facility, capable of serving twelve thousand men, supplied with food and medicine by steamers from the North. The soldiers were tended by male and female nurses—the latter an innovation made possible by the work of Dorothea Dix and Clara Barton, among others. They were also attended by members of the Sanitary Commission and the Christian Commission, who offered such treats as lemonade, reading matter, and religious attentions. There was, of course, a separate hospital for Colored troops, served by doctors of both races, with Black women providing the nursing care.

Chase was one who did recover, though his torn face and empty socket were likely targets of infection. A few days after the battle, his father came down from Portland to take him home. On the train back north, a woman complained hysterically to the conductor, "Don't let him come in here; I can't ride with such a horrid looking creature."[8]

For once in the war, the Confederate wounded probably enjoyed better facilities than the Federals. From their aid stations they could be taken to regular hospitals in Petersburg and Richmond. The situation was particularly fortunate for those Virginians in Weisiger's and Goode's brigades, whose homes were in the Petersburg-Richmond area. Privates Stith and Davis of the 12th were each wounded in the arm, Davis seriously. They were able to walk to the aid station sheltered behind the Plank Road. Surgeons probed their wounds, and they were each given a shot of whiskey and put on an ambulance for transport to the brigade hospital behind their old position. As they passed through downtown Petersburg, Davis's father came out of his house with a bottle of homemade wine for each of them, "and that . . . in addition to the whiskey . . . saved two lives." However, medical supplies of all kinds were in extremely short supply in the Confederacy, which affected the recovery rate for Confederate wounded. Doctors were in short supply as well, and captured Federal army surgeons were pressed into service, by a combination of appeal to the Hippocratic oath and a promise that they would not be sent to some-place like Andersonville.[9]

Wounded White Federal prisoners were tended in the same hospitals as Confederates, but there were no facilities for wounded Black POWs. Colonel Haskell remembered seeing forty or fifty wounded Blacks lying in one of the branches of the lateral ravine where they had been carried after the battle. He tried to induce the "camp negroes" (officers' servants or army cooks) and "colored loafers" from Petersburg to load them onto wagons that would carry them to the rear, but they refused to have any-thing to do with Black Yankees—except to rob and mock them. Haskell thought them callous, but they may have been dramatizing their loyalty in front of a lot of angry White folks. Haskell eventually got his own surgeon to gather a detail that did the job. Black POWs, wounded and un-wounded, were initially held with White enlisted POWs. A Confederate civilian said that he later saw a hundred fifty wounded Blacks left in an open field, stripped of nearly all their clothing. The number is certainly too large, but the description of their condition is accurate. Five captured Federal doctors were detailed to care for them, but they refused to tend Negroes until threatened with transport to a prison camp.[10]

THE TRUCE: JULY 31–AUGUST 1

Once the sun went down, the shooting slacked off. Then it became possi-ble to hear the wounded, those who lay between the lines or lost in the trenches. No-man's-land was thickly strewn with wounded and dead Fed-eral soldiers. "We could hear them crying for relief, but the firing was so severe that none dared go to them either by day or night."

> The air was filled with groans, moans, shrieks and yells. Prayers were offered and curses pronounced. Piteous appeals were made for water, for help, for death. The sounds came from everywhere, dis-tinctly heard from those near by, and growing fainter and more in-distinct until lost in one constant low, faraway moaning sound. . . . I see them now when my eyes are shut, and hear the sounds I cannot describe.

Those wounded who could crawled to their own lines, but sharp-shooters watched for movement by the light of the moon, and a nervous sentry might shoot you just as you reached safety. Perhaps fifty men made it into Willcox's lines that night.[11]

The Confederates used the cover of darkness to strengthen the parapet of the crater. In the process they unearthed the bodies of men from the 18th South Carolina who had been buried by the explosion. Some of these were torn or crushed; others had been smothered in their shelters. Captain Featherston remembered finding eight soldiers lying side by side, buried as they slept. Private Callahan was found standing erect but entirely buried in dirt.

The dead had to be buried close to where they fell—there were far too many for the few available men to haul them out of the way. Sergeant Bernard's squad was tapped for this disagreeable duty. They were marched to the crater through trenches that were "so thick [with corpses] that to walk without stepping upon their bodies or limbs was very difficult." A number of Black soldiers captured in the fighting had been kept near the front, and under Bernard's supervision they were compelled to dig a long trench one hundred feet behind the crater. Into this the bodies of the Union dead were dumped, in stacks three or four high. In the dark a Black soldier mistook the adjutant of the 12th Virginia, sleeping the sleep of exhaustion, for a corpse and dragged him by his ankle almost to the pit before the man awoke. They covered the dead with no more than two or three inches of earth.

The stench of death was already building up, not merely from the bodies and body parts strewn everywhere but from coagulated blood pools and the large quantity of blood that had soaked into the clay. Holes dug by curious soldiers established that the blood went as far as five inches deep in some places. Many of the corpses had lain for hours in the furnace heat of the previous day, the temperature at night was still uncomfortably hot, and the bodies and parts of bodies began very quickly to rot. The stench would grow and thicken through the following day, penetrating and foul beyond the foulness of shit, with a horrible undertone of sweetness, so strong it almost had substance and a livid color. The sky was gray by the time Bernard finished, and his men were hungry—for twenty-four hours they had had little to eat beyond the ration of hardtack they'd taken into combat. They had to wolf down their mess of hardtack and fried pickle pork while breathing in the nauseating odor of the dead.[12]

Meade had no intention of continuing the battle, but first thing in the morning—instead of moving immediately to seek a truce—he reopened his telegraphic war with Burnside. At 8:40 A.M. Chief of Staff Andrew A.

Humphreys admonished Burnside, "The major-general commanding directs me to call your attention to the fact that you have made no report to him on the condition of affairs in your front since he left your headquarters yesterday, and that you have made no reply to the two special communications upon the subject sent you last night at 7.40 and at 10.40. I am also directed to inquire as to the cause of these omissions."

Burnside had had second thoughts about his peevishness the previous night, and answered promptly but indefinitely. It was difficult to get an accurate report of losses, because "rumors are very numerous and exaggerated." He added that it had been quiet on his front, and that "nearly 100 wounded are lying between the lines in our front, which possibly could be brought in by a flag of truce." In fact twice that number may have been out there. It was not until sometime after 9:30 A.M. that Burnside gave Meade the formal request for a truce that Meade had invited the night before.

Meade then addressed a letter to General Lee "asking for a cessation of hostilities sufficiently long to enable us to bring off our wounded and dead." However, instead of delivering the letter immediately, Burnside was to hold it while he approached the commander of the troops immediately opposite to seek a purely informal and local truce. Meade hoped to avoid sending the letter to Lee, because (by protocol) the party asking the truce acknowledges himself to have been defeated. Generals resisted making such admissions for a variety of reasons: to maintain army morale, to avoid adverse political reactions, and to give themselves leverage in negotiations. All of these would have weighed with Meade, to say nothing of the fact that an admission of defeat was galling to his personal and professional pride. But in this case, no reasonable person could have doubted Meade's army had been defeated, and by delaying the delivery of his request he merely delayed the relief of his own wounded.

Burnside compounded the problem by quibbling over whether or not the letter to Lee was to be delivered sealed, and was slapped down for it. As a result the flag of truce did not go out till noon.[13]

The sharpshooting stopped. General Sanders, commanding in the crater, asked for a white handkerchief to raise in answer to the Federals' white flag. A soldier quipped that if he raised his undershirt "they will think we have hoisted a black flag," the sign of "no quarter." Captain Clark, with his orderly, met the Federal officers halfway across—only forty yards from their line—and received Burnside's verbal request for a local truce. Sanders recognized this as a face-saving ploy and rejected it as "not being in accordance with the usages and civilities of war." The Federal officer went back to his lines, was given Meade's formal letter of request, asked for and got another parley, and delivered the letter. Thus another hour or more was wasted.

While Meade's letter was making its way to Lee's headquarters, the flag of truce continued, by mutual agreement between Sanders and Burnside. Sergeant Bernard was surprised to see "a *woman* standing on the Yankee breastworks." It was Clara Barton, who had come down from her hospital at Point of Rocks to help with the wounded. She was particularly concerned for Sergeant Horace Gardner of the 21st Massachusetts, "one of her dearest comrades." She had nursed him when he was wounded earlier in the war, a lonely frightened boy who "seemed to cling to me as he would a sister or brother." But Gardner had been killed, and she was not allowed onto the field.[14]

Until the truce proposal was accepted or rejected, Sanders agreed to an informal arrangement, under which the Federals could distribute water and whiskey to the wounded between the lines, and also to those lying between the Confederate main line and their picket line. The latter were technically inside Confederate lines, although sharpshooter fire prevented their being brought in. No other assistance was allowed until the terms of the truce were agreed to, and the wounded were left to lie untended among the fetid bodies of the dead. In some instances, Confederate officers permitted the Federals to remove Whites who had been wounded, but not Blacks, who made up a substantial percentage of those left lying on the field. They were given water and materials to shelter them from the sun, but these were distributed by the Confederates—no contact with Union soldiers was allowed. General Warren was outraged by the spectacle. Dozens of wounded were lying close to the Confederate lines, there was no firing whatever, yet the Southerners were making no effort to help them. Warren believed the neglect was intentional, because most of the wounded were Black. He asked Meade for permission to open fire if the Confederates continued in that vein, but no one else wanted to break the truce on those grounds.[15]

The informal arrangement persisted till nightfall because the Confederate response was delayed. Lee decided that the communication ought properly to have gone to Beauregard, who was responsible for the Petersburg front. By the time Beauregard received it, not enough daylight was left for the burial of the dead. Rather than extend the truce through the night, Beauregard chose to let hostilities resume until 5:00 A.M. the next morning, when a formal truce would begin. The dignity of the several generals involved, and the "usages and civilities of war," were thus preserved at the cost of another day and night of suffering and death for the wounded.[16]

⸎

While the truce negotiations were going on, Meade kept hectoring Burnside—every order, whether vital or petty, was now "peremptory," no suggestions or demurs allowed. In the late morning of July 31, while the truce negotiations were beginning, Meade arrested Burnside's telegraph operators for the unauthorized taking-off of messages not addressed to IX Corps. Burnside tried to take responsibility: "Whatever they have done . . . was by my direction and for what I conceived to be for the good of the public service. . . . I am entirely responsible for this and am to blame if any one is. They have been active and efficient during the campaign, and should not be made to suffer for what they could not help doing." Chief of Staff Humphreys replied that the commanding general was "surprised to learn that you had given them such orders after the conversation he had with you upon the subject, in which he declined to authorize your doing so." As for the operators, they had disobeyed orders and would be tried for it.

At 6:40 P.M. Burnside sent two telegrams. The first noted that "the flag of truce is still out," because of the large number of burials. The second reported that "the loss in this corps, in the engagement of yesterday, amounts to about 4,500, the great proportion of which was made after the brigade commanders in the crater were made aware of the order to withdraw." Adjutant Williams, speaking for Meade, at once snapped back: "The commanding general directs that you at once withdraw the flag of truce. . . . The commanding general did not anticipate that the flag would be kept out longer than might be necessary to effect an arrangement for the recovery of the wounded or to deliver the letter for General Lee to the officer sent to receive it." Then Chief of Staff Humphreys went to work on the report of losses: "The commanding general requests that you will explain the meaning of the latter part of the dispatch, and again reminds you that he has received no report whatever from you of what occurred after 11 a.m. yesterday." Before Burnside could answer, Williams weighed in: the report of losses was inadequate because it did not "have a statement showing the killed, wounded, and missing, distinguishing under each head between the officers and enlisted men." If they were trying to goad an already infuriated Burnside into some further display of insubordination, they were going about it the right way.

Burnside's response was predictably resentful and ill-considered. In a 9:10 P.M. telegram he explained that the enemy had attacked just after the withdrawal order had been received in the crater, and the officers there had ordered an immediate evacuation, because they knew "they were not to be supported by other troops. . . . In view of the want of confidence in their situation, and the certainty of no support consequent upon the receipt of such an order, of whose moral effects the general commanding cannot be ignorant, I am at a loss to know why the latter part of my dispatch requires explanation." Though the last sentence was somewhat incoherent, its import was clear. The heavy loss that attended the retreat was Meade's fault, because he had ordered the troops withdrawn (showing lack of confidence) and refused to provide the support needed to make the withdrawal safely. If Burnside had failed to explain that in his previous message, it was because he thought the matter too obvious to require explanation.[17]

There was no overlooking a failure of this magnitude, especially when its author had put in writing statements that were both insubordinate and indiscreet. Meade requested a court of inquiry into the failure of the attacks of July 30, 1864, and the tribunal was ordered to convene within the week.

THE POWs IN PETERSBURG, JULY 30–AUGUST 1

The POWs were passing through a different kind of ordeal. They had had to run the gauntlet of artillery fire from their own army's guns and the vindictiveness of Confederate soldiers and rear echelon warriors. Most were robbed of watches, belts, and hats. One Rebel soldier swiped a good felt hat from the colonel of the 4th Rhode Island, and clapped his own ragged slouch onto the colonel's head. Farther on another soldier stole that hat and gave the colonel one still worse. The blockaded South could replace manufactured clothing with homespun, but it was evidently more difficult to produce viable headgear.

The captives were gathered in the low ground behind the Plank Road, where officers were separated from enlisted men, and Black soldiers from White. The Blacks were made to strip down to shirt and drawers—no sign of uniform left—and the able-bodied men were taken away to bury the dead. Lieutenant Bowley was disturbed to note that the words

"Colored officer" were written next to his name, but he was not singled out for particular mistreatment. However, the officers were systematically robbed by their guards, sometimes forcibly, sometimes apologetically ("If I don't take it from you, someone else will"). Officers as well as enlisted men joined the looting. General Bartlett—unable to stand without his wooden leg—was robbed of his general's sash by an officer who threatened him with a sword.

The prisoners were given no food for more than twenty-four hours, and no water until nightfall. A Rebel soldier offered to get them water if they would give him their canteens. The Iron Brigade veteran Lieutenant Beecham "had no confidence in his disinterested kindness, and told my comrades to hold onto their canteens," and was called "a fool, and other pet names" for his trouble. "They loaded the fellow up with canteens, which, for some reason or other, he failed to return." Many men were prostrated by the heat, and were not relieved until after dark, when they were corralled on an island in the Appomattox. The river water slaked their thirst, and was used to cool and revive those felled by heat exhaustion. General Bartlett was depressed and humiliated by his treatment. "We wouldn't treat cattle as we are being treated." He was "crazy" with thirst and drank too much from the river that flowed by their camp. A day later he would be ravaged by dysentery.[18]

That evening Lieutenant General A. P. Hill visited their encampment, and he reappeared the following morning. The savvy Lieutenant Beecham suspected something special was in the works. At 10:00 the next morning the captive officers and enlisted men, Blacks and Whites, were mustered together and arranged in a column of fours. They were then paraded through the streets of Petersburg for the diversion of the civilians and "the humiliation of the Union officers." General Bartlett, the senior captive, was at the head of a column that probably consisted of eight hundred Whites and one hundred Blacks. Both Bowley and Beecham remembered that the Rebels sat the one-legged general on a spavined nag to increase the comic effect, but Bartlett himself said he rode in an ambulance. In either case, the point of the display was to humiliate Bartlett, by presenting the general as a pathetic cripple, hatless and in a filthy uniform, reduced to parity with "his niggers." Behind Bartlett came alternating groups of Black soldiers (wounded and unwounded), barefoot and stripped down to shirts and drawers, and field officers—Colonels Marshall and Weld prominent among them. Junior officers were placed in the same files as the Blacks, "two officers between four 'niggers' " as Lieutenant Hand remembered.[19]

Like a circus parade they were marched down and around all the streets of the town for two hours or more, "taunted by the women, stoned by the boys, and cursed by the men." The merging of officers and men, Whites and Blacks, was (from the Southern point of view) the essence of the humiliation: "See the white and nigger equality soldiers!" "Yanks and niggers sleep in the same bed." Captain Shearman passed a house in which a White woman, flanked by two slave women, called out "That is the way to treat the Yankees, mix them up with the niggers, they are so fond of them, mix them up." Shearman thought the woman herself was caught up in the condition she cursed them with, but he kept it to himself.[20]

Beecham doubted whether the enlisted men were bothered by the association, and the USCT officers were used to marching with Black soldiers. By way of getting their own back, they cheered whenever they passed a building that had been damaged by shell fire. But the officers of the White regiments did feel the humiliation of being associated with Negroes. Beecham thought "it almost broke the hearts of very many of the officers of the white divisions, a majority of whom, I honestly believe, would have been glad to see the officers of the 4th Division hanged or shot, if thereby they could have been relieved from the terrible humiliation of marching through Petersburg with Negro soldiers." Though Beecham's remark may be taken for a rhetorical exaggeration, it suggests that the racial animosity that had led White enlisted men to murder their Black "comrades" had its counterpart among the officers. Beecham believed that racial antipathy had a distinct class bias. The more "aristocratic" the officers, the more they felt the humiliation of being associated with Negroes, and the more likely they were to vent their anger against USCT officers, during their captivity and after. "Of course, they were not all built that way, but the highborn and aristocratic would often go out of their way to . . . call some officer of the 4th Division a 'nigger officer,' with supreme content and lordly satisfaction."[21]

After the march a more systematic effort was made to find the USCT officers. Hand and a group of his colleagues were confronted with a group of Black POWs. Confederate officers tried to induce the Blacks to point out their officers, presumably so they could be disgraced, but the soldiers kept faith with their officers and refused to do so. The officers returned to their island, where the show continued. Citizens of Petersburg gathered across the stream to enjoy the spectacle of Yankee misery and to insult the captives. It was notable that the Confederate soldiers guarding the prisoners were often more sympathetic to their plight than the civilians. One of them explained to Captain Shearman that he wouldn't mistreat a prisoner because he might be one himself some day. Another defended Lieutenant Beecham from a civilian who had gotten the worst of an exchange of insults and was reaching for a gun: "If you'd been whar I was yesterday you wouldn't be 'round heah today fightin' with your mouth and tryin' to shoot some man who's got no gun. . . . Go out to the lines and they'll give you a gun and you'll find plenty of white men and niggahs, too, out thar with guns that'll give you all the shootin' you want."[22]

Black POWs were gathered at Poplar Lawn, an estate within the boundaries of Petersburg. Confederate authorities invited masters from the area to come and reclaim their property. Many did so, though the exact number is not on record. In one case, a Black soldier arranged with a complaisant White man to have the latter claim him (illegitimately) as property—a ploy to avoid the horrors of a prison camp. Many Black POWs were kept with the Confederate army and were used as laborers to build fortifications under fire—a violation of the rules of war. For the Confederate authorities, this practice was both a taunting of the Yankee enemy and a deterrent to Black recruitment. It was a particularly noticeable example of a policy the Lincoln administration had protested, and for which it threatened retaliation. But the administration had never backed the threat with action. Federal officials feared beginning an unlimited exchange of reprisals that might violate the laws of war, that Northern public opinion would not sustain, and that would kill many Union POWs in Confederate hands. So it was Ben Butler, who went his own way in matters of law and policy, who acted on Lincoln's threats. In October, sixty-eight Black POWs from the Crater, and eighty-two taken in later engagements, were put to labor on Confederate earthworks under fire. Butler retaliated by ordering one hundred ten Confederate POWs to labor under the same conditions, and with the same food and quarters as those given the Blacks. He also obtained Grant's endorsement of the policy. General Lee ordered the Blacks returned to POW camps forthwith, and they were never used that way again—at least on the Richmond front.[23]

As POWs, officers fared far better than enlisted men, whether White or Black. Enlisted POWs were sent to camps such as Andersonville, where despicable sanitation and bad food and water killed hundreds of them. The captured officers were sent to smaller facilities scattered around the Confederacy from Danville, Virginia, to Columbia, South Carolina. These prisons were often in old warehouses or jails, where sanitation and food were better than in Andersonville, though still quite bad. Lieutenant Scholl, the German American immigrant who'd served in the 28th USCT, spent six months in captivity and returned "looking like a skeleton."[24] But officers enjoyed a privilege denied to enlisted men—they were not included in the ban on prisoner exchanges instituted by Grant. Many of the officers captured at the Crater were exchanged within two months. Most USCT officers were not treated differently from the others, although since most of them were junior officers, they waited longer for exchange. In general, the higher an officer's rank, the better his treatment and the sooner he would be exchanged—both sides were more tender toward their colonels and generals than toward captains and lieutenants.

BURIAL OF THE DEAD, AUGUST 1

The truce finally began at 5:00 A.M. on August 1. When the flags went up, Captain Featherston witnessed an extraordinary scene: men rose up as if sprouting straight out of the earth, peopling the bleak inhuman landscape left by the fighting. Burial parties came forward, and with them a large number of senior officers, division and brigade, who took advantage of the truce to make or renew acquaintance with their opposite numbers. Their conversations were extremely cordial—except when the subject of Negro soldiers somehow popped into view.[25]

Captain Featherston had an especially friendly chat with General Potter, who offered the Alabaman a good cigar and a sip from a canteen of excellent whiskey. Potter asked Featherston to identify the Southern generals on the scene. When he pointed out the diminutive Mahone, Potter laughed, and commented, "Not much man but a big general." Featherston noticed a remarkably handsome general, identified by Potter as General Ferrero. Potter suggested, "Let me call him up and introduce him." But Featherston refused. "We down South were not in the habit of recognizing as our social equals those who associated with negroes." Potter understood perfectly and said no more.

The closest the enlisted men came to conversation was when, at one moment during the burial, soldiers on both sides of the lines stood on their parapets and began to shout, "Let's all go home!" But most enlisted men on the scene were too busy searching out the wounded and dead, digging burial pits, and hauling bodies and dumping them in. Since both sides assigned nearly all of this duty to Blacks, socialization with Confederate enlisted men was nonexistent. As Sergeant Bernard noted, "We made the negro prisoners carry their dead comrades to the Yankee line, where the Yankees made their negroes bury them."[26]

Many Whites were struck by the fact that after two days in that heat the White and Negro dead had turned the same color—black—and could only be distinguished by the difference of their hair. As Ernest Hemingway observed in "A Natural History of the Dead," "the color change in Caucasian races is from white to yellow, to yellow-green, to black. If left long enough in the heat the flesh comes to resemble coal-tar . . . and it has quite a visible tar-like iridescence." Some Whites felt the transformation symbolized a common humanity and an equality in sacrifice that negated the stigma of race. But most responded with a kind of puzzled dismay, as if realizing for the first time that for them "Negro" and the degradation of bodily death had always been metaphors of each other. Unnoticed at the time was the body of a woman in male disguise lying among the dead. Her sex, but not her identity, would be discovered when the bodies in several of the mass graves were reinterred in 1866.[27]

There were representatives of the Sanitary and Christian commissions on hand, and they went out among the bodies with supplies of medicine and jugs of lemonade, but found after two days that only twenty wounded men were still alive. It was not known how many had been alive when the long wrangle over protocol began. Union sources estimated the number buried between the lines at between two hundred and two hundred thirty. A detail from the 20th Michigan buried one hundred eighty Blacks and thirty Whites between the lines. A Georgia private remembered burying 133 in one "chasm" and 300 in another. An officer of Elliott's Brigade, Beaty, said that his men buried 55 Blacks and 178 Whites in the crater itself. Confederate newspapers estimated that seven hundred dead were found between the lines, a number Bernard thought exaggerated. The judgment was partly subjective, real quantities enlarged by a sense of horror. A Georgia private thought, "the whole face of the Earth was utterly strewn with dead negroes Y[ankees] and our men." His comrade took pride in having "left them thicker than any place that yanks was ever killed on."[28]

Most burials were made on the spot, in ditches or graves midway between the lines, because the dead were already badly decomposed. The smell was over and through everything, heavy in the nostrils, vile, thick, clinging. The four hours scheduled for the truce had to be extended for the work to be completed. The corpses were thrown into piles or stacked crosswise, "blacks whites and all together" three or four layers deep. The covering of earth was necessarily a good deal less than six feet, enough to keep the dead out of sight but not enough to dampen the stench that haunted the area for weeks.[29]

Confederates burying men in the crater suffered the most. Under the hot heavy sun of August those shallow graves and pools of dried blood became "pest-holes [that] filled the whole atmosphere with a foul vapor, which we inhaled at every breath. Green flies without number buzzed audibly all around us and added to the hideousness. . . . Every attempt to eat or even open one's mouth caused nausea." It was worse when Confederate engineers showed up and began digging shafts, searching for the Yankee tunnel and projecting mines of their own. These diggings broke open veins of corpse-rot gas and partly combusted black powder that nearly drove the men from the position.

And of course the war was on again: "When the dead were buried each side returned to their entrenchments, and soon the sharpshooters were firing at each other when and wherever seen."[30]

Part Five

CONSEQUENCES

Chapter 16

Court of Inquiry

AUGUST 6–SEPTEMBER 9, 1864

The Battle of the Crater was, in Grant's words, a "stupendous failure." It was not merely the number of men lost in the operation, but the way they were lost. His staff blamed the defeat on the ineptitude and apparent cowardice displayed by officers and men of IX Corps, and indeed the men of the Army of the Potomac as a whole. "The chances of success were so great—the failure so utter—that all men who understand the whole matter are paralized and petrified." The court of inquiry would apportion the blame and, by blaming, exorcise the embarrassment caused by the affair. The court would not perform the kind of operational analysis that might have improved the army. On those matters, Grant had already made his own analysis and reached his own conclusions—and his was the only opinion that counted.

Grant was disgusted by the defeat, but not unduly dismayed. On August 1, he wrote to Chief of Staff Halleck: "It was the saddest affair I have witnessed in this war. Such opportunity for carrying fortifications I have never seen and do not expect again." However, he did not think the defeat had diminished the strategic advantages enjoyed by his army. Battle losses had not seriously weakened his force. He believed Lee had actually lost more killed and wounded, though the Confederates had taken more prisoners. This served his strategy of draining Confederate manpower by imposing irreplaceable losses, and since he refused to exchange enlisted POWs, the Rebels' haul simply left them with more prisoners to guard and feed.[1]

Grant's tally was incorrect, but his evaluation of losses and gains had merit. Early estimates by Federal officers suggested losses in the Battle of the Crater of 4,400 to 4,500 killed, wounded, and missing, and that number has often been cited by historians. However, those estimates included men who had been separated from their units but later returned. The official tabulation, made some days later, listed 3,826 total casualties, of whom 504 were killed or mortally wounded, 1,881 wounded, and 1,441 missing (most of whom were probably POWs). This was a loss of roughly 23 percent of the engaged force of 16,772 men. The best available estimates of Confederate losses indicate that approximately 9,960 troops were engaged around the crater, and of these *at least* 361 were killed or mortally wounded, 727 wounded, and 403 missing (most of them taken prisoner), for a casualty total of 1,491—15 percent of the number engaged. By these measures the Federals lost twice as many men as the Confederates, and a significantly higher percentage of their force.[2]

However, the Battle of the Crater was not a stand-alone engagement but the culmination of a larger operation that began with the attack at Deep Bottom on July 27th. That part of the operation was a success, not only because it drew Lee's reserves north, but also because it inflicted heavier casualties than were suffered. Federal losses at Deep Bottom totaled 488 killed, wounded, and missing; Confederate losses totaled at least 635. Adding in these figures narrows the differential in losses: a total of 4,314 Federals to 2,126 Confederates. Confederate losses were certainly higher than these figures indicate. Record keeping in Lee's army was spotty, and methods of accounting were defective, so the reported casualty figures always represent a minimum. One Confederate officer estimated the loss at the Crater as three thousand men—certainly too large for that part of the fighting but perhaps appropriate for the total Confederate loss for July 27 to 30. If that was indeed the case, then Lee's percentage of loss (5 percent of his whole force) was equal to Grant's, and might have been slightly higher.[3]

As always, Grant's analysis treated the battle as a phase in an ongoing strategy of offensive operations. He was interested in the question "What went wrong?" only as it offered answers to the question "What next?" He'd drawn the key lesson from the action, and figured out how to apply it, before the battle itself had ended. At 2:15 P.M., while Hartranft's men were still fleeing across no-man's-land, he had written to Meade: "Our experience of to-day proves that fortifications come near holding themselves without troops. . . . With a reasonable amount of artillery and one infantryman to six feet I am confident either party could hold their lines against a direct attack of the other." Instead of seeing this as a deterrent to offensive action, Grant saw in it the germ of the strategy that would ultimately defeat Lee's army. If Confederate entrenchments could be held with a token force, so could Meade's. Therefore, if Lee should dare one of his fearsome counterattacks, Meade should "not hesitate to take out nearly every man to meet such attack." Since the Union had more soldiers than Lee, they could use the shield of their trenches to free large forces to strike at Lee's flanks. Even if they failed to turn those flanks or win a decisive battle, they could incrementally extend their invulnerable trench lines. Every extension of the line would compel Lee to stretch out the infantry in his trenches, until in the end his reserves would be drained and his infantry would be one to every eight feet or every ten, and then a series of powerful columns could shatter the attenuated line like a pane of glass. Moreover, the success of Grant's diversionary thrust north of the James proved that Grant could shift troops from one end of the line to the other much faster than Lee could respond—a tactical advantage he would exploit in the future.[4]

However, the immediate effect of the battle was to confer advantage on General Lee. He still lacked the troop strength to attempt a counteroffensive against Grant, but the losses in IX Corps and the absence of VI Corps made it unlikely that Grant could mount another major assault in the near future. So it was safe to risk sending Kershaw's Division to reinforce Early, whose power to threaten Washington was the best offensive option Lee had. At the least, Early would prevent Grant from recalling the VI and XIX Corps to Petersburg.

Grant *was* forced to postpone for more than two weeks his projected sweep against the Weldon Railroad. The top generals in the Army of the Potomac were caught up in the court of inquiry, and in any case his troops badly needed the rest. But like Lee, Grant had also begun to see the Shenandoah as the theater for a potentially decisive offensive. The events of July—and the demands of Abraham Lincoln—taught Grant to see Petersburg and the valley as integral parts of a single theater-wide operation. In effect, Early's army was now Lee's primary mobile force, the one element of his army still capable of offensive action. But unlike the army at Petersburg, Early's army could not shelter in trenches. It had to fight in the open field. During the first week of August, while the Army of the Potomac prepared for the court of inquiry, Grant began assembling the elements of a new strategic combination. Instead of recalling the VI and XIX Corps for battle at Petersburg, he made them the core of a new Army of the Shenandoah and reinforced that army with three divisions of cavalry. To command the army he chose his energetic and combative cavalry commander, Philip Sheridan—disappointing Meade, who had hoped for the independent command. Sheridan was the antithesis of the Potomac generals, preferring action to correctness of procedure, and Grant gave Sheridan a mission to his liking: to "put himself south of Early and follow him to the death." He gave Sheridan an overwhelming force—thirty-two thousand to Early's fifteen to eighteen thousand—artillery in plenty, and cavalry armed with repeating carbines. And to ensure success, Grant would launch operations against Petersburg coordinated with Sheridan's movements, attacking Lee in strength sufficient to force him to recall Kershaw's Division, and only then sending Sheridan in for the kill.

The Military Investigation, August 6–September 9

That shift of strategy and reordering of commands set the context in which the court of inquiry would do its work. It would have been better if the army could have conducted privately a thorough and searching review of the planning and operations in the Army of the Potomac, with a view to improving its performance—as the army has done in modern times. Grant's staff believed that the organizational structure and command culture of the Army of the Potomac were deeply flawed. But the public and quasi-judicial character of this inquiry put the emphasis on individual culpability, and it was impossible to condemn the system without condemning Meade. Grant understood Meade's limitations, but he had already considered and dismissed the idea of replacing him. Hancock was the only alternative, but his health was questionable, and the Potomac officer corps would not support an outsider from the Western armies. To dismiss Meade now would also be seen as an admission by Grant that his campaign was not going well.

So the court that convened on August 6 was designed to exonerate Meade and make Burnside and his officers scapegoats for the failure. The four officers impaneled to hear testimony were appointed by Meade, and included a member of Meade's staff and a general who (as Burnside saw it) had failed to come to Burnside's support on July 30. Burnside protested, but Meade's choices were confirmed by Grant, Secretary of War Stanton, and President Lincoln.[5]

The prosecutorial atmosphere spooked Colonel Pleasants into going on sick leave to avoid testifying. He had been under severe psychological strain during the digging of the mine. As Potter's aide during the battle, he had tried with increasing desperation and even hysteria to get the attack moving. The fiasco had made his entire investment of labor, reputation, and emotion worthless, even ridiculous, and he expected the army engineers would blame him for the failure. When General Barnard, chief of engineers under Grant, came to consult him about future mining operations, Pleasants blew his top and told him that he'd "see him in h—l first." Four months later he resigned his commission, "a greatly disappointed and disgusted man."[6]

The central issue of the inquiry was between Burnside and Meade. Burnside's defense was that Meade had interfered inappropriately, as when he refused to let the 4th Division lead, and had failed to act positively when he should have. He had denied Burnside, the man at the front, power to employ Warren's supporting force when it was needed, and had refused to come to the front himself (as Warren had requested) to see what needed to be done. Finally, he had ordered Burnside to withdraw, denied him support by Ord's or Warren's troops, and left the field prematurely, making Burnside responsible for the retreat without giving him the means to conduct it. Meade indicted Burnside for insubordinate behavior; for disobeying orders to remove the obstacles and trees in front of his lines; for choosing his spearhead division by lot, and allowing it to fall to an incompetent poltroon like Ledlie; for letting his troops go up in a disorganized manner; for failing to send engineering troops and equipment forward, without which even a victorious column could not have held the crest; for failing to report frequently and accurately, which prevented Meade from gaining a clear picture of conditions at the front; for sending in the 4th Division when he should have known the battle was lost; and for mismanaging the retreat.

Burnside's was a losing case but was not without merit. Meade *had* been too distant from the action to understand what needed to be done. Once it was clear that Burnside's reporting was inaccurate (and perhaps mendacious), Meade ought to have gone to the front to see for himself—as Grant did, twice. He mistrusted Burnside's judgment, yet left the retreat entirely to Burnside, and made himself unavailable for further consultation. It was certainly imprudent to order Warren and Ord to stand down before the retreat was accomplished. Meade denied having ordered Burnside to send in the Negro division after all was lost, but Burnside was able to display his 6:00 A.M. telegraphic dispatch demanding that Burnside send in everyone, "white and black," and rush for the crest.[7]

However, the evidence of Burnside's incompetence was irrefutable. The choice of Ledlie to lead the attack and the way in which he was chosen were utterly irresponsible. Burnside's failure to send engineers with the attacking force, and to prepare paths for artillery to be sent forward, might have had serious consequences if his troops had actually succeeded in capturing Cemetery Hill. His reports to Meade were so scanty, inaccurate, and misleading that they did prevent the army commander from understanding conditions on the field. This was especially true with regard to the withdrawal. Burnside had lobbied Meade to continue the attack instead of considering what he would need to get his men out with minimum losses. He had four hours after his last conference with Meade to assess the situation and ask for support from Warren and Ord if he thought he needed it, but he did not do so. Finally, as the court noted, one of the chief errors was "the want of any competent common head at the scene of the assault, to direct affairs as occurrences should demand." What they had in mind was the failure of any of Burnside's division commanders to accompany their troops into the breach, and Burnside's failure to detail a competent senior officer (or to go himself) to oversee a maneuver involving several divisions.[8]

There was no formal disgrace attached to the court's finding. Burnside remained one of the best-liked of the army's senior generals. He was not formally relieved of command. He simply went on a leave that would never end, and was replaced by John Parke, his longtime chief of staff. The army was bettered by the exchange.

The court also condemned Ledlie for "misbehavior," for losing control of his troops, and for spending all his time in the bombproof. Ferrero too was condemned for "being in a bomb-proof habitually." General Willcox was criticized for not having made a strenuous enough effort to push the attack, and Colonel Bliss for sequestering himself in the rear. Of the division commanders, only Robert Potter escaped criticism.

In Bliss's case they went too far—in Ledlie's not far enough. If Bliss was to be criticized for weak leadership, something should have been said about the failure of Marshall and Bartlett to see to it that their troops went forward in good order—which was their primary responsibility. For their failure to move swiftly beyond the crater they were not culpable, since Ledlie had given them false orders. In Ledlie's case, there was plenty of evidence that he had abdicated all his responsibilities as a commander, had probably been drunk all or part of the time, and was quite likely guilty of cowardice in the face of the enemy. Yet the court spent surprisingly little time on Ledlie. He was allowed to resign without facing a court-martial that would have embarrassed the army. Not until the congressional hearing in the winter of 1864–65 would testimony be taken about Ledlie's behavior in the bombproof. The court did not investigate the orders Ledlie gave his brigadiers, which contradicted those he had had from Burnside. If he had deliberately altered them to evade the task of charging the high ground, he ought to have been shot—as enlisted men guilty of far lesser offenses, such as sleeping on guard, sometimes were. Burnside's telegraphers probably received harsher treatment from the military justice system.

The court said nothing about General Warren's role, perhaps agreeing with him that it had been "insignificant." However, Warren's role had been insignificant because he'd wanted it to be. There were two points at which V Corps might have intervened effectively: by attacking in force in conjunction with Willcox's division to break the Confederate grip south of the breach, or by staging a diversionary attack to cover the final retreat from the crater. Under Meade's operational plan, Warren was to judge whether or not to support Burnside's assault by active measures. From first to last, Warren displayed extreme reluctance to take action, responding ambiguously or passively whenever Meade suggested he ought to attack. He believed that infantry attacking the Confederate lines would be uselessly slaughtered, and he would not attempt it unless Burnside's assault compelled the Confederates to weaken their line or retreat. Although there was no evidence that the Rebels had a fortified secondary line, Warren kept telling himself (as he would later tell the court of inquiry) "that is what the enemy had . . . or ought to have had if they did not." Even after the facts were known, Warren could not bring himself to acknowledge that there had been no second line: "If [the enemy] have been there all this time without that preparation, they are much more unprepared than I think they are." Nor would he believe the reports from Meade's HQ and the army signal stations that Mahone's troops were moving north from Warren's sector. In his testimony he falsely claimed that all the troops sent against the breach came from north of Cemetery Hill, when in fact all but one regiment was drawn from his front. Warren's dilatory behavior went unnoticed, perhaps because it was standard operating procedure in Meade's army.[9]

But it was Meade's battle plan that gave Warren license to drag his feet. Meade had been torn between two contradictory imperatives,

Grant's determination to strike a blow and Lincoln's insistence that casualties be minimized. To reduce the risk of heavy casualties, Meade decided that no forces beyond Burnside's would be committed unless success appeared imminent, and that if the attack went badly, it would be called off as quickly as possible and the troops returned to their lines. That suited the risk-averse Warren, who simply avoided doing anything until it was clear that nothing would do any good.

No one attributed any culpability for the failure to Grant. The lieutenant general's primary areas of responsibility were strategy and the design of large operations, and his performance on this level was highly successful. By diverting Lee's reserves north of the James he had created the conditions under which an assault on Petersburg might have succeeded. His judgments and actions in and around the tactical engagement of July 30 are more questionable. If (as Porter recalled) he thought the assault a failure when he met with Burnside at around 6:30 A.M., he ought to have been more forceful in advising Meade to call it off. There were good reasons for entrusting tactical operations to Meade, and Grant was justified in his reluctance to shortcut the chain of command by giving orders to Meade's subordinates. But he seems to have been exceptionally passive about giving Meade advice, although he had visited the front twice and seen the conditions Meade could only guess at.

Grant himself admitted an error of judgment in acceding to Meade's decision to remove the Colored division from the spearhead assignment. He agreed with Burnside's contention that had the 4th Division led, the assault would probably have succeeded. The freshness and high motivation of the Black troops, combined with the careful training they had been given, would certainly have enabled them to move through the breach without the disorganization that beset Ledlie's men, and this would have given the attack an excellent chance of success. But there are reasons for thinking that that change alone would not have yielded the kind of success the operation had aimed at.

The Federals could not have won by simply pushing a single division up to the Plank Road–Blandford Cemetery line. Unless the substantial Confederate forces holding the shoulders of the breach could have been pushed back, that division itself would have been isolated and destroyed. The mine was not as effective as Burnside had hoped. Its crater had made most of the breach an impassable barrier, and it had not killed or dispersed enough of Elliott's Brigade to allow the shoulders of the breach to be pushed back. Burnside had had the right idea when he'd planned for two regiments to peel off and clear the flanks of the advance. But events proved this was far too small a force for the purpose. To produce a breach of sufficient width, the shoulders would have had to be assailed in coordinated attacks by strong forces from the front as well as from the breach. To achieve such a combination, Burnside would have had to deploy all of Potter's and Willcox's divisions right on the heels of the spearhead's advance. His decision to have the supporting forces queue up in the covered ways made this impossible. Alternatively, V Corps could have advanced in concert with Burnside's men, striking the front held by Colquitt and Goode and preventing the latter from shifting troops to hold the breach. But only Meade could have ordered it done.

Grant and others had assumed that little or nothing stood in the way of Burnside's initial advance, and that all that was required for victory was a rapid dash from the breach to the high ground. However, there were several serious obstacles that any attacker would have had to overcome. The open slope from the breach to the Plank Road was subject to cross fire from artillery on the west and north and to rifle fire from the communication trench labyrinth north of the crater. The 26th South Carolina and 25th North Carolina had occupied the lateral ravine early in the action. It would have required a hard and costly assault to dislodge them, and there were entrenched positions off on the flank (the long covered way) in which they could have rallied. The lateral ravine itself would have been untenable by Union troops, since it could have been enfiladed by the Ellett and Letcher batteries to the north. The 4th Division would have had to rally there under fire and reorganize before renewing their drive for the high ground.

To overcome these and other contingencies that might have arisen, the attacking force would have needed a competent senior division commander on the scene, capable of adjusting and coordinating the movement of two or three divisions. It is not clear that IX Corps had such a general, but in any case Burnside did not order any division commander to command beyond the breach. Finally, even if the 4th Division had taken the high ground, it might have lost it to a counterattack, because Burnside had failed to send engineers to help the spearhead dig in, and had not made paths for artillery to be brought forward.

The Battle of the Crater *could* have been won, and putting the 4th Division in the lead would have made it more likely—but far from certain, given the weaknesses of Meade's battle plan and Burnside's limited skills as a corps commander and tactician.

The Confederates did not inquire into their army's performance. They accepted victory as vindication of the superior courage and prowess of their men, the perfection of their fortifications, and the pusillanimity of Yankees and Negroes. But there were questionable aspects to their victory. Grant had succeeded in enticing Lee to send all of his mobile reserve north of the James—more troops than were required to check Hancock. The three divisions he'd sent prior to July 29 had achieved that much, and Field's Division could have been kept on the south side as a reserve. If it had been, Burnside's attacks would have had no chance at all of success. It is possible that, as Charles Adams said, Grant had "out-generaled Lee"—fooled him into thinking that more than one infantry corps was at Deep Bottom, forty thousand men instead of twenty-five thousand. But it would also have been consistent with Lee's tactics in the Petersburg fighting if he had planned to use Field for a counterattack, to turn the Federal repulse into a serious defeat. In either case, Lee took a calculated risk, and relied on the strength of his defensive arrangements to prevent a breakthrough. He had already reached the conclusion Grant came to on July 30: that trench lines could be held by a minimal allotment of infantry. The Battle of the Crater just barely proved him right—but luck played too large a role in the outcome for the result to be reassuring. If the attack had not been so egregiously mismanaged, it might well have succeeded.

The events of July 27–30 showed that Grant could shift his troops from one end of his line to the other more rapidly than Lee could move his reserve, and that despite previous failures, Grant was determined to strike hard at any opportunity. Bearing all that in mind, Lee would never again risk his entire reserve on a single operation. He would parry Grant's offensives with carefully calibrated force, usually one reinforced infantry division augmented by cavalry.

But Grant retained the initiative, and his tactics forced Lee to spread his force ever thinner. In August, Grant varied the plan of the Crater operation, sending Hancock back to Deep Bottom to threaten Richmond (August 14–16), then—having drawn some of Lee's reserves north—sending Warren and V Corps out beyond the southern end of the trench line to seize Globe Tavern and a piece of the Weldon Railroad (August 18–21). Then he swung Hancock's II Corps all the way around from the extreme right of the line out past Warren on the far left, to extend the Union's control of the Weldon. Lee drove Hancock back at Ream's Station on August 25, but Grant had forced Lee to extend his lines north and south of the James and had cut one of the main supply lines into Petersburg. Lee recalled Kershaw's Division, which left Early's command on September 14. The next day Grant visited Sheridan's headquarters and ordered him to go in. Sheridan routed Early's force at Winchester on September 19 and at Fisher's Hill on September 22, and his troops proceeded to destroy the crops and livestock that made the valley so vital as a source of Confederate supply. In a desperate effort to regain the initiative in the valley, Lee sent Kershaw's Division back to Early for a surprise attack on Sheridan's army at Cedar Creek. On October 19, Sheridan virtually destroyed Early's reinforced army, and with it Lee's ability to mount a major offensive. After that the siege of Petersburg truly was "a matter of time."[10]

While that was happening, Grant kept pressing at Petersburg. On September 29–30 he repeated his patented one-two punch, using Butler's troops to storm Confederate lines north of the James at Fort Harrison and New Market Heights, and then sending V Corps and Potter's division of IX Corps to strike at Lee's southern flank and force another extension of the lines. On October 27, Grant staged simultaneous attacks by Butler north of the James and by Hancock at Hatcher's Run, out beyond Lee's right flank. By the time winter put an end to active operations, the trench lines stretched more than thirty-five miles from one end to the other, so that Lee had to man with the same number of troops a line three times longer than it had been in July. Doubting that he could hold his lines when Grant renewed the offensive in the spring, Lee tried to loosen the siege by storming Fort Stedman (March 25, 1865). The attempt failed, and cost Lee a substantial part of his reserve. When Grant sent Sheridan with the whole Cavalry Corps, supported by V Corps infantry, to sweep around Lee's right flank and cut the last railroad into Petersburg, Lee had to risk the rest of his reserve, cavalry and infantry, to stop him. Sheridan destroyed that force at Five Forks (April 1). The next day Grant ordered an attack along the entire line, and Lee's force was spread too thin to stop it. Three Union corps broke through the trench lines south and west of Petersburg; Richmond and Petersburg were abandoned; and the Army of Northern Virginia began its last desperate retreat to Appomattox and surrender.

EFFECTS ON ARMY MORALE

The officers and men of Mahone's Division took tremendous pride in having saved the army from a ruinous defeat and in having routed a superior force. They had done this under the anxious eye of General Lee himself, whose praise was beyond price. But their achievement came at terrible cost. Of the 2,250 men in the three brigades, official records showed that at least 588 were killed, wounded, or missing, a casualty rate of 26 percent. In reality, their losses were probably a good deal higher. The three brigades of Johnson's Division felt a grim satisfaction in their bitter four-hour struggle to contain the Federal assault, but their losses were even more severe: at least 894 out of the 2,200 who had engaged, more than 40 percent. Elliott's Brigade was virtually wiped out, suffering nearly seven hundred casualties out of fewer than eight hundred fifty officers and men. Only in the artillery was the joy unalloyed: the gunners had held the Federals at bay in the absence of infantry, and their emplacements had proved immune to counter-battery fire.

The impact of the battle cut deeper than any quantification of gain and loss. The fighting had been peculiarly intense and horrible. Nearly every soldier who wrote about the battle in later years rated it the most savage, brutal, and merciless struggle they experienced in the entire war. Even to men inured to the effects of artillery bombardment, the outcome produced by the mine explosion was traumatic. The size of that single blast, the numbers destroyed at one blow, the horrible dismemberments it produced, and the uniquely awful thought of dozens of men buried alive—all of these combined to make the mine explosion seem an extraordinary escalation in the murderousness, cruelty, and destructive power of the Federal war effort. This demonstration of Yankee cruelty made some Confederates more determined to resist, while others were intimidated. Lieutenant Hightower of the 20th Georgia was glad to be transferred away from Petersburg: "This way they have got blowing up people I dont believe in it." One Confederate officer declared that "no one thing during the war produced such a demoralizing influence among our troops. . . . From that day desertions became more frequent, and from the uncertain horrors which that even threw around services 'in front' the greatest dissatisfaction began to prevail in all ranks of the army."[11]

Reaction was similar to that other Yankee innovation, the use of Black troops against the Army of Northern Virginia. Lieutenant Colonel William Pegram wished the Federals would send more Blacks into the field because "it has a splendid effect on our men," intensifying their commitment to the cause and their energy on the battlefield. It also increased the bitterness of Southern soldiers toward the Northern people. Hospital workers in Richmond noted that after the Crater, Southern soldiers no longer showed the kindness and chivalry toward Federal wounded that had been displayed in earlier fights. On the other hand, the increased use of Black troops affected the disposition to desert among soldiers whose homes were in regions threatened by invasion. These men were not opting out of the struggle, but they were withdrawing their service from the national army and its cause in order to protect a home interest.[12]

In the Federal army, the effects of the defeat were most strongly felt in the units immediately involved. Morale in IX Corps plummeted. All four divisions had been driven from the field, and 25 percent of the corps had become casualties. The 1st Division lost both brigadiers, and its commander was disgraced. IX Corps would need a month to rebuild its numbers and replace lost or disgraced officers, and until the end of September, the corps would man the trenches while others mounted offensives. Among the enlisted men, there was grief for their losses and chagrin for their bad performance and loss of face among their peers. As Charles Francis Adams sardonically put it, "It is agreed that the thing was a perfect success, except that it did not succeed [because] our troops behaved shamefully."

But even in IX Corps the effect was not permanent. There remained, as before, a hard core of officers and men whose responses were shaped by a solid commitment to their unit and the war. Colonel Cummings of the 17th Vermont had a surgeon's certificate for medical leave but felt "I *must* get the regiment in some shape before applying for leave." The 17th lost every officer it had taken into the fight. The historian of the 31st Maine summed it up in a way that acknowledged the defeat and put it in perspective: it was "a sorry day's work for us, and nothing gained." But they had been at war a long time, had experienced defeat before, and knew there would be other days and chances to improve their record.[13]

The battle left IX Corps infantry with an undeserved reputation for cowardice, which later historians have tended to perpetuate. Their most substantive weakness was one that had in fact become universal in the armies before Richmond, affecting even such elite combat units as II Corps: an extreme reluctance to make frontal assaults, and a discouragement that led many to give up on an engagement at the first sign of crisis. The problem in IX Corps was its abysmal leadership at the division and corps levels. Still, despite the utter breakdown of command on July 30, most soldiers in most units kept trying to get the job done. The numerous volunteers who repeatedly ran the gauntlet to bring resupply to the troops in the breach, when they might have stayed safe after regaining their own lines, reflect a devotion to cause and comrades second to none.

There were some strong performances on July 30 that were difficult to appreciate at the time. Simon Griffin's brigade, led by Griffin and Colonel White, had done most of the fighting north of the crater, and Griffin's achievement in shifting the direction of his attack while closely engaged was remarkable. The commanders of the Michigan regiments in Humphrey's brigade showed initiative and willingness to close with the enemy in the most dire circumstances, as did Colonel Weld of the 56th Massachusetts north of the crater. Hartranft did well to hold the defense together, although he was ineffective in mounting the offensive demanded by the operation.

The enlisted men and the regimental officers were able to forgive themselves for bad performance by shifting the blame to convenient scapegoats: the generals and the Negroes. There was universal agreement that Ledlie was the chief culprit, a cowardly incompetent and drunkard. The soldiers' liking for Burnside vied with their recognition that none of their generals had come forward to help them. On the other hand, Meade could be excoriated without qualification, for spoiling Burnside's plan, forcing White troops to do what the Blacks had been trained for, and abandoning the field in the middle of the fighting.

The recovery of morale in IX Corps and the army as a whole was facilitated by the scapegoating of the 4th Division. The Blacks were blamed for having precipitated the panicky rout that had driven Griffin's, Bliss's, and Bell's brigades from the field, and for confounding the defense of the crater by piling in on top of the Whites already there. Alvin Voris, an officer in Butler's Army of the James, spoke to Bell just after the battle, and was told that "the black rascals got scared and dashed back on our troops with fixed bayonets, and so disorganized the white troops. . . . All join in saying that the 'nigger' did verry [sic] badly and had no excuse for it." (Voris himself was well-disposed to Blacks, and hoped to command a USCT regiment.) This belief was especially favored by the officers of the routed regiments, and by their brigade and division commanders, whose actions would be scrutinized by the court of inquiry. Their testimony turned the court of inquiry into an investigation of the strengths and weaknesses of Black soldiers, as well as a tribunal on the performance of general officers. It became customary in descriptions of the battle to describe the timing of events in relation to "the stampede of the darkies." In contrast General Hartranft, who came out of the battle with some credit, described the Blacks as having been no more or less disordered by conditions around the crater than any troops would have been.[14]

The blame game was not really rational. Some of those who blamed the Blacks for the rout also blamed Meade for having removed the Colored troops from the spearhead role. Captain Charles Adams caught the paradox precisely when he noted that "all who dislike black troops shoulder the blame onto them—not that I can find with any show of cause. They seem to have behaved just as well and just as badly as the rest and to have suffered more severely." On the other hand, General Grant and a number of other senior officers, including General Ord, declared under oath their belief that the 4th Division had had the training and had displayed the élan needed to make the attack a success.[15]

The Performance of the 4th Division

An accurate assessment of the performance of the 4th Division ought to have been of greater concern to the court of inquiry, since the future use of Black troops was in question. But that very fact led the officers involved to ask what the battle had shown about racial character, rather than assessing the division's performance relative to the rest of IX Corps and relative to other units with comparable training and experience.

The most significant factor in the 4th Division's performance was not that its men were Black but that its units were "green." Not only did individual soldiers lack combat experience, officers and men had no experience of operating as part of a brigade or division. The overall arc of their performance was exactly what the army would expect of a rookie outfit: they attacked with energy but had a limited repertoire of responses to battlefield surprises and reverses, which led them to break under Mahone's attack and to be difficult to rally. However, in many crucial respects their performance matched that of the best troops on the field.

Their morale withstood the denigration implicit in their shift from spearhead to reserve; the long hours of waiting in the covered way while an unseen battle raged outside; the sight of wounded and demoralized men hurrying to the rear. When the opportunity came to make their assault, they went forward with considerable élan, despite the heavy fire as they crossed no-man's-land. They were able to adapt their formations to the unexpected circumstances they faced, and were able to maintain a high degree of regimental and even brigade cohesion as they worked their way through the traffic jam and into action. Like the brigades that preceded them, they lost squads and platoons of men to the crater and to the maze of trenches, and the jam-up prevented one regiment in each brigade from getting to the front. But they were able to bring more men through the clog and into effective action than any of the brigades that had preceded them—despite the fact that the crowding was more severe and enemy fire more intense than it had been when the brigades of Marshall, Bartlett, Griffin, and Bliss had advanced. The training they had undergone was undoubtedly one of the key factors in their success.

Having made the passage, Sigfried's brigade mounted the most successful assault of the day, an improvised pincers movement that drove the Carolina troops back and won the day's largest haul of prisoners and battle flags. Then, like Griffin's brigade before it, Sigfried's brigade was reorganized and reoriented under fire to attack the high ground to the west. Thomas's brigade came later, when crowding and confusion were worse, but Thomas was also able to get most of his brigade through the jam and into a position from which it could fight. After Thomas's first assault was broken up, his troops were willing to attempt another. So much for the worries expressed by Burnside and Loring that Colored troops would not attempt an attack if they saw that White men had failed before them.

Both brigades attempted an advance in conjunction with Griffin's, and were broken by Mahone's well-timed counterattack. Confederates asserted, and many Union officers agreed, that the Blacks had been terrified by the sight of enraged White men charging them with bayonets. As John Wise put it, "when our men, in frenzy, rushed upon them and drove the cold steel into them, they did not show the stubborn power of endurance for which the Anglo-Saxon is preeminent, nor do I believe they ever will on any field." Yet these same Black troops had just succeeded in storming positions that had balked White troops for hours, against Anglo Saxons as angry and well armed as Mahone's. They broke under circumstances that would probably have broken any unit in the army: their attack was weak and badly organized, their line officers decimated, their combat power weakened by casualties and the disorganization of passing the trenches.[16]

The regiments that broke were unable to rally. That was to be expected with green troops, and it was certainly the case that many of them fled until they were back behind Fort Morton. However, as many observers noted, there were White troops in plenty fleeing with them.[17]

Contrary to expectations, large numbers of Black troops *did* rally after Mahone's attack, as individuals and squads, with and without their White officers—just as White troops were expected to do. Some Blacks stood and fought to the last in their original positions; others retreated to the crater and rallied there. These men then formed the backbone of the force that defended the crater to the last, performing tasks that White troops feared to undertake. Race may have played some role in their re-sponse: they believed that the enemy would not grant them quarter. But they were also in the unique position of having to fear a stab in the back from their White comrades as well as murder by the enemy. Charles Fran-cis Adams had written that "after all a negro is not the equal of the white man. . . . He has not the mental vigor and energy, he cannot stand up against adversity. . . . Retreat, defeat and exposure would tell on them more than on whites. . . . He cannot fight for life like a white man." But as Private Bird of the 12th Virginia said, the Blacks in the crater "fought like bulldogs, and died like soldiers."[18]

The level of casualties suffered by the 4th Division offers a final meas-ure of the share of the fighting they carried. The 1st Division, which at-tacked first and spent the longest time under fire, suffered a little less than 18 percent killed, wounded, and missing—the lowest casualty rate in IX Corps. The 3rd Division casualty rate was slightly higher. The 2nd Divi-sion, whose two brigades tried to break out north of the crater, lost 23 percent of those engaged. The 4th Division, which was engaged for the shortest period, lost 31 percent. Of the 504 in the corps that were listed as killed in action, 209 were from the 4th Division—41 percent of those killed. The 4th Division were good soldiers, and they performed as well as or better than any of the other divisions on the field.[19]

Their soldierly quality is also attested by the fact that, despite their losses and the supposed trauma of their confrontation with Mahone's Di-vision, they continued to effectively perform the military and other work assigned them—including combat—when an army command grown leery of Black troops allowed them to fight. In addition to regular service in the trenches, the whole division participated in the August battles for the Weldon Railroad, and most of the regiments were in the actions at Fort Sedgwick and Poplar Grove Church in the fall of 1864, and at Hatcher's Run in the spring of 1865. In December the wishes of Meade and Butler were granted: all Black troops in the Army of the Potomac were trans-ferred to the Army of the James and combined in the all-Black XXV Corps. All the regiments in Sigfried's brigade saw action in the campaign against Fort Fisher in Wilmington, North Carolina, and joined in the last skirmishes before the surrender of Johnston's army on April 16, 1865. Thomas's regiments participated in the final assault on Richmond and were the first infantry to enter the Confederate capital. The 19th, 23rd, and 31st USCT joined in the pursuit of Lee's army to its surrender at Ap-pomattox.[20]

POLITICAL RESULTS: THE NORTH

The scapegoating of the Colored troops may have helped the White soldiers of IX Corps recover their morale, but its political implications were harmful. It was inevitable that the 4th Division's performance would be seen as a test of the soldierly qualities of the Negro race, and an answer to the question of whether Blacks were worthy of full citizenship.

That question was politicized as soon as the partisan newspapers digested the preliminary dispatches. The *New York Herald,* which took a conservative Democratic line in the election, began coverage on August 2. Its correspondent first described the Colored division favorably: their "splendid discipline could not but be observed, and in the early part of the contest no soldiers behaved more gallantly." The article went on to note that the Blacks had broken when faced with enraged Rebels who'd attacked "with the fury of demons," and their panic had then infected the White troops. That treatment was too favorable for editor James Gordon Bennett, who vehemently opposed the use of Black troops and any measure looking toward racial equality. On August 3 the *Herald* reported that the White troops were angry and out of patience with the Black troops, and with the abolitionist "fanatics who have forced this miserable material into our armies."[21]

> We must blame . . . the President and his whole Cabinet, with its nigger-worshipping policy. They who have insisted against all opposition that niggers should enter the army are even more to blame than all the others. Niggers are not fit for soldiers. They can dig, and drive mules; they cannot fight, and will not fight.[22]

The Republican *New York Times* made the best of a bad business. Their front-page headline on August 2 admitted the failure of a "Desperate Attempt to Carry the Enemy's Position," and reported that "The Colored Troops [Were] Charged with the Failure." No mention was made of the failure of Ledlie's troops to advance. On the contrary, the 14th NYHA was credited with leading a gallant attempt to storm the crest, which "nearly gained the summit [despite] a withering fire." The Colored division was said to have advanced after the repulse of the 14th, to have "moved out gallantly" and gained a hundred yards. Then the 39th Maryland USCT broke and spread panic through the whole force—which was checked when "the white soldiers recovered their stamina" and made their stand at the crater. Thus the *Times* also put the onus of defeat on the Black troops, though it limited the rebuke by (falsely) attributing the panic to a single regiment.[23]

Reaction in the African American communities of the North was supportive of the troops and defensive about their behavior. In New Jersey the Black press and the Republican press condemned the insulting language of the *Herald* and pointed to the genuine achievements of Black troops while urging continuation of Lincoln's policies. Indiana Republican newspapers dismissed the *Herald*'s views as typical of the Copperhead press. One African American paper argued that the Blacks seemed to have done no worse than the Whites, and "if they do as well as white men we ought to be satisfied." More positive views gained circulation as letters from the soldiers and their officers were printed. Sergeant Payne of the 27th USCT described his brigade's advance as "one of the most daring charges ever made since the commencement of the rebellion," a charge that would have succeeded if not for the prejudice of White generals who had refused to send reinforcements, and "the white soldiers [who] lay in their pits, and did nothing to support our men." Garland White, the chaplain of the 28th, condemned as cowardly and slanderous the claim of the *Herald* editors and other "foul-hearted buzzards" that the Colored troops had "acted cowardly." It was "a calumny heaped upon an innocent and brave people, laboring under disadvantages unparalleled in the history of civilized warfare."

However, even within the African American community, the evident failure of the attack required a scapegoat. A sergeant major in the 4th USCT of Hinks's victorious division was angry and aggrieved that the 4th Division had sullied the race's reputation and diminished their prospects for future action: "Broke and *run*! Devil blame 'em!" Even Garland White believed that the regiments that broke "were principally raised in Slave States. They did not stand up to the work like those from the Free States."[24]

For Lincoln, it was one of the worst moments in a bad summer. The Crater fiasco tainted Grant's reputation and caused people to doubt the will and ability of the soldiers themselves. The Illinois clergyman who presided at the funeral of Colonel Bross believed "it spread a gloom over all the land. It was widely felt, as a result, that we were making no progress in the war, and were likely to make none." The Democrats, taking their cue from Bennett's *Herald* and Manton Marble's New York *World,* were claiming that Lincoln had made this a war for "nigger equality" and that the Crater had proved that integrating the army had degraded it. The War Democrats and conservative Republicans in Lincoln's coalition were pressuring him to back away from the Emancipation Proclamation or to circumscribe its implications. Lincoln could not win the election without their support, but he also believed he could not win the war without Black soldiers. At the end of August he judged that "unless some great change takes place [I will be] *badly beaten,*" and he asked his cabinet members to sign a secret memorandum pledging their support to win the war and save the Union by inauguration day, since his successor "will have secured his election on such ground that he cannot possibly save it afterward." The nation was spared that disastrous possibility by Sherman's victory at Atlanta and Sheridan's in the Shenandoah, which transformed public opinion.[25]

THE QUESTION OF ATROCITY

The court of inquiry never addressed the aspect of the battle that, in later years, became most notorious: the killing of a considerable number of wounded men, disarmed men, and POWs after they had surrendered. Yet it is this element of atrocity that makes the Crater unique among the major battles of the Civil War. (Fort Pillow and Plymouth were small-scale actions.)

Black units at the Crater suffered a much higher proportion of dead to wounded than was typical in Civil War battles. On average, the ratio of wounded to dead was 4.8 to 1. In the Battle of the Crater, the overall ratio for Union troops was 3.7 to 1—but for Black troops it was 1.8 to 1. The latter figure might be taken as an indication of the hard fighting done by the Blacks. It is significant that the ratio of killed to wounded Confederates was 2 to 1. The presence of Blacks heightened the intensity of what was, by all accounts, one of the most murderous infantry combats of the war. Participants frequently remarked on the extraordinary number of corpses packed onto that small field, and the large percentage of dead as opposed to wounded. Others noted the unusually large number of casualties caused by bayonets and rifle butts. Trench fighting accounts for much of this. In the open field, troops could break or retreat before crossing bayonets with the enemy. But once a trench was entered, combat was at close quarters and escape or evasion was difficult. Many encounters involved troops blundering into one another around blind corners. In all of these situations, men tended to fight until killed or severely wounded.

And when the combat was between White and Black, men fought desperately, believing that the enemy would not grant quarter—an expectation that became a self-fulfilling prophecy.[26]

Modern historians of the battle have generally acknowledged that such killings occurred but usually mention them at the very end of the action in the crater itself. This is understandable, given the difficulty of reducing the events of the battle to a coherent narrative. However, this procedure leaves the impression that the killings were localized and limited to soldiers maddened by the last moments of fighting. If my account of troop movements and the timing of assaults is correct, then these killings occurred early and late, at several different places on the field, and included the deliberate murder of wounded men after surrender, and of POWs by rear echelon troops.

Few historians note that the initial massacre occurred when Sigfried's brigade stormed the positions held by the remnant of Elliott's Brigade. Several officers, including Hall, Bates, and Bowley, declare that their Black soldiers killed some prisoners and were with difficulty restrained from killing more. From these and other sources we also know that officers of Sigfried's brigade gave their men "Fort Pillow! No quarter!" as a battle cry. However, these officers quickly intervened to stop their men from carrying out the threat, and more than one hundred POWs were sent to the rear by Sigfried's brigade. Confederate massacres of wounded or disarmed Black troops involved more killing, in part because as victors the Confederates had more opportunity. These killings occurred over a longer period of time, at several points on the battlefield: by Weisiger's Brigade (and others) in the trenches north of the crater; by elements of three brigades in the northern lobe of the crater; by Sanders's Alabama Brigade in the southern lobe of the crater; and by various troops in the Confederate rear, who shot individual POWs as they passed by.

Whatever the precise number, the ways in which the killings occurred qualify as atrocities—perhaps (under modern codes) as war crimes. In any case, they qualify as violations of the moral and legal codes that govern (and governed) our society. In the heat and confusion of a combat assault, it is not uncommon for soldiers to kill enemies who are trying to surrender. The rage of battle cannot simply be switched on and off. But soldiers at the scene on both sides in the Battle of the Crater testify that wounded and unarmed men were deliberately killed after it was clear that combat had ended, and there is no palliating the murders of POWs committed by troops in the rear.

The issue of responsibility for the massacres is defined most suc-
cinctly by Noble Brooks, the Georgia private: "Oh! the depravity of the
human heart; that would cause men to cry out 'no quarters' in battle, or
not show any when asked for."[27] Before the killing began, orders were
given. There is unambiguous testimony that Sigfried and some of his regimental commanders gave orders that, explicitly or implicitly, told their
troops not to expect or grant quarter, that Mahone gave a "no quarter" instruction to each of his brigades as it went into action, and that some
brigade or regimental commanders did the same. But for such orders to
have effect, men must also be willing to obey them—to reject the appeal to
mercy when it is finally made, face-to-face. As we have seen, there were
many officers and men on both sides who actively or passively refused to
execute those orders.

Participants in and witnesses to these events offered two explana-
tions, which were also partial justifications, for the killings. The first was
that the killings were morally legitimate acts of revenge for atrocities committed by the enemy. Sigfried's men thought of themselves as avengers of
the massacre at Fort Pillow, and of the oppression and humiliation of enslavement. Many of Mahone's troops were told that Elliott's men had
been killed by Negroes crying "No quarter!" Modern readers may be inclined to sympathize with the feelings of the Black soldiers, but if they do
so, they must grant the moral equivalency of the vengeance exacted in the
name of Elliott's men.

However, the revenge rationale applies only to those Confederates
who got the word from survivors, from Mahone, or from their officers. As
the accounts by George Bernard and John Featherston make clear, many
of Weisiger's and Sanders's men had no idea they were fighting Negroes
until they came face-to-face in combat. Other Confederate participants
insisted as a matter of principle that they needed no orders or specific
premise of vengeance to motivate and justify the murder of Blacks taken in
arms, that their response was the natural and spontaneous reaction of any
true White man to the racial threat, and they exulted in the killings. It's
possible that some of this vaunting reflected a desire to be seen as an ideal
Confederate and defender of White supremacy. However, such boasts
would not have been made unless the soldiers had believed that their society would find such sentiments praiseworthy.

The idea that the races were naturally and innately hateful to one another was the second and most prevalent form of explanation. Confederate accounts affirm that Southern Whites regarded any manifestation of

Black defiance with rage, hatred, and reflexive or instinctual violence. The slave system created a culture in which racial antipathy and mutual fear was rampant and often deadly. The only Civil War battles in which regular forces refused to grant quarter to the enemy involved Confederates and Black Union troops. The exceptions are those massacres perpetrated by *irregular* units on the Missouri-Kansas border. In this case, the fact that the city of Petersburg, with its large civilian population, was the objective of the attack made Confederates think of the nightmare scenario in which helpless women and children were threatened by maddened Negroes.[28] Some Federal officers subscribed to a similar idea: that Blacks were indeed "savage" by temperament and were naturally disposed to wreak terrible vengeance on their former masters. But this concept of Negro character was offset by the other, more prevalent half of the racial stereotype, which imagined Black men as innately docile and servile, readily giving way to the superior race. The primary reason the Union officers gave their troops the "no quarter" instruction was to overcome that supposed docility and motivate them to fight with absolute determination.

However, for the Federals "no quarter" was a motivational ploy, and one that was contrary to official policy and to the ethical system of Northern culture. When USCT officers saw their troops acting out "no quarter," they tried to stop the killing, and in at least one instance an officer shot a Black soldier who refused to stop. Confederate officers responded in radically different ways, with some actively trying to stop the killing, others ignoring it, and others approving or joining in. But in general, when the Confederates said "no quarter," they meant it. The summary killing of armed Blacks and their White abettors was the logical extension of the slave codes that governed their society, which demanded instant condign punishment, without benefit of trial, for defiant or rebellious slaves. The stated policy of the Confederate government was to treat Black soldiers and their White officers as criminals liable to enslavement and/or summary execution. The threat of retaliation against Confederate POWs deterred the open execution of these policies, but official letters of instruction from the Confederate War Department indicated a preference for killing USCT captives "red-handed." Thus officers and men who sanctioned or joined in the killing at the Crater were fulfilling the spirit and intent of their government's policies.

The parading and public humiliation of captured officers and men was also a violation of the ethical norms of American society and "civilized warfare." Under the modern law of war, such behavior is formally proscribed—one of the indictments leveled against Saddam Hussein after the Gulf War was that he had made a public display of captured servicemen. No such law existed in 1864, but Confederate authorities understood that this treatment was not according to the "usages and courtesies" of war. The Confederates did it to dramatize the principle that those who used Negroes as soldiers or associated with them were not entitled to the courtesies accorded "decent" men. The idea came from high up the chain of command: the parade was organized by A. P. Hill, at the time Lee's senior corps commander. It is noteworthy that, despite the publicity of this display and the widespread acknowledgment that Black troops had been murdered, General Lee never addressed the issues raised by such events. "Honor can turn a blind eye when the subject is thought to be beneath recognition." His silence was permissive.[29]

Thus Confederate policy and propaganda must bear the chief responsibility for creating that "mutual assumption of the Black Flag" that made Blacks and Whites willing (in Private Noble's phrase) to "cry out 'no quarters' in battle, [and] not show any when asked for." The basic rationale for those Confederate policies was the overriding need to identify the cause of the Confederacy with the preservation of White supremacy. In that sense, the Battle of the Crater was a godsend for the Confederate government. The role played by the Black troops highlighted the distinctly racial character of the war, and dramatized the stakes of battle. "Reunion" now carried with it the threat of civil equality between the races—or worse, a regime in which Negroes were empowered as the instruments of coercion to subjugate and degrade the White South. The Richmond papers hailed Mahone's men for having saved their streets from massacre and their women from rape. The *Examiner* claimed that all of the Black troops were either stolen or runaway slaves, "black rascals" who had themselves cried "no quarter," and that killing them out of hand was therefore justified. Although the captured Blacks were probably worth half a million dollars on the auction block, it was "an outrage to common sense, and a direct encouragement to atrocious barbarism" to take any of them alive. On the other hand, Fort Pillow was "a good beginning in the right direction." The Richmond *Whig* thought the process should continue "until every negro has been slaughtered." In that context, it is easy to see why Captain Featherston thought a Fort Pillow–type massacre an exemplary punishment for "whites and negroes together" in arms, and apologized to his wife for allowing any Black POWs to reach the rear alive.[30]

But President Davis had to weigh the symbolism of White supremacy against the Confederacy's material necessities. The exhaustion of the South's White manpower could only be offset by somehow increasing the military use of Black manpower. Over the course of the summer and fall, Davis was drawn back to the proposal Cleburne had made in January 1864: to tap the Confederacy's own resources of Black manpower by recruiting a select number of slaves into the military, with compensation to their owners and a promise of freedom to the enlistee after his term of faithful service. In its most poignant and painful terms, the question for Davis was whether the Confederacy should surrender the institution for whose sake it went to war, in order to win that war and achieve independence. Opposition was fierce to a proposal that was widely seen as the first step on a slippery slope to universal emancipation, but the measure had support outside the cotton states, and when General Lee endorsed the idea, its passage was assured. The Richmond *Whig*, which had called for the wholesale slaughter of free Negroes in August 1864, supported the policy. Let a quarter of a million Black men be enlisted and "present them with their freedom and the privilege of remaining in the States, and arm, equip, drill and fight them. We believe that the negroes, identified with us by interest, and fighting for their freedom here, would be faithfull and reliable soldiers, and . . . could be depended upon for much of the hardest fighting."[31]

Ideological purists such as Howell Cobb might have objected that "if the negro will make a soldier, then our whole theory of slavery is wrong." But the performance of Black troops at the Crater, and in subsequent battles around Richmond, was experimental proof that Blacks *would* make soldiers. Davis's answer to Cobb was a warning that the Confederacy's epitaph might be: "Died of a Theory."[32]

But Davis had waited too long. A few weeks after the enabling legislation was passed, Richmond fell.

Chapter 17

Epitaphs

In the winter of 1864–65 the Joint Committee on the Conduct of the War conducted its own investigation of the Crater, which was implicitly critical of Meade for his handling of the mine and the Colored division, and his absence from the front. This time Colonel Pleasants was willing to testify: he did not think the committee would be out to get him. However, their findings—and the memory of the battle itself—were eclipsed by the dramatic events that closed the war: Sherman's march through the Carolinas, the capture of Fort Fisher, Grant's final victory at Petersburg, and Lee's surrender.

At Fort Fisher, Ben Butler plagiarized Burnside's mine, exploding a ship full of gunpowder under the ramparts. The explosion fizzled, Butler abandoned the attack, and—since Lincoln had been safely reelected—Grant fired him. Butler would serve ten years as a Radical congressman, leading the fight for President Johnson's impeachment and for civil rights for the freedmen. Anathema to conservatives of both parties, obscured by clouds of scandal, he would end his career as the presidential candidate of the populist Greenback party in 1884.

Meade commanded the Army of the Potomac till the end of the war. Afterward, out of favor with the Republican Congress, and the prestige of Gettysburg diminished by his questionable performance under Grant, his postwar career would be embittered by controversy and the sense that his service and sacrifice were unappreciated.

The JCCW hearings gratified Burnside by giving a more sympathetic hearing to his side of the case, but the verdict of his peers, the public, and history was against him. No matter. He remained well liked even by his critics and was a favorite son to the people of Rhode Island. He served three terms as governor and was twice elected U.S. senator, dying in office in 1881.

Although Willcox and Ferrero had been criticized by the court of inquiry, both remained in divisional command. The judgment against Ferrero was apparently reconsidered within the army even before the JCCW hearing, and his testimony there helped restore his reputation. Willcox stayed in the service after the war, and Ferrero returned to his dance hall business in New York City. Robert Potter also retained his command. He was desperately wounded in the final attack on Petersburg, on April 2, 1865, but recovered and returned to the practice of law.

James Ledlie resumed his career as an engineer, working for the Union Pacific during the building of the transcontinental railroad. A siding in Nevada was named in his honor. He later headed his own railroad corporation, and died in 1882 at age sixty, a prominent and prosperous businessman.

Joshua Sigfried resigned his commission after the battle and returned to civilian life. Henry Thomas commanded a brigade of Colored troops in the Army of the James until the war's end, and in recognition of his service was given brevet (temporary) promotions to brigadier and major general of volunteers. His account of the 4th Division's role in the battle was published in the great historical compendium *Battles and Leaders of the Civil War*. After the war he reverted to his Regular Army rank of captain in the 11th Infantry. He retired as a major in 1891 and died six years later.[1]

Seymour Hall and Delevan Bates recovered from their wounds and returned to active service, leading their regiments in the Appomattox campaign and the postwar expedition to the Rio Grande, which forced the French to withdraw support for the puppet state they had established in Mexico. Bates availed himself of the Homestead Act to take up a homestead in Nebraska, and had a long career as a businessman and civic leader in his community. Hall moved to Missouri and was active in reconstruction politics there, before settling in Kansas.[2]

Freeman Bowley spent seven months in captivity, starving and suffering from scurvy, and failed in several attempted escapes before his parole and exchange in March 1865. After the war he was turned down for a commission in the Regulars; he moved to San Francisco (1867–68) and worked as a fireman on the Southern Pacific Railroad, the western half of the transcontinental railroad then being driven to completion. In the 1890s he felt impelled to write his memoirs of service in the 30th

USCT—the values for which he and his Black soldiers had fought were being forgotten or traduced by a nation that was permitting the former Confederacy to reestablish White supremacy and Black subjection. Bowley spent his working life shoveling coal into the furnaces of the SP's locomotives, and died in 1903. Two of his sons realized his thwarted hope of a commission in the Regulars. One retired from the army as a lieutenant colonel, the other as a lieutenant general.[3]

Frank Bartlett spent two months as a POW. He suffered from dysentery, with high fever and interminable bouts of diarrhea that led him to despair of survival. Without his artificial leg, or even a set of crutches, he had to "hop" from place to place leaning on a comrade's shoulder. His sense of helplessness and humiliation was extreme, and he attributed his mistreatment to having been captured in company with Negroes. But his health improved, and after his exchange at the end of September he was appointed to command the 1st Division of IX Corps, a post he held till the end of the war. On July 21, 1865, he was the central figure when Harvard University paid tribute to its alumni who had served in battle. There was a splendid ceremony, attended by such eminences as Ralph Waldo Emerson, James Russell Lowell, and Charles Sumner. Bartlett's emotions were so strong he could barely speak. His friend Herman Melville paid tribute in a poem titled "The College Colonel," published the following year. Melville saw in him the spiritual alienation of the man who has outlived his own heroism, whose experience of helpless suffering has discredited the belief that men can control their destiny.

> But all through the Seven Days' Fight,
>   And deep in the Wilderness grim,
> And in the field-hospital tent,
>   And Petersburg crater, and dim
> Lean brooding in Libby, there came—
>   Ah heaven!—what *truth* to him!

Bartlett had some success as a businessman—for a while ran the Tredegar Iron Works in Richmond—but never recovered. He died in 1876 at the age of thirty-six.[4]

On the Confederate side, Bushrod Johnson had been almost as ineffective in division command as Ledlie. But there was a shortage of senior officers, and Johnson was retained until the fall of Richmond. After the war he ran a preparatory school in Nashville, but the school went bankrupt and Johnson ended his days in poverty as a farmer in Illinois.

Colonel David Weisiger recovered from his wound and was promoted to brigadier general. After the war he worked as a cashier in a Petersburg bank.

General John Caldwell Calhoun Sanders, commander of the Alabama Brigade, lived for only three weeks after the Crater. In the fighting for the Weldon Railroad on August 21 a bullet tore through his thighs, severing both femoral arteries, and he bled to death. He was twenty-four years old.[5]

Stephen Elliott spent the winter of 1864–65 convalescing, and then joined Johnston's army in its futile defense of the Carolinas. In one of the war's last battles Elliott was wounded again. After the surrender he returned to his home in the Sea Islands to find his lands confiscated for nonpayment of taxes, and turned over to his former slaves. This was one of the few successful attempts to provide freedmen with the forty acres and a mule they needed to become economically self-supporting. His former slaves remembered Elliott as a good master and treated him kindly, even offered to lend him money. But they wanted it understood that they now met him not as chattels but as citizens. "They were delighted to see me, and treated me with overflowing affection. They waited on me as before, gave me beautiful breakfasts and splendid dinners . . . [but] they firmly and respectfully informed me: 'We own this land now. Put it out of your head it will ever be yours again.' " Elliott returned to his Charleston home and won election to the state legislature that fall. But he never really recovered from his wounds, and they killed him in February 1866.[6]

Colonel McMaster had a distinguished postwar career as a lawyer, businessman, and educator. He helped found the first public school system in Columbia, South Carolina.[7]

Colonels William Pegram and John Haskell, the young artillerymen, had done more than most to check the Federal advance. Yet neither would receive the coveted promotion to general. An artillery battalion was not a general's command, and the artillery could not afford to lose officers of their quality. Pegram was killed beside his guns at Five Forks in April 1865—he was twenty-four. After a brief period as a Mississippi planter, John Haskell returned to his native South Carolina and married Sarah Hampton, and after her death married her cousin Lucy Hampton. Sarah was the daughter of Wade Hampton, the ex-Confederate general and wealthy planter who was leading the fight to "redeem" his state from its reconstruction government. Hampton was elected in 1876 after a political campaign in which vigilante organizations (the Red Shirts, Rifle Clubs, etc.) used violence to intimidate Blacks who supported the government. Haskell entered the redeemed legislature as a Hampton supporter in 1877, and was regularly reelected until his retirement in 1890.

❦

The irony of Southern history is that by making war to save slavery, the Confederacy destroyed it. The irony for the Union is that in winning its war for free labor, it created a new financial and industrial order in which free labor principles no longer applied. The wealth and economic activity generated by the war taught a generation of managers, bankers, and entrepreneurs how to conceive, capitalize, and run great enterprises. The unregulated postwar economy would enable them to consolidate ownership and management of the nation's banking, mining, transportation, and manufacturing into huge corporations. The men who had fought for free labor would find that in the new order of big business it was impossible for a large number of wage workers—let alone a majority—to earn their way out of the working class. The postwar decades would be marked by the often violent struggle of workers to resist their reduction to proletarian status.

Two veterans of the Crater would play prominent roles in those struggles.

John Hartranft was elected governor of Pennsylvania on a pro-labor platform. In 1877 he was faced with a strike by railroad workers in Pittsburgh—part of a nationwide railroad strike that paralyzed the nation's transportation network and appeared to many to signal for a new civil war, not between North and South but between capital and labor. Hartranft sent in militia units from other cities to break the strike, and the action made him a national hero.

Henry Pleasants returned to the Pottsville coalfields but abandoned engineering to take charge of the Coal and Iron Police, an arm of the corporation headed by B. F. Gowen that was consolidating ownership and management of the industry in the Schuylkill region. Gowen was working to eliminate the system under which skilled miners were treated as independent contractors, in order to reduce all miners to wage workers. During the Long Strike of 1873–74, Pleasants worked with the Pinkerton National Detective Agency in its campaign to discredit the unions by linking them with the terrorist Molly Maguires. There were probably some veterans of the 48th among the miners whose unions Pleasants helped break. There were no veterans among the Mollies who were tried and executed, but many men in the 48th were from the same region, and bore the same last names as the Mollies: Dolan, Fisher, Boyle, O'Brien, Dougherty, Gibbons, Kane, Kell(e)y, Kerrigan, O'Neil, Monaghan, Duffy, Carroll, O'Donnell.[8]

⸜⸜⸝⸝

White Southerners in the postwar era struggled to reconcile their desire to reestablish White supremacy with their need to modernize the Southern economy and share in the commercial prosperity of the nation. Among the most interesting figures in that struggle was William Mahone, the hero of the Crater. Right after Appomattox he regained the presidency of the Norfolk and Petersburg Railroad and immediately began rebuilding the line. Railroad businessmen could not prosper without playing politics to win the land grants, tax assistance, and franchises on which they depended. Mahone built a strong political machine to defend his railroad interests and played a leading role in the complex and devious machinations that produced a "reconstructed" state constitution. His success led Virginians to recognize him as "our railroad Bismarck."[9]

Mahone worked hard to create a new South, with a diversified economy and a working class to match. His principles were opposed by conservative Bourbon Democrats, who sought to preserve the old plantation-based economy. In 1879 Mahone took leadership of a reform faction, the Readjusters, whose policy of industrial development required the diffusion of education and a larger share of prosperity to working-class Whites—and to Blacks. Mahone did not question the fundamental soundness of White supremacy, or the policies that segregated Blacks and Whites. But African Americans still had the vote in Virginia, so Mahone welcomed Black leaders to his party and his administration, and included in his platform the upgrading of Black public schools.[10]

Thus the man who had told his soldiers at the Battle of the Crater to grant no quarter to Negroes in arms now presided over one of the last successes of reconstruction. He was elected to the Senate on the Readjuster ticket in 1880, served one term, and died in 1895. He was buried in Blandford Cemetery, on the hill overlooking the battlefield.

The African Americans

The individual fates of those Black soldiers who fought at the Crater and outlived the war are nearly impossible to follow. The service of the USCT regiments was not committed to public memory as the deeds of White regiments were. White regiments typically came from and returned to a particular community, which preserved the memory of their service. Former officers usually took the lead in organizing regular reunions and compiling a regimental history—which typically recounted the deeds of *named* individuals.

The Maryland regiments of the 4th Division had that kind of community base, but the other units drew men from all over the states that formed them, and from refugee and contraband camps. Color, not community, was the basis of organization. Moreover, the officers of the USCT were not from the same communities as their troops—often they were not even from the same states. (The reunions they attended were of the White "home" regiments from which they had transferred.) The 43rd USCT was the only regiment in the division for which a unit history was written. Although it contains short biographies of all the officers, only one Black soldier is mentioned by name. When the division's officers published accounts of their individual experiences, they almost never mentioned individual Black soldiers by name, even when recording some act of extraordinary bravery or dedication. Even in the eyes of their friends, race overrode individuality.

On average, veterans fared better than most other Blacks after the war. They tended to have higher literacy rates, and were more likely to move from the country to cities and towns. The confidence and pride they'd gained through service had something to do with this outcome, but there were also material benefits to having served. Many had learned to read and write while in the army, or had acquired skills useful in civilian life (blacksmithing, construction work, cooking). They and their survivors also benefited from the Federal veterans' pensions—when they could collect them. Many could not, because of clerical errors that erased or misfiled their service records. In many cases the name under which the soldier had enrolled was a misspelled or corrupted version of his actual name. The name of Prestley Dorsey of the 43rd USCT was transmuted to Dawson, which caused the government—in its periodic attempts to eliminate fraud from a much-abused system—to take his pension away, restore it, and then take it away again. Fugitive slaves often enlisted under false names, fearing that their owners might otherwise recover them. Soldiers' widows could have a hard time collecting a pension, because their marriages were often unrecorded—since slaves in most states had been unable to marry.[11]

Veterans also came home from military service with partially healed wounds, illnesses, and disabilities. A picture of Private Lewis Martin of the 29th USCT shows a young Black man sitting in a chair. Most of his right arm is missing, and what remains of his amputated left leg is crossed over his right knee. Martin had been a slave in Arkansas before the war, and presumably lacked any private means of support. He would have received a pension for his disability, but without the support of family or community would still have found it very hard to make his way in the "work or starve" postwar economy.[12]

Nearly all the men who served in the 4th Division had already been living in the border states or Free States when they enlisted. Since the vast majority probably returned to these regions after the war, they would have escaped the poverty and violence that marked the lives of freedmen in the Deep South during reconstruction. However, they were still denied full civil rights in the North, and the moral claim they made as men who had fought for the Union was offset by deep and abiding racial prejudice.

The 28th USCT had left Indiana with a promise: "Show yourselves worthy soldiers [and] the petty prejudices that weak and wicked men have endeavored to excite against you will be forever swallowed up in the gratitude of a nation that will own and applaud your heroic deeds." But when the regiment returned to Indianapolis, they found the state's infamous Black Codes still on the books. Indeed, now that the ex-slaves were free to come north, the public was more than ever determined to enforce its prohibition against Black settlement. Returning soldiers were threatened with prosecution as illegal immigrants, and a proposal to give Blacks the vote was condemned as incitement to a "war of races."

So-called moderates proposed to resolve the problem by reviving the moribund American Colonization Society and sending the Blacks back to Africa. Governor Morton was able to win the exemption of veterans from the immigration law, but it was not until the passage of the Thirteenth Amendment at the end of 1865 that Indiana Blacks won such basic rights as that of testifying under oath and serving on juries. In Ohio a statewide referendum rejected the extension of voting rights to Negroes. The Democratic legislature tried to rescind its endorsement of the XIV Amendment when they realized that it required states to guarantee the equal protection of the laws to all their citizens, regardless of race.[13]

But the experience of fighting for "their" country gave many of the USCT veterans a sharper sense of their merit and of their power. At a time when Ohio Republicans were uncertain whether to grant Blacks the right to vote, a sergeant in the 27th was writing: "I wonder, as the Southern black man has got sense enough to fight for his country, if he ain't got sense enough to vote, whether he is educated or not. . . . It seems to me, if he knew where to strike with his steel and firearms, he will also know how to strike with his vote."[14]

None of the officers who served in the 4th Division was especially prominent in reconstruction. The strongest and most radical advocacy of Black civil rights was put forward by Chaplain Mickley in the postscript to his history of the 43rd USCT (1866). He demanded full civil rights for the newly freed slaves, including the right to vote, asking "What are Freedmen without citizenship?" Those who opposed equal rights, or proposed delaying them till the race was better prepared, were "Catalines and Judas Iscariots," defamers of a "loyal race," who should be punished as traitors.[15]

But when White opinion in the North began to turn against reconstruction and Negro rights, the reminiscences and memoirs published by 4th Division officers, or delivered as addresses at public meetings, offered a staunch and uncompromising defense of their soldiers, and of the race they represented. Robert Beecham used his memoir to ridicule and refute the prevailing "theories and ideas" of Black inferiority, and he embedded in it a brief history of Black military service from the American Revolution forward. Colonel's Thomas's article in *Battles and Leaders* placed his affirmation of the courage and dedication of his troops in the canonical compilation of military sources. Colonel Bates, and Lieutenants Bowley and Proctor used the columns of the *National Tribune,* the leading veterans' newspaper, to defend the courage of Black troops at the Crater. In 1907 Proctor sneered at the fashionable racism of so-called Progressives who had joined Southerners in defaming Black infantrymen after the "Brownsville Raid": it is "quite the fad when a party cannot find anything to hit or scold to make a shy at the colored troops."[16]

Captain Wallace Bartlett's contribution to the cause was more concrete. He joined the 19th USCT just after the end of the war and commanded I Company for nearly a year, while the 19th and most of XXV Corps were on the Rio Grande. Bartlett later settled in Maryland, which was home to most of his soldiers. In the early 1880s he began buying up property in a rural area between Baltimore and Washington, D.C., and invited USCT veterans there. In 1891 he incorporated North Brentwood as the first African American township in the county. "The town was settled by black families seeking, through home ownership, some control over their lives in a segregated society. In spite of significant drawbacks . . .

these early owners developed their own political and social institutions, and created a successful community. . . . The surviving historic buildings illustrate the forms and styles of buildings typically constructed in working-class suburban communities of the period, and many have been preserved through methods that clearly reflect the efforts and hardships of a working-class minority community."[17]

Most veterans of the USCT made their way without philanthropic assistance. In Ellicott City, then a rural town northwest of Baltimore, veterans from Maryland's three USCT regiments established the Ellicott City Colored School to provide free education to Black students. This Black community also proudly identified itself as the home of Decatur Dorsey, color sergeant of the 39th USCT, winner of the Medal of Honor at the Battle of the Crater. Dorsey lived for a while in Maryland but eventually moved to Hoboken, New Jersey, where he died in 1891 at the age of fifty-one. He was buried in an unmarked grave, which was discovered in 1984 and moved to a more prominent location, with full military honors and a headstone paid for by the federal government.[18]

WHAT SHALL MEN REMEMBER?

The Battle of the Crater was shaped by politics, and so was its history. This was a battle Northern historians and writers preferred to minimize or forget, not simply because it was a defeat but because it so forcibly displayed the intransigence and complexity of the race question that puzzled and ultimately repelled them. George Kilmer's article "The Dash into the Crater," which described the murder of Blacks by both Confederate *and* Union soldiers, was published in *The Century* magazine as part of the series that later became the canonical *Battles and Leaders of the Civil War*. But Kilmer's account was left out when the articles were published in book form.

Despite the valor and moral commitment symbolized by the officers of the USCT, the North was unwilling to develop and maintain a truly radical program of reconstruction. It was not simply that Northern Whites were unwilling to recognize the equal entitlement of Blacks to the rights of free labor. Among the North's social and cultural elites there was a sharp turn against the premises of free labor itself. By the 1870s, opinion makers such as Charles Francis Adams and editor E. L. Godkin of *The Nation* were questioning whether working-class Whites could be trusted with the ballot. And even among Northerners philanthropically disposed toward the freedmen, the basic premises of White supremacy remained prevalent. So it is hardly surprising that Northern support for Black civil rights was too weak to offset the White South's determined and violent resistance to reconstruction. The South was willing to threaten, and perhaps to wage, a "war of races" to reestablish White supremacy. The North was *not* willing to take the Black side in such a war.[19]

In contrast, the Battle of the Crater was perfectly congruent with the Southern myth of the Lost Cause—a version of Civil War history that allowed Southerners to accept the practical failure of the Confederacy while still exalting the social and spiritual values of the old South. Central to that mythology was the need to justify the new order of Jim Crow, in which Blacks would be systematically stripped of those civil liberties they had gained during reconstruction. It was vital to this ideology that Blacks be seen not merely as incompetent citizens but as an active menace to White society, requiring suppression by a harsh legal regime and the terror threat of lynching. Southern accounts published during this period characterize the 4th Division as "crazed" or "drunken negroes," yelling "No quarter!" and killing their prisoners. They attribute the rout of the Blacks to a panic terror induced by the appearance of Mahone's avenging infantry—as if a Black soldier would become unhinged at the mere sight of angry White men. They praise and even vaunt the murder of Black POWs after the battle as justified punishment and (in William Pegram's words) a necessary policy. In effect, justification of the massacre at the Crater symbolically justified the use of lynching to terrorize Blacks and keep them in submission in the contemporary South.[20]

In the last decades of the nineteenth century, Americans began to see the great achievement of the Civil War as the creation of a unified American nation-state capable of striving for mastery among the great powers. The war was the crucible of a new national identity, symbolized by the reconciliation of veterans in blue and gray, shaking hands across "the stone wall" at Gettysburg or a Petersburg parapet. Black soldiers played no part in such ceremonies. Indeed, the reconciliation was largely at their expense. Nowhere was that clearer than in the meetings and ceremonies that occurred at the site of the Crater battlefield. Confederate veterans began holding reunions there in the early 1870s, many of them sponsored by William Mahone, whose political standing was enhanced by these reminders of his moment of glory. The role played by Black troops was rarely acknowledged, and then only to disparage it. That tendency was actually exacerbated when Northern veterans began touring the site in the mid-1870s. They too preferred to make no mention of the USCT, perhaps in deference to their hosts, perhaps because they too considered the presence or actions of the Black troops shameful. While African Americans in the area did memorialize their soldiers' deeds, they did so in places segregated from the White public sphere.[21]

The final erasure of the USCT from the commemoration of the battle came in 1903, when the battle was reenacted as part of the campaign to establish a national battlefield park. On this occasion, the only mention of the USCT was by Colonel William Stewart (61st Virginia), who referred to the "brutal malice of negro soldiers." No Blacks participated in the reenactment, and no USCT unit was in any way represented. The idea was to Jim-Crow public memory and give a united America a history "on the White basis." That was the history Americans would learn for the next sixty or seventy years.

The crater has been preserved as part of the Petersburg National Battlefield park. Its sheer sides and jagged boulders have been softened and rounded by weathering, leaving a hollow in the grassy slope instead of a pit. The field is dotted with monuments to those who fought there, honoring regiments by marking the places where they stood, or failed to stand. Some monuments have been raised by veterans' organizations, some by state governments. South Carolina's United Daughters of the Confederacy had one built for Elliott's Brigade, and there is an obelisk to honor Mahone. There is a monument to the 2nd Pennsylvania Provisional Heavy Artillery, which got farther forward than any of Ledlie's other regiments.[22]

There is no monument to the memory of the African American troops who fought and died in the crater.

Notes

PREFACE

1. Ulysses S. Grant, *Papers,* Vol. 11, pp. 361–3.

CHAPTER 1. STALEMATE: PETERSBURG, JUNE 21, 1864

1. Allen D. Albert, *History of the Forty-fifth Regiment,* p. 294; Bruce Catton, *Bruce Catton's Civil War: Stillness at Appomattox,* pp. 572–3.
2. Charles Austin, 14th NYHA, http://freepages.genealogy.rootsweb.com/~snugaza/austin/june181864.html
3. *OR* 40:2, pp. 167, 179, 205.
4. Charles F. Adams, Jr. *A Cycle of Adams Letters,* Vol. 2, p. 155.
5. James M. McPherson, *Battle Cry of Freedom,* pp. 742–4.
6. Catton, *Stillness,* p. 577; Stephen M. Weld, *War Diary and Letters,* p. 318.
7. Earl J. Hess, *The Union Soldier in Battle,* p. 63 and ch. 5; Charles F. Adams, pp. 154–6.
8. Gary W. Gallagher, *The Confederate War,* pp. 28–30, 35, 38.
9. Gallagher, pp. 26, 31–2, 34; Douglas Southall Freeman, ed., *Lee's Dispatches,* pp. 154–8; J. Tracy Power, *Lee's Miserables,* pp. 3–4, 38, 57, 76.
10. Power, p. 5; Hess, pp. 2–3, 102–3; Gallagher, pp. 57, 87.
11. Keith Wilson, ed., *Honor in Command,* p. 2; Reid Mitchell, *Civil War Soldiers,* p. 173 and Bertram Wyatt-Brown, *Honor and Violence in the Old South,* chs. 2–4.
12. Power, p. 87; Gallagher, pp. 3, 57–8, 73; McPherson, *For Cause and Comrades* and *What They Fought For.*
13. For a full discussion of these issues see Eric Foner, *Free Soil, Free Labor, Free Men* and Bertram Wyatt-Brown, *Honor and Violence in the Old South.*
14. Hess, p. 101; Gallagher, p. 105; Joseph Glatthaar, *Forged in Battle,* p. 25.
15. McPherson, *Battle Cry,* pp. 242–3.
16. Byron M. Cutcheon, *The Story of the Twentieth Michigan,* p. 138; Lyman Jackman, *History of the Sixth New Hampshire,* pp. 302–3; William Marvel, *Burnside,* p. 390.

17. John W. De Forest, *A Volunteer's Adventures,* p. 116; Warren Wilkinson, *Mother, May You Never See,* p. 144.
18. Oliver C. Bosbyshell, *The 48th in the War,* p. 163.

CHAPTER 2. "WITH AS LITTLE BLOODSHED AS POSSIBLE": PARAMETERS FOR A FEDERAL OFFENSIVE, JUNE 21-23, 1864

1. Horace K. Porter, *Campaigning with Grant,* p. 217.
2. See William S. McFeely, *Grant: A Biography,* ch. 9, and Stephen Taaffe, *Commanding the Army of the Potomac.*
3. Porter, pp. 218–23; McPherson, *Battle Cry,* p. 560.
4. Theodore Lyman, *With Grant and Meade,* p. 192.
5. Benjamin F. Butler, *Private and Official Correspondence,* Vol. 4, pp. 428, 435, 451, 510–2.
6. Marvel, *Burnside,* pp. 5–6, 12–5, 32.
7. Bosbyshell, p. 41. Burnside was always willing to listen to advice—while an operation was in planning—though as a listener he lacked discrimination. He often discussed his plans with Robert, his elderly Black manservant, because he believed Robert always took *his* interests to heart. (Belief in the selfless loyalty of Black servants was not restricted to Southern planters.)
8. *OR* 40:2, p. 284.
9. Marvel, *Burnside,* pp. 390–1; Bosbyshell, pp. 166–7; Michael A. Cavanaugh and William Marvel, *The Petersburg Campaign: The Battle of the Crater,* pp. 5–6, 9.

CHAPTER 3: THE MINERS, JUNE 25-JULY 2, 1864

1. Jim Corrigan, *The 48th Pennsylvania,* ch. 3; Cavanaugh, ch. 1; Joseph Gould, *The Story of the Forty-eighth,* pp. 22, 69–70, 142–5, 197–207; Henry Pleasants, Jr., *Tragedy of the Crater,* pp. 15–6; Bosbyshell, pp. 157, 163. For Rozas see http://en.wikipedia.org/wiki/Juan_Manuel_de_Rosas
2. Kevin Kenny, *Making Sense of the Molly Maguires,* pp. 48–9, 57–65.
3. Kenny, pp. 44, 70; Wayne G. Broehl, Jr., *The Molly Maguires,* pp. 85–6.
4. Kenny, pp. 74–83.
5. Ibid., pp. 289–302; Gould, pp. 399 ff.
6. Kenny, pp. 82–3, 87–8, 91, 94, 101; Broehl, pp. 86–93; Bosbyshell, ch. 10; Gould, p. 18.
7. Bosbyshell, p. 167; Cavanaugh, pp. 5–6; Gould, p. 166; Corrigan, pp. 33–5.
8. Corrigan, pp. 35–8; Bosbyshell, pp. 146–7, 156, 168; Gould pp. 167, 171.
9. James J. Chase, *Charge at Day-break,* p. 8; Jackman, ch. 17, pp. 300–4; Wilkinson, pp. 191–2, 194.
10. Albert, pp. 144–5.
11. http://freepages.genealogy.rootsweb.com/~snugaza/austin/index.html

Wilkinson, pp. 204, 208; Edward O. Lord, *History of the Ninth New Hampshire,* p. 466; De Forest, pp. 116–8.

12. Lord, pp. 463–4, 466–7.

13. De Forest, p. 118; Lord, pp. 457, 461; Jackman, pp. 302–3, 307–8.

14. Wilkinson, pp. 191–2, 196, 200, 202; Jackman, p. 456.

15. Albert, p. 144–5; Jackman, pp. 303, 308; Lord, pp. 459, 461, 464.

16. George W. Whitman, *Civil War Letters,* pp. 66–8, 79, 123–5; http://www
   .dmna.state.ny.us/historic/reghist/civil/infantry/51stInf/51stInfCWN.htm

17. Jackman, p. 306; Lord, p. 459.

18. Albert, pp. 144–5; Jackman pp. 304–8; Cutcheon, ch. 22.

19. The modern instruments had telescopes that pivoted 180 degrees, so observations
   could be made in both directions without having to rotate the whole apparatus.

20. Barnard to Pleasants, and v/v, *OR* 40:Part 2, pp. 611–2; Gould, pp. 209–10.

21. *OR* 40:2, pp. 598–9.

22. *OR* 40:1, pp. 629–30.

23. Corrigan, p. 35; Gould, p. 363; William H. Powell, "The Battle of the Petersburg
   Crater," in *Battles and Leaders,* p. 545. Cavanaugh p. 8 says they hit quicksand
   first on July 2 and then marl on July 5. But Pleasants couldn't have told Duane he
   was two hundred fifty feet in unless he had already gone past the marl.

24. United States. Congress. *Report of the Committee,* pp. 1–3.

CHAPTER 4. CONFEDERATE STRATEGY: THE BEST DEFENSE. . . , JUNE 21–JULY 5, 1864

1. Freeman, *Lee's Dispatches,* pp. 253–7; on Lee's character and career see Freeman, *R. E. Lee* and Alan T. Nolan, *Lee Considered.*

2. Freeman, *R. E. Lee's Lieutenants,* Vol. 3, p. 498.

3. Power, p. 59; Jefferson Davis, *Papers,* Vol. 10, p. 556.

4. To calm Davis's concerns about the defense of Richmond, Lee insisted troop
   strength was of less concern than "our ability to procure supplies for the army."
   Lack of supply "will oblige me to attack Gen Grant in his entrenchments." He
   thought his chances of success would be slim, and "a want of success, would in
   my opinion be almost fatal." Davis, *Papers,* Vol. 10, pp. 484–5; Steven E. Woodworth, *Davis and Lee at War,* pp. 296, 304.

5. Freeman, *Lee's Lieutenants,* Vol. 3, 513–4; Power, pp. 38, 54–5, 59, 70. Technically, Beauregard commanded the divisions of Pickett, Hoke, and Johnson, but
   Pickett had been detailed from the Army of Northern Virginia (ANV). Mahone's
   Division, which held the right of Beauregard's front, was administratively part of
   III Corps, ANV. However, Lee was effectively in command of all units, though he
   usually consulted and in some matters deferred to Beauregard.

6. Freeman, *Lee's Lieutenants,* Vol. 3, pp. 450–67.

7. Power, pp. 112–3, 121.

8. Cavanaugh, pp. 10–1; Noah Andre Trudeau, *The Last Citadel,* pp. 99–100, 102.

9. Woodworth, pp. 300–1.

10. Power, pp. 125, 131. Sanders's name is sometimes given as "Saunders" in the sources.

11. Power, pp. 117, 123; DeWitt Boyd Stone, Jr., *Wandering to Glory,* p. 180.

12. *OR* 40:1, p. 621.

13. Nelson M. Blake, *William Mahone,* ch. 1, pp. 34, 38.

14. John Sergeant Wise, *The End of an Era,* pp. 320–6.

15. The names of Confederate brigades or divisions are capitalized (e.g., Elliott's Brigade, Johnson's Division), while those in the Union army are not. Federal units were identified by number, while the Confederates named them for the commander. This can be confusing, because a unit *officially* commanded by one general might have been temporarily commanded by another. For example, at the Crater, the unit officially designated as Wise's Brigade was commanded by Colonel Goode.

16. 8th Alabama, http://www.37thtexas.org/html/CoI8thAla.html and http://www .37thtexas.org/html/gerfus1.html; 10th Alabama, http://home.earthlink.net/ ~larsrbl/CW/10ALInfpage.htm; 3rd Georgia, http://www.3gvi.org/ga3hist8 .html; 61st Virginia, http://www.nkclifton.com/61streg2.htm

17. W. B. Judkins, "History of Co. G, 22nd Georgia," pp. 2–4, 12–6, 39, 84 at http://www.mindspring.com/~jcherepy/memoir/judkins.txt

18. Fred L. Ray, *Shock Troops of the Confederacy,* pp. 131–2, 148–50, 207–15. http://www.mahonessharpshooters.org/Index/Unit_History.html

19. William D. Henderson, *12th Virginia Infantry,* pp. 1–6, 49; George S. Bernard, *War Talks,* Introduction and p. 155.

20. Cavanaugh, p. 93; Corrigan, pp. 89–90; Wise, pp. 358–9; Ezra J. Warner, *Generals in Gray,* pp. 157–8.

21. http://members.aol.com/jweaver300/grayson/wise.htm

22. Wise, pp. 346–51; Power, p. 127.

23. Stone, pp. 12, 15–6, 23, 175, 180.

24. Ibid., p. 174.

25. David Logan, *"A Rising Star of Promise,"* pp. xvi–iii, 18–9, 128–9; Stone, pp. 97, 138, 174.

26. Willie Lee Rose's *Rehearsal for Reconstruction* is a detailed study of the project that makes frequent reference to the Elliott family and its holdings.

27. Stone, pp. 180–1; Power, p. 129.

28. Stone, pp. 12, 166, 177–9, 181–3. Because Pegram's battery was located there, it was also known as Pegram's Salient.

29. Wise, pp. 351–2; Corrigan, p. 40; *OR* 40:3, pp. 772, 776–7; Power, pp. 128–9; Cavanaugh, pp. 10–2. Douglas refers to Elliott's as "Pegram's Salient" because the battery there was commanded by Captain Richard Pegram.

30. Freeman, *Lee's Lieutenants,* Vol. 3, p. 464; Power, p. 119.

31. Power, pp. 131–2.

32. Woodworth, p. 305; Power, p. 113. For Early's campaign see Edward J. Stack-pole, *Sheridan in the Shenandoah*, chs. 2–3.

CHAPTER 5. BURNSIDE SELECTS THE SPEARHEAD, JULY 5–9, 1864

1. Cavanaugh, ch. 2.
2. Jackman, pp. 205–6; Lord, pp. 6, 10–1; Fox, *Regimental Losses*, p. 142.
3. http://www.jewishvirtuallibrary.org/jsource/biography/acohn.html http://www.acjna.org/acjna/articles_detail.aspx?id=241 http://jewish-history .com/civilwar/simonwolf.html Cohn's feat is remarkable because troops in such a crisis generally refused to recognize orders given by officers from other regiments, let alone NCOs.
4. Wilkinson, pp. 116, 119; Warner, *Generals in Blue*, p. 277; http://www .civilwararchive.com/Unreghst/unnyinf2.htm#17 Weld, *War Diary*, pp. 311–2, 339, 344; Francis W. Palfrey, *Memoir of William Francis Bartlett*, pp. 112, 116; Corrigan, pp. 58–9.
5. Wilkinson, "*Mother, May You Never . . . ,*" pp. 403 ff.
6. Palfrey, pp. 1–5, 5, 11–2, 70, 76–80, 135–43, 225; Wilkinson, chs. 7–8.
7. Wilkinson, p. 197; Oates, *A Woman of Valor*, p. 243. Barton's cousin Clara, founder of the American Red Cross, also served at Petersburg, organizing hospitals for the Army of the James.
8. U.S. Congress, *Report*, p. 23.
9. Warner, *Generals in Blue*, pp. 150–1 http://library.morrisville.edu/local _history/sites/gar_post/ferrero.html Gould, pp. 363–4.
10. Bosbyshell, pp. 146–7; Warner, *Generals in Blue*, p. 502.
11. Ferrero's plan is a variation on the innovative tactics used by Emory Upton to storm trenches at Spotsylvania. It has been described in various ways, by participants and by later historians. Bates and Hall (the commanders directly involved) recalled that their regiments were assigned the lead roles, and trained to peel off left and right. Henry G. Thomas, "The Colored Troops at Petersburg," in *Battles and Leaders*, Vol. 4, p. 563; Delevan Bates, "A Day with the Colored Troops," p. 6; Henry Seymour Hall, "Mine Run to Petersburg," *War Talks*, pp. 219–22; Corrigan, p. 53; U.S. Congress, *Report*, pp. 119–20.
12. Grant, *Papers*, Vol. 11, p. 250.
13. http://aotw.org/officers.php?officer_id=1106 Hall, pp. 220–1; Jeremiah Marion Mickley, *The Forty-third Regiment*, pp. 12–5; H. G. Thomas, p. 563; Griffith, *Battle Tactics*, p. 97; Hess, pp. 152–3.
14. Hess, pp. 114–5, 152–3.

CHAPTER 6. "GUIDE ON DE ARMY": AFRICAN AMERICANS GO TO WAR

1. H. G. Thomas, pp. 563–4; Wilson, pp. 62–3, 69.
2. H. G. Thomas, pp. 563–4.

3. Charles F. Adams, pp. 167–8; Glatthaar, pp. 13–8, 38–42; J. C. Adams, "Battle of the Crater," *National Tribune,* June 25, 1903 p. 1.

4. Glatthaar, pp. 39, 49.

5. McPherson, *Battle Cry,* pp. 566–7. Although propaganda exaggerated some aspects of Fort Pillow, careful analysis by modern historians has confirmed that mass killing of surrendered troops did occur. See John Cimprich, *Fort Pillow* and Andrew Ward, *River Run Red.*

6. Glatthaar, p. 10; William J. Jackson, *New Jerseyans in the Civil War,* p. 161.

7. Hall, p. 216.

8. Theodore Lyman, pp. 102, 180.

9. Glatthaar, pp. 56–7, 87.

10. Ibid., pp. 10–2; Bosbyshell, pp. 146–7, 156; Jackman, pp. 114, 138, 204; Gould, pp. 167, 171.

11. Catton, *Never Call Retreat,* pp. 110–5; Glatthaar, p. 12; Robert F. Crawford, ed., "The Civil War Letters of S. Rodman," *Delaware History* 31:2, 1984, p. 92.

12. Wilson, pp. 45–8, 60, 64–5.

13. C. M. Tyler, *Memorials of Lieut. George H. Walcott,* pp. 5–6.

14. Robert Beecham, *As If It Were Glory,* pp. 144, 164–8.

15. Glatthaar, pp. 79, 87, 96–7, 197–8.

16. Ibid., p. 83.

17. Charles F. Adams, pp. 194–5, 216–9; Glatthaar, p. 84.

18. Glatthaar, pp. 65, 70; http://home.nycap.rr.com/civilwar/usctblakely.htm

19. Tyler, p. 50. Young Lieutenant Walcott of the 30th savored the crowd's hostility because it showed that Southerners "fear the negro soldiers." Christian though he was, the thought did not displease him. But his service was brief: he died of a camp disease, probably typhoid, on July 10.

20. Kevin Conley Ruffner, *Maryland's Blue & Gray,* p. 58; James H. Rickard, "Services with Colored Troops," pp. 14–5; Ruffner, p. 58. On Dobbs see http://www.pa-roots.com/~pacw/reserves/11thres/11threscok.html and http://www.interment.net/data/us/ks/leavenworth/leavenat/leaven_dodum.htm. Thanks to the Jefferson, Erie, and Crawford (Pennsylvania) county historical societies for this information.

21. For a full discussion see Glatthaar, chs. 3–4.

22. Glatthaar pp. 271–2 gives the breakdown for sample companies in two of the regiments. For answers to my inquiries, thanks to the Maryland State Historical Association; the historical associations of Charles County and Howard County; the African American Heritage Society of Charles County, Inc.; Howard County Center of African American Culture; St. Mary's County Historical Society; and Susan G. Pearl, historian, Prince George's County Historical Society.

23. See the roster of enlistees at http://www.msa.md.gov/msa/speccol/3096/html/00010001.html#alphD for Prestley Dorsey, see http://www.afrigeneas.com/library/dawson_article.html for Decatur Dorsey, see http://www.nps.gov/archive/pete/mahan/edbiosdd.html

24. Wilson, p. 82.

25. Rickard, pp. 9–13, 20–2; Crawford, p. 109; Wilson, pp. 92–3.

26. From a sample company raised at the same time and place, in Glatthaar, pp. 71, 272; http://www.correctionhistory.org/html/chronicl/nycdoc/html/usct01.html; Ira Berlin, *Freedom: A Documentary History of Emancipation,* Vol. 1, p. 523. For Asians see http://members.aol.com/gordonkwok/cacwpart14.html

27. Laurence M. Hauptman, *Between Two Fires,* pp. 148–51.

28. William Blair and William Pencak, eds., *Making and Remaking Pennsylvania's Civil War,* pp. 143–5.

29. Glatthaar, pp. 72, 84, 91; Jackson, p. 180; Blair and Pencak, pp. 146–7; Brenna King, Pennsylvania Historical Society.

30. Hall, pp. 218–9; Mickley, pp. 71–3.

31. Mickley, Introduction and pp. 12–36, 69–71, 148–9.

32. Ibid., pp. 72–3; Hall, pp. 218–9.

33. Blair and Pencak, pp. 150–2.

34. Versalle F. Washington, *Eagles on Their Buttons,* pp. 2–3, 16, 36–7; http://www.angelfire.com/oh/chillicothe http://www.washingtonch.k12.oh.us/mapsite/usctcw/lest/contents/History/hisusct.htm http://www.correctionhistory.org/html/chronicl/nycdoc/html/usct01.html

35. Glatthaar, pp. 115, 228 (includes sample company); Washington, pp. 13–4.

36. William R Forstchen, *The 28th United States Colored Troops,* pp. 43–4, 46; E. Miller, *Black Civil War Soldiers,* pp. 7–9.

37. Forstchen, pp. 39, 41, 47, 54–7; E. Miller, pp. 5–7, 10–3, 22–3; Glatthaar, p. 181; http://civilwarindiana.com/black_soldiers.html

38. Forstchen, pp. 45, 51–7; E. Miller, pp. 12, 2–3, 29; Glatthaar, pp. 70, 77, 272.

39. Glatthaar, p. 272; E. Miller, pp. 14–20, 24, 26, 29–31; Forstchen, pp. 74–5.

40. E. Miller, pp. 36, 46; Forstchen, pp. 87–8; Martin Öfele, *German-Speaking Officers,* pp. 42, 53, 69–70, 173–4.

41. E. Miller, pp. 12–3, 34–6; *Memorial of Colonel John A. Bross,* pp. 10–1, 21.

42. E. Miller, p. 23.

43. Ibid., pp. 38–40; *Memorial,* pp. 10–1; Forstchen, p. 40.

44. Glatthaar, p. 155; C. F. Adams, p. 154.

45. Greiner, *Subdued by the Sword,* pp. 8, 55, 89, 104, 197; Frederick Phisterer, *New York in the War,* p. 128. Comradeship also played a role in the decision to transfer. Three regimental commanders came from the 121st New York: Colonels H. Seymour Hall (43rd), Cleaveland Campbell (23rd), and Delevan Bates (30th). And there were similar instances of group transfer among the junior officers.

46. Wilson, pp. 102, 121. Lt. Bowley says the training began on July 2—probably an error of memory.

47. See W. J. Hardee, *Rifle and Light Infantry Tactics* (1855), available online at http://www.usregulars.com/hardeehome.html#school%20of%20the%20soldier Bernard, p. 141.

48. Griffith, p. 101.

49. Hall, p. 221.

50. Hess, pp. 114–5; Howard C. Westwood, *Black Troops*, p. 419; Wilson, p. 58.

51. Hall, p. 221.

52. Philip Katcher, *The Complete Civil War*, p. 55; Weld, *War Diary*, pp. 311–2.

53. Hess, p. 84.

54. Westwood, pp. 426–7.

CHAPTER 7. THE POLITICS OF RACE:
WASHINGTON AND RICHMOND, JULY 1864

1. McPherson, *Battle Cry,* pp. 558–9, 565, 620 ff, 699–713, 762, 766–71; Bruce Catton, *Terrible Swift Sword*, p. 383; Catton, *Never Call Retreat,* pp. 5, 110–5, 272–81; Davis, *Papers*, p. 407.

2. Stephen A. Douglas, quoted in Lincoln, *Speeches,* Vol. 1, p. 598, and contrast Lincoln, Vol. 1, pp. 717–8; McPherson, *Battle Cry,* p. 560; Charles B. Dew, *Apostles of Disunion,* pp. 11, 28–9; Alexander H. Stephens, "Cornerstone Address, March 21, 1861," in *The Rebellion Record: A Diary of American Events with Documents, Narratives, Illustrative Incidents, Poetry, etc.,* ed. Frank Moore, Vol. 1, pp. 44–6.

3. Iver Bernstein's *New York City Draft Riots* is the best full-length study.

4. McPherson, *Battle Cry,* pp. 600–11, 789–90; Catton, *Never Call Retreat,* pp. 164, 264; Jackson, p. 161. For a study of the "Miscegenation" hoax see Forrest G. Wood, *Black Scare.*

5. Catton, *Never Call Retreat,* pp. 264–5, 352–62.

6. Lincoln, *Speeches,* Vol. 2, pp. 498–9.

7. Lincoln, *Speeches,* Vol. 2, pp. 612–3.

8. Davis, *Jefferson Davis: The Essential Writings,* p. 197.

9. Wise, pp. 26, 36–7, 76, 139–41, 145, 346–8.

10. David M. Potter, *The Impending Crisis,* ch. 1; D. W. Meinig, *The Shaping of America,* Vol. 1, pp. 139, 397, and Vol. 2, pp. 278, 292; Wilbur Zelinsky, *Cultural Geography of the United States,* p. 122; James H. Webb, *Born Fighting,* Pt. V, chs. 3–4.

11. Davis, *Papers,* Vol. 10, p. 506; McPherson, *Battle Cry,* p. 690.

12. For a detailed discussion of these issues see David Williams, *Rich Man's War,* especially chs. 1–3; McPherson, *Battle Cry,* pp. 439–42, 611–20; Gallagher, pp. 22–3; Davis, *Papers,* Vol. 10, pp. 365–6, 511, 515; Bruce Levine, *Confederate Emancipation,* pp. 23–4. The situation was exacerbated in the cotton states by the fact that while other forms of property (land, businesses) lost value, slave property maintained or increased its value because so much labor power had been drained off by the army. See for example David Logan, "*A Rising Star of Promise,* "pp. 128–9.

13. McPherson, *Battle Cry,* pp. 242–3; Dew, pp. 11, 28–9, 76–7.

14. Catton, *Terrible,* pp. 444–5; Dew, pp. 13, 78–9; Davis, *Jefferson Davis: The Essential Writings,* pp. 290–1; Thomas Jefferson, "Notes on Virginia," in A. Koch and W. Peden, eds., *The Life and Selected Writings of Thomas Jefferson,* p. 256.

15. Levine, pp. 17, 25.

16. Robert F. Durden, *The Gray and the Black,* pp. 58–60, 102–3; Levine, p. 26.

17. Durden, pp. 184–5; Bruce Catton, *Coming Fury,* pp. 203–4.

18. E. Miller, pp. 38–40; *Memorial,* pp. 10–1; Forstchen, p. 40.

19. McPherson, *Battle Cry,* pp. 566, 634; Catton, *Terrible,* pp. 444–5.

20. Bill I. Wiley, *Johnny Reb,* p. 314.

21. William W. Holden, *Memoirs,* pp. 39–41; Durden, pp. 95–6; McPherson, *Battle Cry,* pp. 695–9.

22. Wayne K. Durrill, *War of Another Kind,* chs. 3 and 8 and epilogue; for the Plymouth campaign see Weymouth T. Jordan and Gerald W. Thomas, "Massacre at Plymouth," in G.J.W. Urwin, ed., *Black Flag over Dixie,* pp. 153–202.

23. For the 26th North Carolina see http://www.26nc.org/History/26th-Full-History/26th-full-history-chapter-5.html for 25th North Carolina see http://home.att.net/~jddlhd/index.html

24. Jordan and Thomas, pp. 167–8.

25. Ibid., pp. 155–7, 171–5, 184, 190.

26. Ibid., p. 167.

27. *OR* 40:3, pp. 301, 598; Power, pp. 128–9; Cavanaugh, p. 11.

CHAPTER 8. SETTING THE STAGE, JULY 15–29, 1864

1. Bosbyshell, p. 168.

2. Corrigan, p. 41; *OR* 40:3, p. 772; Cavanaugh, pp. 10–12.

3. Freeman, *Lee's Lieutenants,* pp. 541–2; Wise, pp. 351–2; Stone, p. 182–3.

4. Stone, p. 183.

5. U.S. Congress, *Report,* pp. 3, 240.

6. David Donald, *Lincoln,* pp. 521–3; Stackpole, pp. 85–6; Lincoln, *Speeches,* Vol. 2, p. 609; Grant, *Papers,* Vol. 11, pp. 262–3. Lincoln also intercepted a telegram Grant sent to Sherman and sent a sharply worded instruction, which implied closer and more critical surveillance of Grant.

7. Grant, *Papers,* Vol. 11, p. 306.

8. U.S. Congress, *Report,* pp. 33, 47–8.

9. Grant, *Papers,* Vol. 11, pp. 266–78; for the Deep Bottom operations see Cavanaugh, ch. 3.

10. U.S. Congress, *Report,* pp. 46–51.

11. Ibid., pp. 15–6, 87–8, 239–41; Corrigan, p. 45. Burnside says the tunnel is 522 feet; actual length was 511 feet.

12. U.S. Congress, *Report,* pp. 239–41.

13. The point of having the outer line wheel by companies was to get some riflemen facing the enemy as soon as possible, to defend against enfilade.

14. U.S. Congress, *Report,* pp. 157, 239–41.

15. *OR* 40:1, pp. 762–3, 767; Freeman, *R. E. Lee,* pp. 465–7.

16. U.S. Congress, *Report,* pp. 157–8.

17. Corrigan, p. 47; *OR* 40:2, p. 529.

18. U.S. Congress, *Report,* p. 17.

19. Ibid., pp. 42, 57. Meade gave two slightly different versions of his statement, but the gist is the same in both cases.

20. Cavanaugh, pp. 143–4.

21. Trudeau, p. 79.

22. U.S. Congress, *Report,* p. 5.

23. Ibid., p. 160.

24. Ibid., pp. 18, 160, 241.

25. Ibid., pp. 160, 164.

26. Corrigan, p. 60.

27. U.S. Congress, *Report,* p. 160; Cavanaugh, p. 23.

28. U.S. Congress, *Report,* pp. 142–3.

29. Ibid., pp. 160, 124; Wilkinson, p. 237; Porter, pp. 268–9.

CHAPTER 9. PREPARATION FOR BATTLE, JULY 29, 1864

1. For a full account of the operation see Cavanaugh, ch. 3; U.S. Congress, *Report,* pp. 238–40; Corrigan, p. 62.

2. Ulysses S. Grant, *Memoirs and Selected Letters,* pp. 543, 701–2; *OR* 40:2 6/23/64; Lyman, p. 147; Stephen Taaffe, pp. 127–8.

3. U.S. Congress, *Report,* pp. 81, 119–21, 195–9.

4. Ibid., p. 155; *OR* 40:1, pp. 158–9.

5. U.S. Congress, *Report,* pp. 39–41.

6. Thomas Livermore, *Numbers and Losses,* pp. 116–7; Cavanaugh, pp. 39, 128–9.

7. Source references to key features of the terrain (e.g., "the ravine," "the crest," "the cavalier") are subjective and not always clear. There were several important ravines, crests, and cavalier trenches, and it often requires a careful tracing of movements and angles of vision to establish which is being referred to. For the sake of clarity I have assigned unique names to the most important features of the terrain, below and on the map on p. 183, The IX Corps Attacks. The best map of the battlefield is in Time-Life Books, *Echoes of Glory,* p. 175, and compare Gould, p. 231. See also Corrigan, pp. 74, 95; Cutcheon, p. 141; Powell, p. 554; F. W. McMaster, "The Battle of the Crater," p. 122; B. L. Beaty, "The Battle of the Crater," p. 50.

8. John Cheves Haskell, *The Haskell Memoirs,* p. 72; for a list of Confederate artillery see Cavanaugh, Appendix E.

9. P. M. Vance, "Incidents of the Crater Battle," p. 178. For Confederate dispositions see John Cannan, *The Crater*, p. 82; Cavanaugh, pp. 39, 44; and Time-Life, p. 175. Ransom's Brigade had served under Hoke in the Plymouth campaign but was assigned to Johnson's Division at Petersburg.

10. Stone, p. 195; Robert W. Barnwell, "A View on the Crater Battle," p. 177; Austin C. Dobbins, *Grandfather's Journal*, pp. 205–6; Gary Loderhouse, *Far, Far from Home*, p. 79.

11. Bernard, p. 150.

12. Oates, pp. 259–60.

13. Jackman, pp. 311–2; Marvel, *Race*, p. 259.

14. Peter Dalton, *Union vs. Dis-Union*, pp. 12, 80; Henry Clarence Houston, *Thirty-second Maine;* DeAnne Blanton and Lauren M. Cook, *They Fought Like Demons*, p. 23.

15. Chase, pp. 4, 8–13.

16. http://51stnewyorkinfantry.tripod.com/ContentsPage.htm

17. Wilkinson, pp. 116, 119; Warner, *Generals in Blue*, p. 277; http://www.civilwararchive.com/Unreghst/unnyinf2.htm#17 Weld, *War Diary*, pp. 311–2, 339, 344; Palfrey, pp. 112, 116; Corrigan, pp. 58–9.

18. Palfrey, pp. 1–2, 112–6; R. Miller, *Harvard's Civil War*, pp. 10–1.

19. Wilkinson, pp. 228, 238–9.

20. Palfrey, pp. 118–9.

21. Cannan, p. 90.

22. Rickard, p. 26; E. Miller, pp. 65–6.

23. Wilson, pp. 121–3.

24. Ibid., p. 122; Cavanaugh, pp. 169–70; Bates, "A Day." I've paraphrased Bates's version of dialect.

25. Cavanaugh, p. 26; Beecham, pp. 180–1; Hall, p. 222; H. G. Thomas, p. 563; Freeman S. Bowley, "The Crater."

26. Cavanaugh, pp. 26–7, 37; 57; U.S. Congress, *Report*, pp. 173, 239; Cannan, p. 51; Jeff Kinard, *The Battle of the Crater*, p. 49; Charles H. Houghton, "In the Crater," p. 561.

27. Weld, *War Diary*, pp. 351–3; Wilkinson, pp. 228, 239–43; Corrigan, p. 63.

28. U.S. Congress, *Report*, pp. 103–5; Wilson, pp. 122–3; Cutcheon, p. 141. These statements correct the map in Cavanaugh, p. 38, which puts the reserves in the railroad cut, rather than behind Fort Morton. Sigfried's brigade was first assembled in the railroad cut, and then moved to the rear of Fort Morton at 3:00 A.M.

29. Emory M. Thomas, *Robert E. Lee*, pp. 224–5; P. M. Vance, p. 178.

30. Cutcheon, pp. 137–8; Herek, *These Men*, p. 216. Bowley, "The Crater," calls them Chippewa, but a number of tribes were represented. In his memoirs, Bowley refers to "Indians." Wilson, pp. 117, 139; Hauptman, pp. 126–33. On the other Michigan regiments in the brigade see David T. Hardy, "A Tale of Two Regiments," http://www.hardylaw.net/2d_27th_Mich_Inf Fox, pp. 381, 391.

31. U.S. Congress, *Report,* p. 204; Cutcheon, pp. 137–8.

32. Wilson, pp. 121–2.

33. U.S. Congress, *Report,* pp. 242–3.

34. For the mine's part in the operation see Corrigan, pp. 65–8.

35. U.S. Congress, *Report,* p. 206; Cutcheon, pp. 138–9.

36. Houston, pp. 312–4; Corrigan, p. 68; Chase, p. 16.

37. U.S. Congress, *Report,* pp. 243–4; Cannan, pp. 55–6; Cavanaugh, p. 26.

38. H. G. Thomas, p. 564; Delevan Bates, "War Reminiscences," http://www
.usgennet.org/usa/ne/topic/military/CW/bates/batenws5.html

39. Rickard, p. 26; Edwin S. Redkey, ed., *A Grand Army of Black Men,* p. 111.

40. Hall, p. 235; H. G. Thomas, p. 564.

Chapter 10. Into the Breach, 4:45–7:30 a.m.

1. Cutcheon, p. 139; Cavanaugh, p. 40; Weld, "The Petersburg Mine," p. 208;
Powell, p. 551; Beaty, pp. 52–3; Régis de Trobriand, *Four Years,* p. 618. Events
during this part of the action are covered in Cavanaugh, ch. 4; Cannan, ch. 8;
Alan Axelrod, *The Horrid Pit,* ch. 7.

2. George L. Kilmer, "The Dash into the Crater," p. 774; Cavanaugh, p. 41; Cannan, p. 83; Houghton, p. 561; Wilkinson, p. 245.

3. Cannan, p. 85; Oates, p. 261; Mary Daughtry, *Gray Cavalier,* p. 199; Wilkinson,
pp. 245–7; Houghton, pp. 561–2; Kilmer, pp. 774–5. Weld, "The Petersburg
Mine," pp. 208–9.

4. Porter, pp. 263–4; Lyman, p. 199. These sources disagree on the timing of
Grant's two trips to the front. Though Porter's memory of specifics is detailed,
his book was written many years later and he seems to have conflated encounters
that can only have occurred on the earlier trip (i.e., the meeting with Colonel
Thomas) with later events. Lyman's account is based on a diary written at the
time.

5. Wise, p. 355; Robert N. Rosen, *Jewish Confederates,* pp. 189–91; Power, p. 136.

6. Cavanaugh, pp. 40–1; Stone, p. 189; Bosbyshell, p. 175.

7. Cavanaugh, pp. 41–3; Stone, pp. 189–93.

8. Weld, *War Diary,* p. 353–6; Weld, "The Petersburg Mine," p. 209; Corrigan, p. 73.

9. For the initial movement to the breach see Wilkinson, pp. 247–8; Houghton, pp.
561–2; Cannan, pp. 84, 89–90; Weld, *War Diary,* p. 353–6; Weld, "The Petersburg Mine," p. 209; Corrigan, p. 73; Gould, p. 230; Bosbyshell, pp. 175–6; Cavanaugh, pp. 40–1. Union observers estimated the crater was as wide as one
hundred seventy feet—probably including the zone of extreme destruction just
outside the crater proper. After the battle, Confederate Henry Douglas was able
to define the borders of the crater; he measured the width as 125 feet.

10. Cavanaugh, p. 99; Cannan, pp. 91–3; Weld, "The Petersburg Mine," p. 209;
U.S. Congress, *Report,* pp. 20, 104.

11. Houghton, p. 562.

12. Wilkinson, p. 251, says Bartlett was in the left lobe, but Weld places him in the right.

13. Houghton, p. 562; Kilmer, p. 775; Cannan, p. 84. Kilmer's account compresses the time sequence so that it appears the guns in the wrecked battery were restored early in the battle, when in fact it was not until 8:30–9:00 A.M. that they were able to fire. The estimate of effective troop strength is based on unit strengths in Cavanaugh, pp. 128–9. Ledlie's division sent about 3,660 men into the action. Nearly a third of these were in the crater and unable to fight. The remainder were distributed among three fighting positions: Weld's on the right; the defensive line across the face of the crater; and Marshall's on the left, which cannot have contained more than 1,200. Many of these were engaged in repairing the battery, and others were unable to advance through the trenches or unwilling to leave cover.

14. Weld, "The Petersburg Mine," pp. 209–10; Stone, pp. 190–1.

15. Estimates based on F. W. McMaster, pp. 119–30; Cavanaugh, pp. 128–9.

16. *OR* 40:1, pp. 280–1; Corrigan, p. 69.

17. Corrigan, pp. 80–1; Haskell, pp. 72–3; Cavanaugh, pp. 42–3.

18. Barnwell, p. 177; Bernard, pp. 228–9.

19. Haskell, Foreword and p. 35.

20. Stone, pp. 190–2; Houghton, p. 562; Cavanaugh, p. 34; Barnwell, pp. 177–8; Corrigan, pp. 79–80.

21. Stone, pp. 192–4; Cavanaugh, pp. 43–6.

22. U.S. Congress, *Report,* pp. 104–5; Cavanaugh, p. 49.

23. Cannan, pp. 101–6; Cavanaugh, pp. 44–6; Cutcheon, pp. 140–1.

24. Cannan, pp. 95–6; Wilkinson, pp. 250–1; U.S. Congress, *Report,* p. 20; Powell, pp. 551–3.

25. U.S. Congress, *Report,* p. 99; Cutcheon, pp. 140–1.

26. Cannan, p. 83; Chase, pp. 16–7.

27. For Griffin's movements see Cavanaugh, ch. 4; Cannan, chs. 8–9, especially pp. 92–4, 101–4; Sumner U. Shearman, "Battle of the Crater," pp. 12–3; Chase, pp. 19–20; Lord, pp. 490–1, 496–7.

28. Cavanaugh, pp. 42–4; Cannan, pp. 94–5.

29. Cannan, p. 103; Stone, p. 194.

30. U.S. Congress, *Report,* p. 100; Chase, pp. 19–20; Cavanaugh, pp. 45, 49; Houston, pp. 312–6.

31. Cavanaugh, p. 44; Wilson, p. 128; and Stone, p. 194, disagree on how far this drive went. Cutcheon, pp. 140–1, says they were at the foot of the "hill," presumably the ridge descending from the cemetery. It might have appeared so from Cutcheon's point of view, but no other observer saw it that way. Confederates on the main line say Griffin never got more than fifty yards from the crater. Observers from the Plank Road, reporting at various times (some much later in the

morning), say the advance stretched between one hundred and two hundred yards north of the crater. I have attempted to correlate these observations and make allowances for differences due to the angle of vision, the imprecision of memory, and the time of day they were made. I am satisfied that the reports of Federal advances more than fifty to seventy-five yards from the crater reflect the two advances made *after* Griffin's initial drive: the attacks by Griffin and Bliss between 6:30 and 7:00 A.M., and the attack by Sigfried's brigade between 7:30 and 8:30 A.M.

32. Powell, p. 553; Cannan, pp. 93–4.
33. Powell, pp. 555–6.
34. Cannan, p. 111; Porter, p. 264; U.S. Congress, *Report,* p. 123; Beecham, p. 182; H. G. Thomas, p. 564.

CHAPTER 11. AT HEADQUARTERS, 5:40–7:50 A.M.

1. U.S. Congress, *Report,* pp. 144, 244. *OR* 40:3, pp. 657–8 gives 5:10 A.M. as the time of Burnside's reply. Either there was a transcription error or Burnside's dispatch was delayed.
2. Lyman, p. 199; U.S. Congress, *Report,* pp. 245, 253, 255.
3. U.S. Congress, *Report,* pp. 147–8, 181, 255–6; Cannan, p. 63.
4. U.S. Congress, *Report,* pp. 245–6, 256–7.
5. Ibid., p. 105, contradicts Cavanaugh, p. 49.
6. *OR* 40:3, p. 663; Cannan, pp. 61–3.
7. *OR* 40:3, p. 663; U.S. Congress, *Report,* p. 245; Corrigan, p. 86.
8. U.S. Congress, *Report,* p. 246.
9. Porter, pp. 266–7; U.S. Congress, *Report,* p. 123. As Porter remembered it, Grant then added, "There is now no chance of success. These troops must be immediately withdrawn. It is slaughter to leave them there." Coming from the lieutenant general commanding, these words would have seemed to be a positive order. However, this exchange is not corroborated by any other source. It is possible that Porter misremembered the exchange, strengthening what may have been a suggestion or concern into a definitive verdict; or he may have conflated Grant's criticism at this early moment with a more dire evaluation reached after his second visit to the front, between 8:15 and 9:15 A.M. It is hard to believe that if Grant thought a "slaughter" was impending, he would not have told Meade— especially in view of Lincoln's strong and repeated injunctions against risking heavy losses. If Grant was willing to defer to Burnside's view that it was still possible to succeed, it does not seem likely that he thought the battle hopeless.
10. Freeman, *R. E. Lee,* p. 475; Rogers, "The Crater Battle," p. 12; Gould, p. 247.
11. Bernard, pp. 150–1; Cavanaugh, pp. 53–4.
12. Rosen, p. 198; Cavanaugh, pp. 48, 53; Freeman, *R. E. Lee,* pp. 467–9, 471; Bernard, pp. 150–1. Wise, pp. 361, 367, has a different sequence.

13. Wise, pp. 366-8.
14. U.S. Congress, *Report,* p. 21.
15. Ibid., pp. 99–100; Corrigan, p. 73; Bosbyshell, p. 172.
16. Jackman, pp. 318–24.
17. Powell, pp. 554-5.
18. U.S. Congress, *Report,* p. 99; Cavanaugh, p. 45.
19. Powell, p. 554; *OR* 40:3, p. 663.
20. Cannan, pp. 103–4; Cavanaugh, pp. 44–50; Whitman, pp. 127–8; Corrigan, pp. 84–5; *OR* 40:1, pp. 554–6.
21. Colonel White, leading Griffin's advance, informed the brigade commander that he could do nothing more unless Ledlie's men advanced in support. Griffin sent back to say they were advancing—but he had been misled by the rising clatter of musketry from the south, where Willcox's men were trying to clear the south side of the breach. Cavanaugh, p. 45–6.
22. U.S. Congress, *Report,* pp. 108–9.
23. Whitman, pp. 127–8; Stone, p. 194; Corrigan, pp. 84–7; Cannan, pp. 103–7; Cavanaugh, pp. 47–50; Beaty, pp. 49, 51, 53; Hall, p. 224.
24. Chase, pp. 21, 28, 22–4; Corrigan, pp. 98–9; U.S. Congress, *Report,* p. 203.
25. U.S. Congress, *Report,* pp. 164, 172, 224–5, 253.
26. Cannan, p. 65; U.S. Congress, *Report,* pp. 181, 265. At the court of inquiry Warren would still insist on his view that there was a second line, and that the reinforcements came from north of the James, although by then it was clear that both assertions were false.
27. Cavanaugh, p. 49; U.S. Congress, *Report,* pp. 21, 94, 161.
28. U.S. Congress, *Report,* pp. 257–8; Cavanaugh, pp. 49–51.
29. U.S. Congress, *Report,* p. 29.
30. Ibid., pp. 29–30, 247.
31. The exchange is in Ibid., pp. 29–30, 247–9.
32. Lyman, p. 200; Cavanaugh, pp. 52–3; Cannan, p. 71; Porter, pp. 264–7.

Chapter 12. The Charge of the Colored Division, 7:00–8:30 A.M.

1. For this phase of the operation see Cavanaugh, ch. 5; Axelrod, ch. 8; Cannan, chs. 10–11; Bernard, *War Talks,* pp. 193ff, 213–7; Freeman, *Lee,* p. 470–1.
2. U.S. Congress, *Report,* pp. 20, 105, 206–7; Cannan, pp. 107–12; Wilkinson, pp. 253–4; Corrigan, pp. 94–5. There is disagreement about the precise timing of the orders to Ferrero. The first was most likely sent after Meade's 6:30 telegram that ordered all troops "black and white" to attack. But Ferrero was unable and/or unwilling to advance until the peremptory order conveyed by Loring at 7:30 A.M.
3. *OR* 40:1, p. 595.
4. E. Miller, p. 67; H. G. Thomas, p. 564; Wilson, pp. 125–6.

5. Redkey, pp. 110–12.

6. Hall, pp. 222–3 and Bowley (in Wilson, p. 130) disagree on which regiment led. Hall's account is more persuasive, and is consistent with the testimony of Bates ("A Day," p. 6) and Van Buren (U.S. Congress, *Report,* p. 109). Bowley's version and (perhaps) his memory seem to have been influenced by Hall's memoir. Since the regiments did not go up together, Bowley (whose company was toward the rear of the regiment) would not have seen the 43rd ahead as he approached the Rebel line, and he had been told the 30th would lead the attack—as it would have under the tactics developed by Bates and Hall.

7. Hall, pp. 222–3; Cutcheon, p. 142; Wilson, pp. 126–7.

8. Cannan, pp. 117–9.

9. Hess, pp. 17, 22; Hall, pp. 228–9.

10. Cannan, p. 114.

11. Ibid., p. 115; Hall, pp. 236–9.

12. Hall, pp. 223–5, 228–9; Bates, "A Day," p. 6.

13. Bates, "A Day," p. 6; Wilson, p. 129.

14. Hess, p. 15; Cavanaugh, p. 56; Corrigan, pp. 95–6; Wilson, p. 130.

15. U.S. Congress, *Report,* p. 109. Bates, writing many years later, says he spoke to Van Buren after the assault. But Van Buren's account was given right after the battle, so it is probably more accurate on the time sequence. Bates's memory seems to have merged several phases of his advance into a single movement. Bates, "A Day," p. 6.

16. Wilson, pp. 131–2; Power, pp. 138–9; Stone, p. 196; Edward Alexander, *Fighting for the Confederacy,* p. 462.

17. E. Miller, p. 69; Bowley, "The Crater"; Wilson, p. 131; Cavanaugh, p. 58 and footnote on pp. 169–70.

18. Corrigan, pp. 95–6; D. E. Proctor, "The Massacre in the Crater," p. 6.

19. Forstchen, p. 126; E. Thomas, p. 342.

20. Cavanaugh, pp. 56–7, says Bates's movement was facilitated by Turner's attack on the right. But Turner (*OR* 40:1, p. 699) says his troops didn't attack there till after the 4th Division went forward. So it was Hall's efforts that made Bates's attack. See also Stone, p. 194; Power, p. 137; *OR* 40:1, pp. 596–7.

21. Hall says one hundred fifty prisoners were taken; Bates says two hundred fifty, which seems high. Van Buren credits Bates with all the captures, but he did not consult with Hall nor see his attack.

22. Hall, pp. 224–5; Proctor, p. 6.

23. H. G. Thomas, p. 563; E. Miller, p. 71; Hall, pp. 243–4.

24. U.S. Congress, *Report,* pp. 100–1.

25. Reese quote in Forstchen, p. 137; U.S. Congress, *Report,* p. 109.

26. U.S. Congress, *Report,* pp. 109, 216; *OR* 40:1, pp. 554–6.

27. U.S. Congress, *Report,* pp. 109, 208; H. G. Thomas, p. 556–7; Beecham, pp. 182–3; *OR* 40:1, p. 598.

28. H. G. Thomas, pp. 564–5; U.S. Congress, *Report,* p. 208; *OR* 40:1, p. 598.

29. U.S. Congress, *Report,* p. 109.

30. Cutcheon, pp. 142–3; Cannan, pp. 107–8.

31. For the maneuvers of Humphrey's brigade see Cavanaugh, pp. 51–3; Cannan, pp. 107–8; Cutcheon, p. 142; U.S. Congress, *Report,* pp. 21, 90–1; Herek, pp. 218, 220–2.

32. Cavanaugh, p. 51.

33. Ibid., p. 85; Wise, pp. 362–3; Blake, p. 56.

34. Cavanaugh, p. 87.

35. Bernard, p. 190; William H. Etheredge, "Another Story of the Crater Battle," p. 167.

36. For Mahone's counterattack see Cannan, pp. 121–6; Cavanaugh, ch. 5; Bernard, pp. 151–4, 190; Etheredge, p. 167; William Stewart, "Carnage at the Crater," p. 41.

CHAPTER 13. MAHONE'S COUNTERATTACK, 9:00–11:00 A.M.

1. H. G. Thomas, pp. 564–5; *OR* 40:1, p. 598–9; Beecham, p. 183; U.S. Congress, *Report,* p. 210.

2. Kilmer, p. 775.

3. Hall, pp. 234, 239.

4. Wilson, p. 134.

5. U.S. Congress, *Report,* p. 210; Hess, p. 22; E. Miller, pp. 70–2; H. G. Thomas, p. 565; *Memorial,* pp. 17–9.

6. U.S. Congress, *Report,* p. 216; *OR* 40:1, pp. 595–7; Öfele, p. 174.

7. Bernard, p. 188; Stewart, pp. 41–2; Rogers, pp. 12–4.

8. Bernard, pp. 154–5; Cavanaugh, p. 88; Ray, pp. 214–5, 225, 250, 304, 313. http://www.cfspress.com/sharpshooters/articles2.html#Anchor-Furthe-16931

9. Bowley, "The Crater," p. 6; Wilson, p. 134; Proctor, p. 6.

10. U.S. Congress, *Report,* p. 216; H. G. Thomas, pp. 565–7; *OR* 40:1, pp. 598–9; Bernard, p. 156; Bowley, "The Crater," p. 6.

11. H. G. Thomas, pp. 566–7; *OR* 40:1, p. 598–9; Beecham, p. 188.

12. U.S. Congress, *Report,* p. 216; H. G. Thomas, pp. 565–7; *OR* 40:1, pp. 542, 598–9; Bernard, p. 156; Bowley, "The Crater," p. 6; Herek, p. 224; Cutcheon, pp. 142–3; Proctor, p. 6.

13. Forstchen, p. 133; Walter Taylor, *Four Years with General Lee,* pp. 259–60. Colonel Taylor, Lee's aide, praised the man as the only Union soldier who understood the proper objective of the attack, and had the will to carry it through— a bit of sarcasm, since Taylor clearly thought the man's actions a symptom of Negro stupidity. It is too bad no one ever asked the soldier himself about it.

14. *OR* 40:1, p. 598–9; Bernard, pp. 155–6.

15. H. G. Thomas, p. 567; *OR* 40:1, pp. 598–9.

16. Frank Kenfield, "Captured by the Rebels," p. 233; Lord, pp. 498, 502; Etheredge, p. 167.

17. Bernard, p. 188; Houston, pp. 313–6; Lord, p. 502; William D. Henderson, *41st Virginia Infantry*, p. 70.

18. Weld, *War Diary*, p. 356.

19. Bernard, p. 156.

20. Ibid., p. 187; Etheredge, p. 167; Stewart, pp. 41–2; George Burkhardt, *Confederate Rage*, p. 166.

21. Kenfield, p. 233; Bernard, pp. 158–60.

22. Cannan, pp. 125–9; Weld, *War Diary*, pp. 356–7.

23. Bowley, "The Crater," p. 6; Proctor, p. 6; Wilson, p. 134.

24. Wilson, p. 134.

25. Ibid.; Mickley, pp. 28–42, 74–5; *OR* 40:1, pp. 596–7; Hall, p. 239. Seagrave was also shot seven times but not killed outright; he was taken prisoner, was exchanged, and died ten months later. Beaty, p. 58, indicates that troops who had come down from the lateral ravine (12th Virginia and 26th South Carolina) joined in the fighting here.

26. Hall, pp. 233, 239; see Dorsey's citation at http://www.army.mil/cmh-pg/html/moh/civwaral.html: "Planted his colors on the Confederate works in advance of his regiment, and when the regiment was driven back to the Union works he carried the colors there and bravely rallied the men."

27. Whitman, p. 128; http://51stnewyorkinfantry.tripod.com/ContentsPage.htm

28. Hall, p. 239; Peter S. Carmichael, *Lee's Young Artillerist*, pp. 130–1.

29. *OR* 40:1, pp. 596–7.

30. U.S. Congress, *Report*, p. 180.

31. Jackman, p. 322.

32. U.S. Congress, *Report*, pp. 101, 221–3.

33. Proctor, p. 6.

34. Cannan, p. 135; Hall, p. 236; Lord, p. 498.

35. Bowley, "The Crater," p. 6; Wilson, pp. 135–6.

36. Bowley, "The Crater," p. 6.

37. *OR* 40:1, pp. 554–5; Wilson, p. 136; Bowley, "The Crater," p. 6, differs slightly.

38. *OR* 40:1, pp. 554–6. For Wilkins's citation see http://www.army.mil/cmh-pg/html/moh/civwarmz.html for Hogan, http://www.army.mil/cmh-pg/html/moh/civwaral.html

39. Cannan, pp. 129–30; Bernard, pp. 187–8.

40. Bernard, pp. 158–60, 191–2.

41. Haskell, pp. 75–7; Cavanaugh, pp. 90–2; Power, p. 137; Beaty, p. 57; George S. Burkhardt, pp. 166–8.

42. Etheredge, p. 167; Cavanaugh, pp. 90–2; Kilmer, pp. 775–6; Rickard, p. 28; Hess, pp. 28–9.

43. U.S. Congress, *Report*, p. 258.

CHAPTER 14. "THEY FOUGHT LIKE BULLDOGS, AND DIED LIKE SOLDIERS":
LAST STAND IN THE CRATER, 8:45 A.M.–2:30 P.M.

1. U.S. Congress, *Report,* pp. 154–5, 248–9, 258–9; Marvel, *Burnside,* p. 406; Cavanaugh, p. 92; C. F. Adams, p. 171.
2. Lyman, pp. 200–1; Cavanaugh, pp. 92–3; U.S. Congress, *Report,* p. 145.
3. *OR* 40:3, p. 663.
4. Cannan, pp. 24, 71–6; U.S. Congress, *Report,* pp. 165–6, 248–50; Cavanaugh, pp. 92–3; *OR* 40:3, p. 663.
5. The order was also attributed to General Willcox. Cavanaugh, p. 97; U.S. Congress, *Report,* p. 21; Herek, p. 226.
6. Beecham, pp. 188–9.
7. This very rough estimate is based on the number of MIA for units that did most of their fighting in or near the crater, and on estimates of the numbers of troops brought into the position by Ledlie's initial advance and the reinforcement from Willcox's division. Hartranft brought perhaps 1,200 troops to the ruined fort, of which no more than 1,000 were still in line; the three Michigan regiments brought 200 into the position. Thomas's brigade lost in total 253 MIA and 54 KIA—probably 200+ remained to fight in and around the crater, and were lost there. Lieutenant Bowley does not mention any troops other than his own company (no more than thirty) who made their way from Sigfried's command to the crater. The 45th Pennsylvania and elements of other regiments from Potter's division also wound up in the crater—perhaps two hundred to three hundred men (based on MIA figures). Ledlie's division took 3,600 into action, but it suffered the lightest casualties of the four divisions. Of these, sixty-five were KIA and three hundred fifty MIA, most of the latter captured, and of these perhaps one hundred were taken when Weld's position was overrun—so perhaps three hundred were lost in the crater itself. However, it is impossible to say how many of Ledlie's troops were still in the breach at this point in the action, and made their escape as the position was overrun. In the end, nine hundred Federals were captured in the crater itself. Cavanaugh, pp. 94–5; Cannan, pp. 134–5.
8. Cannan, p. 135; Hall, p. 236.
9. Bowley, "The Crater," p. 6; *OR* 40:1, pp. 554–6; Bernard, p. 162; Vance, p. 179; Wilson, p. 137.
10. Cavanaugh, pp. 93–4.
11. Hess, pp. 15–6; Katcher, p. 59.
12. Cannan, p. 134; Albert, pp. 155–6; Forstchen, p. 140, Bowley, p. 6.
13. Cavanaugh, pp. 95–6; Lord, pp. 466–7, 505–7, 510. Bowley, "The Crater," p. 6, erroneously identifies him as a sergeant of the 31st Maine.
14. Cavanaugh, pp. 94–5; Cannan, pp. 134–5; Bowley, "The Crater," p. 6; *OR* 40:1, pp. 555–6.
15. Bernard, pp. 161–2.

16. Hess, pp. 28–9; Cavanaugh, p. 95.

17. Bowley, "The Crater," p. 6.

18. Cavanaugh, pp. 94–5; Bowley, "The Crater," p. 6; Wilson, p. 137; Hess, p. 39.

19. Houghton, p. 559; Palfrey, pp. 119–22.

20. Bowley, "The Crater," p. 6; Houghton, p. 558; Cavanaugh, p. 96.

21. Herek, p. 224; Cavanaugh, p. 96; *OR* 40:1, pp. 555–6.

22. *OR* 40:3, pp. 663–4; U.S. Congress, *Report,* pp. 20–1, 205; Cavanaugh, p. 97.

23. Bowley, "The Crater," p. 6; Kilmer, p. 776.

24. *OR* 40:1, pp. 555–6.

25. Lord, pp. 491–3; Wilkinson, pp. 202, 255–61; Cannan, p. 134.

26. *OR* 40:1, pp. 555–6; Cavanaugh, p. 96; Houghton, p. 562.

27. Houghton, p.562; Kilmer, p. 776.

28. Cannan, p. 135; Hall, p. 236. See also Robert Poirier, "*By the Blood of Our Alumni,*" p. 223.

29. Bowley, "The Crater," p. 6.

30. Herek, pp. 225–6; Cutcheon, pp. 143–4.

31. Warner, *Generals in Gray,* p. 268.

32. Cavanaugh, pp. 97–9.

33. John C. Featherston, "Incidents of the Battle of the Crater," pp. 107–8; Wise, pp. 365–6. See Featherston's letter to his wife at http://www.aphillcsa.com/accountcrater1.html his narrative of the battle is at that site and http://www.aphillcsa.com/accountcrater2.html

34. Featherston, "Incidents," p. 107; Vance, pp. 178–9; Cavanaugh, p. 98.

35. Featherston, http://www.aphillcsa.com/accountcrater1.html

36. *OR* 40:1, p. 556.

37. Featherston, "Incidents," pp. 107–8; Palfrey, pp. 119–22; Cavanaugh, pp. 98–9.

38. Featherston, "Incidents," p. 108, claimed he heard "Yankee officers in the fort trying to encourage their men, telling them among other things to 'remember Fort Pillow.' " He took this as a spur and a justification of vengeance: "In that fort Forrest's men had found whites and negroes together. History tells what they did for them." It seems unlikely (though it is surely possible) that Federal officers would still be using that battle cry in the face of what most must now have recognized as certain defeat. "Fort Pillow" had the same significance for them that it had for Featherston: they believed that Forrest's men had not only massacred surrendering Black troops, but had also refused quarter to the Whites who fought alongside them. Featherston was recalling this moment many years later, and his memory may have been colored by the need to rationalize what happened after the Confederates stormed the crater. In a letter to his wife, dated August 9, 1864, he does not mention hearing these words himself. "The enemy," he says, "*have* shouted 'No quarters!' We then gave them what they justly deserved [italics mine]." Perhaps, like Stewart, he had heard the story of Sigfried's attack from South Carolina troops who had escaped to the rear—either before or after

the battle. In any case, as he himself says, the Alabamans did not need orders to tell them to deny quarter to Blacks.

39. Cavanaugh, pp. 98–9; Bowley, "The Crater," p. 6; Marvel, *Race,* p. 270; Burkhardt, ch. 12; Bryce Suderow, "The Battle of the Crater: The Civil War's Worst Massacre," in G.J.W. Urwin, ed., *Black Flag over Dixie,* ch. 9; Kilmer, p. 776.

40. Cavanaugh, p. 99; Wilson, pp. 139–40; Urwin, p. 205.

41. Power, p. 139; Burkhardt, pp. 168–9; Haskell, pp. 77–8; Albert, p. 220; Wilson, pp. 140–1; Featherston, "Incidents," p. 108; Cavanaugh, p. 102; Jordan and Thomas, p. 168.

42. Featherston, "Incidents," p. 108; Palfrey, p. 122; Urwin, p. 205; Jordan and Thomas, p. 168.

43. Cannan, p. 140; Cavanaugh, pp. 99–100; U.S. Congress, *Report,* p. 205; Freeman, *R. E. Lee,* p. 476.

44. Herek, pp. 226–8; Cavanaugh, p. 100; http://www.hardylaw.net/2d_27th _Mich_Inf

45. Vance, p. 179.

46. Stone, p. 201; Featherston, "Incidents," p. 108; Cavanaugh, p. 100; George Clark, "Alabamians in the Crater Battle," http://americancivilwar.50megs.com/ 1895/art9506.html

47. Power, p. 139.

48. Rickard, p. 29.

49. Burkhardt, pp. 169–70.

50. Carmichael, pp. 130–1; Power, p. 139; Alexander, p. 462.

51. Alexander, p. 462; Stewart, pp. 41–2; Haskell, pp. 78–9.

52. Cannan, p. 144.

CHAPTER 15. FLAG OF TRUCE, JULY 30–AUGUST 1, 1864

1. Bernard, p. 163; Featherston, "Incidents," p. 108; Cavanaugh, p. 102.

2. *OR* 40:3, pp. 667–8; Cavanaugh, pp. 102–3, 128; Cannan, p. 76; Marvel, *Race,* p. 278.

3. U.S. Congress, *Report,* pp. 24–5.

4. *OR* 40:3, pp.637–40; U.S. Congress, *Report,* pp. 250–1, 259.

5. Cavanaugh, pp. 128–9; Forstchen, p. 146. The medical director of IX Corps reported treating 93 officers and 1,300 enlisted men on July 30, out of a total 1,646 reported wounded in the corps (1,881 for all units engaged). Some fifty wounded managed to crawl into Union lines that night, and when the truce was finally granted on August 2, only about twenty wounded were still alive between the lines. Union officers reported burying two hundred twenty of their soldiers during the truce (many of whom had no doubt been killed outright). The Confederates buried hundreds more but made no exact tally, and they tended to in-

clude bodies buried behind their lines. Any wounded Confederates left between the lines would have been POWs hit while being taken back to the Union lines. If these figures are correct, then there were at least three hundred lying between the lines when the fighting ended. If we assume that two men were wounded for every one killed—an atypically high ratio reflecting intense combat—then some two hundred wounded would have been alive when the major fighting ended at 3:00 P.M. on July 30. More than half of these were left to die without treatment because of the delay in starting the truce.

6. Hess, pp. 32–5, 45; Albert, p. 385; Hauptman, p. 141.

7. Lord, pp. 505–8.

8. Chase, pp. 24, 28; Hauptman, p. 157.

9. Bernard, p. 189.

10. Haskell, pp. 79–80; Cavanaugh, pp. 106–7; Albert, pp. 116, 296–300, 324 ff.

11. *OR* 40:3, p. 707; Featherston, "Incidents," p. 108; Bernard, pp. 163–4; Stone, p. 201; Hess, p. 22. The description is from Gettysburg.

12. Power, p. 136; Bosbyshell, pp. 175–6; Featherston, "Incidents," p. 108; Bernard, pp. 163–4; Stone, p. 201.

13. *OR* 40:3, pp. 701–3.

14. Featherston, "Incidents," p. 108; *OR* 40:3, p. 699; Bernard, p. 165; Oates, pp. 262–3.

15. Axelrod, p. 224; Crawford, p. 108.

16. Cavanaugh, p. 104.

17. *OR* 40:3, pp. 703–7.

18. Shearman, p. 15; Bowley, "The Crater," p. 6; Wilson, pp. 137–8; Palfrey, p. 119; Beecham, p. 191.

19. Beecham recalled that there were eleven hundred Whites and five hundred Blacks in the column, which is wildly overstated. (He may have taken his figures from published statistics of the total reported "missing" after the battle.) It is more likely that there were a hundred or so Blacks and perhaps eight hundred Whites. Beecham, p. 192; Hall, p. 231; Wilson, pp. 149–50.

20. Hall, p. 231; Shearman, pp. 15–7.

21. Beecham, pp. 192–3.

22. Ibid., p. 193; Hall, p. 231.

23. Wise, pp. 368–71; Washington, p. 60.

24. Forstchen, p. 142.

25. Power, p. 230.

26. Herek, p. 230; Featherston, "Incidents," p. 108; Bernard, p. 165.

27. Ernest Hemingway, "A Natural History of the Dead," p. 337; Hess, pp. 40–1; Oates, p. 263; Blanton and Cook, p. 108; Albert, p. 148.

28. Herek, p. 230; Beaty, p. 57; Power, p. 138.

29. Featherston, "Incidents," p. 108; Hess, pp. 40–1.

30. Featherston, "Incidents," p. 108; Cavanaugh, pp. 107–8; Stone, pp. 201–2.

CHAPTER 16. COURT OF INQUIRY, AUGUST 6–SEPTEMBER 9, 1864

1. Grant, *Papers,* Vol. 11, pp. 361–3.

2. Cavanaugh, pp. 128–9 and 143–4, is definitive on casualties; Livermore, pp. 116–7, gives higher figures.

3. Bosbyshell, p. 171. Percentage assumes the average Union strength for July was about 77,300 and the Confederate strength 57,000.

4. *OR* 40:3, pp. 338–9; Grant, *Papers,* Vol. 11, pp. 353–4, indicates it was not received by Meade until 10:00 P.M.

5. Grant, *Papers,* Vol. 11, p. 363; C. F. Adams, pp. 172–3; Cavanaugh, pp. 108–11.

6. Bosbyshell, pp. 176–7.

7. U.S. Congress, *Report,* pp. 57 ff, 65. For Meade's testimony see pp. 139–52; Burnside's cross-examination of Meade and his own testimony are on pp. 152–73.

8. Ibid., pp. 230–2.

9. Ibid., pp. 94–5, 181, 265; Cannan, p. 65.

10. Donald, p. 520; Stackpole, pp. 103–8, 146–9, 153–74, 180–5.

11. Power, pp. 108, 135–40, 262; Bosbyshell, p. 171. Statistics don't quite bear this out: desertions had reached a high in July and decreased somewhat during the month after the Crater. Mark Weitz, *More Damning Than Slaughter,* p. 246. But statistics are not everything: General Lee certainly thought that rates of desertion between July 30 and August 30 threatened his army's ability to maintain the field.

12. Carmichael, p. 130; Cavanaugh, p. 105.

13. Jeffrey D Marshall, ed., *War of the People,* pp. 250–1; C. F. Adams, p. 172.

14. Alvin C. Voris, *A Citizen-Soldier's Civil War,* p. 205; U.S. Congress, *Report,* pp. 33–4, 203, 223.

15. U.S. Congress, *Report,* pp. 125, 172–3, 210.

16. Wise, p. 366.

17. It was this flow of refugees that supposedly caused Bell's brigade to break. Other Federal formations faced with a similar rout either stemmed it or opened ranks to let the fugitives pass through. The court of inquiry ought to have asked why Bell's men broke, instead of accepting Turner's assertion that the Blacks were to blame.

18. C. F. Adams, pp. 216–9; Suderow, in Urwin, *Black Flag,* p. 205.

19. Cavanaugh, p. 128; Forstchen, p. 146, cites higher losses; Hauptman, p. 157.

20. H. G. Thomas, p. 567; for regimental histories see index in the Civil War Archive, http://www.civilwararchive.com/unioncol.htm

21. Forstchen, pp. 148–9.

22. *New York Herald,* August 4, 1864, p. 4; *New York Herald,* August 6, 1864, p. 4.

23. *The New York Times,* "The Assault—Its Character and Results," August 2, 1864, p. 1.

24. Jackson, p. 182; Forstchen, pp. 149–51; Redkey, pp. 110–5; Edward Longacre, *Regiment of Slaves,* p. 107.

25. Donald, p. 529; *Memorial,* p. 15.

26. Forty-two were MIA for reasons other than capture. Confederate officers reported seeing one hundred fifty wounded Blacks lying in a field a day or two after the battle, but this was an estimate rather than an actual count. Suderow, in Urwin, pp. 206–7; Cavanaugh, pp. 128–9.

27. Power, p. 139.

28. See Burkhardt, passim.

29. Peter Wallenstein and Bertram Wyatt-Brown, *Virginia's Civil War,* p. 35.

30. Forstchen, pp. 132, 142–3; Carmichael, p. 130; Featherston, "Incidents," pp. 107–8.

31. Durden, p. 75.

32. Levine, pp. 112–5.

Chapter 17. Epitaphs

1. Biographies of Butler, Meade, Potter, Willcox, H. G. Thomas, and Ledlie in Warner, *Generals in Blue;* for Ledlie see http://www.nevadaweb.com/cnt/cc/bmtn.html

2. Greiner, pp. 197–8; http://aotw.org/officers.php?officer_id=1106

3. Wilson, pp. xxi, xxv, 3, 167. For his son the general see http://www.arlingtoncemetery.net/ajbowley.htm

4. Palfrey, pp. 119–20; R. Miller, pp. 2–4; Warner, *Generals in Blue,* pp. 24–5.

5. Warner, *Generals in Gray,* pp. 157–8, 268, 330.

6. Rose, pp. 347–8; Warner, *Generals in Gray,* p. 82.

7. Stone, p. 287.

8. Kenny, pp. 48–9, 82.

9. Blake, pp. 72–4, 83–7, 91, 97–104; Carl N. Degler, *The Other South,* p. 274.

10. Foner, p. 592; Degler, pp. 276–7.

11. The most complete treatment is Donald R. Shaffer, *After the Glory.* See Forstchen, pp. 228–9; E. Miller, ch. 6; http://www.afrigeneas.com/library/dawson_article.html

12. http://civilwarmemory.typepad.com/civil_war_memory/my_civil_war/index.html

13. Forstchen, pp. 56–7, 220–2; Washington, p. 79.

14. Glatthaar, p. 228; Washington, pp. 3–14.

15. Mickley, pp. 85–8.

16. Beecham, ch. 9; Proctor, p. 6.

17. See the application for Federal funding of a historic district, http://mdmunicipal.org/cities/index.cfm?townname=Brentwood&page=home.

18. There is a historical marker honoring Dorsey and the Ellicott City Colored

School: see http://www.visithowardcounty.com/history/trails.html For Dorsey's later life see http://www.nps.gov/archive/pete/mahan/edbiosdd.html and Nicholas Acocella, "Famous Hobokenites: Decatur Dorsey: Civil War Sergeant from Hoboken Won Medal of Honor." at http://www.hudsonreporter.com/site/news.cfm ?newsid=15203888&BRD=1291&PAG=461&dept_id=551343&rfi=6

19. Richard Slotkin, *The Fatal Environment,* ch. 19.

20. Haskell's account (pp. 77–8) of the post-Crater massacre is an almost perfect allegory of the ideology of the movement to "redeem" the South from reconstruction. The moral of the fable is that the "Bourbon" aristocrat is the Negro's only safe reliance. Poor Whites will lynch him, Yankees will cheat and betray him, his own people will prove too selfish and weak to aid him.

21. Kevin M. Levin, "The Battle of the Crater, National Reunion, and the Creation of the Petersburg National Military Park: 1864–1937," pp. 3–6.

22. Cannan, pp. 156–8.

Selected Bibliography

Adams, Charles Francis, Jr., et al. *A Cycle of Adams Letters, 1861–1865.* Volume 2. Edited by Worthington Chauncey Ford. Boston: Houghton Mifflin Co., 1920.

Adams, J. C. "Battle of the Crater," *National Tribune,* June 25, 1903.

Albert, Allen D. *History of the Forty-fifth Regiment Pennsylvania Veteran Volunteer Infantry 1861–1865.* Williamsport, Pa.: Grit Publishing Co., 1912.

Alexander, Edward Porter. *Fighting for the Confederacy: The Personal Recollections of General Edward Porter Alexander.* Edited by Gary W. Gallagher. Chapel Hill: University of North Carolina Press, 1989.

Axelrod, Alan. *The Horrid Pit: The Battle of the Crater, the Civil War's Cruelest Mission.* N.Y.: Carroll & Graf Publishers, 2007.

Barnwell, Robert W. "A View on the Crater Battle," *Confederate Veteran 33*:5, 1925, pp. 176–8.

Bates, Delevan. "A Day with the Colored Troops," *National Tribune,* January 30, 1908, p. 6.

———. "War Reminiscences," http://usgennet.org/usa/ne/topic/military/ CW/bates/ batenws5.html

Beaty, B. L. "The Battle of the Crater," in Joshua Hilary Hudson, ed., *Sketches and Reminiscences.* Columbia, S.C.: The State Company, 1903, pp. 46–61.

Beecham, Robert. *As If It Were Glory: Robert Beecham's Civil War from the Iron Brigade to the Black Regiments.* Edited by Michael E. Stevens. Madison, Wis.: Madison House, 1998.

Berlin, Ira, Joseph P. Reidy, and Leslie S. Rowland, eds. *Freedom's Soldiers: The Black Military Experience in the Civil War.* Cambridge, U.K.: Cambridge University Press, 1998.

Bernard, George S., ed. *War Talks of Confederate Veterans.* Petersburg, Va.: Fenn & Owen, Publishers, 1892.

Bernstein, Iver. *The New York City Draft Riots: Their Significance for American Society and Politics in the Age of the Civil War.* N.Y.: Oxford University Press, 1990.

Billings, John D. *Hardtack and Coffee, or the Unwritten Story of Army Life.* Williamstown, Mass.: Corner House Publishers, 1973.

Blair, William, and William Pencak, eds. *Making and Remaking Pennsylvania's Civil War.* University Park: Pennsylvania State University Press, 2001.

Blair, William. *Virginia's Private War: Feeding Body and Soul in the Confederacy, 1861–1865.* N.Y.: Oxford University Press, 1998.

Blake, Nelson M. *William Mahone of Virginia: Soldier and Political Insurgent.* Richmond, Va.: Garret & Massie, 1935.

Blanton, DeAnne and Lauren M. Cook. *They Fought Like Demons: Women Soldiers in the American Civil War.* Baton Rouge: Louisiana State University Press, 2002.

Bosbyshell, Oliver Christian. *The 48th in the War. Being a Narrative of the Campaigns of the 48th Regiment, Infantry, Pennsylvania Veteran Volunteers, During the War of the Rebellion.* Philadelphia: Avil Printing Company, 1895.

Bowley, Freeman S. (Free R. Bawley [*sic*]), "The Crater," *National Tribune,* November 6, 1884.

———. "The Petersburg Mine," War Paper No. 3, California MOLLUS (November 6, 1889), pp. 1–17.

Broehl, Wayne G., Jr. *The Molly Maguires.* Cambridge, Mass.: Harvard University Press, 1964.

Brown, William Wells. *The Negro in the American Rebellion: His Heroism and His Fidelity.* Edited by John D. Smith. Athens: Ohio University Press, 2003.

Burkhardt, George S. *Confederate Rage, Yankee Wrath: No Quarter in the Civil War.* Carbondale: Southern Illinois University Press, 2007.

Butler, Benjamin F. *Private and Official Correspondence of Gen. Benjamin F. Butler During the Period of the Civil War.* Volume 4. Norwood, Mass.: Plimpton Press, 1917.

Cannan, John. *The Crater: Burnside's Assault on the Confederate Trenches, July 30, 1864.* Cambridge, Mass.: Da Capo Press, 2002.

Carmichael, Peter S. *Lee's Young Artillerist: William R.J. Pegram.* Charlottesville: University Press of Virginia, 1995.

Catton, Bruce. *Bruce Catton's Civil War: A Stillness at Appomattox.* N.Y.: Fairfax Press, 1984.

———. *The Coming Fury. The Centennial History of the Civil War,* Volume 1. N.Y.: Doubleday & Co., 1961.

———. *Never Call Retreat: The Centennial History of the Civil War,* Volume 3. N.Y.: Doubleday and Co., 1965.

———. *Terrible Swift Sword. The Centennial History of the Civil War,* Volume 2. N.Y.: Doubleday & Co., 1963.

Cavanaugh, Michael A. and William Marvel. *The Petersburg Campaign: The Battle of the Crater, "The Horrid Pit," June 25–August 6, 1864.* 2nd Edition. Lynchburg, Va.: H. E. Howard, Inc., 1989.

Chambers, H. A. "The Bloody Crater," *Confederate Veteran* 31:5, May 1923, pp. 174–7.

Chase, James Judson. *The Charge at Day-break: Scenes and Incidents at the Battle of the Mine Explosion, Near Petersburg, Va., July 30th, 1864.* Lewiston, Maine: Journal Office, 1875.

Chester, Thomas Morris and R.J.M. Blackett. *Thomas Morris Chester, Black Civil War Correspondent: His Dispatches from the Virginia Front.* Cambridge, Mass.: Da Capo Press, 1989.

Cimprich, John. *Fort Pillow, a Civil War Massacre, and Public Memory.* Baton Rouge: Louisiana State University Press, 2005.

Cleaves, Freeman. *Meade of Gettysburg.* Norman: University of Oklahoma Press, 1960.

Copp, Elbridge J. *Reminiscences of the War of the Rebellion, 1861–1865.* Nashua, N.H.: Telegraph Publishing, 1911.

Cornish, Dudley Taylor. *The Sable Arm: Negro Troops in the Union Army, 1861–1865.* N.Y.: W. W. Norton Co., 1966.

Corrigan, Jim. *The 48th Pennsylvania in the Battle of the Crater: A Regiment of Coal Miners Who Tunneled Under the Enemy.* Jefferson, N.C.: McFarland & Co., Inc., 2006.

Crawford, Robert F., ed. "The Civil War Letters of S. Rodman and Linton Smith," *Delaware History* 31:2, 1984, pp. 86–116.

Cutcheon, Byron M. *The Story of the Twentieth Michigan Infantry, July 15th, 1862, to May 30th, 1865.* Lansing, Mich.: Robert Smith Printing Co., 1904.

Dalton, Peter. *Union vs. Dis-Union: The Contribution of a Small Maine Town to the American Civil War, 1861–1865.* Union Publishing Co., 1993.

Daughtry, Mary. *Gray Cavalier: The Life and Wars of General W.H.F. "Rooney" Lee.* Cambridge, Mass.: Da Capo Press, 2002.

Davis, Jefferson. *Jefferson Davis: The Essential Writings.* Edited by William J. Cooper, Jr. N.Y.: Modern Library, 2003.

Davis, Jefferson. *The Papers of Jefferson Davis, Volume 10, October 1863–August 1864.* Edited by Lynda Lasswell Crist, et al. Baton Rouge: Louisiana State University Press, 1999.

Day, W. A. "Battle of the Crater," *Confederate Veteran* 11:8, 1903, pp. 355–6.

De Forest, John William. *A Volunteer's Adventures: A Union Captain's Record of the Civil War.* Edited by James H. Croushore. New Haven: Yale University Press, 1946.

Degler, Carl N. *The Other South: Southern Dissenters in the Nineteenth Century.* N.Y.: Harper & Row, 1974.

Dell, Christopher. *Lincoln and the War Democrats: The Grand Erosion of Conservative Tradition.* Rutherford, N.J.: Fairleigh Dickinson University Press, 1975.

Dew, Charles B. *Apostles of Disunion: Southern Secession Commissioners and the Causes of the Civil War.* Charlottesville: University Press of Virginia, 2001.

Dirck, Brian R. *Lincoln & Davis: Imagining America, 1809–1865*. Lawrence: University Press of Kansas, 2001.

Dobbins, Austin C. *Grandfather's Journal: Company B, Sixteenth Mississippi Infantry Volunteers, Harris' Brigade, Mahone's Division, Hill's Corps, A.N.V. May 27, 1861– July 15, 1865*. Dayton, Ohio: Morningside, 1988.

Donald, David Herbert. *Lincoln*. N.Y.: Simon & Schuster, 1995.

Durden, Robert F. *The Gray and the Black: The Confederate Debate on Emancipation*. Baton Rouge: Louisiana State University Press, 1972.

Durrill, Wayne K. *War of Another Kind: A Southern Community in the Great Rebellion*. N.Y.: Oxford University Press, 1990.

Dyer, Frederick H. *Compendium of the War of the Rebellion*. 2 Volumes. Dayton, Ohio: Morningside Press, 1994.

Etheredge, William H. "Another Story of the Crater Battle," *Confederate Veteran* 15:4, 1907, p. 167.

Featherston, John C. "Incidents of the Battle of the Crater," *Confederate Veteran* 14:3, 1906, pp. 107–8.

Floyd, N. J. "Concerning the Battle of the Crater," *Confederate Veteran* 16:4, 1908, p. 159.

Folsom, James M. "Heroes and Martyrs of Georgia," http://www.3gvi.org/ga3hist8.html

Foner, Eric. *Free Soil, Free Labor, Free Men: The Ideology of the Republican Party Before the Civil War*. N.Y.: Oxford University Press, 1970.

Foner, Eric. *Reconstruction: America's Unfinished Revolution, 1863–1877*. N.Y.: Harper & Row, 1988.

Forstchen, William R. *The 28th United States Colored Troops: Indiana's African-Americans Go to War, 1863–1865*. Dissertation, Purdue University, 1994.

Fox, William F. *Regimental Losses in the American Civil War, 1861–1865*. Albany: Albany Publishing Co., 1889.

Frank, Joseph Allan. *With Ballot and Bayonet: The Political Socialization of American Civil War Soldiers*. Athens: University of Georgia Press, 1998.

Freeman, Douglas Southall, ed. *Lee's Dispatches: Unpublished Letters of General Robert E. Lee, C.S.A. to Jefferson Davis and the War Department of the Confederate States of America, 1862–65*. N.Y.: G. P. Putnam's Sons, 1957.

Freeman, Douglas Southall. *Lee's Lieutenants: A Study in Command. Volume 3, Gettysburg to Appomattox*. N.Y.: Charles Scribner's Sons, 1944.

———. *R. E. Lee: A Biography*. Volume 3. N.Y.: Charles Scribner's Sons, 1935.

Freidel, Frank, ed. *Union Pamphlets of the Civil War, 1861–1865*. Volume II. Cambridge, Mass.: Belknap Press of Harvard University Press, 1967.

Gallagher, Gary W. *The Confederate War*. Cambridge, Mass.: Harvard University Press, 1997.

Glatthaar, Joseph T. *Forged in Battle: The Civil War Alliance of Black Soldiers and White Officers*. N.Y.: Free Press, 1990.

Goff, Richard D. *Confederate Supply*. Durham, N.C.: Duke University Press, 1969.

Gould, Joseph. *The Story of the Forty-eighth: A Record of the Campaigns of the Forty-eighth Regiment Pennsylvania Veteran Volunteer Infantry*. Philadelphia: Alfred M. Slocum, 1908.

Grant, Ulysses S. *Memoirs and Selected Letters*. N.Y.: Library of America, 1990.

———. *The Papers of Ulysses S. Grant. Volume 11: June 1–August 15, 1864*. Edited by John Y. Simon. Carbondale: Southern Illinois University Press, 1984.

Greiner, James M. *Subdued by the Sword: A Line Officer in the 121st New York Volunteers*. Albany: State University of New York Press, 2003.

Griffith, Paddy. *Battle Tactics of the Civil War*. New Haven: Yale University Press, 1987.

Hagerman, Edward. *The American Civil War and the Origins of Modern Warfare: Ideas, Organization, and Field Command*. Bloomington: Indiana University Press, 1988.

Hall, Henry Seymour. "Mine Run to Petersburg," *War Talks in Kansas*, Kansas MOLLUS (1906), pp. 219–49.

Hammett, Hugh B. *Hilary Abner Herbert: A Southerner Returns to the Union*. Philadelphia: American Philosophical Society, 1976.

Haskell, John Cheves. *The Haskell Memoirs*. Edited by Gilbert E. Govan and James W. Livingood. N.Y.: G. P. Putnam, 1960.

Hauptman, Laurence M. *Between Two Fires: American Indians in the Civil War*. N.Y.: Free Press, 1995.

Hemingway, Ernest. "A Natural History of the Dead," *The Complete Short Stories of Ernest Hemingway*, N.Y.: Simon & Schuster, 1987.

Henderson, William D. *12th Virginia Infantry*. Lynchburg, Va.: H. E. Howard, 1985.

———. *41st Virginia Infantry*. Lynchburg, Va.: H. E. Howard, 1986.

Herek, Raymond J. *These Men Have Seen Hard Service: The First Michigan Sharpshooters in the Civil War*. Detroit, Mich.: Wayne State University Press, 1998.

Hess, Earl J. *The Union Soldier in Battle: Enduring the Ordeal of Combat*. Lawrence: University Press of Kansas, 1997.

Higginson, Thomas W. *The Complete Civil War Journal and Selected Letters of Thomas Wentworth Higginson*. Edited by Christopher Looby. Chicago: University of Chicago Press, 2000.

Holden, William W. *Memoirs of William W. Holden*. http://docsouth.unc.edu/fpn/holden/holden.html

Holt, David. *A Mississippi Rebel in the Army of Northern Virginia: The Civil War Memoirs of Private David Holt*. Edited by Thomas D. Cockrell and Michael B. Ballard. Baton Rouge: Louisiana State University Press, 1995.

Houghton, Charles H. "In the Crater," in R. U. Johnson and C. C. Buel, eds., *Battles and Leaders of the Civil War*. Volume 4. N.Y.: The Century Co., 1884–1888, pp. 561–2.

Houston, Henry Clarence. *The Thirty-second Maine Regiment of Infantry Volunteers: An Historical Sketch*. Portland, Maine: Southworth Brothers, 1903.

Jackman, Lyman. *History of the Sixth New Hampshire Regiment in the War for the Union*. Concord, N.H.: Republican Press Assoc., 1891.

Jackson, William J. *New Jerseyans in the Civil War: For Union and Liberty*. New Brunswick, N.J.: Rutgers University Press, 2000.

Jefferson, Thomas. *The Life and Selected Writings of Thomas Jefferson*. Edited by Adrienne Koch and William Peden. N.Y.: Modern Library, 1944.

Jones, Archer. *Civil War Command and Strategy: The Process of Victory and Defeat*. N.Y.: Free Press, 1992.

Jordan, Ervin L. *Black Confederates and Afro-Yankees in Civil War Virginia*. Charlottesville: University Press of Virginia, 1995.

Judkins, W. B. "History of Co. G, 22nd Georgia," http://www.mindspring.com/~jcherepy/memoir/judkins.txt

Katcher, Philip. *The Complete Civil War*. London: Cassell, 2005.

Kenfield, Frank. "Captured by the Rebels," in *Vermont History*. Volume 36, Issue 4, 1968, pp. 230-5.

Kenny, Kevin. *Making Sense of the Molly Maguires*. N.Y.: Oxford University Press, 1998.

Kilmer, George L. "The Dash into the Crater," *The Century* magazine (September 1887), pp. 774-6.

Kinard, Jeff. *The Battle of the Crater*. Abilene, Tex.: McWhiney Foundation Press, 1995.

Levin, Kevin M. "The Battle of the Crater, National Reunion, and the Creation of the Petersburg National Military Park: 1864-1937," *Virginia Social Science Journal*, 2006, Vol. 41, pages 1-14.

Levine, Bruce. *Confederate Emancipation: Southern Plans to Free and Arm Slaves During the Civil War*. N.Y.: Oxford University Press, 2006.

Lincoln, Abraham. *The Collected Works of Abraham Lincoln*. Edited by Roy P. Basler. Volume VII. New Brunswick, N.J.: Rutgers University Press, 1953.

———. *Speeches and Writings*. Two Volumes. N.Y.: Library of America, 1989.

Livermore, Thomas L. *Numbers and Losses in the Civil War in America: 1861-1865*. Bloomington: Indiana University Press, 1957.

Loderhouse, Gary. *Far, Far from Home : The Ninth Florida Regiment in the Confederate Army*. Carmel, Ind.: Guild Press, 1999.

Logan, David. *"A Rising Star of Promise": The Civil War Odyssey of David Jackson Logan, 17th South Carolina Volunteers, 1861-1864*. Edited by Samuel N. Thomas, Jr., and Jason H. Silverman. Campbell, Calif.: Da Capo Press, 1998.

Longacre, Edward G. *A Regiment of Slaves: The 4th United States Colored Infantry, 1863-1866*. Mechanicsburg, Pa.: Stackpole Books, 2003.

Lord, Edward O. *History of the Ninth New Hampshire Volunteers in the War of the Rebellion*. Concord, N.H.: 1895.

Lyman, Theodore. *With Grant & Meade from the Wilderness to Appomattox.* Edited by George R. Agassiz. Lincoln: University of Nebraska Press, 1994.

Marshall, Jeffrey D., ed. *A War of the People: Vermont Civil War Letters.* Hanover, N.H.: University Press of New England, 1999.

Marvel, William. *Burnside.* Chapel Hill: University of North Carolina Press, 1991.

———. *Race of the Soil: The Ninth New Hampshire Regiment in the Civil War.* Wilmington, N.C.: Broadfoot Publishing Co., 1988.

Maryland Commission on Publication of the Histories of the Maryland Volunteers During the Civil War. *History and Roster of Maryland Volunteers, War of 1861–5.* Baltimore, Press of Guggenheimer, Weil & Co., 1898–99.

McAlpine, Newton. "Sketch of Company I, 61st Virginia Infantry, Mahone's Brigade, C.S.A.," *Southern Historical Society Papers,* Volume 24 (1896), pp. 98–108.

McClelen, Bailey George. *I Saw the Elephant: The Civil War Experiences of Bailey George McClelen, Company D, 10th Alabama Infantry Regiment.*

McFeely, William S. *Grant: A Biography.* N.Y.: W. W. Norton and Co., 1982.

McMaster, F. W. "The Battle of the Crater, July 30, 1864," *Southern Historical Society Papers,* Volume 10 (1882), pp. 119–30.

McPherson, James M. *Battle Cry of Freedom: The Civil War Era.* N.Y.: Oxford University Press, 1988.

———. *For Cause and Comrades: Why Men Fought the Civil War.* N.Y.: Oxford University Press, 1997.

———. *What They Fought For, 1861–1865.* Baton Rouge: Louisiana State University Press, 1994.

Meade, George Gordon. *The Life and Letters of George Gordon Meade, Major-General United States Army.* Volume 2. N.Y.: Charles Scribner's Sons, 1913.

Meinig, D. W. *The Shaping of America: A Geographical Perspective on 500 Years of History, Volume 1, Atlantic America, 1492–1800.* New Haven: Yale University Press, 1986.

———. *The Shaping of America: A Geographical Perspective on 500 Years of History, Volume 2, Continental America, 1800–1867.* New Haven: Yale University Press, 1993.

Memorial of Colonel John A. Bross, Twenty-ninth U.S. Colored Troops, Who Fell in Leading the Assault on Petersburgh, July 30, 1864. By a Friend. Chicago: Tribune Book and Job Office, 1865.

Mickley, Jeremiah Marion. *The Forty-third Regiment United States Colored Troops.* Gettysburg, Pa.: J. E. Wible, printer, 1866.

Miller, Edward A., Jr. *The Black Civil War Soldiers of Illinois: The Story of the Twenty-ninth U.S. Colored Infantry.* Columbia: University of South Carolina Press, 1998.

Miller, Richard F. *Harvard's Civil War: A History of the Twentieth Massachusetts Volunteer Infantry.* Hanover, N.H.: University Press of New England, 2005.

Mitchell, Reid. *Civil War Soldiers.* N.Y.: Viking Press, 1988.

Montgomery, David. *Beyond Equality: Labor and the Radical Republicans, 1862-1872.* Urbana: University of Illinois Press, 1981.

Nolan, Alan. T. *Lee Considered: General Robert E. Lee and Civil War History.* Chapel Hill: University of North Carolina Press, 1991.

Oates, Stephen B. *A Woman of Valor: Clara Barton and the Civil War.* N.Y.: Free Press, 1994.

Öfele, Martin W. *German-Speaking Officers in the U.S. Colored Troops, 1863-1867.* Gainesville: University Press of Florida, 2004.

OR 40—see below, United States. War Department. *The War of the Rebellion.*

Palfrey, Francis W. *Memoir of William Francis Bartlett.* Boston: Houghton, Osgood and Co., 1878.

Phisterer, Frederick. *New York in the War of the Rebellion 1861 to 1865.* Albany: Weed, Parsons & Co., 1890.

Pleasants, Henry, Jr. Tragedy of the Crater [n.p.]: Christopher Publishing, 1938.

———. *Inferno at Petersburg.* [n.p.]:Chilton Book Co., 1961.

Poirier, Robert. *"By the Blood of Our Alumni": Norwich University Citizen Soldiers in the Army of the Potomac.* Norwich, Vt.: Savas Woodbury, 1999.

Porter, Horace K. *Campaigning with Grant.* N.Y.: The Century Co., 1906.

Potter, David M. *The Impending Crisis, 1848-1861.* Completed and edited by Don E. Fehrenbacher. N.Y.: Harper & Row, 1976.

Powell, William H. "The Battle of the Petersburg Crater," in R. U. Johnson and C. C. Buel, eds., *Battles and Leaders of the Civil War.* Volume 4. N.Y.: The Century Co., 1884-1888, pp. 545-60.

Power, J. Tracy. *Lee's Miserables: Life in the Army of Northern Virginia from the Wilderness to Appomattox.* Chapel Hill: University of North Carolina Press, 1998.

Proctor, D. E. "The Massacre in the Crater," *National Tribune,* Oct. 17, 1907, p. 6.

Rable, George C. *But There Was No Peace: The Role of Violence in the Politics of Reconstruction.* Athens: University of Georgia Press, 1984.

———. *The Confederate Republic: A Revolution Against Politics.* Chapel Hill: University of North Carolina Press, 1994.

Radley, Kenneth. *Rebel Watchdog: The Confederate States Army Provost Guard.* Baton Rouge: Louisiana State University Press, 1989.

Ray, Fred L. *Shock Troops of the Confederacy: The Sharpshooter Battalions of the Army of Northern Virginia.* Asheville, N.C.: CFS Press, 2006.

Redkey, Edwin S., ed. *A Grand Army of Black Men: Letters from African-American Soldiers in the Union Army, 1861-1865.* Cambridge, U.K.: Cambridge University Press, 1992.

Rickard, James H. "Services with Colored Troops in Burnside's Corps," *Personal Narratives of the Events of the War of the Rebellion, Being Papers Read Before the Rhode Island Soldiers and Sailors Historical Society, 5th Series, No. 1* (1894), pp. 1-43.

Roberts, Agatha Louise. *As They Remembered: The Story of the Forty-fifth Pennsylvania Veteran Volunteer Infantry Regiment, 1861–1865*. N.Y.: William-Frederick Press, 1964.

Rogers, George T. "The Crater Battle, 30th July, 1864," *Confederate Veteran* 3:1, 1895, pp. 12–14.

Rose, Willie Lee. *Rehearsal for Reconstruction: The Port Royal Experiment*. N.Y.: Oxford University Press, 1964.

Rosen, Robert N. *The Jewish Confederates*. Columbia: University of South Carolina Press, 2000.

Ruffner, Kevin Conley. *Maryland's Blue & Gray: A Border State's Union and Confederate Junior Officer Corps*. Baton Rouge: Louisiana State University Press, 1997.

Sanders, Charles W., Jr. *While in the Hands of the Enemy: Military Prisons of the Civil War*. Baton Rouge: Louisiana State University Press, 2005.

Shaffer, Donald R. *After the Glory: The Struggles of Black Civil War Veterans*. Lawrence: University Press of Kansas, 2004.

Shaw, Charles A. *A History of the 14th Regiment N.Y. Heavy Artillery in the Civil War from 1863 to 1865*. Mt. Kisco, N.Y.: North Westchester Pub. Co., 1918.

Shearman, Sumner U. "Battle of the Crater and Experiences of Prison Life," *Personal Narratives of the Events of the War of the Rebellion, Being Papers Read Before the Rhode Island Soldiers and Sailors Historical Society, 5th Series, No. 8* (1898), pp. 5–38.

Silver, James W. *Confederate Morale and Church Propaganda*. Tuscaloosa, Ala.: Confederate Publishing Co., Inc., 1957.

Slotkin, Richard. *The Fatal Environment: The Myth of the Frontier in the Age of Industrialization, 1800–1890*. Norman: University of Oklahoma Press, 1985, 1994.

Stackpole, Edward J. *Sheridan in the Shenandoah: Jubal Early's Nemesis*. N.Y.: Bonanza Books, 1946.

Stephens, Alexander H. "Cornerstone Address, March 21, 1861," in Frank Moore, ed., *The Rebellion Record: A Diary of American Events with Documents, Narratives, Illustrative Incidents, Poetry, Etc.* N.Y.: O. P. Putnam, 1862, Vol. 1, pp. 44–6.

Stewart, William. "Carnage at the Crater," *Confederate Veteran* 1:2, 1893, pp. 41–2.

Stone, DeWitt Boyd, Jr., ed. *Wandering to Glory: Confederate Veterans Remember Evans' Brigade*. Columbia: University of South Carolina Press, 2002.

Taaffe, Stephen. *Commanding the Army of the Potomac*. Lawrence: University Press of Kansas, 2006.

Tap, Bruce. *Over Lincoln's Shoulder: The Committee on the Conduct of the War*. Lawrence: University Press of Kansas, 1998.

Taylor, Walter H. *Four Years with General Lee*. Edited by James I. Robertson, Jr. Bloomington: Indiana University Press, 1996.

Taylor, William R. *Cavalier and Yankee: The Old South and American National Character*. N.Y.: G. Braziller, 1961.

Thomas, Emory M. *Robert E. Lee: A Biography*. N.Y.: W. W. Norton, 1995.

Thomas, Henry Goddard. "The Colored Troops at Petersburg," in R. U. Johnson and C. C. Buel, eds., *Battles and Leaders of the Civil War*. Volume 4. N.Y.: The Century Co., 1884–1888, pp. 563–7.

Thrash, A. B. "Vivid Reminiscence of the Crater," *Confederate Veteran* 14:11, 1906, pp. 508–9.

Time-Life Books. *Echoes of Glory: The Illustrated Atlas of the Civil War*. Alexandria, Va.: Time-Life Books, 1991.

Trask, Benjamin H. *16th Virginia Infantry*. Lynchburg, Va.: H. E. Howard, 1986.

———. *61st Virginia Infantry*. Lynchburg, Va.: H. E. Howard, 1988.

Trobriand, Régis de. *Four Years with the Army of the Potomac*. Translated by George K. Dauchy. Boston: Ticknor and Co., 1889.

Trudeau, Noah Andre. *The Last Citadel: Petersburg, Virginia, June 1864–April 1865*. Baton Rouge: Louisiana State University Press, 1991.

Tyler, Charles Mellen. *Memorials of Lieut. George H. Walcott, Late of the 30th U.S. Colored Troops*. Boston: Massachusetts Sabbath School, 1865.

United States. Congress. *Report of the Committee on the Conduct of the War on the Attack on Petersburg, on the 30th Day of July, 1864*. Washington: Government Printing Office, 1865.

United States. War Department. *Atlas to Accompany the Official Records of the Union and Confederate Armies*. Washington: Government Printing Office, 1891–95.

———. *The War of the Rebellion: A Compilation of the Official Records of the Union and Confederate Armies*. Volume 40, Parts 1–3. Washington: Government Printing Office, 1892. http://cdl.library.cornell.edu/moa/ browse.monographs/ waro.html [Abbreviated as *OR* 40:1, 2, 3]

Urwin, Gregory J. W., ed. *Black Flag over Dixie: Racial Atrocities and Reprisals in the Civil War*. Carbondale: Southern Illinois University Press, 2004.

Vance, P. M. "Incidents of the Crater Battle," *Confederate Veteran* 14:4, 1906, pp. 178–9.

Voris, Alvin C. *A Citizen-Soldier's Civil War: The Letters of Brevet Major General Alvin C. Voris*. Edited by Jerome Mushkat. De Kalb: Northern Illinois University Press, 2002.

Waite, Otis F. B. *New Hampshire in the Great Rebellion*. Claremont, N.H.: Tracy, Chase & Co., 1870.

Wallenstein, Peter and Bertram Wyatt-Brown, eds. *Virginia's Civil War*. Charlottesville: University of Virginia Press, 2005.

Ward, Andrew. *River Run Red: The Fort Pillow Massacre in the American Civil War*. New York: Viking, 2005.

Warner, Ezra J. *Generals in Blue: Lives of the Union Commanders*. Baton Rouge: Louisiana State University Press, 1992.

——. *Generals in Gray: Lives of the Confederate Commanders.* Baton Rouge: Louisiana State University Press, 1987.

Washington, Versalle F. *Eagles on Their Buttons: A Black Infantry Regiment in the Civil War.* Columbia: University of Missouri Press, 1999.

Webb, James H. *Born Fighting: How the Scots-Irish Shaped America.* N.Y.: Broadway Books, 2005.

Weitz, Mark A. *More Damning Than Slaughter: Desertion in the Confederate Army.* Lincoln: University of Nebraska Press, 2005.

Weld, Stephen Minot. "The Petersburg Mine," *Papers of the Military Historical Society of Massachusetts,* Volume 5 (1906), pp. 207–19.

——. *War Diary and Letters of Stephen Minot Weld, 1861–1865.* 2nd Edition. Boston: Massachusetts Historical Society, 1979.

Westwood, Howard C. *Black Troops, White Commanders, and Freedmen During the Civil War.* Carbondale: Southern Illinois University Press, 1992.

Whitman, George W. *Civil War Letters of George Washington Whitman.* Edited by Jerome M. Loving. Durham, N.C.: Duke University Press, 1975.

Wiley, Bell I. and James I. Robertson. *The Life of Johnny Reb: The Common Soldier of the Confederacy.* Baton Rouge: Louisiana State University Press, 2007.

Wilkinson, Warren. *Mother, May You Never See the Sights I Have Seen: The Fifty-seventh Massachusetts Veteran Volunteers in the Last Year of the Civil War.* N.Y.: William Morrow, 1990.

Williams, Alfred B. *Hampton and His Red Shirts: South Carolina's Deliverance in 1876.* Freeport, N.Y.: Books for Libraries, 1970.

Williams, David. *Rich Man's War: Class, Caste, and Confederate Defeat in the Lower Chattahoochee Valley.* Athens: University of Georgia Press, 1998.

Wilson, Keith, ed. *Honor in Command: Lt. Freeman S. Bowley's Civil War Service in the 30th United States Colored Infantry.* Gainesville: University Press of Florida, 2006.

Wise, John Sergeant. *The End of an Era.* Boston: Elibron Classics, 1989.

Wood, Forrest G. *Black Scare: The Racist Response to Emancipation and Reconstruction.* Berkeley: University of California Press, 1968.

Woodworth, Steven E. *Davis and Lee at War.* Lawrence: University Press of Kansas, 1995.

Wyatt-Brown, Bertram. *Honor and Violence in the Old South.* N.Y.: Oxford University Press, 1986.

Zelinsky, Wilbur. *Cultural Geography of the United States.* Englewood Cliffs, N.J.: Prentice-Hall, Inc., 1973.

Index

ABOUT THE AUTHOR

RICHARD SLOTKIN has established a reputation as one of the preeminent cultural critics of our times. His award-winning trilogy on the myth of the frontier in America, which includes *Regeneration Through Violence, The Fatal Environment,* and *Gunfighter Nation,* offers an original and highly provocative interpretation of our national experience. He has also published three historical novels: *The Crater, The Return of Henry Starr,* and *Abe: A Novel of the Young Lincoln.* He is the Olin Professor of English and American Studies at Wesleyan University.